THE PRINCIPLES AND PRACTICE OF MARKETING

THE PRINCIPLES AND PRACTICE OF MARKETING

JOHN FRAIN

MA, MTech, PhD(Econ), DipM, FIEx
Principal
South Mersey College, Liverpool

PITMAN

PITMAN PUBLISHING LIMITED
128 Long Acre, London WC2E 9AN

A Longman Group Company

© J Frain, 1986

First published in Great Britain 1986

British Library Cataloguing in Publication Data
Frain, John
  The principles and practice of marketing.
  1. Marketing
  I. Title
  658.8   HF5415

ISBN 0 273 02583 X

Typeset in Great Britain at The Bath Press, Avon

Printed and bound in Hong Kong

CONTENTS

PREFACE

The kind response to my earlier work *Introduction to Marketing* prompted the publisher to suggest a longer book at a higher level of treatment. This work is intended for undergraduate students of business studies at universities and polytechnics, for students on B/TEC HND and HNC courses and for examination candidates of the Institute of Marketing, the Institute of Export and similar bodies. It is also hoped that students on such post-experience courses as the Diploma in Management Studies, as well as Marketing practitioners, will find value in what is written here.

The book's case for shelf space among the other titles on this subject is based on the fact that, in addition to its survey of the field, it offers, hopefully, interesting examples of the marketing of services and ideas and of non-profit marketing, as well as dealing with export marketing at greater length than is usual in books of this type. Over a number of years, the author's own students have also suggested that it would be helpful to see the marketing function set in the context of broader organisational issues – hence the sections on organisation theory and objective setting in Chapter 2 and other parts of the book.

Marketing is a vast study – a distillation of many insights, a bumper bundle of the fruits of much experience. So an author quarrying his material from this field finds himself indebted to many organisations and many individuals. Among the organisations that have been generous with material in copyright are: the British Market Research Bureau Ltd, Business Books Ltd, C.A.C.I. Market Analysis Division, Haymarket Publishing Ltd, Her Majesty's Stationery office, A.C. Nielsen Ltd, Prentice-Hall International Inc., Research Services Ltd, and Taylor Nelson Associates Ltd. The Netherlands–British Chamber of Commerce kindly agreed to the reproduction of the chart of its services which appears on Page 455.

At the individual level, Julia Lacey, Mike Cuthbert and Robin Ebers must be thanked for surveying appropriate sections of the book as must Alan Broadaway, for the suggestions he made for additions to the content. It is also a pleasant task to acknowledge the debt due to the many authors whose works are referred to in the text.

J. K. Galbraith once wrote that:

'Authorship of any sort is a fantastic indulgence of the ego. It is well, no doubt, to reflect on how much one owes to others'. In this context, mention must be made of the publishers – Tania Hackett and David Carpenter should be thanked for their support, but mostly for their patience.

Any errors or omissions to be found in the work are the sole responsibility of the author.

John Frain, 1986

1 MARKETING: AN INTRODUCTION TO THE CONCEPT

Objectives

In this introductory Chapter we shall look at the meaning of marketing, how it developed and why it is a mistake to confuse it with selling. We shall see how it can assist organisations to plan their activities, study some examples of its success and reflect on why it can sometimes fail. Finally, we shall look at how marketing might assume a broader role.

Introduction

A conversation about marketing

Some years ago, the author visited a television programme company. As part of a research project, the author was to interview the producer of a series of programmes. This series had met with acclaim. One newspaper critic considered it the most colossal concept he had ever come across on television.

The author was ushered into a dark, cinema-like studio. The producer was watching a screen intently. After the transmission he turned and smiled.

'I'm sorry for the delay, but those are the rushes of a recently completed programme. I wanted to see whether I had got a particular point across.'

It is fatal to be tactless at the beginning of an interview but these remarks had prompted a question. So when the conversation was under way, the author asked as politely as possible:

'When you wonder whether a particular point has got across, how can you judge other people's perception of it?'

He looked and shook his head slightly to convey that he did

not quite understand. Set out below is part of the conversation which followed.

AUTHOR: The viewer's mind is not a blank slate on which you can make impressions. Your television programme is a 'stimulus object', as the psychologist would say. People have quite different perceptions of the same stimulus object.

PRODUCER: Mm. How do their perceptions differ?

AUTHOR: By selective perception, for example. People tend to interpret information in a way which supports rather than challenges their own beliefs. So the point you wish to put across could be selectively distorted. People also tend to hold on only to that information which fits their preconceptions.

(The office clock hesitated in its ticking)

PRODUCER: I don't think any of us here have even considered communications in the way you mention.

AUTHOR: May I mention something else?

PRODUCER: Yes, of course – it's good to have another viewpoint.

AUTHOR: I hope you'll forgive me for this, but I just wonder whether a studio of the type I've just seen in which you, a captive audience of one, are dominated by the screen, is a suitable situation in which to judge the impact of a television programme.

PRODUCER: I don't follow you.

AUTHOR: Television programmes come into the home on a relatively small screen. People are talking, making phone calls, eating meals, washing up, attending to their hobbies. Your programme is just one element among many. And the viewing process itself is a sociological process.

PRODUCER: Sociological? . . .

AUTHOR: Most of your audience watch television in groups – rarely alone. The nature of those groups and the fact that viewers are invariably members of groups has implications for the way your programme is received. The family, for instance, is a primary group. Primary groups have a great deal of influence on an individual's opinions and values.

PRODUCER: (laughing) With all the mistakes we've made, I am beginning to doubt whether the series was a success or not.

AUTHOR: It was wonderful – because it was a brilliant idea – for which the viewing public was ready. The things I'm talking about might increase the acceptability of ideas that perhaps aren't so brilliant – and I think they'll *increase* the brilliance of the brilliant programme.

PRODUCER: I've quite forgotten now where we were in this discussion – but I'm genuinely interested in what you're saying. Any other thoughts?

AUTHOR: I think it follows that a period actually in a home observing a family watching TV might be part of a training programme for producers. Unless, of course, you've got that kind of information through your market research department.

PRODUCER: Market research?... Market research... Is that an American idea?

AUTHOR: It's a function within marketing. In your case it would tell you quite a lot about your audience – its interests, likes and dislikes and how well they might understand ideas you were trying to put across. Knowing all that would help you in making programmes.

PRODUCER: But TV people are creative... they must say what they have to say. Making programmes by numbers, pushing buttons on a computer... that would be creative death.

AUTHOR: Why do you think that?

PRODUCER: Surely, it's obvious. We're not marketing soap powder!

AUTHOR: Well, just let me pursue that for a minute. You use the word 'marketing'... what does that mean to you?

PRODUCER: Selling. Probably high pressure selling.

AUTHOR: I think selling is part of it... part of a broader operation called marketing.

PRODUCER: Suppose we say it's buying and selling... like in a market place – which is where marketing goes on.

AUTHOR: I think if we said that it's more about buying than selling, we may be getting closer to my interpretation of marketing. One of its basic ideas is to start from what the customer needs rather than from what we would like to give them, assuming the two aren't the same. In fact, on marketing and selling one writer says that they're words with opposite meanings. With the concept of selling, for instance, a company produces a product then tries various methods of selling to persuade you and me to buy it... which is bending demand to fit the supply, whereas under the marketing concept the company bends its supply to the nature of the demand... an opposite process. That's where the market research comes in – giving information about the market – and that needn't be a block to creativity. You could actually argue that it's a bigger challenge to plan and design something against a background of stated information and objectives than to leave creative people free to follow their own fancy in the hope that they'll come up with something that appeals to somebody. After all, you as producer are responsible for the resources involved.

PRODUCER: This is an interesting conversation although I don't follow everything you say. Actually, I remember that you came to interview me. Are you happy for us to continue on these lines?

AUTHOR: Yes – I came to interview you about the extent to which the type of marketing I've described shapes the production of television programmes ... so this is very useful.

PRODUCER: You describe marketing in a way I've never heard before.

AUTHOR: Perhaps that's because marketing, in the sense I describe it, is a concept that's been badly marketed. Not that I'm alone with the idea – lots of organisations have adopted it as an approach and done well out of it.

PRODUCER: But how would you define it?

AUTHOR: There are any number of definitions. What they boil down to is that the most productive way to use resources – people, finance, raw materials – is to concentrate on the needs of the buyer. Winning the buyer's support – which means the user's support for your product or your service, or your idea, is a process one might call *market induced flow* and it's particularly sensible when the nature of demand is changing. Most markets are changing, these days.

PRODUCER: What you've discovered about us so far is that we're making programmes but not actually marketing, in your sense.

AUTHOR: Your current series has been magnificent and leaves no room for criticism. But in a general sense what I have learned so far suggests a process the marketing man would describe as *production orientation*.

PRODUCER: What's wrong with production orientation? I'm paid to be a *producer*!

AUTHOR: In this sense, production orientation means that the organisation plans its production with greater regard for its production techniques or its past experience rather than for its customer. The expression is marketing jargon, if you like. *Market or user orientation*, on the other hand, means that every decision is made with the satisfaction of the ultimate user in mind. User needs and satisfaction is the starting point and the organisation's operations and management are conducted from that standpoint.

PRODUCER: So marketing, as you define it, means putting the priority on the customer ... (?)

AUTHOR: In essence, yes. Then a lot of things flow from that which the marketing man has to know about.

And so the conversation went on. At the end of it, the author had some grounds for thinking perhaps he had corrected, for one person at least, some of the commonly mistaken beliefs about marketing. It is interesting that in the part of the conversation which is set out above, the television producer revealed some of these general misconceptions:

1   that marketing means selling, and nothing more;
2   that it is only related to fast-moving consumer products ('we're not marketing soap powder!');
3   that because it implies planning, it must be a depersonalised process, leaving no room for creative people ('pushing buttons on a computer ... would be creative death').

To explain why these notions are mistaken, the next Section describes more fully the meaning of marketing as it was touched upon in the conversation with the TV producer.

The meaning of marketing

Perhaps marketing is misunderstood because it is frequently thought of as one of the activities in which an organisation engages rather than as an attitude to how the organisation should operate. In effect, the layman believes it is merely to do with selling and is therefore something that is done by sales personnel. Those with a little more knowledge, usually of the business world, see it as having a broader role – being concerned with advertising and sales promotion as well as the efforts of salesmen. Even now, too few people would understand Peter Drucker[1] when he says that the aim of marketing is to make selling superfluous.

To illustrate what he has in mind consider the following definitions of marketing, as applied to business organisations:

Marketing is the management function which organises and directs all those business activities involved in assessing and converting customer purchasing power into effective demand for a specific product or service, and in moving the product or service to the final consumer or user so as to achieve the profit target or other objectives set by a company.[2]

Marketing is seen as being the primary management function that co-ordinates the activities involved in developing and manufacturing suitable products for specified markets, converting consumer purchasing power into effective demand, and in moving the products to the user in order to attain corporate objectives ... the scope of marketing demands that the marketing manager be concerned with profitability (preferably expressed as a rate of return on investment) and hence with sales revenue and costs.[3]

The marketing concept says that a firm should focus all its efforts on satisfying its customers, at a profit.[4]

Other definitions of marketing can be found in the literature but central to all of them is the idea that, as far as business organisations are concerned, two fundamental elements should be found in their operating policies:

1   that the organisations should bring themselves into mutually satisfactory relationships with the users of their products or services, and
2   based upon these relationships, organisations must then strive to attain their objectives which, in the business world, are usually expressed in terms of return-on-investment.

As a way of doing business, this takes us beyond selling, important though selling is. Professor Philip Kotler,[5] an authoritative writer in the field suggests that:

Selling is only the tip of the marketing iceberg. It is only one of several functions that marketers perform, and often not the most important one. If the marketer does a good job of identifying consumer needs, developing appropriate products, and pricing, distributing and promoting them effectively, these goods will sell very easily.

Another writer observes that:

The distinction between marketing and sales is highlighted by the distinction between strategy and tactics – marketing is basically a study of strategy, whereas selling is essentially a tactical operation.[6]

For his part, Kotler believes that, given the marketing approach:

The amount of promotion and hard selling will not have to be intense.

User orientation

The grounds for this view might best be explained by referring to *user orientation* – a phrase with which marketers are very familiar. To understand its importance, it must be compared to *production orientation*, a phrase which the author also used in his conversation with the TV producer. Figs. 1.1 and 1.2 below might

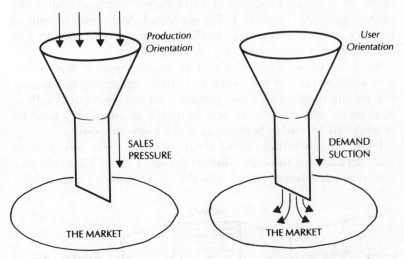

Fig. 1.1   Production orientation   Fig. 1.2   User-orientation and
         and sales pressure   demand suction
                                           (market-induced flow)

help us here. Production orientation applies to the organisation which plans its output with greater regard for:

     its established production techniques
     its existing management experience
     its existing knowledge of raw materials and components
     the current skills of its labour force, than for
     the actual and potential preferences of users.

On the other hand, the firm adopting the user orientation philosophy is very sensitive to the changing form of user needs and wants. And this sensitivity conditions its approach to planning for the market.

In the author's previous work, *Introduction to Marketing*, he described how,[7] as in Fig. 1.1 above, a production-oriented firm might be thought of as one attempting to dispose of its production by 'force-pumping' it into the top end of a funnel. And in effect, it says to its sales people 'this is what we like producing – go out and sell it'. The user oriented firm, as depicted in Fig. 1.2, is doing something quite different. Its output is being 'suction drawn' from the bottom of the funnel by a process of market induced flow. To enable this to happen it will have deduced, by a prior examination of market needs using techniques of marketing research, that a benevolent vacuum exists in the market ready to draw in products or services with characteristics the user judges to be important. These characteristics may be related to price, colour, durability, quality, economy, size, output etc, and alone or in some appealing combination.

So these ideas are at the root of Kotler's notion that, given a product or service with such in-built acceptability to the market, selling it could be a less intense (and thus less costly) affair. And so we can see why an organisation's *selling policy* must be subordinate to, and dependent upon, its *marketing policy*.

For the reader with a technical turn of mind, the words pressure and suction used in connection with Figs. 1.1 and 1.2 might give rise to another image (Fig. 1.3) – that of a 'balance valve', which

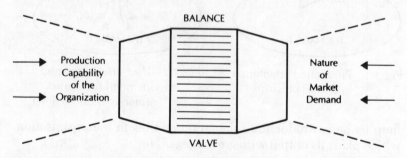

Fig. 1.3   *The marketing concept as a balance valve*

equalises the thrust of the organisations production capability on the one hand and the nature of its market demand on the other. This and many other pictures could be used to fix the vision of marketing as, in the words of yet another writer,

A method of managing a business so that each critical business decision – whether by the Sales Department, the Maintenance Department, the Production Department, or the Financial Department – is made with the full, prior knowledge of the impact of that decision on the Customer.

The next Section traces the development of the marketing approach, with particular reference to the British experience.

The development of the marketing approach

Every schoolboy knows that during the period 1760–1830, the British economy was transformed from its dependence on agriculture to a basis of industrial activity. The spectacular expansion of output, particularly from 1780 onwards, was achieved by the *division of labour* applied to production processes. This increased job specialisation gave rise to the need for *exchange* and around this fundamental need for exchange there emerged an elaborate web of work organisations – in production, in distribution and in finance.

To some extent, the increase in Britain's population served as a market for this growth in production (in the century from 1750, the population of England and Wales trebled from its base of $6\frac{1}{2}$ million). Yet population growth at home could not, of itself, sustain the industrial and commercial plenitude which developed at this time. The principal factor underlying Britain's growth was the development of her international trade. This was based on her monopoly supply position to the countries of the undeveloped world, many of which were part of the Empire and Commonwealth. So that although her pre-eminence as an industrial power began to wane from the third quarter of the nineteenth century (in face of competition from Germany and the United States) until almost the mid-twentieth century Britain's trade continued to 'follow the flag'.

The period to 1914 was one in which international competitors were making great strides. Britain continued to prosper, however, with expansion based on her trade in coal, cotton, wool, steel and engineering products. Moreover, whole new industries appeared, based on the bicycle, the motor car, the electrical appliance. At this point in time, as Baker[8] has written, production orientation was no bad thing for demand exceeded supply, user needs were readily identifiable and preoccupation with production volume actually did the users a service as it put luxury goods within the reach of many more pockets.

As a result of World War I, Britain was forced to sell off many of her overseas investments. The general economic depression of the post-war period was aggravated in Britain's case because the demand for her main export, coal, declined as other countries began to exploit their own resources. Also, the War itself had interrupted the links with her overseas markets. She subsequently discovered these were being serviced by new competitors, among which Japan was prominent. But ... the decline in Britain's older industries was being abated to some extent by the appearance of still more new industries based on electrical engineering, artificial fibres, the radio and the telephone.

The emergence of marketing

The motor car industry had by this time become firmly established and it gave the national workforce experience of the techniques of mass production. With the outbreak of World War II, this experience was further developed as the economy moved to the purposes of war production. In addition, the demand for munitions, aircraft, ships, tanks and military vehicles brought a fresh impulse to Britain's 'depressed areas'.

At this time too, because *more* was *better*, production orientation was no detriment to the economy and the author believes that it was at precisely this period that a development of great relevance took place. This was the evolution of the 'Sunday soviets'. These were meetings at which Services chiefs discussed in detail with their suppliers design and development aspects of the products they were requisitioning for war purposes. It is a fact that many of the management techniques currently used in industry and commerce were developed and applied in the context of World War II, those of operational research being but one example. Who is to say that the user-orientation philosophy which began to be talked about ten years later did not, for all practical purposes, emerge via the Sunday soviets?

Without doubt too, it was in the post-1945 period that several trends combined to create a situation in which the marketing concept could take root.

The UK population expanded to 50 million people. The mass of these people achieved greater living standards and purchasing power than ever before. For almost 30 years after the War there was virtual full employment. Because of the increase in the number of working wives, the two-income family became more the rule than the exception. Standards of health and education improved markedly.

All of this made for a situation in which proportionately less of the family budget was spent on the necessities of life and proportionately more on such items as furniture, motor cars, refrigerators, washing machines, UK and foreign travel, communication (particularly by telephone) and entertainment. Moreover, as people became better off in real terms they became more discriminating as buyers, so that *consumer sovereignty* and *consumer choice* emerged as the bed-fellows of *consumer affluence*.

It was in the late 1950s that the business world began to talk of the marketing concept. For then it came to be appreciated that while science and technology were generating more and more ideas for faster and more cost effective production, the stability of the markets for many products and services was being undermined by changing economic and social forces. So that here were new production techniques with the capability of delivering either a higher standard of living or a mountain of waste, depending upon whether what they produced was in phase with the changing composition of user needs and wants.

Industrialists now had acquired a more powerful productive weapon but with it they had perforce to hit a moving target. In the context of mass production requiring mass consumption it became advisable to consider market induced flow – a process by which information on user preferences was to be incorporated at the beginning rather than the end of the cycle of product development, production, distribution and consumption. And this information was to be acquired by business organisations through the use of *marketing research*.

The American influence

The reader will recall that, in the conversation reported at the beginning of this Chapter, the TV producer asked whether marketing was 'an American idea'. Now those writers who claim that marketing is an age-old idea remind us that it was the British economist, Adam Smith[9] writing in the eighteenth century, who suggested that:

Consumption is the sole end and purpose of all production; and the interest of the producer ought to be attended to, only in so far as it may be necessary for promoting that of the consumer.

For the historical reasons set out earlier, Smith's maxim was not widely adopted by the British business community, and notwithstanding what has also been said about the Sunday soviets it must be owned that the first practical evidence of widespread adoption of the marketing concept emerged from the United

States. The reason is not hard to discover. The economy of the United States was the first to be faced with the danger of over-production.

In his book *America*, an expanded version of his television series, Alistair Cooke[10] makes some interesting comments:

... that America, after the First World War, had vaulted into the position of the World's creditor nation; that its unscathed industries achieved miracles of production on the first great assembly lines; that it had the highest average income of any country; that it made more steel than Europe; and that Henry Ford built a motor car for Everyman.

Intriguingly, he adds:

... Ford made his radical breakthrough by thinking first of the needs of hundreds of thousands of consumers.

From Cooke's description of American economic development it becomes clear how that country's experience influenced marketing activity throughout the world. It is also fascinating to see how part of the vocabulary of marketing (e.g. 'branding', 'trade fair') emerged from the winning of the wild frontier. Unhappily, further speculation on this cannot detain us here.

The British experience

Towards the end of the 1950s then, the marketing concept began to be applied in Britain. Early successes for it were recorded in the field of consumer products – both consumables (e.g. food, drink, confectionery) and durables (e.g. television sets, washing machines, motor vehicles). A considerable amount of American reading matter on the subject began to appear in the libraries and bookshops. In 1959, a British textbook, *Marketing* written by business consultant, Colin McIver, pioneered the development of this country's own literature. At about this time the Incorporated Sales Managers' Association changed its title to the Institute of Marketing and Sales Management and shortly afterwards became, simply, the Institute of Marketing.

By the mid-1960s a number of UK consumer goods companies had become acquainted with the philosophy and it next gained a footing in the field of industrial goods. An early UK work in this context was the *Marketing of Industrial Products*, edited by another consultant, Aubrey Wilson, and published in 1965. That same year, the country's first Professorship in Marketing was established at the University of Lancaster.

The marketing of services

By the middle of the decade too, a number of service organisations notably in the banking, insurance and hotel sectors became interested in the marketing way of doing business. As the application of marketing to banking services provides an interesting case study of the UK experience it is now briefly described.

It had become obvious to the clearing banks that Britain's affluent society contained many thousands of potential customers, not least among the skilled and semi-skilled manual workers. Yet although some of this segment of the population was now being paid by cheque, it was still generally guarded in its outlook towards banks and the banking process. It was regarded too widely still as a service for 'them' but not for 'us', 'them' being the upper middle classes. In an earlier time they had owned a substantial part of the nation's wealth but their fortunes were being eroded by death duties and other forms of social engineering as both ends of the financial spectrum were being pulled in towards the middle.

Yet to the newly affluent, bank premises were uninviting. From the high-street pavements, through the semi-screened windows, marbled columns, decorated ceilings and polished wooden counters gave the 'package' an austere, dated look. If one was dexterous enough, one could glimpse booths in which customers prepared deposit slips with all the secrecy of the confessional. The bank manager was still visualised as the stern figure of the melodramas – reliably severe with the improvident, without mercy to the defaulters.

So it was that television advertisements began to appear extolling the virtues of 'the friendly bank manager'. Behind large windows which now extended to the pavement, premises were extensively re-designed. In an effort to disperse the mystique, transactions were now open to view. Powerful corporate symbols, in the shape of unicorns, black horses and other devices provided a distinctive image for each separate banking organisation. The subsequent moves by the banks into the fields of insurance services, house mortgages and credit cards provided other evidence of the sector's response to the composition of new consumer needs, as did each bank's interest in the student market.

Today, one of the clearing banks, 'the listening bank' emphasises in its advertising the reliable level of attention it pays to consumer needs. Not that the business community is ignored. As technology changes the structure of industry, rendering some firms redundant but opening up new opportunities, especially in the fields of electronics, information processing and personal services, the banks are keen to offer advice and help in 'starting your own business' or 'making a small business bigger'.

The banking sector has thus produced a number of interesting examples of the application of the marketing concept. The sector's responsiveness to the market and its flexibility is all the more notable in a field traditionally marked by caution and conservatism – as the student of economic history knows this is an outlook rooted in the fact that some of the sector's most spectacular failures have been due to high-risk diversification.

User orientation in the banks is still developing. Towards the end of the 1970s it was announced that Barclays Bank was about to begin 'a programme of humanisation'.[11] This related to the introduction of an open-plan 'banking hall' at Milton Keynes in Buckinghamshire. It was intended to provide a 'barrier-free atmosphere for customers and staff'. Cash transactions are transferred to and from the open area on the ground floor using automatic dispensers which are sealed in time-lock safes within open counters. Pneumatic tubes connect the banking hall to a secure area on the first floor of the premises. It is a system which enables customers to meet and talk freely with staff whereas the glass counter panels while formerly necessary for security were a barrier to communication.

Following the success of the concept in the banking sector, UK insurance companies and organisations in the hotel and catering industry began to consider the marketing approach. A number, in applying it, were able to capitalise on the opportunities offered by the increasing expenditures on personal and business services. In 1972, Aubrey Wilson, writer and consultant, produced a volume on *The Marketing of Professional Services*. For the purpose of his book, Wilson[12] defined services as incorporating not only 'facilitating services' (finance, storage, transport, promotion and insurance) but also 'advisory and consultative services' (all services providing general or specific technical expertise and intelligence).

Metamarketing

At about this time, Professor Kotler[13] describing the scene in the United States, remarked on the growing importance of the concept to *non-profit organisations*. This had become especially so in the fields of health, education and welfare. He reasoned, therefore, that *all* organisations – churches, museums, libraries and hospitals as well as industrial and commercial organisations – face marketing-like tasks, because all organisations, both 'profit' and 'non-profit' have 'customers' and 'products'. Their functions include the task of *managing exchange processes* and they are all engaged in 'furthering' (i.e. advancing the cause of) something. Kotler coined the term *metamarketing* to describe the processes involved in attempting to develop and maintain exchange relationships for products, services, institutions, places or causes.

It is not fitting to talk of 'adequate return-on-investment' in the context of applying marketing to non-profit organisations. In that setting it is more appropriate to think of marketing's capacity to reduce waste. Through 'in-built' acceptability' there is a better chance of improving the productivity of scarce factors of production. And with the world's supplies of non-renewable resources (oil, coal, natural gas and minerals) fast being depleted, it is possible to perceive marketing with a social role.

Social marketing

Writing in 1973, British author Norman Marcus[14] in referring to the fact that every industrial society pollutes its natural surroundings and tramps heavily on its wildlife and wilderness, believed that:

Criticism in society of commercial marketing is likely to be mounting substantially in the years ahead.

He was sure that the environmentalist lobby would see to that and he argued that social marketing might well be the process to return the environment to its 'pre-industrial purity'. Marketing, as applied to business, could be said to contribute to the quality of life because its objective was to satisfy human needs and to co-ordinate production and consumption. But social marketing concerned with 'safety and health, the encouragement of fraternity and the abolition of selfish behaviour and prejudice', went further than the current activities of profit or even non-profit organisations engaged merely in providing goods and services. Social marketing could 'market propositions which concern living and new attitudes to life by utilising tried and proven marketing techniques'.

The purpose of this book is to describe the marketing techniques to which Marcus refers and to outline how marketing draws upon insights provided by the social sciences, by financial and cost accountancy and by logical and quantitative analysis.

For now, the foregoing survey of the evolution of the marketing concept has traced its application to consumer products, industrial products and services of all kinds. The idea of its application to social causes has also been touched upon. The philosophy of marketing has been pervasive enough, in fact, for Kotler,[15] in one of his recent works, to record it under several classifications:

conversional marketing
stimulational marketing
developmental marketing
remarketing
synchromarketing
maintenance marketing
demarketing
countermarketing.

The reader wishing to understand the meanings attached to these classifications is referred to Kotler's works in the bibliography.

Marketing in action

Industrialised economies such as those of the United States, Western Europe and Japan can now reflect upon decades of experience with the marketing approach. Has it been successful? What examples of success can be provided? When and where has it failed? What are the reasons for its failures? This Section deals with such questions.

The application of marketing: case histories of success

1   The Armstrong Patents Company Ltd

Writing on international marketing ten years ago, the author well remembers describing the success of this small British organisation in the Swedish market. Its shock absorbers were specifically and painstakingly matched to the road conditions there. Through its surveys, the company was able to learn whether and to what extent the market was satisfied with existing shock absorbers under varying road conditions. Its own prototypes were then tested on no fewer than 20 makes of motor car. To be successful in Sweden, a rich market full of discriminating users, the individual firm has to innovate.

The Armstrong case history was highly significant and demonstrated a number of important points:

1   that the marketing concept can be applied just as effectively by a small firm producing industrial goods as by the multinational in the consumer goods field;

2   that successful innovation can be generated by intelligent, conscientious research into user needs;

3   that there are certain key stages in such research, viz:

   (a) assessment of whether existing products are satisfactory to the market (e.g. re: specification, performance and price);

   (b) assessment of weaknesses in competitive products that present an opportunity for a firm's own product development;

   (c) determination of the *product strategy* (e.g. modifications) that makes for market acceptability;

   (d) assessment of the *market segment** in which it is best for the organisation to operate.

2   The Fisher Price Company

Throughout the years of its existence, *Marketing*, the monthly journal of Britain's Institute of Marketing has featured any number of success stories. The June 1979 issue told the story of Fisher Price.[16] The company began, in a small way, as recently as 1972. On the verge of the 1980s, it had become one of the best known names in the British toy industry. Its success is considered to have been based upon:

   an excellent product range and excellent packaging;

   a marketing strategy carefully directed at appropriate segments of the market;

   efficient selling to the retail trade;

   efficiency of the efforts taken to ensure that retailers, in turn, were able to sell their stocks of Fisher Price toys.

* Market segmentation is explained in Chapter 4.

This last activity, known in the vernacular as *merchandising*, may rely upon the use of attractive packaging, showcards, dispensers etc, or special offers at the point-of-sale. The operations involved in siting display material and keeping it fully stocked, either through an organisation's own sales personnel or through its training programme for the retailers' staff, are also part of the merchandising function.

By 1979, Fisher Price were finding merchandising a costly business – the expenditure on salesmen and on the design, production and setting-up of display material was rising markedly. To compound the problem, there was increasing competition for the retailer's space and the large multiple organisations were exercising an increasing control over what the individual retail branch could display.

The company asked a well-known consultancy, Marketing Improvements Ltd, to devise a computer based merchandising 'package'. This was required to achieve the following objectives:

1   provide a display, cheap and simple to erect and suitable for any size of retail outlet;
2   provide an adequate plan for layout of the display;
3   ensure that sales and profit objectives were attained;
4   ensure that as much available shelf space as possible was utilised;
5   reduce the number of 'out-of-stock' situations by equalising the rate of depletion of all products involved;
6   determine stock levels and calculate the cost of fully merchandising the display at pre-determined levels.

When the package was developed, it enabled the sales personnel or the store managers to input basic data from each outlet via a portable terminal and a telephone link to the computer. Using the mathematical technique, *integer programming* (a variant of linear programming), and at a cost of approximately 50p per outlet, the company can produce via this programme a specific display for each retailer, based on only those products the retailer wishes to stock, given the dimensions of the available space and details of any special requirements relating to shelving.

The Fisher Price example provides an excellent illustration of marketing in action. Its *Computerised Planned Merchandising for Profit Scheme* shows how the computer can assist the planning and operation of marketing. Now that microprocessing places inexpensive but powerful computing capacity within the reach of marketing departments, large and small, this is a case history of increased significance.

3 Pittards Leather

No doubt most leather tanneries in the UK work hard to produce leathers to the best possible quality and specification. To the tanner's customers, however – manufacturers of shoes, handbags and other leather goods – leather is just a raw material. One UK tanner, Pittards Leather, decided to change all that by undertaking a revolutionary marketing exercise. With the help of its advertising agency, it first conducted an extensive survey on user attitudes to leather – 'user', in this context, meaning the leather-buying public. Thus the company was able to devise a market strategy based on reliable 'consumer research'. It also led to another singular outcome for the leather tanning industry – the creation of a brand name, simply, Pittards. The leather trade journals carried advertisements identifying Pittards as 'the leather that helps your profit'.

Thus it came about that, in the latter part of the 1970s, with the rest of the leather industry in severe recession, the Pittards group substantially increased its sales volume. The advertising agency was also intrigued to note that Pittards was a company that took enormous pains to service its customers. It decided to emphasise this fact in trade press advertising: one advertisement highlighted the occasion when the firm delivered a consignment of leather to a customer with an urgent order to complete. The transfer was effected at 7 am on the Severn Bridge!

The advertising campaign set out to affirm the following facts:

1   the company's close collaboration with its customers in devising leathers that will meet their needs;
2   the company's close and continuing attention to trends and fashions in the consumer market, again to the obvious benefit of Pittards' customers;
3   the company's high level of service and readiness to help in emergencies.

All of these points were made in the context that Pittards is the 'leather that helps your profit'.

Subsequent marketing strategy has been based on the idea of helping Pittards' customers to sell to their customers. For example, consumer research had demonstrated that:

1   the typical user was not particularly sure about the different qualities of leather nor on how it differed from good synthetics; and
2   user information on the care and maintenance of leather was also lacking.

The firm produced a range of tags, bearing the brand name Pittards. These were intended for manufacturers to fix to their own products and they also contained instructions for cleaning and general care of the leather. In the main UK sales regions a television campaign helped to create *brand awareness*, advising the public to: 'Look for this label on anything leather you buy. Pittards – very clever leather'.

In describing this case history, journalist Julia Piper[17] has recorded that Pittards achieved an increase in turnover from £10.6 million to £26 million, between 1974 and 1977, 'because of its forward looking marketing policies in a traditional industry'.

To the student of marketing, the Pittards case history provides an interesting example of how a strategy of *non-price competition* can effectively counter threats from the opposition in the market, including, in this instance, opposition from cheap, subsidised imports.

Note: Before considering other examples of marketing in action, the reader will find it useful to study the next Section.

What business are we in?

In 1964, an article appeared which has been described[18] as 'perhaps the literature's most vivid description of the role of the marketing concept in managerial thinking'.

Written by Theodore Levitt and entitled 'Marketing Myopia', its impact was such that subsequently most courses on marketing management began with the delegates being entreated to ask themselves: 'What business are we in'?

Levitt pointed out that 'every major industry was once a growth industry. But some that are now riding a wave of growth enthusiasm are very much in the shadow of decline ... In every case the reason growth is threatened, slowed or stopped is not because the market is saturated. It is because there has been a failure of management'.

The railroads declined, according to Levitt, at a time when the market for passenger and freight transport was growing

because those responsible for the policies of the railroad companies incorrectly defined the business they were in as the railroad business rather than the transportation business. Had they
concluded they were in the transportation business they would
have taken advantage of the lucrative market opportunities that
were filled by cars, trucks and aeroplanes. But the railroads
'defined their industry wrong' because they were 'product-
oriented instead of customer oriented'.

No industry was free from the shadow of obsolescence. 'In the
case of electronics', argued Levitt 'the greatest danger which faces
the glamorous new companies in this field is not that they do
not pay enough attention to research and development, but that
they pay too much attention to it... they are growing up under
conditions that come dangerously close to creating the illusion
that a superior product will sell itself... Having created a successful company by making a superior product, it is not surprising
that management continues to be oriented toward the product
rather than the people who consume it. It develops the philosophy that continued growth is a matter of continued product innovation and improvement'.

4 United Biscuits

The case history of this group's performance provides a good
example of the importance of Levitt's question, 'What business
are we in'?

United Biscuits incorporates such well-established manufacturers as McVities, Meredith and Drew, Kemps, Carrs of Carlisle
and Macfarlane Lang. In a general sense, the history of the group
is interesting enough because it demonstrates how a cluster of
small family businesses was brought together within a unified
management structure with rationalised methods of sales and
production and the introduction of up-to-date marketing techniques.

Beyond this, however, and as the journal Marketing[19] describes,
the group was asking itself 'what business are we in'? as long
ago as 1964. And furthermore, it recognised the answer as being
'the convenience food market' for reliance upon the generally
static biscuit market would have been of no value to the development of the group. In deciding its strategy for growth, objectives
were set with the emphasis on the long-term rather than on short-
term returns.

Overseas markets were scoured for additions to the product range (TUC, Krackawheat, Ry-King). An intensive effort was made to enter the 'own-brand' market of the retail food chains. KP nuts, potato crisps and various types of savoury snacks contributed to further growth. The policy was so successful that by the end of the 1970s, sales turnover of the group's food division was approximately £800 million – twenty times the 1964 figure.

In the meantime, the group had noted that in the United States 50 per cent by value of food is actually eaten outside the home, resulting in the food supermarkets losing substantial turnover to the 'fast-food' outlets. United Biscuits foresaw that the trend would come to Britain and, having already entered into the prepared frozen food business (King Harry pizzas) next purchased the Wimpy franchise from the J. Lyons organisation. The group also purchased the Pizzaland chain of outlets in spite of keen competition from the Spillers group. The surge in profitability which accompanied its entry into the fast food and the catering fields would never have been obtained had the group relied solely upon the sales of its original product, biscuits. 'Marketing myopia' is an epithet which would be curiously out-of-place if applied to United Biscuits.

Note: Recognising the importance of Levitt's question has provided more than one company with a formula for success. Another current example is The British Petroleum Company plc. A substantial part of its recent success, as described by the Chief Executive of Deutsche BP, its German subsidiary, is that it sees itself as an energy rather than an oil company. Its diversification into coal and natural gas has made an important contribution to the flexibility of this multinational enterprise as well as mitigating the effects of the oil crisis on its profit performance.

5　The Black and Decker Company

By the end of the 1970s, the Black and Decker Company had secured no less than 95 per cent of its markets. Despite the impregnability of its position, the UK Prices Commission concluded its investigation of the Black and Decker monopoly with the judgment that the consumer was in no way being exploited.

There have been fundamental changes in the market for DIY power tools and other products. Tom Lester[20] believes, however, that it is the firm's user orientation which has helped it to move its annual turnover, during the decade of the 1970s, from £10 million to £65 million, with a further annual total of £23 million being despatched to export markets.

The Black and Decker drill, with its attachments, so widely advertised on television, provided the basis for the company's success. Now, however, one UK household in every two possesses at least one power drill so that the original market is, in substance, only a replacement market.

Awareness of market changes enabled Black and Decker to steer a course from this static market to several new growing markets, which it came to dominate with such products as 'integral' power tools (sanders and saws), the DIY Workmate bench and a number of garden care items, including hedge trimmers, lawn trimmers, lawn mowers and lawn rakers.

Thirty years ago, when Black and Decker entered the market for DIY drills and attachments, it was so successful that it forced two well-established competitors (Wolf; Bridges) to concentrate on small market segments at the top of the price range. Today, in its expanded activities, it still has to counter competition, notably from the USA and Japan, but it continues to do so successfully. Lester concludes that: 'there are not many companies which have organised themselves ... to take advantage of the new opportunities at the same time as continuing to exploit the old ones so effectively'.

So far as marketing activities are concerned, the company is best known for its television advertising. Less evident, but equally important, is the way in which Black and Decker constantly up-dates its information on the user. In this, careful analysis of guarantee cards plays a large part. Distribution policy is based upon data which even improves upon that available to the distributors themselves: days and dates of purchase and sales by type of outlet being carefully examined.

The high volume automated production, coupled with an enlightened personnel policy on security of employment, mean that marketing targets have to be met each month (for stock levels are kept very low). A significant strategy in this regard is a confident approach to pricing and discount policies, for these are based on the anticipated cost structures which will result from the achievement of high-volume production. This seemingly high-risk concept is one that is reaping rewards and it has an in-built safety aspect provided by the extensive market information accumulated by the company.

6   *International Paint Marine Coatings (IPMC)*

In 1978, the International Paint Company obtained one of the UK's annual Marketing Awards. This was due to the success of its marine division (IPMC). According to journalist Michael Rines[21] IPMC had 'recently extended its world lead as a result of a brilliant technological innovation supremely well marketed'.

Through its world wide associates and subsidiaries IPMC has served international merchant shipping for almost a century and currently holds approximately one third of the world market for marine paint. Fundamental to its importance as a supplier is its expertise in the technology of anti-fouling paints. These are designed to prevent the accumulation of barnacles and weeds on the underwater hulls of vessels – which reduces speed and necessitates frequent visits to drydocks for cleaning and maintenance. The anti-fouling paints release biocide to deter these accumulations but, in the past, the effective period of such treatment has been limited to 18 months or so. The problem has assumed even greater importance as fleet owners, faced with rising interest rates and increasing inflation have sought to use their capital investment in vessels more intensively.

When IPMC carefully studied changing trends in its markets, it discovered that:

1   new developments in corrosion prevention were rendering obsolete the established methods of anti-fouling treatment;
2   the major proportion of related drydock costs was being taken up in preparing hull surfaces for painting;
3   increasing the number of coats of anti-fouling paints did not increase the life of the treatment to the same proportion;
4   the build-up of coats actually caused detachment of the paint and roughness of the hull – factors which, over time, contributed to 'drag' on vessels and hence, to increased fuel costs.

IPMC succeeded in developing a water soluble copolymer varnish which increased the life of the treatment to two years or more. Also, doubling the thickness of the varnish effectively doubled the life of the treatment. Here, the solubility of the varnish was important in that the 'polishing' action of the sea water upon it constantly exposed successive films of biocide so that the anti-fouling treatment stayed effective throughout the whole of its thickness. This polishing away of the surface also dispensed with the need for expensive surface preparation, since there was now no build-up of coatings and thus no detachment and roughness.

IPMC thus knew it had a product with in-built acceptability so far as client needs were concerned. The problem was how to disarm shipowners' suspicions in marketing it, since they could hardly be expected to put their faith in a paint that was actually soluble in water. The solubility, moreover, could be seen as one way of ensuring that the supplier would be guaranteed continuity of sales!

The marketing organisation based its appeal on a cost/benefit analysis approach. Shipowners were exhorted to: 'Use SPC (self-polishing copolymer) and save 12 per cent on fuel over a two year in-service period'.

The marketing task was not merely to sell a much more expensive product but to convince clients that the extra preparation time and the extra cost in applying the paint were worthwhile. The marketing team thus became involved in shipowners' problems at a new, more profound level. As a result, it gained appreciable knowledge of many aspects of ships' operations, including chartering, voyage patterns, the cost of ships being out of commission and the monitoring of the vessels' performance. Sales personnel were accordingly trained not just to sell paint but to sell cost savings. Each salesman was taught how to prepare a cost-benefit analysis and to use it during a sales presentation.

A film, translated into 14 languages and accompanied by brochures and newsheets emphasised this problem-solving approach. It was distributed world-wide.

Since 1974, the company's success has been such as to vindicate both the product and the approach adopted to market it. The marketing strategy is to sell a solution to a problem rather than to sell a product. It is a client-centred strategy, based on an accurate understanding of the market. The strategy is one which IPMC's main Japanese competitor has now also adopted and is one which, as Rines concludes, 'all industrial goods marketers should strive to do'.

Note: The above case histories demonstrate that the marketing approach, when applied to business organisations does not pre-suppose a specific category of product (it is for industrial goods as well as consumer goods). Nor does its application require the organisation to be of a given minimum size (it is for small firms as well as big ones). It is not difficult to find such case histories and a significant number of studies drawn from the fields of services and non-profit organisations are now becoming available. Some examples are given later in this volume.

Marketing: the failures

It appears then that marketing can be a powerful factor in company planning. But would it be true to say that the coming of the concept has met with unabridged success? The answer must be 'No'.

Foster[22] advances clear and obviously sound reasons for 'Why marketing can fail'. Apart from the fact that its greater or lesser success will be influenced by the quality of the personnel in the marketing department, he points out that its alleged failure can stem from what marketing is, what techniques it employs and what these can and cannot achieve. Moreover, the value of marketing research, for example, must be weighed against the costs it will entail. Nor is it necessary to commission possibly costly external research when an intelligent scrutiny of the organisation's own internal statistics might prove just as adequate (the use to which Black and Decker put their user guarantee cards is a good example).

Spasmodic use of marketing techniques can also lead to disillusion – better a planned, continuing and constantly up-dated programme of research than some ambitious one-off research project not really related to the organisation's objectives. Foster also makes the point, with which all observers of the marketing scene will agree, that there have been innumerable instances where, because it seemed fashionable to do so, the title of the appropriate executives has been changed from 'sales manager' to 'marketing manager' but this is all that has changed. The organisations concerned have then continued to go about their business in a production-oriented manner.

The author can vouch for the accuracy of this last observation, and go even further perhaps – for he recalls discussing the marketing approach with the chairman of a UK public limited company. The chairman requested the author not to emphasise the strategic role of marketing when conducting a seminar within the company. It transpired that he had recently transferred an executive out of the post of sales manager to the newly designed post of marketing manager. The employee concerned could 'do very little harm' there because the post had such limited authority.

Giles[23] and other writers have emphasised the importance of *organisational integration*. Here again, unless this receives proper attention from senior management, the marketing approach may be doomed to failure. The marketing approach requires a know-ledge of user needs to be incorporated at the product development stage and into the subsequent stage of production. This means that, in a general sense, research and development personnel and production personnel are just as involved in the marketing pro-cess as the sales personnel. The organisation's efforts must there-fore be integrated so as to attain marketing objectives. The essence of the philosophy is contained in the statement[24] that marketing is a process in which 'the point of origin is consumer demand; and all relevant activities in research, manufacturing, sales and advertising should be co-ordinated by the marketer to the single end of satisfying consumer demand – at a profit'.

If communication within the organisation is at fault, the intro-duction of the marketing approach may generate doubt and possi-bly dissension. Production and other personnel may come to believe that the more strategic role being given to the 'sales func-tion' is really a diminution of their own role.

Two points are relevant here:

1   It is often the case that sales executives assume the marketing role, but this need not be the invariable rule. It could, for instance, be argued that where complex technical products require research and development and/or production executives to maintain con-tinuous contact with customers, the marketing function could just as reasonably be left with these executives. Similarly, since marketing is to do with 'return-on-investment' and since this implies that cost-consciousness, particularly within the distribu-tion function, must be raised to a new, high level, a case could be made for the marketing function to be the responsibility of a financial manager.

To any sales-minded reader, these propositions may seem fanci-ful but they do demonstrate that there is some room for debate. At least one British writer[25] has planned and produced a market-ing textbook with accountants in mind. It is indisputable that sales managers frequently do succeed in marketing – but then, so do accountants and lawyers and engineers. In fact, where sales personnel have been seen to fail in the role, the argument runs that this is because selling is a verbal culture and many sales people find the more analytical role required of them in marketing a strange and stressful one. The thought is that they could have been more profitably left to get on with the important business of selling.

2   The second point is that too often, the fearful reaction to marketing has been because, in some organisations, too large a role has been claimed for it – as though marketing was, in essence, 'the business' and all other functions were there to serve it. In this sense, some confusion has arisen over the distinction between *marketing* and *corporate planning*. In the words of management consultant, John Argenti:[26]

This arises because in most corporate plans one of the crucially important strategies involves products or markets or both. It is difficult to imagine a corporate plan that does not include a product-market strategy, but this does not mean that they are the same thing. Whereas marketing is solely or mainly concerned with products, markets, customers, promotion, distribution and so on, corporate planning includes everything: production, research, people, finance, tax and anything else, so long as it is sufficiently important to the future of the company to warrant attention in the plan.

The moral is that self-aggrandisement can be self-defeating.

If marketing's failures have been due, on occasions, to lack of effective internal communication it is equally true that external communication of its ideas has also been faulty. One recalls J. K. Galbraith's[27] entertaining essay on 'The Language of Economics', in which he says:

Among the social sciences, and indeed among all reputable fields of learning, economics occupies a special place for the reproach that is inspired by its language. The literate layman regularly proclaims his discontent with the way in which economists express themselves. Other scholars emerge from the eccentricities of their own terminology to condemn the economist for a special commitment to obscurity. If an economist writes a book or even an article in clear English, he need say nothing. He will be praised for avoiding jargon – and also for risking the rebuke of his professional colleagues in doing so.

Perhaps the language of marketing has been more of a hindrance than a help in winning acceptance for it. Had marketing practitioners, teachers and writers, including this writer, read this paragraph of Galbraith's as a daily exercise, many more followers would have been won for the cause. It is certain that the marketing way is vital to the survival of many businesses. Yet it does such businesses no service if, from motives of 'professionalism' or 'academic respectability', we bring them news of 'methodological breakthroughs' and talk of 'scalar interactions'. Had we ourselves been more customer-oriented (itself an ugly enough description) we would perhaps have pondered on how 'cross elasticity of demand' and 'cognitive dissonance' would be regarded by the harassed businessperson with an urgent problem to solve.

Marketing is essentially a simple notion. Only the communicators have made it complex. We would have done well to remember the Churchillian line that: 'the short words are best and the old words are the best of all'.

Before concluding this Section, it would be useful to return to another observation of Douglas Foster[28] – for he is undoubtedly correct when he says that marketing is not simply a matter of producing what the market wants. The secret of success, according to Foster, is to establish what products the firm is best able to make and, from market research information, the firm can persuade its customers to buy: 'Marketing then becomes the art of doing what is possible to obtain optimum profit at minimum cost'.

In other words, the realistic strategy is grounded in these questions:

1   what can be produced, from existing assets, that possesses in-built acceptability?
2   if additional capital expenditure is necessary, will it be affordable and profitable?

Whither marketing?

This chapter has explained the marketing concept, described something of its history and said something of the successes and failures that can be recorded for it. Where does marketing go from here?

This writer believes there are many UK organisations, and particularly small businesses, that have not yet adopted the marketing approach and could do so with advantage. In early 1982, the National Economic Development Office issued a report[29] in which lack of commitment to marketing was highlighted as 'the single most important constraint in improving UK and overseas market shares'.

Beyond tangible products, David Schwartz reminds us[30] that such 'intangibles' as health care and entertainment require marketing too. And since marketing is intended to meet either commercial or non-commercial objectives, non-profit organisations must also perform marketing activities. He adds that universities in the United States use advertising and other promotional techniques to market continuing education programmes. Charitable organisations perform marketing activities to win public support and (even) 'the mounting of an evangelical crusade requires careful marketing planning and execution'. He points out that as we extend our understanding of marketing, of what it is and what it will do, so we shall come to appreciate the role for it in the exchange of concepts and ideas.

If marketing does assume a broader role in the UK it may well be along these lines. Changes in the climate or environment surrounding every organisation, commercial or otherwise, bring threat or opportunity. In the next chapter some illustrations are provided from both the profit and non-profit sectors of Britain's economy. In the non-profit sector, the author frequently hears talk, in universities and other institutions of higher learning, of 'the need to market our services' – a trend which is all to the good.

Reflecting on the American experience Stanton[31] is concerned about whether we are 'marketing the wrong things'. Social and economic resources are becoming scarce. This raises questions about the influence that marketing has on the allocation of these resources. He wonders how reasonable it is for marketing to be occupied with promoting the sale of motor cars and high fashion and outboard motors when the benefits to society of education, urban services, slum clearance and the elimination of air and water pollution go unpromoted.

In describing the *societal marketing concept*, Kotler[32] queries whether:

... the pure marketing concept constitutes an adequate business philosophy in an age of environmental deterioration, resource shortages, explosive population growth, worldwide inflation and neglected social services.

He believes[33] that:

The societal marketing concept is a consumers' needs orientation backed by integrated marketing aimed at generating consumer satisfaction and *long-run consumer welfare* as the key to satisfying organisational goals.

We shall have an opportunity to consider the ways in which organisations can generate long-run consumer welfare, as this book progresses.

Self-assessment questions

1 Someone says to you: 'Marketing is just another name for selling'. How would you answer?
2 Explain how the marketing approach assists organisations to adapt to change. Why, in some instances, was 'production orientation' no bad thing?
3 Define: (a) social marketing; (b) merchandising; (c) organisational integration; (d) market-induced flow; (e) return-on-investment.
4 Explain why marketing can fail.
5 Distinguish between marketing and corporate planning.
6 Outline the ways in which UK banking organisations have successfully adopted the marketing philosophy.

References

1 Drucker, Peter. *Management: tasks, responsibilities, practices* New York, Harper & Row, 1973, pp. 64–65
2 Institute of Marketing. Definition of September 1966, In *Marketing in a competitive economy* London, Cassell/Associated Business Programmes, 3rd edn, 1971, p. 47
3 Wilson, R. M. S. *Management controls in marketing* London, William Heinemann Ltd, 1973, p. 4
4 McCarthy, E. Jerome. *Basic marketing: a managerial approach* 6th edn, Homewood, Illinois, Richard D. Irwin, 1978, p. 29
5 Kotler, Philip. *Principles of marketing* 2nd edn, Englewood Cliffs, NJ, Prentice-Hall, 1983, p. 6
6 *Management controls in marketing* (see Reference 3) p. 4
7 Frain, John. *Introduction to marketing* 2nd edn, Plymouth, Macdonald & Evans Ltd, 1983, pp. 2–3
8 Baker, Michael J. *Marketing: theory and practice* London and Basingstoke. Macmillan, 1979, p. 9
9 Smith, Adam, from his treatise: *Enquiry into the nature and causes of the wealth of nations*, 1776
10 Cooke, Alistair. *America* London: British Broadcasting Corporation, 1973, pp. 316–317
11 Collins, David. Face to face at Barclays *The Sunday Telegraph*, 12 August 1979

12 Wilson, Aubrey. *The marketing of professional services* London, McGraw-Hill Book Company (UK) Limited, 1972, p. 3

13 Kotler, Philip. Metamarketing: the furthering of organisations, persons, places and causes *Marketing Forum*, UK Institute of Marketing, July–August 1971, pp. 13–23

14 Marcus, Norman. *Marketing concepts and strategies in the next decade* Ch. 10, Social Marketing, (ed. Roger, Leslie W.), London, Cassell/Associated Business Programmes Ltd, 1973, p. 219

15 Kotler, Philip. *Marketing Management-Analysis, Planning and Control* 4th edn, Englewood Cliffs, NJ, Prentice-Hall Inc, 1980, pp. 23–26

16 Melkman, Alan. Fisher-Price's electronic shelf-appeal *Marketing*, London: Haymarket Publishing Ltd, (on behalf of the Institute of Marketing), June, 1979, pp. 26–30

17 Piper, Julia. How Pittards put a brand on its leather *Marketing*, August, 1979, pp. 17–20

18 Enis, Ben M. and Cox, Keith K. Marketing strategy, *Marketing classics*, Boston: Allyn and Bacon, Inc, 1969, p. 340

19 Lester, Tom. The boss who took on the pickets, (profile of Sir Hector Laing) *Marketing*, April, 1979, pp. 35–36

20 Lester, Tom. Why Black and Decker takes the lion's share, *Marketing* May, 1979, pp. 23–26

21 Rines, Michael. IPC's underwater winner, *Marketing* November, 1978, pp. 21–24

22 Foster, Douglas. *Mastering marketing* London, The Macmillan Press Ltd, 1982, pp. 5–7

23 Giles, G. B. *Marketing* 3rd edn, Plymouth, Macdonald & Evans Ltd, 1978, p. 4

24 McIver, Colin. *Marketing* 2nd edn, London, Business Publications Ltd, 1964, p. 5

25 Williamson, R. J. *Marketing for accountants and managers* London, William Heinemann Ltd, 1979

26 Argenti, John. *Practical Corporate Planning* London, George Allen & Unwin, 1980, pp. 6–7

27 Galbraith, J. K. *A Contemporary Guide to Economics, Peace and Laughter* London, André Deutsch Ltd, 1971, p. 26

28 *Mastering marketing* p. 5

29 Cannon, Tom and Willis, Michael. Why marketing barriers are hard to jump, *The Guardian*, 30 April, 1982 on Industrial performance, trade performance and marketing (NEDO report)

30 Schwartz, David J. *Marketing today–a basic approach* 3rd edn, New York, Harcourt, Brace, Jovanovich Inc, 1981, p. 4

31 Stanton, William J. *Fundamentals of marketing* 6th edn, New York, McGraw-Hill Book Company, 1981, p. 7

32 *Principles of marketing* p. 20

33 Kotler, Philip. *Marketing for nonprofit organisations* Englewood Cliffs, New Jersey, Prentice-Hall Inc, 1975, p. 47

2 THE MARKETING ENVIRONMENT AND THE MARKETING PROCESS

Objectives

An organisation is affected by a number of influences which make up its 'environment'. Moreover, the environment can be friendly or hostile to what the organisation is trying to do – it can pose threats or opportunities.

We shall see in this Chapter how the marketing manager, by mixing 'ingredients', or resources, and directing these to a target market, attempts to achieve the objectives the organisation has set for itself.

Introduction

Arnold Ceramics – an organisation and its environment

Arnold Ceramics is a well-known British company which manufactures tableware. Its factory premises are situated in Card Street, Potterstown, North Staffordshire. The company was founded more than two hundred years ago by Enoch Arnold (a contemporary of the great Josiah Wedgwood). Since that time, Arnold's fine tableware, characterised by the famous 'bottle-oven' trademark, has found its way to practically every part of the world. Some of the firm's younger directors feel that the trademark has a curiously dated look and reflects inaccurately upon the company and its modern production techniques. The most frequent and inconclusive debates in the boardroom centre on the trademark, for the more senior directors feel that to dispense with it would be to effectively dispense with the great goodwill which has accumulated around it in over two centuries of successful trading.

The process of making this famous tableware, as an economist would describe it, is depicted in Fig. 2.1. From this it can be seen that *economic inputs* in the form of:

natural resources – e.g. clays, glazes, water, energy;
labour   – of various types and levels of skill;
capital items   – e.g. factory premises, machinery and kilns (in which to bake or fire the ware),

are brought together in a production process. This process results in an *output* of tableware (of the design and quality upon which Arnold's reputation has been based).

The environment

Fig. 2.1 also suggests, however, that this production process does not stand alone. It is actually part of a larger system. It can be seen that at the boundaries of the inner system (the production process) there are several influences at work:

- economic
- political
- demographic
- technological
- legal
- competitive,

which have a bearing on the way in which the inner system (the Arnold sub-system) will operate.

Economic influences

For example, under the bundle of boundary conditions labelled economic influences, Arnold's activity will be clearly affected by changes in the value of money (the inflation rate), by the general level of economic prosperity, and by the cost of resources. All of these factors will play a part in determining the market price of Arnold's tableware and hence, the nature and extent of the demand for it. In this respect, one of the firm's greatest concerns has been the soaring cost of energy, particularly since the OPEC price rises of the mid and late 1970s.

Political influences

These bear significantly upon the Arnold operations. For example, traditionally, the UK ceramics industry has been regarded by

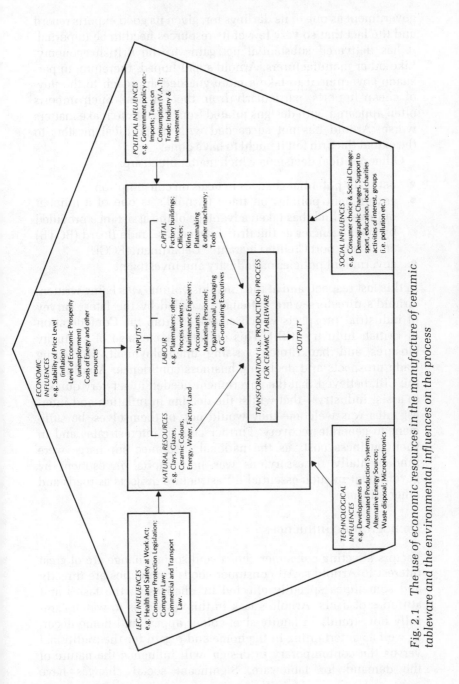

Fig. 2.1   The use of economic resources in the manufacture of ceramic tableware and the environmental influences on the process

POLITICAL INFLUENCES
e.g. Government policy on:-
Imports; Taxes on
Consumption (V.A.T);
Trade; Industry &
Investment

SOCIAL INFLUENCES
e.g. Consumer choice & Social Change:
Demographic Changes, Support to
sport, education, local charities
activities of interest, groups
(i.e. pollution etc.)

*ECONOMIC
INFLUENCES*
e.g. Stability of Price Level
(inflation)
Level of Economic Prosperity
(unemployment)
Costs of Energy and other
resources

"INPUTS"

CAPITAL
Factory buildings;
Offices;
Kilns;
Platemaking
& other machinery;
Tools

LABOUR
e.g. Platemakers; other
Process workers;
Maintenance Engineers;
Accountants;
Marketing Personnel;
Organisational, Managing
& Co-ordinating Executives

*TRANSFORMATION (i.e. PRODUCTION) PROCESS
FOR CERAMIC TABLEWARE*

"OUTPUT"

NATURAL RESOURCES
e.g. Clays, Glazes,
Ceramic Colours,
Energy, Water, Factory Land

*TECHNOLOGICAL
INFLUENCES*
e.g. Developments in
Automated Production Systems;
Alternative Energy Sources;
Waste disposal ; Microelectronics

LEGAL INFLUENCES
e.g. Health and Safety at Work Act;
Consumer Protection Legislation;
Company Law;
Commercial and Transport
Law.

government as one of its darlings for, given its good exports record and the fact that so very few of its resources need to be imported, it has delivered substantial net gains to the British economy. Like other manufacturers, Arnold's had hoped, therefore, to persuade government to take a more guarded approach to the flow of cheap imports, particularly from the Far East. Such imports often appeared with designs pirated from the UK, to make matters worse. Arnold has not succeeded with its political masters to the extent the firm felt it ought to have done.

Other political decisions which matter much are:

- actual or potential changes in taxes on consumption
- government policies on trade (Arnold's is one of a number of firms which has taken advantage of the assistance provided by such agencies as the British Overseas Trade Board (BOTB) and the Export Credits Guarantee Department (ECGD)
- government policies on industry and investment

In this last respect, and at the time this volume was being written, Arnold's directors were extremely worried by the latest survey of industrial prospects which emanated from the Confederation of British Industry (CBI). This outlined a message of company closures and bankruptcies, rising unemployment, worsening trade prospects and declining business confidence. Arnold, like the CBI, believed that the government needed to act very quickly to assist industry – that whilst the decline in inflation and interest rates was welcome they would not, of themselves, be sufficient to generate recovery. Further cuts in interest rates and in such business costs as the national insurance surcharge were fundamentally necessary, as was new capital investment by government in such essential infrastructure projects as roads and other utilities.

Demographic influences

Factors affecting consumer choice and social change are of great interest to Arnold's. All consumer goods companies are directly and sometimes speedily affected by changes in the tastes and attitudes of users. Arnold's task in this respect is to watch carefully how trends in family size, colour appeal and home decor, as well as entertaining in the home and regard for the traditional versus the contemporary in design, will influence the nature of the demand for tableware. Significant social changes have included the phenomenon of *consumerism*, which has expressed itself in a reaction against overpriced, inadequate and unsafe products. A trend towards simplification has led users away from complicated designs and products. The reaction known as 'anti-bigness' has shown itself as a dislike for big companies, big brands and big communications media. An increasing number of people have expressed their concern for the environment and are worried about the waste of finite resources. Arnold's must search for cheaper, cleaner and more cost effective ways of producing their tableware not only because it makes good commercial sense but also because nowadays there is a social obligation for it to do so.

Technological influences

The two centuries since the inception of the company have seen its techniques of production move from their basis in craft skills to a basis of applied engineering. The factory at Potterstown is considered by many to be one of the most up-to-date in the industry. Although its products are relatively expensive and of good quality, the firm caters for a mass market. Consequently, mass production techniques have been perfected in order to transform the basic raw material into items of tableware. Similarly the old type bottle-ovens, which required 72 hours firing with solid fuel, have been swept away in favour of gas fired tunnel kilns and electrically heated moving-belt furnaces, requiring only a fraction of this time to complete their firing cycle.

Yet Arnold's recognise that new developments in computing and communications have now brought the possibility of fully automated production systems to even small firms. Families of automatic transfer machines and robots may soon make the push-button ceramics factory more the rule than the exception. Arnold's must stay abreast of these developments if they are to remain competitive. They must similarly keep themselves informed on progress in the search for new sources of energy, on new methods for the disposal of industrial waste, and on developments in management information systems, electronic message systems and the automated office.

Legal influences

The period since 1945 has been one of burgeoning legislation. This has affected all aspects of life, not least its industrial and commercial aspects. Legislation concerning trade descriptions, consumer protection, consumer credit, contract terms, hire purchase, pricing and price marking, monopolies and restrictive practices, copyright and patents and trade marks must be mentioned in this context.

Other legal influences are designed to ensure that employers take adequate steps to ensure the health and safety of workers, that business organisations operate within the provisions of company law and that, as employers, they observe the provisions of labour law, relating to such matters as contracts of employment, equal pay, discrimination in employment, trade union membership and redundancy payments. As we shall see in Chapter 13, Arnold's must also observe various legal requirements in all their international markets. And, of course, since the United Kingdom is a member of the European Community, the law of the Community, as expressed through the treaties and the delegated legislation stemming from Community institutions (the Council, the Commission and the European Court of Justice) influences Arnold's operations.

Since any changes in the legal environment are likely to consist of increased, rather than decreased, intervention in business operations, this is an environmental factor to which Arnold's will have to devote close attention.

Competition

All of the above influences are usually described as uncontrollable elements in the organisation's environment. It is just possible that the individual firm may have some effect on the operation of one or other of these influences – for example, by effective lobbying of government for change in its industrial policies. However, it is usually more realistic for the business organisation to consider that these are influences outside its own control. The organisation must therefore learn to exist within the environment that these influences help to create but so adjust its policies and operations as to minimise the threats and maximise the opportunities provided by the environment. More of how the organisation may develop an appropriate strategy for this later in this Chapter – for now, let us remember that no listing of the uncontrollable elements is complete without mentioning competition.

Arnold's face *direct* competition from a number of UK manufacturers producing good quality, relatively expensive tableware of a similar type. The young housewife and the bride-to-be have a wide range from which to choose. They are, if anything, less loyal to one particular manufacturer or brand than were their mothers and grandmothers. Mention has already been made of cheap foreign imports and although these are not directly comparable to Arnold's output they do constitute an increased threat in times of economic recession and high unemployment.

This competition has also to be faced in the key overseas markets of the USA, Western Europe and Scandinavia, where there is also additional direct competition from well-established local manufacturers, many of whom pay careful attention to their designs and product development policies so as to maintain a continuing appeal to highly discriminating users. Moreover, these richer markets are the ones that are characterised by national impatience. Because of the range of choice available to them, users will not wait very long for a particular brand or a particular design. Arnold's have to take significant steps to ensure their ware is available when it is needed as a consequence of this (see Chapter 13 on international marketing).

So it can be seen that in this competitive environment, the appearance of an intriguing new product from a rival organisation can affect the most carefully prepared marketing plan. Consequential adjustments may have to be made in all phases of Arnold's operations.

Then there is the *indirect* competition provided by all the other items which compete for a family's discretionary expenditure:

- from other items of tableware – silver, linen, glassware
- from other 'homemaking' items – furniture, carpets, washing machines
- from other items of general expenditure – school fees, clothing, car repairs and the foreign holiday

Organisation theory

The foregoing notes on the Arnold organisation provide us with an insight into the role of management. It is a role that can be thought of as:

1 the co-ordination of scarce resources
2 in pursuit of certain objectives

3 the process taking place within an *environment*, in which a number of factors, economic, demographic, political etc are at work.

Fig. 2.1 attempts to depict the situation as it relates to Arnold Ceramics, a business organisation pursuing profit objectives. As we shall see later, such an image is equally useful for non-profit organisations. In passing, it should also be noted that the environmental influences which have been described are not discrete. A government may take, for example, some *political* standpoint on the activities of trade unions. This may show itself via some *legal* enactment giving the unions more, or less, freedom according to government's ideology and it may accordingly have implications for management in one direction or another.

The concept of an organisation operating in an environment has its roots in a field of study called *organisation theory*. Although its ideas are still being developed, it might be useful to briefly consider some of them, for their relevance for the marketing concept and the marketing process can then be distinguished.

Early work in the field is linked with *Frederick Winslow Taylor (1856–1917)*, an American engineer. He was mainly interested in how organisations work internally. Taylor examined the ways in which work was carried out, the amount of specialisation that was involved and the manner in which work operations were controlled and co-ordinated. He concluded that the most important tasks for management were:

1 the discovery of the most effective methods of performing jobs;
2 the determination of the most effective methods of controlling the work force.

His so-called *classical approach* was based on the belief that the organisation's objectives would best be attained through the worker co-operation stemming from the provision of continuing, well-paid employment. This was the best incentive for workers. He also emphasised that, within the work situation, maximum specialisation was essential.

During the period 1927–32, significant research was undertaken by *Elton Mayo* at the Hawthorne Works of the Western Electric Company, in Chicago. Unlike Taylor, Mayo and others came to believe that co-operation was not automatically achieved by providing well-paid employment and issuing orders. Mayo's *human relations approach* constituted the next step forward in organisation theory. It was important to involve the work groups in the decision-making processes. Solutions to problems were more likely to be found by examining the needs of the workers rather than by merely scrutinising the jobs they did. The 'job-centred' approach of Taylor was discarded in favour of an 'employee-centred' approach which drew a great deal of its philosophy from sociology and social psychology.

1938 saw the next development when *Chester Barnard*, an executive of the Bell Telephone Company, expressed the view that organisations could not be considered merely as groups of workers co-ordinated to achieve some specific goal. The organisation extended beyond these internal groups and comprised investors, suppliers and customers as well as workers. Moreover, he suggested that 'the organisation is influenced in its workings by external ('environmental') forces' – such as the government, the trade unions and the forces of the market for its products or services.

Barnard's views, which came to be known as the *systems approach* are still in vogue. The reader can identify them in the operations of Arnold Ceramics, as just described. The systems approach can be seen to derive its central ideas from biology and the physical sciences. Man's own bodily system continually adjusts to changes in the physical environment so that body temperature and blood sugar are maintained within the quite narrow tolerances necessary to avoid damage or death. And thus, an organisation must react to, and adapt to, changes in its environment if it is to maintain itself in being.

How is the organisation to inform itself of changes in its environment? The human organism achieves this by a system of *feedback*. It possesses a number of sensing devices – the eyes, the skin, the nervous system – which enable it to monitor environmental change. This feedback principle – the use of information to warn the system how it is functioning in relation to its environment, is also central to the systems approach in organisation theory. As we shall see in Chapter 3 a *marketing information system*, utilising the techniques of marketing research, is intrinsically important to both profit and non-profit organisations in obtaining this feedback. Marketing research becomes even more important when the organisation's markets are undergoing rapid change.

The stakeholder theory

What has been described above is an organisation within an environment which nowadays is typically subject to change, with such change being caused by environmental influences outside the control of the organisation. The organisation maintains itself in being by a process of adaptation relying on feedback in the shape of information obtained for it by the techniques of marketing research. A collateral idea to the systems approach to organisations is the *stakeholder theory* which suggests that the objectives of the organisation should not stem from the organisation exclusively but from the claims upon it of its various 'stakeholders' – its employees, suppliers, shareholders, distributors, consumers, the general public, central and local government – all parties who have a 'stake' in its well-being and are affected by its operations. The proposed objectives should constitute a reasonable balance of all their 'claims' upon the organisation.

Mention of such relevant third parties as suppliers and distributors is helpful at this stage for Stanton[1] is one of a number of writers who would go further than the representation of the organisational environment provided by Fig. 2.1. Stanton firstly describes a company's complete marketing system as 'a framework of internal resources operating within a set of external forces' and he finds it useful to think of:

non marketing resources	(production, finance, research & development, personnel etc)
↓	
helping to establish a *'marketing mix'*	(of product planning, price structures, distribution systems and promotional activities)
↓	
which is operating within a set of *macroenvironmental forces*	(i.e. the political, technological and other influences mentioned earlier in this Chapter).

Stanton goes on to suggest that there are three further environmental forces, which although they are clearly external to the organisation should nevertheless be regarded as part of its marketing system. These are:

the market itself

the organisation's suppliers

the organisation's 'marketing intermediaries' (i.e. its distributors and sales agents)

He reasons that these three forces constitute an *external micro environment* and that whilst these are usually considered as non controllable forces they are in fact different in kind from the broader forces operating upon the organisation and stemming from the economic system as a whole (i.e. the 'macroenvironment'). When one considers the way in which the average individual organisation can influence the market (e.g. through promotional activities), its suppliers (through its specifications and negotiating policies) and its intermediaries (e.g. through its distribution policies) and compares this with its virtual impotence relative to the economic system as a whole, the reasoning behind Stanton's classification becomes clear enough.

Thus we have an overall system in which the organisation utilises its *internal resources* (capital equipment, finance, operative and management skills, research and development etc) and applies these to the raw materials and other products and services received from suppliers in order to develop a marketing mix which is then transferred to the market with the assistance of marketing intermediaries (distributors, agents, transport organisations etc). Fig. 2.2 is an attempt to depict this in the case of Arnold Ceramics and it can be seen that the whole of this activity takes place within a framework of broader forces making for change.

The marketing process and the marketing mix

We know one thing for certain about most of the markets of today – their common characteristic is that they are undergoing rapid change. In fact, the *rate of change* continues to accelerate so that, of itself, it constitutes, in the words of Alvin Toffler,[2] 'an elemental force'. In Toffler's notable social study *Future Shock* he feels moved to speak of:

the roaring current of change, a current so powerful today that it overturns institutions, shifts our values and shrivels our roots.

In the section of his study, strikingly entitled 'The death of permanence' he suggests that:

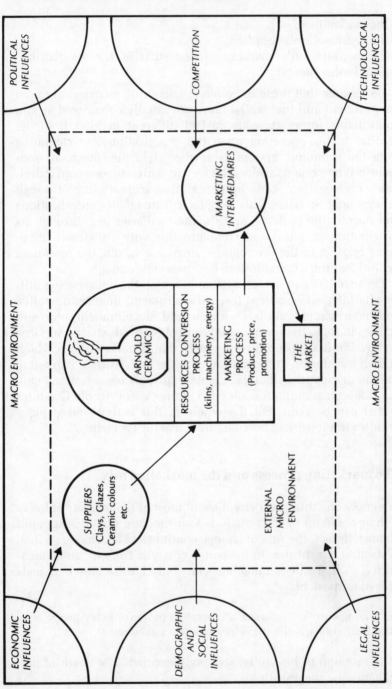

Fig. 2.2   The complete marketing system (including the micro and macro environments)

between now and the twenty-first century millions of ordinary, psychologically normal people will face an abrupt collision with the future. Citizens of the world's richest and most technically advanced nations, many of them, will find it increasingly painful to keep up with the incessant demand for change that characterises our time. For them, the future will have arrived too soon.

Toffler's work was first published in Great Britain in 1970. Since then, of course, the pace of change has quickened even further.

Organisational objectives

Figuratively speaking, the idea of rapid change in the environment can be thought of as a turbulent sea with the ship of organisation ploughing through it towards its objectives. There is a management team on the bridge and in that team none has a more crucial role than the head of marketing. Plotting the route to its objectives means that the team must ask itself four questions:

Where are we going?

Resolving the answer to this question can be done in a number of ways, for the organisation might set out its objectives as, for example:

1   a rate of return on the resources it will employ (return on investment)
2   as an excess of its revenues over its costs (profit);
3   as a rate of growth of sales per annum;
4   or simply, as 'survival'.

How will we get there?

The answer to this question will help to fix the methods (i.e. the 'policies') by which the objectives will be achieved. If, for instance, Arnold Ceramics were to set out its objectives in terms of *sales growth* [as in 3 above] then it might try to attain a target figure of growth by:

1   increasing the number of products it makes and sells;
2   increasing the number of markets to which it sells;
3   increasing the number of sales representatives it employs;
4   a combination of some or all of these policies.

When will we get there?

Here the organisation is setting itself a time period against which its success or failure will be judged, for example, 'In the next financial year our objective will be to increase the rate of return on investment by 2 per cent'.

In order to help the organisation to really decide where it is going objectives will be devised over a lengthy time scale. This means that:

● some objectives will be set out in detail for attainment in the immediate future (*proximate objectives*);
● some, for the medium term (1 to 5 years perhaps), which will not be set out in so much detail (*medium term objectives*);
● some of the objectives will be set out in 'broad brush' style for attainment in the longer term (*visionary objectives*).

Visionary objectives describe the organisation's ultimate destination. Arnold Ceramics may set itself the visionary objective of being the best quality, medium priced tableware manufacturer in Europe. On the other hand, if it decides that this field is too crowded with competition it may decide to diversify into industrial ceramics or into architectural ceramics. The important point to note here is that whatever the visionary objectives may be, the proximate and the medium-term objectives will be so related to them that the attainment of earlier objectives is a step towards the fulfilment of those in the longer-term.

How will we know when we've arrived?

Whatever the organisation achieves must be measured. In economic organisations, the unit of measurement is invariably money (e.g. 'a short term profit objective before interest and taxation, of £1 million'.) On the other hand, the unit could be expressed in percentage terms ('an increase of 2 per cent in profits') or in terms of volume of production or sales, or perhaps as a share of the market. The non-profit organisation might set itself an increase in the rate of usage of its services – a library, for example, might express its intention of increasing its book issues by 5 per cent. The significance of this question is that progress can be regularly checked, using the appropriate unit of measurement and, if necessary, corrective action can be taken in good time.

Unfortunately, the process of setting objectives cannot be

treated at greater length in this work. Suffice it to add that objectives have been defined as 'the fundamental purpose for an organisation's existence' and, in fact, are so crucial to it that failure to achieve its objectives means that the organisation itself has failed.

The purpose of providing this simple outline is to demonstrate that once the organisation's general objectives are set, plans can be devised for all the functional areas of the organisation – the marketing plan, the manpower plan, the production plan etc. And such a sequence of planning is logical for, as the marketing concept implies, all activity must stem from the requirements of the market. Fig 2.3 which expresses, as an example, the relationship between the marketing plan and the manpower plan is intended to demonstrate this organic linkage between parts of an organisation striving to attain certain objectives.

The role of marketing management

When the strategic objectives for the whole organisation have been established, a marketing plan can be developed:

1   to serve the attainment of these objectives and
2   to provide a basis from which plans for the other parts of the organisation can be devised.

The process of planning for marketing is described in detail in Chapter 11, but it is important at this stage at least to outline how marketing management approaches the task. McCarthy[3] suggests that the nature of the management job can be generally thought of as comprising three basic duties:

1   to set up a general plan (strategy) for the organisation;
2   to direct the execution of this plan;
3   to evaluate, analyse and control the plan in actual operation.

These duties fittingly describe the role of marketing management within the marketing function but let us at this stage primarily consider the marketing manager's contribution to the organisation's general plan. In helping here, and following the systems approach described earlier, marketing executives must consider how the environment will influence future operations, for to quote Kotler:[4]

Modern marketing theory holds that the key to an organisation's success

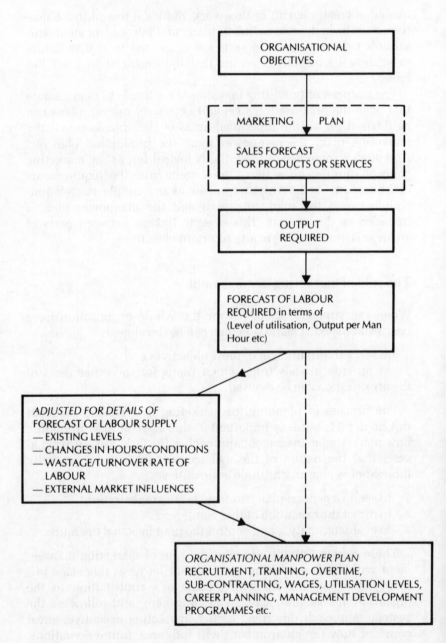

Fig. 2.3   *The marketing plan and the manpower plan*

is the ability to make timely and appropriate adaptations to a complex and ever changing environment.

The environment must be thought about for ways in which change may endanger present operations or bring with it prospects for new growth. This is what is usually termed *opportunity and threat analysis*. It is relatively easy to visualise how *technological change* can bring threats or opportunities. The table below, takes another example, that of *demographic change*. If the demand for a product or service is related in some significant way to the age of users then the importance of the trends described below need no emphasis.

The changing structure of the UK population

1   According to figures published by the Government Actuary, whilst the total UK population continues to grow each decade, the rate of growth in the 1970s has been considerably less than the average rate of growth per decade for the period 1941–1971.

2   The next important point to note is the change in the age composition of the population since the 1940s. When the year 1981 is compared with 1951, for example, the *Under 15* age group declined slightly (11.3 : 11.4 million) whereas there was an increase in the *45–74* age group (17.6 million : 15.8 million) and in the *75 and over* age group (3.2 : 1.8 million). Moreover, as the index numbers below (reproduced from official statistics) clearly show, future projections indicate a continued decline in the 'Under 15' segment and an increasing proportion of old people in the population.

Projected population by age
Index numbers (1976 = 100)

	1976 (base)	1981	1991	2001	2011
0–14	100	88	89	98	87
15–29	100	104	104	87	101
30–44	100	109	119	130	109
45–59	100	97	94	87	99
60–74	100	98	94	87	99
75 and over	100	112	127	103	124
All ages	100	99	101	103	103

3   With changes in the age profile come changes in the patterns of demand for goods and services. A declining birth rate means reduced need for primary schools, school books and other supplies, teachers, children's and teenage clothes, perambulators, baby care products, soft drinks, transistor radios and cinema admissions. There would be an increased need for financial, medical and welfare support for the aged and a higher level of demand for health care products and services.

The general objectives for the organisation are derived from a consideration of threats and opportunities. The actions that are necessary to achieve the objectives – what is termed 'fixing the strategy' – can then be decided. In its turn this will point towards the organisational functions required to carry out the actions and how best these should be related to each other (organisational structure). Finally, systems must be established to examine results and to take appropriate further actions. Such a monitoring process acts as a feedback mechanism to all parts of the organisation and may call for further adjustments. Fig. 2.4 is a simple diagram to depict the process.

The marketing strategy

Let us imagine that the marketing manager has identified opportunities which fit within a framework of the resources the organisation has available, for here we must remember Foster's[5] point in Chapter 1 that 'Marketing... becomes the art of doing what is possible to obtain optimum profit at minimum cost.' Once the organisation has developed general objectives based upon these opportunities, it next becomes possible to develop a marketing strategy by which they can be exploited.

McCarthy[6] describes the *marketing strategy* as consisting of 'two distinct yet interrelated parts':

1   the identification of a *target market* – that relatively homogeneous group of users to which the organisation will direct its appeal (a process known as *market segmentation*);
2   the *marketing mix* – the determination of a mixture of variables which the organisation will combine in order to satisfy this target market.

The sections which follow explain these two parts of marketing strategy.

Marketing segmentation

The *total market* for a product or service consists of the total estimated sales of that product or service during a given period of time, usually one year. Thus, the total UK market for ceramic tableware consists of the aggregate number of teasets, dinnersets

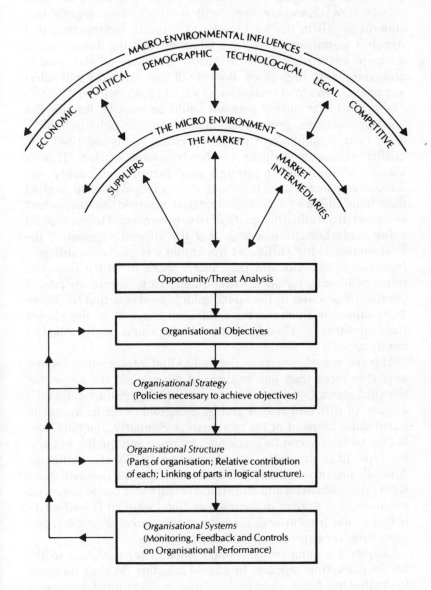

Fig. 2.4   Creative alignment of the organisation with its environment

and related items that will be bought in the UK during one year. In very few cases, however, will the individual organisation attempt to sell to the total market. We recall, for instance, that Arnold Ceramics produces fine tableware and the description is no mere advertising puff – it means tableware of high quality and consequent high price. Because of this, Arnold's will select a *segment* of the total market to which its appeal will be directed. The typical user in that segment could be broadly described as 'the upper-income, professional/managerial class of householder'. Even then, Arnold's will not be operating in the most affluent, quality-conscious segment of the tableware market. This is because while Arnold's certainly manufacture high quality products, the material used is earthenware, a less expensive product than bone china – a ceramic material reserved for the richest and most discriminating group of tableware users. The main point being made here, however, is that the affluent segment of the total market being cultivated by Arnold's is markedly different from other segments and particularly those in which manufacturers producing cheaper, lower-quality earthenware operate. A parallel illustration in the motor vehicle market is that the Rover 2600 saloon is intended for a different segment of the market than the Maestro, although both vehicles could be described as family cars.

This is not to say that the individual organisation cannot appeal to more than one segment of the market. We know that the Ford Motor Company, like its competitors, produces and sells a range of different makes and models, each with its appeal to a particular segment of the total market. Similarly, the total market for tableware can be segmented by price and quality but also by *type* (e.g. domestic and institutional). So that although Arnold's produce a range of fine tableware for the domestic market, a range of heavier and more durable tableware is also produced and marketed. Known in the trade as 'hotel ware', it is well established in the institutional segment of the market. Fig. 2.5 represents Arnold's approach to its market segments.

Chapter 4 emphasises the importance of segmentation to the whole marketing process. In concluding this Section suffice it to say that few firms, apart perhaps from multinational companies in the soft drinks market, have attempted to satisfy the total market for a product or service. Such a policy would, in most cases, only serve to support the old adage that 'to run in all directions at once is to go nowhere'.

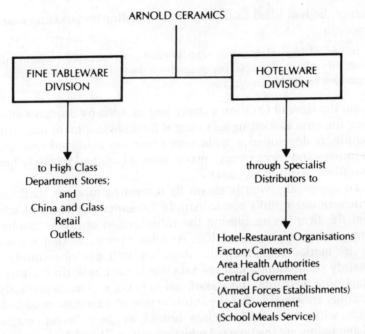

Fig. 2.5   *Arnold Ceramics – segmentation of UK tableware market*

Organisations adopt the policy of segmentation for two main reasons:

1   in order to match their own finite resources to market opportunities;
2   to provide guidelines for the development of an appropriate marketing mix.

The marketing mix is a notion we shall now consider.

The marketing mix

In a study concerned with manufacturers' marketing costs, Professor James Culliton[7] once described the business executive as a 'mixer of ingredients'. He imagined the executive sometimes following an established recipe, sometimes adapting a recipe to the ingredients available and on occasions experimenting with ingredients never previously tried.

Writing in 1964, Neil H. Borden[8] reflected how, fifteen years earlier, he had liked Culliton's idea of calling a marketing executive:

a 'mixer' of ingredients, one who is constantly engaged in fashioning creatively a mix of marketing procedures and policies in his efforts to produce a profitable enterprise.

From the time of Culliton's study and assisted by Borden's advocacy the term marketing mix caught the imagination of marketing people. It developed a wide usage because it helped managers to understand more clearly procedures which had formerly been described in duller language.

To appreciate what is meant by marketing mix, we shall now return in our mind's eye to Arnold Ceramics. We shall imagine that the firm is considering the introduction of a new product. Now as has been said earlier, Arnolds operate in that segment of the market which, at this stage, we will describe simply as 'mainly professional, managerial class households' (in Chapter 3, Marketing Research, the classification is defined more precisely). Arnolds are considering the introduction of a new range of tableware with these middle-class homes as their 'target' market. Listed below are the types of question they will seek to answer.

Category 1

- What shapes of tableware (i.e. what blend of the aesthetic and the functional) should be considered?
- What types of decorative design should be considered?
- What type of brand name will best reflect the quality and other characteristics of this tableware?
- How should the ware be packaged and presented?
- Within the range, what varieties of selection should be provided? (e.g. teasets – 18 piece, 21 piece? dinner sets – 48 piece, 56 piece?
  Starter sets for the young marrieds and for the gift trade?)
- What after-sales service should be provided? (e.g. replacement items for breakages)
- What instructions (if any) ought to be provided with the product?
  (re use of detergents, exposure to oven temperatures, etc)
- Should any warranties be provided on the stability of the glaze and decoration?

Category 2

- What is the established price-level (i.e. 'confidence-level') for this type of tableware?
- What price(s) should be charged for a standard assortment (i.e. teaset, dinner set)?
- What price(s) should be charged for individual pieces?
- Should there be a recommended retail selling price or should prices in different types of outlet be left to find their own level?
- Should an 'introductory offer' price be used to help establish the range?
- What profit margins should be offered to distributors (wholesale, retail)?
- What discounts should be offered to distributors (a) for the purchase of 'quantities' (b) for prompt settlement of invoices?
- What pricing strategies should be adopted for international markets?
- What should be the policy for transport costs (carriage paid, carriage forward etc)?

Category 3

- How should the range be distributed to users – via china and glass retailers? mail order houses? department stores?
- Should all possible points of sale be approached or should a more selective type of distribution be adopted?
- Should there be a wholesaler stage in the distribution channels?
- If so, how many wholesalers are required? Should they be selected by geography, size of firm, type of products handled or some combination of these criteria?
- What service level should be provided to users (speed of delivery, availability of standard consignments, replacement pieces)?
- How best should storage and transportation be organised?

Category 4

- What proportion of promotional activity will be allotted to:
  (a) Arnolds' own sales personnel
  (b) advertising in the mass media

    (c) advertising to distributors

    (d) point-of-sale presentation and display?

- What creative approach seems most suitable for this range? (i.e. what product features ought to be emphasised – quality? durability? design? value for money? etc)
- What mass medium is the most appropriate for advertising? (television? homemaker magazines? women's press? credit card publications, e.g. Barclaycard magazine? colour supplements? if more than one type of medium is used what balance between media is appropriate?)
- What are the most appropriate sizes of advertisement at successive stages of the promotion campaign?
- What frequency of advertisement insertion should be adopted?
- Should advertising be in full colour? monotone? or some proportion of each? in what media? at what stages of the campaign?
- Is there a secondary market? (e.g. buyers of gifts for the young marrieds)
- If so, should some aspect of promotional policy and expenditure pay attention to it?

The reader will see that the questions have been grouped into categories according to their subject matter. Thus:

Category 1 – deals with the *product* itself

Category 2 – deals with the aspects of *price*

Category 3 – deals with *distribution* (or *place*)

Category 4 – deals with aspects of *promotion*

It is useful at this point to quote McCarthy[9] who stated that:

an analysis of the problems that face both large and small companies shows that it is possible to reduce the number of variables in the marketing mix to four basic ones: product, place, promotion and price.

So it is that marketing executives tend to think of the marketing mix as comprising the 4 P's. In effect, this writer has rearranged the 4 P's into a sequence of:

PRODUCT

PRICE

PLACE

PROMOTION

since, for practical purposes, this seems a more logical sequence. This comment, however, gives rise to a warning note. The student of marketing should not be led, by talk of a sequence, into thinking of these four variables as separate and isolated from each other. What must be emphasised at this point is *the interrelationship and interdependence of all the variables*. For example, it is impossible to settle some aspects of product policy without considering their implications for price. The pattern of distribution (i.e. the place policy) will also be affected by the decisions on price, as will the type and extent of promotion activity. Thus, any sequence of presenting the 4 Ps is no more than a nicety to assist their recall. Moreover, no sequence is intended to emphasise the importance of one variable compared to the others.

McCarthy makes two further important points. His first is that the selection of a target market and the development of a marketing mix are also interrelated and that no marketing manager can think of these as separate tasks. They are tasks which must be undertaken in combination and they must also be related to the organisation's objectives, which are in turn governed by the scale of the organisation's resources.

How the marketing management process fits within an integrated approach to operating an organisation can perhaps be demonstrated by Fig 2.6.

The solid lines in the diagram indicate those tasks which are the sole responsibility of marketing management. The broken lines show those tasks where, along with others, the marketing manager will make a contribution to establishing the objectives and defining the general lines of policy for the development of the organisation. The feedback loop indicates how results are measured against plans and subsequently fed back to the various operational areas so that adjustments to plans can be made if necessary. (For example, when the marketing plan has been put into operation, some change in competitive activity may require adaptations to the original plan if objectives are still to be attained. Similarly, sales may exceed expectations or be less than the forecast. Again, adaptations to the plan may be required.)

McCarthy's second point is that the customer (and by this he means the user) must be the focal point for the development of the marketing mix. This is, after all, what the marketing concept implies. If we return to the example of Arnold Ceramics' proposal to introduce a new range of tableware, the particular segment of the market around which the marketing mix is evolved is that of the middle-class housewife. Fig. 2.7 attempts to illustrate how the organisation *co-ordinates a set of controllable variables* (the marketing mix) whilst it is itself operating within a

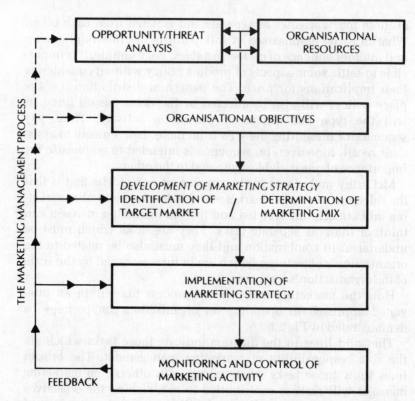

Fig. 2.6 *The marketing management process within an organisation's operations*

framework of uncontrollable variables (the environment). The focal point for its activity is the housewife who buys on behalf of the middle-class professional/managerial type households which constitute the target market.

Before leaving this introduction to the marketing mix it might be helpful to note some additional points:

1 *The balance of ingredients in the mix will be governed by the type of product.* For example, products with a high fashion content (e.g. ladies' clothes) may require emphasis on product development and design and on promotion whereas a product in consistent demand as an industrial raw material (e.g. china clay) may require less emphasis on these variables because such factors as price and availability (i.e. place) are more important to the user.

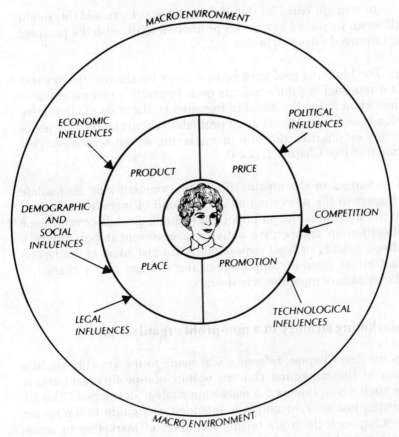

Fig. 2.7 A marketing strategy within an environmental system

2   *The blend of ingredients is not static.* In order to achieve objectives it may have to be varied from time to time and an evaluation of performance will indicate how best the mix should be varied (Arnold's may at some stage, for example, be led to wonder to what extent an increase in the number of distributive outlets would be accompanied by an increase in sales and profits beyond the consequent increase in distribution costs – an illustration of a possible change in the place variable);

– or the firm might ask itself whether increased expenditure in improving product quality or design might be offset by an increase in market share, possibly allowing also for some decrease in promotional expenditure;

– or it might consider that if the price was increased this might allow an increased budget for promotion again with the prospect of improved sales and profits.

3　*The planning goal must be to achieve maximum effectiveness at a reasonable commensurate cost.* In practice this necessitates that when fixing the blend of ingredients, the costs of alternative blends and their effects upon profitability must be thought about – this emphasises the role of marketing as the *revenue-buying function* (see Chapter 1, p. 29).

4　*Changes in the organisation's environment may necessitate changes in the marketing mix.* The blend of ingredients is fixed in the short term but an important technological discovery, some alteration in competitive activity, a government policy which affects pricing or legal requirements are just some of the factors that might force a reappraisal of the strategy and a change in the balance of ingredients in the mix.

Marketing strategy in a non-profit organisation

In the first Chapter, reference was made to the growing application of the marketing concept within non-profit organisations. In such cases, how is the marketing strategy developed? The following imaginary example is intended as a guide to the reader. In Chapter 6 there are further examples of marketing in action on non-profit lines.

Adult Education in Brightshire – A Case Study

Edward (Ted) Turner has just been appointed Adult Education Organiser for the Brightshire County Council. His brief is a simple one – to develop the county's adult education provision in a no-growth financial situation. In effect, this means making improved use of existing resources.

Ted was struck by something said to him at the selection interview. The chairman of the panel, a successful local businessman remarked: 'In my view, the whole thing needs marketing properly'.

He had taken this as serious advice and had done some background reading on the subject. In consequence, he was about to embark upon the two distinct but interrelated parts of the marketing strategy, namely:

1   the identification of a target market;
2   the determination of the marketing mix.

It should be explained to the reader that in the educational system of England and Wales, 'adult education' is usually taken to mean *non-vocational* education. This is in contrast to those many courses available at Universities, Polytechnics and Colleges where students of mature years can study for degrees and professional qualifications in order to improve their career prospects. Adult education courses typically encompass leisure and recreation subjects, cultural subjects, social and manual skills. Although there are some courses which lead to formal qualifications (at the GCE A Level, for example) by far the greater part of adult education provision is intended to provide for what may be described as hobbies, interest and enrichment.

The target market

Ted Turner is experienced enough to know that in talking of 'the market for adult education', it is misleading to think of a single, homogeneous market. The 'market' is, in reality, an aggregation of a number of minority markets. These usually comprise:

1   *the market for the development of manual skills* consisting of such popular 'perennials' as DIY, car maintenance, flower arranging, typing, gardening and cookery;

2   *the market for 'enrichment'* in which courses on literature, the arts, music, painting, pottery, local history and archaeology are well-established favourites;

3   *the market for 'health and beauty'* which includes sport, yoga, classes on diet, skin care, deportment and a host of other popular subjects;

4   *the market for social skills* including public speaking and debating, group dynamics and

5   *other specialised markets* which include pre-retirement

courses, 'languages for businessmen', and courses on setting up playgroups.

Turner realises that he will need to study carefully the features of the county's 'catchment' for adult education. This will include the geographical distribution of its population as well as its age composition and social and economic structure. Scrutiny of the data on courses previously offered, their numerical support, wastage rates and comparative costs will also be important.

He has decided to organise discussion groups among existing students. He hopes these will generate an 'item pool' for a questionnaire to be distributed among fairly large samples of users and non-users of the adult education service. In this way, he hopes to develop a programme which, because it will pay careful attention to the views expressed in the questionnaires, will then possess a content and structure with 'in-built acceptability'. His objective will be to ensure that existing students are satisfied with current provision whilst at the same time providing sufficient incentive for new users to try the service.

The marketing mix

Although he hopes to preserve enough finance to undertake some experimental work in markets and courses, he realises that the mix must recognise the relative importance of the various current market segments. For each segment to be covered by the programme a mix will have to be developed based on the considerations set out below.

PRODUCT   Very simply, he must determine whether the courses currently on offer are what the market requires in terms of their content, structure, duration and teaching method. Questions he has drafted are as follows: how popular is each course in terms of its initial recruitment? what is the subsequent wastage rate? what steps have already been taken to evaluate the courses being offered? what do the users (i.e. the students) think? is the mode of providing the courses (e.g. day-time, half-day and evening, evening only) appropriate to the needs of the market(s)? what scope is there for offering new courses? and in what new modes (e.g. Saturday courses, week-end residential courses)?

PRICE   Decisions here are crucial, for what is being offered must be judged as 'value for money' by the user, but at the same time

Turner's expenditure must stay within the budgets approved by the County Council. Above and beyond the revenue estimates, however, it has been agreed that the organiser can retain for further development any surpluses obtained by operating courses on a 'self-balancing' basis (which roughly approximates to full cost). In this sense, Ted Turner has commercial decisions to make. He has a quantum of funding from the Local Authority but if he wishes to develop the service beyond its present level he must generate sufficient surpluses to do so.

Therefore, he must investigate:

1 the extent to which demand depends upon price (i.e. price elasticity of demand)

2 the established 'confidence-level' on price (i.e. what is the price per course or per session or per hour's tuition which existing users have come to regard as reasonable)? What room is there for increasing prices? Would the user pay an additional sum for materials used, over and above the tuition fee? If so, how best should prices be calculated – as a compound fee or as a tuition fee with materials to be charged separately?

3 how the existing pricing policy relates to the information obtained under 1 and 2. Here a judgment has to be made based on a recognition that provision is already being paid for to some extent by rates and taxes and yet any opportunity of generating reasonable surpluses for further development should be seriously considered.

PLACE   The main issue here revolves upon three factors:

1 the availability of courses within reasonable travelling distance for students;

2 the necessity to maintain viable numbers on all courses at all centres being operated;

3 the fixed and variable costs of operating both courses and centres.

A reasonable balance must be struck between availability of courses and the need to operate within approved financial estimates. In the matter of distribution of courses it should be mentioned here that Ted Turner has available to him within the County boundaries:

(a) three local Colleges of Further Education
(b) the premises of 18 Upper Schools
(c) Sandywell Hall, a large country house on the fringes of the County (in some state of disrepair but suitable for mounting

residential courses should there prove to be a demand for these)

(d) a number of small village halls, eminently suitable for the teaching of craft skills and recreational pursuits.

From his deliberations he aims to produce a plan describing:

- the number and type of centres to be operated;
- the number and type of courses in each centre;
- the comparative costs of operating courses at the various types of centre;
- the minimum numbers of students which would justify operating each centre.

Among the data he will have to study carefully are: the geographical distribution of the County population; the demographic characteristics of the population (e.g. age, sex and social grade composition for matching with characteristics of existing users – in terms of actual and potential recruitment to courses); transport and communications data (particularly concerning rural areas); planned developments (if any) likely to affect course provision (e.g. housing clearance schemes, projected new estates, new industrial development and similar data as revealed by the County Structure Plan).

PROMOTION   The County Library service has produced for Ted Turner a number of text books on marketing. From these he has discovered that the promotion variable in the marketing mix (which is usually labelled *marketing communications*) is taken to comprise four elements:

1 *advertising* which denotes the purchase and use of space in newspapers and magazines, and time on television and commercial radio, as well as outdoor and cinema advertising;

2 *sales promotion* which includes point-of-sale display material, catalogues, brochures, in-store demonstrations and exhibitions;

3 *publicity* which is the creation of a favourable 'atmosphere' for the sale of a product or service by means of 'free publicity', e.g. editorial articles in the press media and programmes on radio and television in which the organisation, its products or services, processes, discoveries etc receive favourable mention; and,

4   *personal selling* which consists of personal interviews, telephone selling etc in which the organisation's sales personnel directly negotiate with its customers.

He feels able to consider the personal selling function first because he knows that if the Adult Education service is to succeed in its objectives, he and his 'centre-heads' (the people who will share with him the responsibility for the programme) will have a great deal of selling to do, not only to the enquirers in enrolment week but also by going out 'to the market'. He intends to ensure that by talking to Womens' Institute meetings, and at meetings of Rotary and the Townswomens' Guilds, as many people as possible know about the programmes the service intends to offer. Ted realises, moreover, that this will be a two-way process and that while he and his colleagues are selling the service they ought also to obtain quite a number of ideas for possible courses.

In considering the other three elements of his marketing communications he is clear that:

1   the budget for promotion is small and it therefore becomes doubly important for promotion to be undertaken with clear objectives on what it should achieve;
2   every item of expenditure will have to be tested for its value and there must be great emphasis on generating as much free publicity as possible – through newspaper articles and 'mentions', on radio and television, of interesting students and courses.

A question that he finds intriguing is to do with the balance between the various elements in communications activity. In the past, this programme has consisted of:

1   the purchase, each September, of large spaces in local newspapers to announce the year's courses and their locations;
2   the purchase and distribution of a large number of folders to provide, for existing and potential students, details of courses and locations – these being usually placed in libraries, municipal offices, job centres, citizens' advice bureaux, in addition to the adult education centres;
3   the purchase and display of a small number of posters for use in the same locations as the folders.

Ted Turner wonders whether it might be sensible to scale down expenditure on other items in order to improve the folder. At the moment this is produced on a duplicator and has a dull 'institutional' appearance. As he remarks to one of his colleagues: 'No-one would ever believe that we did anything that wasn't deadly dull from the look of this folder'.

He also wonders about the media the service has never used – exhibitions for example. Here he recalls being most impressed with the work produced in some of the handicraft classes – in woodwork, needlework, embroidery, flower arranging and DIY. He was also gratified to learn that a member of a literary appreciation class and a member of a local history class have recently had work published. He believes that an inexpensive but appealing exhibition of students' work could easily be mounted in the foyers of the County Libraries. Also, he feels that some funds should be reserved for experimentation. What would be the effect of door-to-door distribution of a letter and folder – perhaps on one of the many large housing estates to be found near the centres but from which the service appears to draw little or no custom?

These musings lead him to consider a more general point. He knows the cliché that 'adult education is primarily a middle-class activity'. He wonders about his present recruitment. Do the middle classes predominate? If so, why do courses draw so little support from the housing estates? Ought the programme to be altered if this will attract the less affluent? At the end of this self-questioning, he realises that perhaps like many marketing executives before him he has isolated a fundamental problem – what is the size of the attainable market in relation to the current market? – and if he reaches towards the attainable market to what extent will he cease to appeal to the current market? With a wry smile he concludes that although his own task is a long way from marketing detergents or micro-computers, it is no less of a marketing task for all that.

At the end of these preliminary thoughts he is reminded that on the shelves of a technical college library he discovered a research monograph by Midgley[10] on managing new products. In this the author drew attention to the fact that the importance of interpersonal influence on the adoption of new products is a factor which marketers have too frequently neglected. This leads him to wonder if he can enlist the help of present students in the promotional exercise. He decides that discussions with them, during their coffee breaks, will be an important part of his action plan.

Self-assessment questions

1   Consider any type of organisation with which you are familiar and describe the environmental influences which act upon it.

2   What significance has marketing research for the systems approach to management?

3   What do you understand by the term marketing strategy?

4   Why do organisations typically adopt a policy of market segmentation?

5   In what sense did Culliton describe the business executive as a 'mixer of ingredients'? How did Borden adopt the idea?

6   How is the balance of ingredients in the marketing mix influenced by the product or service?

7   Consider how a marketing mix might be developed for a non-profit organisation.

References

1   Stanton, William J. *Fundamentals of marketing* 6th edn, New York, McGraw Hill Book Company, 1981, pp. 20–32

2   Toffler, Alvin. *Future shock* London, Pan Books, 1971, p. 11

3   McCarthy, E. Jerome. *Basic marketing: a managerial approach* 6th edn, Homewood, Illinois, Richard D. Irwin, p. 33

4   Kotler, Philip. *Marketing management – analysis, planning and control* 4th edn, Englewood Cliffs, NJ, Prentice-Hall, 1980, p. 95

5   Foster, Douglas. *Mastering marketing* London, The Macmillan Press Ltd, 1982, p. 5

6   *Basic marketing: a managerial approach* p. 35

7   Culliton, James W. *The management of marketing costs* (research bulletin) Boston; Division of Research, Graduate School of Business Administration, Harvard University, 1948

8   Borden, Neil H. The concept of the marketing mix reprinted from *Journal of Advertising Research*, 1964. In *Marketing Classics* (Enis, B. and Cox, K.) Boston; Allyn and Bacon, 1969, p. 365

9   *Basic marketing: a managerial approach* p. 39

3 THE MARKETING INFORMATION SYSTEM AND MARKETING RESEARCH

Objectives

Managing an organisation means making decisions and the better the information available the better the prospect of sound decisions. We are now about to examine the function of a marketing information system and how it might be designed. The role of marketing research, the uses to which it is typically applied, the types of data it generates and the services that are available are all described. The procedures upon which marketing research is based are considered and thoughts are offered on the design of research surveys.

The marketing information system

Information and the decision making process

When a pilot is at the controls of his aircraft he is constantly monitoring its performance on such factors as air speed, height and attitude, making adjustments when necessary to its engine revolutions, control surfaces and rate of climb or descent so that the flight can continue safely towards a destination and an e.t.a. (estimated time of arrival). The task of piloting the plane centres on his receiving information through the instrument panels on his flight deck, enabling him to *make decisions* on how best the complex man-machine organisation, i.e. the aircraft he is flying can be made to proceed through its environment towards its objective.

In many ways, managing a business is like piloting an aircraft. To control the business effectively, our friends at Arnold Ceramics (Chapter 2) need a great deal of information from internal sources, related to matters such as:

per time period	sales costs; production output rates; volume of orders received; volume of orders despatched; cash flow etc.

This is comparable to the *internal* information the pilot receives on the plane's progress (speed, height etc) relative to its use of resources (as indicated to him through the fuel gauges and the oil pressure displays). Of course, he must also receive a great deal of *external* information on such environmental matters as visibility, weather conditions and landing conditions at the destination and intermediate airports, if he is to make any required adjustments to the performance of the aircraft. Similarly, the directors of Arnold's need environmental information on any changes in:

- general trading conditions and economic outlook;
- activities of competitors;
- consumer responses to promotional campaigns;
- other aspects of user behaviour,
  if they are to steer their organisation towards its objectives.

In fact, the word *cybernetics* when used in the context of management theory has been called, in convenient shorthand terms, 'the art of steersmanship'. A. M. Ampère[1] first used the term Cybernetique when alluding to the area of the social sciences concerned with the art of government. More recently, Norbert Wiener[2] has used the anglicised form of the term to describe the study of 'control and communication in the animal and the machine'. It is now well settled that cybernetics is concerned with the theory of information flow in control systems.

So what have we said so far? That in steering their organisation through its environment, the managers must have a flow of information within a control system – conceptually, this is identical to the pilot's instrument panel, for management needs an adequate set of instruments with which to 'fly' the company.

Recognising the salience of up-to-date, relevant information in the quality of decision making, an increasing number of organisations have established a management information system (MIS), as an information base for decision making in all functional areas – finance, marketing, production, personnel, administration. Our purpose in this Chapter is to consider a major component part, or sub-system, of the overall management system – the marketing information system.

The marketing information system (MkIS)

A well-established definition is that of Brien and Stafford[3]:

A structured, interacting complex of persons, machines and procedures designed to generate an orderly flow of pertinent information collected from both intra- and extra-firm sources for use as the bases for decision-making in specific responsibility areas of marketing management.

Philip Kotler's[4] conception is very close to this:

A marketing information system is a continuing and interacting structure of people, equipment and procedures designed to gather, sort, analyse, evaluate and distribute pertinent, timely and accurate information for use by marketing decision makers to improve their marketing planning, execution and control.

Note that both definitions incorporate the notion of *pertinence*. The objective of establishing the system is not to deluge the unfortunate marketing executive with mountains of statistical print-outs so that the 'system' constitutes a block to decision making. The objective is to make speedier and better decisions based on an accurate and up-to-date flow of *relevant* information and today this is becoming easier and more economical, due to the fact that developments in microelectronics, computing and telecommunications are revolutionising the handling, processing and storage of information.

Not that the design of such a system is any easy task and certainly *ad hoc* or piece-meal development of a number of unco-ordinated, incompatible systems serving the various functional areas of marketing – sales, advertising, physical distribution etc – would be totally self-defeating. Costs would outweigh benefits and the quality of decision-making would probably be impaired.

Designing the system

In Chapter 2 we considered the systems concept by way of which the organisation maintains itself in being by adapting to changes in its environment. The feedback principle – the use of information to warn the system how it is functioning in relation to its environment – is central to this approach. The design of the system must be such as to assist progress to organisational objectives, which is why British author, Gordon Oliver,[5] talks of:

the rigorously planned and integrated system which is embedded in the very design of the organisation structure. It should be clear that information management is intimately connected with organisational structure. Presumably the organisation has been designed to accomplish tasks – to take decisions. Information is central to decision taking and so information flows to decision takers.

Now this is not to say that, whilst the individual executive cannot be allowed to do 'his own thing', the system should not be user-oriented. In fact the information technologist would say that unless the system is 'user friendly' it is already about to fail.

Kotler[6] suggests that the organisation 'should design the marketing information system in a way that reconciles what executives would like to have, what executives really need and what is economically feasible to offer', with the information being precisely related to the major decisions which marketing managers have to make – the decisions concerning the product, place, price and promotional aspects of market performance. He therefore proposes that the system design should be based on a survey of user needs, covering such issues as:

* types of decisions being taken;
* types of information needed to make the decisions;
* types of information presently being supplied regularly;
* types of information which would be liked but which are not yet being supplied;
* types of special studies being periodically requested;
* types of information required daily, weekly, monthly, yearly;
* types of magazines, trade reports required regularly;
* types of special topic on which information is thought useful;
* types of data analysis programmes to be made available.

Kotler's questionnaire would also ask respondents for details of 'the four most helpful improvements that could be made in the present marketing information system'. Thus would the system acquire the necessary *in-built acceptability*.

Kotler writes clearly and forcefully on the benefits to be derived from the MkIS approach and cites a study of 193 major US companies[7] which revealed that 77 per cent of them had either installed or were installing such a system. He describes the four major sub-systems which comprise the overall MkIS these being:

1   the *internal reports system* supplying current data to management on sales, costs, stocks, cash flow and accounts (receivable and payable);

2   the *marketing intelligence system* which provides data on developments in the external marketing environment and includes the scrutiny of newspapers and trade publications, reports from sales representatives and distributors, the purchase of information from specialist organisations (e.g. The AC Nielsen Company) and the establishment of a bureau within the organisation to collect and disseminate such marketing intelligence;

3   the *marketing research system* which enables management to commission specific studies on marketing situations, resulting in reports to assist decision making (a process which is described at some length in the pages which follow), and

4   the *analytical marketing system* by means of which marketing data and marketing issues can be analysed by logical and quantitative techniques, the *statistical bank* of such a sub-system comprising advanced procedures for the examination of data relationships and reliability, whilst the *model bank* comprises models of inter-related variables which can be manipulated in such a way that the influence of individual variables upon outcomes, e.g. sales volume, net profit etc can be studied.

And so, if we consider what has been said in this textbook up to this point:

●   Chapter 1 has discussed marketing as a philosophy of attaining objectives through concentration on the customer;
●   Chapter 2 has described the 'environment' in which organisational activity takes place and the way in which changes in that environment can affect progress to objectives;

- Chapter 3 (so far) has described the planning and control of marketing operations in a sophisticated manner through the management of information which is relevant, accurate, up-to-date and orderly in its flow, so enabling the organisation not only to monitor progress but to react to events as they happen and, if necessary, take appropriate actions.

Thus, the marketing executive depicted below at his work station within the marketing information system is not different

from the pilot on the flight deck looking carefully at his instrument display and making adjustments to the controls. The analogy is not a bad one, in fact.

One recognises why Marion Harper Jr[8] once said:

To manage a business well is to manage its future, and to manage the future is to manage information.

The reader will appreciate how the first of Kotler's sub-systems – the internal reports system, can be used to monitor and control marketing operations. The storage and retrieval of data and the manipulation of that data statistically and financially, can yield important information on the performance of:

- individual products;
- individual markets;
- sales representatives (individually and collectively)
- advertising campaigns etc,

and their contribution to organisational objectives (which is, typically, a target rate of return on investment).

After what has been said in Chapter 2, the reader will also clearly understand why information on the external environment should be provided by the marketing intelligence system – the second of Kotler's four sub-systems. Reference will be made to his fourth sub-system, the analytical marketing system, from time to time as the book progresses.

The remainder of this Chapter will be taken up with the third of Kotler's sub-systems. The scope and function of marketing research will be described, while Chapters 4 and 5 will provide examples of its processes in action. One caveat – where Kotler would incorporate the purchase of information from specialist organisations (i.e. syndicated research) within his marketing intelligence system – it will be described here as part of the marketing research system, as befits practice in the United Kingdom.

Marketing research

Introduction

Many writers claim that the process is as old as the hills. Lawrence Lockley[9] expains that even the children of Israel sent out interviewers to sample the market of Canaan. He tells us that, more recently, the application of marketing research to marketing and advertising problems probably had its genesis in 1879 when, in a crude but formal way, the NW Ayer organisation used a survey technique in attempting to fit a proposed advertising schedule to the needs of the Nichols-Shepard Company, manufacturers of agricultural machinery.

How is it defined today? A business-bound definition comes to us from The American Marketing Association[10] which proposes that marketing research is:

the systematic gathering, recording and analysing of data about problems relating to the marketing of goods and services.

A broader role is provided by the Code of Practice of the International Chamber of Commerce and European Society for Opinion and Marketing Research:[11]

The term marketing research is defined as the systematic collection and objective recording, classification, analysis and presentation of data concerning the behaviour, needs, attitudes, opinions, motivations, etc of individuals and organisations (commercial enterprises, public bodies etc) within the context of their economic, social, political and everyday activities.

While this definition can be criticised for its language (and its length) it is nevertheless very useful, for it not only describes the processes involved – it indicates that in its broadest role it includes *social* research and *industrial* marketing research

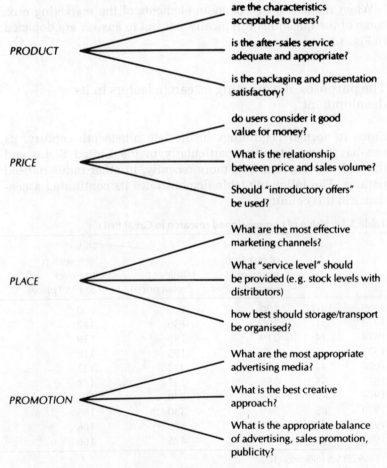

PRODUCT
- are the characteristics acceptable to users?
- is the after-sales service adequate and appropriate?
- is the packaging and presentation satisfactory?

PRICE
- do users consider it good value for money?
- What is the relationship between price and sales volume?
- Should "introductory offers" be used?

PLACE
- What are the most effective marketing channels?
- What "service level" should be provided (e.g. stock levels with distributors)
- how best should storage/transport be organised?

PROMOTION
- What are the most appropriate advertising media?
- What is the best creative approach?
- What is the appropriate balance of advertising, sales promotion, publicity?

Fig. 3.1   Marketing research and the marketing mix

(because organisations as well as individuals come within its purview).

Often, the terms marketing research and market research are used interchangeably and this is not correct, for as Oliver[12] explains, market research describes the characteristics of markets (i.e. users) whereas marketing research is to do with any research relevant to marketing operations, including 'studies on advertising, packaging, distribution, sales force activities, pricing and products as well as market studies'. Market research is therefore one aspect of marketing research, albeit an important one. In turn, marketing research is but one input, albeit an important one, to the organisation's marketing information system.

When related to one or more elements of the marketing mix, some of the questions it typically sets out to answer are depicted in Fig. 3.1.

The purposes of marketing research; factors in its development

Since its formal beginnings in the late nineteenth century, its use has grown steadily, particularly in the United States and the United Kingdom, and more recently, in other industrialised nations. The following table demonstrates its continuing ascendance in this country.

Table 3.1   Value of commissioned research in Great Britain

	£m	Index* of research turnover at current prices	Index of retail prices	Index* of research turnover at 1969 prices
1969	14-17	100	100	100
1973	31	200	136	147
1974	34	219	158	139
1975	36	232	196	118
1976	43	277	229	121
1977	55	355	257	138
1978	72	.465	278	167
1979	85	549	330	166
1980	98	631	379	166
1981	109	707	425	166

* 1969 (£15.5 million) = 100

Source: *Campaign* 9 July 1982

Writing in July 1982 Valerie Farbridge, chairman of the UK's Market Research Society, was able to record that based on the value of research commissioned, the size of the industry had increased in 12 years from £16 million to £100 million, in the number of people the industry employs, from 3000 to 5000 (excluding interviewers and coders) and in the number of companies carrying out the research, from 95 to 210 research agencies.

To understand the reasons for the trend it is enough just to consider the purpose of marketing research which is to increase the quality of decision making in conditions of uncertainty by increasing awareness of, and interest in, the customer. Enough has already been said of the dynamic nature of markets for the reader to recognise how that uncertainty arises. Research enables the costs and benefits of alternative courses of action to be assessed with, hopefully, a much greater degree of accuracy than by guesswork and optimism, thus leading to better decisions.

In one survey[13] which examined the marketing research activities of 800 companies, the following ten types figured very prominently:

Type of activity	Percentage of companies
Measurement of market potentials	93
Determination of market characteristics	93
Market-share analysis	92
Competitive-product studies	85
Short-range forecasting (up to 1 year)	85
Studies of business trends	86
Long-range forecasting (over 1 year)	82
Pricing studies	81
Testing of existing products	75
Studies of advertising effectiveness	67

(The reader should note that sales forecasting, a highly important research activity, is dealt with separately in Chapter 10.)

Although the data on these activities is taken from a US survey, the author's experience leads him to suggest that the pattern of activities undertaken by British companies would not be distinctly different from the outline provided by this particular survey.

Scientific method

There are a number of definitions of science. A general and reasonable one is that it means 'an objective investigation of empirical phenomena' – of the observations which derive from our experience. It is also true to say that whenever a branch of supposed factual knowledge is rejected by science, it is always on the basis of its methodology. It is important to adopt scientific method in attempts to interpret marketing phenomena because sound decision making must be based on *facts* – the truth of the situation – not on the prejudices of the researcher or the rationalisations of the marketing executive. As the above definition declares, the investigation must be *objective*, otherwise undertaking the research in the first place could not be justified.

Now, of course, it is not as easy to apply scientific method in the social sciences as it is in the physical sciences. For one thing, our knowledge of human behaviour is nowhere near as well developed as we would wish it to be. In attempting to understand behaviour in the market place and to classify types of consumer, for example, there has been a traditional reliance on the theroretical insights of a number of fields of study including economics, psychology and sociology. More recently attempts have been made to derive new understanding and new classifications by actually studying what happens in the market place rather than rely on importing insights from the behavioural sciences. But this does not mean that an interpretive theory of consumer behaviour has been perfected – indeed many would say that such an objective is illusory.

Another point advanced in defence of the 'intuitive' school of management is that the time and expense implied by the scientific method, given the dynamic rate of change of most markets, is hardly justified. By the time we know the true facts about the market, the market will have changed anyway. So why bother? We will return to these issues near to the end of this chapter. In the meantime, the continuing growth in the value of commissioned research in Great Britain (Table 1) demonstrates the confidence which an increasing number of managements place in the findings of marketing research. To justify such confidence it is important that research is undertaken with thoroughness and care and in this regard it has been claimed[14] that standards in Britain 'are higher than anywhere else in the world'. Good decision making depends upon the provision of the most objective and reliable data it is possible to provide. This, in turn, relies heavily upon the application of scientific method.

As David Schwartz[15] reminds us, the scientific method has four basic characteristics:

1   *rationality* – in all stages of the research process rationality, not emotionalism, must be the keynote, with theories, hypotheses and proposed solutions to problems being rigorously tested;

2   *objectivity* – the search for data must not be conditioned by the desire to keep prejudices warm or to substantiate pre-judgments but to discover the situation as it really is – which in turn implies a willingness to discover and face up to unpalatable findings, if necessary; bias must not affect either the design of the research or the interpretation of its results;

3   *precision* – the research must be executed thoroughly, the acquisition of accurate data should be the objective and the results should be stated with clarity and exactitude;

4   *honest interpretation* – it is sometimes said that if four executives read the same research report they will interpret it in ways which support what they 'always believed' – even though this results in four different interpretations: here is the danger; honest interpretation is an important characteristic of the scientific method.

In a typical marketing research project, the scientific method follows distinct stages. For example, suppose Arnold Ceramics discover that their sales of tableware begin to decline. They commission a marketing research survey to discover why – could it be the price? the packaging? something to do with quality or competition from imports? At the first stage, the *observation stage*, discussions are conducted with housewives and others who are typical users of this grade of tableware. This leads the research agency to *formulate the hypothesis* (second stage) that the designs and colours currently available from Arnolds are felt by many (and particularly the young, first-time buyers) to be too traditional, making them difficult to co-ordinate with contemporary tastes in furnishings and interior decor. Typically, the research agency would now attempt to establish a significant quantitative basis for this tentative hypothesis and they might well do this by the use of a questionnaire with a sample of users – a sample large enough and representative enough to validly reflect the opinions of the total population of actual and potential users of such types of tableware (i.e. the market). If such a survey confirms the tentative hypothesis generated by the discussion group then the agency would settle for it and in its report to Arnolds express this view, citing the evidence for it, statistical and otherwise.

This then brings us to the third stage where some outcome is *predicted* if some action is taken. Clearly in this case the proposition will be that if Arnolds re-design their tableware along contemporary lines, the level of sales will increase. Now of course, ultimately, there is no way of verifying this prediction other than in the market place. Accordingly, Arnolds will probably arrange to pilot-test the limited-quantity production of a redesigned range through a limited area try-out (a 'test market'), or through utilising the services of a major distributor. With the second method, care must be taken not to alienate other distributors who may react against what they consider to be the 'preferential treatment' of a competitor. Usually if it is explained to them that the limited distribution is being undertaken for the purposes of marketing research, which will ultimately benefit all distributors, misunderstanding and ill-will can be avoided. The distributor chosen for the experiment would probably be one with a national network of outlets who, through computer analysis of his own sales, could forecast what his eventual sales, perhaps for the first year and at least one subsequent year, might be. Knowing what proportion of their normal sales is usually taken up by this distributor would enable Arnolds to make a reasonable forecast of what their initial sales of the new range might be. Of course, if after testing the hypothesis empirically in this way, it is found not to be well grounded, then the scientific method would require the whole process to be repeated – with some alternative hypothesis being formulated and tested.

The above is necessarily a simplified and abbreviated outline of a research project but it illustrates the application of scientific method to marketing problems, such method being founded upon the stages of:

1   Observation – to ascertain the facts of a situation in an objective way so as to lead to a definition of the problem;
2   Formulation of hypothesis: this may be in the two steps of (a) the tentative hypothesis, which is then (b) verified, perhaps by quantitative examination of a larger and more representative

sample of users, the data so acquired being rigorously tested for its validity;

3 Based on this hypothesis, the prediction of some outcome if certain action is taken (e.g. 'it appears that if you re-design the tableware along these lines, sales will increase');

4 The testing of the hypothesis (usually under conditions which, as rigorously as possible, can be made to represent the opportunities and the pitfalls of full-scale marketing).

Now we are still some distance away from the precision of the physical sciences, where we can say that by adding type X acid to type Y solid we will generate type Z gas... but we are also some distance away from the 'method' of solving marketing problems which relies on the rationalisations and 'experience' of managers – a 'method' which is notoriously fallible, especially in markets undergoing change. (As a footnote for the interested reader – the author has used the selected distributor/computer analysis approach of market testing for new product development and found it a low-cost, helpful aid to decision-making).

The scope of marketing research

We have seen earlier (p. 75) how marketing research, an important input to the marketing information system (MkIS), can be used to answer questions about the development of the various elements in the marketing mix. It might now be useful to say more about the scope of such research as an aid to decision making and to indicate some other areas, beyond the mix itself, where it is typically valuable to marketing activities. Before doing so, however, it seems logical at this point to define some of the marketing research terms in general use.

1 *Data*: derived from the Latin verb 'dare' (to give) – data means 'facts given' – in effect 'given facts' (note that the word data is plural in form, the singular for which is datum).

It is from these given facts that other facts may be deduced. For example, through the processes of statistical analysis *raw data* is often treated methodically so as to yield *information*.

2 *Internal data*: drawn from the firm's own records and typically including sales by products, sales by territories, 'calendar sales (i.e. sales per time period) – such data would relate to what Kotler

described as the 'internal reports sub-system' of the marketing information system. Trends of sales over previous years; the profit earning capacity of various products; selling and administrative expenses per product; data on cash flow, raw materials usage, production capacity and costs and manpower costs are just some of the internal data which have important implications for marketing activity. When combined with and compared with *external data* (see 5) it can be used to monitor progress to marketing/profit objectives and to make forecasts of future peformance. Before defining external data, however, other classifications of data must be described.

3 *Primary data*: earlier in this Chapter we saw how a research agency, acting on behalf of Arnold Ceramics, conducted a research survey among tableware users in order to discover why Arnolds' sales had begun to decline. The data obtained by the survey was primary data – it was collected as a result of the investigation of a particular problem and it bore directly upon that problem.

Another point here – since that data was accumulated as the result of a self-contained, 'once-only' investigation, this would be termed *ad hoc research* in contrast to *continuous research* (see 6).

4 *Secondary data*: it is frequently the case that data has not been collected especially for the solution of a particular problem, but it is nevertheless of value in solving that problem. This is termed secondary data. It can frequently be obtained at a fraction of the cost of primary data and it derives from both internal and external sources. The internal sources (i.e. from within the organisation) can be deduced from the description of these types of data in 2, (above). The systematic analysis of such data is very valuable and can often assist in the subsequent formulation of research objectives. Types of sources of external data include Departments of HM Government, banks, trade associations, professional bodies, universities, commercial research organisations and the press (e.g. *The Financial Times* surveys).

Secondary data from such sources usually takes the form of published statistics on economic trends, volumes of production, expenditure on consumer goods, statistics on imports and exports, changes in regional dispersions of population, numbers of retail outlets, sales volume by types of retail outlet – the list is endless and the reader has only to obtain a booklet on HM

Government's statistical services (e.g. *Profit from Facts*, HMSO) to realise how much secondary data is available in the UK.

This type of data is very often useful in providing an outline of changes in the market environment, in market size, in patterns of distribution, in the composition of user needs etc. Chapter 13 (International marketing) provides a list of sources of secondary data relevant to the export trade (p. 453–4). This list is but one example of the richness and variety of the secondary data available.

The examination and analysis of secondary data is usually called 'desk research'. Occasionally, desk research may, of itself, be sufficient to solve a marketing problem. More frequently, and if it provides sufficient encouragement for the organisation to do so, it precedes the use of a research project to obtain primary data.

In conducting desk research care must be taken to ensure that the data obtained:

(a) is relevant to the problem in hand;
(b) is accurate enough for its intended purpose;
(c) is up-to-date.

The reader should also bear in mind that secondary data from abroad, especially from Third World countries, is not nearly as reliable as that provided by UK sources.

5 *External data*: this can now be better understood since it can comprise secondary data, from the published sources just described, primary data or a combination of both these data. For example, an analysis of secondary data on the volume, value and type of goods being imported into a foreign market may suggest to a would-be exporter that a market exists there for his own product. He may then decide to undertake a research survey among users in the foreign country in order to obtain primary data on whether and how his product should be re-styled for maximum acceptability there.

6 *Continuous data*: we have seen in 3 how primary data can be furnished by the ad-hoc, self-contained research project. Another important source of data is the continuous research method. Examples here are:

(a) the services of the AC Nielsen Company Ltd, which through *shop audit research* provide subscribers with continuous, reliable and comprehensive facts on market size, market shares, product performance, competitive activity, current store and consumer promotions, advertising activity, packaging and retail prices.

(b) the 'Family Food Panel' of Taylor Nelson Associates, which provides clients with continuous data obtained from a panel of 2000 housewives. Through the completion of diaries on foods served, how prepared, form in which obtained (fresh, tinned, bottled etc), brand served, flavour served etc, clients obtain data of direct relevance to the modification and improvement of existing products, the development of new products and the developent of marketing strategies.

(c) the services of The Economist Intelligence Unit, which provides a great deal of continuous data including quarterly reviews of multinational business; European trends, international tourism, motor business etc and whose monthly publication *Retail Business* covers markets, marketing and distribution in the UK.

Note: All of the examples of continuous data given here are described at greater length in the author's work *Introduction to Marketing*, 2nd edition 1983. See bibliography for further details.

7   *Syndicated research*: the results of research carried out by the retail audit method, the consumer panel method and other types of research often conducted on a routinised, repetitive basis can be purchased by way of subscription and are therefore termed syndicated research. Carrying out research on this basis enables the costs to be shared and since the overall results are made available generally and often include data on the performance of competitors, the individual organisation can monitor its own performance in comparison to the trends of the total market and the performance of competitors. Syndicated research is clearly a useful method of monitoring changes in the marketing environment, including the comparative importance of various types of distribution.

Another example of a syndicated research service is the *Target Group Index (TGI)* of the British Market Research Bureau Ltd. This is a national product and media survey which measures 'heavy' to 'light' usage for over 2500 branded products in more than 200 fast-moving consumer product fields. Information is collected from 24 000 adults each year in this national survey. It also includes an examination of media usage, covering 141 newspapers and magazines, ITV viewing, commercial radio, 'outdoor' media (i.e. posters etc) and the cinema. This enables an advertiser to match media coverage to actual product usage rather than building media schedules on more generalised classifications (e.g. demography – age, sex, income group) which may or may not be relevant to purchasing behaviour for the marketer's product.

It is interesting that a significant growth area in recent times has been in continuous subscription and *omnibus research* (see 10). According to Valerie Farbridge[16] in her helpful interpretation of the 1981 figures in Table 1, this growth has been particularly noticeable in *buyer-syndicated services...* 'Here manufacturers are banding together to research areas of mutual interest, to reduce the overheads. Consumer panels have been set up and retail audits have been extended.'

(In Chapter 7, where distribution planning is considered, we shall see how co-operative research is also developing between manufacturers and distributors.)

8 *Quantitative data*: this is alternatively termed 'hard' data by marketing practitioners and it comprises those research findings that are expressed in the form of numbers. For example, a readership survey of national newspapers would provide a great deal of quantitative data on the numbers and types of people who read particular newspapers, the length of time they had been reading particular papers, and the method by which they obtained their newspapers (i.e. by collection or delivery).

9 *Qualitative data*: but such a survey might also contain a great deal of qualitative data, sometimes called 'soft' data. Whilst quantitative data typically indicates what people buy, qualitative data, resulting from an exploration of user attitudes and motivations attempts to throw some light on why they buy what they do. Qualitative data in the newspaper survey would deal with the feelings and preferences of readers, the nature of their perceptions and their 'response functions' to advertising.

Qualitative research relies on the techniques of applied behavioural science for its methodology and typically includes 'depth' interviews, attitude scaling techniques and psycho-physical measures. Again, according to Valerie Farbridge,[17] this is currently a growth area. She writes: 'The other growth area is qualitative research. The number of companies supplying this has increased enormously in a year. Research buyers have a very wide choice and the services offered are often sophisticated, of high quality and geared to marketing decisions.'

10 *Omnibus* surveys: increasingly popular, these are surveys operated on a regular basis by research organisations. A single survey sets out to obtain information on a wide variety of products and services but the individual client 'buys' questions to be included in the survey.

'Access', the continuous research survey operated by the British Market Research Bureau (BMRB) utilises a nationally representative sample of 1250 adults aged 15 and over. Charges to clients are made on the basis of 'question units' (i.e. one question with six pre-coded answers), discounts being available to clients who require only minority samples within the main survey.

Now that a number of marketing research terms have been explained, we can consider the scope of marketing research activities. The schematic on p. 75 is a useful starting point, illustrating as it does the types of information frequently required in relation to the four components of the marketing mix. But how is this information actually obtained in practice?... and what other types of question are usually referred to the research function? The Section which follows provides some examples which it is hoped will illustrate marketing research in action.

Example 1

The 'Sabine' service is available for a stipulated fee to clients of the AC Nielsen Company of Oxford. It is intended to assist clients to focus on particular product situations in order to isolate a marketing or sales problem and find possible solutions. The service is based on statistical analysis of marketing data, sophisticated computing support enabling the clients to obtain proposed solutions very speedily.

For example, a manufacturer of carbonated drinks had introduced a new, additional style of packaging in order 'to make his product more versatile and so increase sales'. This new packaging seemed to draw from ('cannibalise') the sales of the product in its original packaging and the manufacturer required confirmation of whether or not this was happening.

The analysis conducted by Nielsen was based on data for two periods, at a year's interval from each other, the data being segmented according to whether retail stockists were handling either or both of the two types of packaging.

The analysis (outlined in Fig. 3.2) showed that the new package increased total brand sales dramatically in stores where both types of package were stocked. Although the rate of sale per store of the original packaging showed some reduction, the main reason for the apparent drawing off (cannibalisation) of sales was a reduction of the percentage of retail outlets stocking the original packaging (lost distribution).

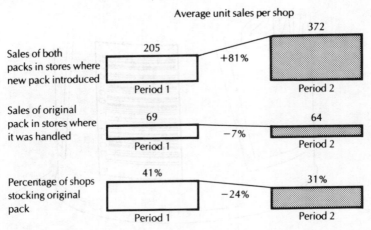

Fig. 3.2   A Sabine analysis for carbonated drinks (Source: The AC Nielsen Company)

The manufacturer accordingly decided to widen the availability of the product in its new packaging and to emphasise to retailers the need to keep both types of packaging in stock.

Example 2

Moving on from the product, let us now think about pricing.

On the can illustrated in Fig. 3.3, we can see a panel containing a pattern of parallel lines of various thicknesses. We recognise this as the computer bar-code. This bar code will be 'read' by a computer, at the check-out till in the retail store, by the use of either a 'wand' or a laser beam. The beam reads the pattern which represents a unique number for each product. When the computer has rapidly searched its memory for the current price, allowing for special offers or discounts, this is relayed to the check-out point along with a short product description. The price is displayed to the user through a visual display panel and recorded on the till roll. There are obvious benefits to the consumer – speed and accuracy (no need for lengthy examination of price lists at the till). The retailer has a constantly moving 'picture' of sales per product, by combinations of sizes, colours, flavours etc in order to make decisions on re-stocking, re-ordering from suppliers and distribution of supplies from central warehouse to retail branches. But, of course, what such a volume of

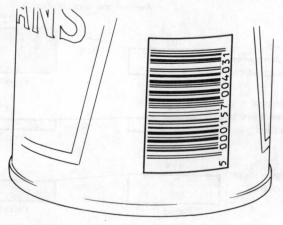

Fig. 3.3   Computer bar coding

data being captured at check-outs provides, when harnessed by appropriate systems, is a marketing information system, owned and operated by the distributor in the marketing channel – a *channel marketing information system* into which the manufacturer can 'tap' his own needs for data retrieval. For example, a manufacturer wishing to change the price of his product or introduce a discount or a promotional offer would clearly like to know what effect this might have on sales. By co-operation, and through a channel marketing information system, he can try out the strategy in a limited area – town, city, TV region or other appropriate 'test market', subsequently analysing the results against the possibilities of full-scale national marketing.

Example 3

After the product and the price elements of the marketing mix, let us think of the place factor – distribution.

The importance of research into patterns of distribution, and particularly concerning changes in those patterns was clearly signified by an article in The Guardian newspaper (15 October, 1983). It began:

A revolution has been taking place in the way books are sold. A rapidly growing proportion of total sales now take place not across the counters of Foyles or Blackwells, but through the check-outs of Marks & Spencer, Boots or Sainsburys. And a lot of these new high street outlets have built their sales mainly or entirely on 'own brand' books.

And, of course, this is only part of a more extensive picture in which it can be seen that the traditional grocers have recently taken a great deal of trade from other specialist shops, including off-licences, retail pharmacies, greengrocers and butchers. The major grocery chains have continued their expansion by developing new product ranges, such as DIY and gardening products. Specialist facilities have been incorporated within their outlets (e.g. in-store bakeries, meat and cheese counters), so that what were once classified as *multiple* outlets, with a *specialist* range of products (i.e. food) have now become rather similar to the traditional department store with all things to be found 'under one roof'. In order to provide a widening range of products and services, some of the UK's major grocers have built 'superstores' (defined as any grocery outlet with 25 000 square feet or more

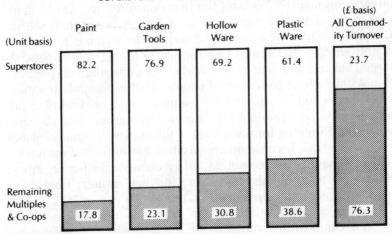

SUPERSTORE HOMECARE SALES SHARES (%)

(Unit basis)	Paint	Garden Tools	Hollow Ware	Plastic Ware	(£ basis) All Commodity Turnover
Superstores	82.2	76.9	69.2	61.4	23.7
Remaining Multiples & Co-ops	17.8	23.1	30.8	38.6	76.3

Source: Nielsen

Fig. 3.4   *Diversification of superstores into non-food areas*

of selling area floor-space, on any number of floors). During the year 1980, these superstores increased their sales revenue by almost 28 per cent.

As Fig. 3.4 indicates, the trend for diversification of the superstores into the non-food areas has been particularly significant in the DIY and gardening sector – for whilst superstores account for less than a quarter of the all-commodity turnover of the multiples and co-operatives, they have obtained a highly significant share of sales of paint, garden tools, hollow ware (pots, pans etc) and plastic ware (food boxes, cleaning utensils etc).

It might be thought that the comments in this Section describe a trend or an issue in distribution rather than provide an example of marketing research in action. What they do exemplify is the importance of continuous research services, provided by organisations such as Nielsen, and based on the techniques of shop audit research. With increasingly rapid and significant developments in information technology these techniques are also changing, but always in the direction of speedier retrieval of data for decision making. This can only be to the good when distribution policy has consistently to be reviewed by marketing executives.

Example 4

In the schematic on p. 75, under the heading 'Promotion', the following question is posed: 'What are the most appropriate advertising media?' To state the question fully, we would then add the words '... for my product/service.' As we shall see in Chapter 4, marketing a product or service is not so much a matter of introducing that product or service to 'a market', in general terms, but to a segment of the market – a particular sub-population within a total collection of people. That sub-population may be characterised by one or more features – such as chronological age, terminal educational age, sex, income group, life style or whatever. Reaching for a segment of the market also makes good economic sense, because no organisation has unlimited resources and in spending on promotion, all efficient marketing organisations attempt to obtain good value for their money. How does marketing research help them to do this?

Here are two illustrations.

1   The composition and size of the audience for television, including television advertising is continuously monitored by arrangements under the aegis of the Broadcasters' Audience

Research Board (BARB) Ltd... a joint Company of the British Broadcasting Corporation and the Independent Television Companies Association (ITCA). The system is operated by Audits of Great Britain Ltd (AGB), at the present time, and is based on electronic meters attached to a representative sample of television sets, supported by diaries recording the personal viewing of members of the household. For audience reaction research, the BBC and ITCA have agreed to use the mechanism of the BBC Daily Survey, suitably adapted to provide for the needs of both television systems.

2   The Target Group Index (TGI) is produced by the British Market Research Bureau (BMRB) and is available on subscription to advertisers, advertising agencies and media owners. It is a national product and media survey and it collects information from 24 000 adults each year. It measures heavy to light usage for over 2500 brands in more than 200 consumer product fields and also measures user activity in such services areas as banking, building societies, airlines, holidays and retail outlets. It also analyses the readership composition of 141 newspapers and magazines, weight of ITV viewing and listening to commercial radio as well as exposure to outdoor media and the cinema. Moreover, the characteristics of the population surveyed include social grade, household income and other 'special breakdowns' – e.g. terminal educational age, working status, home ownership, size of household, marital status (i.e. the 'demographics'). TGI is a single source measurement and therefore all elements of the survey can be cross-referenced, e.g. media usage related to product usage; brand usage related to demographics etc.

Clearly, expenditure on promotion is not the invariable 'hit or miss' affair that the critics of marketing would have us believe.

Example 5

All of the examples given in this Section have been based on continuous research services. Such services are very significant and their popularity with marketing organisations increases, as has been said earlier. However, the importance of ad hoc research must not be overlooked. The term ad hoc is in some senses, unfortunate, particularly if it conveys the idea of a survey which is scrambled together and badly managed. The ad hoc survey must be meticulously planned and rigorously conducted and the knowledgeable marketing organisation emphasises the 'checks and balances' to safeguard research quality, whether it conducts such research itself or commissions it externally. In the latter case it will seek an organisation of the required experience and reputation. Ad hoc surveys are often surveys of the market – whether for market selection, market appraisal or the formulation of marketing policy.

An organisation such as the Economist Intelligence Unit, for instance, is well suited, through its international organisation and experience, to conduct detailed market investigations in most countries, if the sponsor of the research is considering entering one or more foreign markets.

The EIU would provide a research report indicating market size, nature and potential as related to the environmental background and, where required, information on inter-market comparability.

Factors such as:

- sales/consumption patterns;
- competition and competitors;
- market shares;
- prices, margins and discounts;
- distribution patterns;
- market regulations and controls;
- product specifications, packaging;
- presentation etc,

would all be covered in such an ad hoc survey. Where the research was conducted for the purposes of industrial marketing, guidance would be provided on the conditions and prospects in user industries and organisations.

Marketing research procedures

Now that we have some appreciation of why marketing research is carried out, we ought to consider how it is conducted and we must therefore look at the process of sampling as this is at the root of most marketing research work.

The theory of sampling

If Arnold Ceramics want to modify their tableware for greater acceptability by the market they could interview all the housewives who purchase their products – i.e. carry out a census of their users. In practice this would be inordinately expensive and therefore it would be out of the question because of *cost* considerations. It would also take a great deal of *time*, and when markets are changing so rapidly, time is often of the essence. The third point is that it is not necessary, for information gained from a representative number of users – i.e. a sample, can not only be obtained more quickly and economically, but it can also be highly reliable, as the survey can be conducted more thoroughly than if the available resources were to be used in conducting a census of the user population. However, we have to remember that in marketing research we are examining the data drawn from a sample in order to learn something about the population from which the sample is drawn. Now here we have a difficulty because any measurement based upon a sample can never be totally accurate – it can only provide an *estimate*, which may be more or less close to the true situation in the population being studied, but it is unlikely to be precisely accurate. To understand why we must think about the issue of sampling error.

Sampling error

As we can learn from any basic book on statistical theory, when we produce some measurement on the basis of a sample it is important to qualify the measurement in terms of its likely accuracy and the risk of its being incorrect by more than a given amount. First of all, the *standard error* of the estimate from the sample is the measure of the extent to which its accuracy may be influenced by chance. To give an example, suppose 90 per cent of the users interviewed in a sample survey conducted on behalf of Arnold Ceramics say that they believe the patterns on Arnolds tableware to be unattractive, and where this sample result (90 per cent) is denoted by the value p, then the standard error to be applied to value p is calculated from the following formula:

$$\text{Standard error } (p) = \sqrt{\frac{p(100 - p)}{n}}$$

i.e. $\sqrt{\dfrac{p \times q}{n}}$

where p = the sample estimate
  q = the alternative estimate (100 − p)
  n = the number of respondents in the sample.

Therefore in the Arnold's example, assuming a sample size of 100,

$$\text{Standard error } (p) = \sqrt{\frac{90 \times 10}{100}} = \sqrt{9}$$

$$= 3 \text{ percentage points}$$

Limits of confidence

It is now possible to use this calculated value in order to qualify the sample estimate with regard to its probable accuracy. The research organisation acting on behalf of Arnold's would make the statement in terms of limits of confidence. For example, 'We are x per cent confident that the true population value lies between 87 per cent and 93 per cent (i.e. $p \pm$ the standard error calculated above, or 90 per cent $\pm$ 3 per cent).

In fact, if we call the value of the standard error sigma, purely for the purposes of description, statistical theory enables us to tabulate the limits of confidence for large samples $(n > 30)$ as follows:

Level of confidence	Multiplier of standard error (Arnolds example)
68%	1 ×sigma 87%–93%
95%	2 ×sigma 84%–96%
99.7%	3 ×sigma 81%–99%

Taking the Arnold's example, then, the research organisation would say that the true population values would be between the percentages stated to the far right of the above data, these values being related to the stated levels of confidence. Thus it can be seen that as the limit of confidence increases, so does the 'spread' of possible values for the population.

Note: in sampling activity, the word 'population' denotes the total group from which the sample is drawn – in this case, the users of Arnolds tableware. The word should not be taken to mean the UK population, unless of course the sample frame, i.e. the list of people from which the sample is taken, is indeed the UK population.

The problem of bias in sampling

So far we have been looking at the standard error – the error which is endemic to sampling operations and which measures the inaccuracies which might arise purely because of the element of chance. This has implications for *sample size*, of course, in that the larger the sample we devise and use, the smaller will be the standard error – increasing the size of the sample increases the accuracy of the estimate. But this is not a 1:1 relationship, for to *halve* the standard error we would need to use a sample increased to *four times* its original size (since the standard error varies inversely with the square root of the sample size).

The question of *costs: benefits*, or more precisely, *costs: increments in accuracy*, is an important factor in marketing research and exercises the minds of the marketing practitioners in ways we shall discuss later in the chapter. The point to be made at this juncture is that whilst sampling error (i.e. the standard error) can be measured, providing the method used allows every member of the population under investigation an equal chance of being included in the sample, sampling error is not the only possible component of total error in a sample survey. Non-sampling error (or bias) derives from faults in sample design, and within the constraints of time and money, these must be rigorously guarded against if the survey data is to have any reliability. For example, bias may be introduced if:

1   the sampling frame for the population in question is inaccurate or incomplete;
2   the results are unrepresentative due to non-response from some sections of the sample;
3   the field workers carrying out the survey take insufficient care in the selection of respondents, e.g. if they take only the most convenient respondents this may bias the sample.
4   questions are ambiguously worded on the survey prompt list or questionnaire, or if they are posed by the interviewer in a way which biases the response.

So it can be seen that the accuracy of estimates can be affected by research of poor quality. Points 2, 3 and 4 above, in so far as they involve interviewers, can be minimised by clear and comprehensive briefing prior to the survey being conducted. Ambiguity in the wording of questions is usually overcome by *pilot testing* the questionnaire on a small but valid sample of respondents prior to the main survey work.

Types of sample

1   *Random (probability) sample.* In this type of sample every

member of the population being investigated has an equal chance, or probability, of being selected for the sample. The valid theoretical basis of probability sampling makes possible the use of the mathematics of probability, e.g. the calculation of the standard error. The approach necessitates a comprehensive and up-to-date listing of the population from which the sample is drawn and this is by no means easy. In consumer research, the Electoral Register can be used for the sampling frame but it becomes out of date from the day of its compilation. Membership lists of professional bodies, clubs and societies are perhaps less 'perishable' in this regard, but the danger is still there. Each member of the sample is selected by the application of random numbers to the sampling frame (either by using a computer or a table of random numbers). Another method is the *equal interval method* where the sampling interval is calculated by dividing the number of respondents in the proposed sample into the number of elements in the sampling list. Where, for example, it is proposed to interview 2000 members of a professional body containing 30 000 current members, each 15th member would be selected for the sample, since $30\,000/2000 = 15$

Of course, the very randomness of the method means that the chosen respondents may be geographically scattered and 'call back' may be necessary before the respondent is finally available for interview. Therefore the cost of this method has to be set against the fact that the validity of the techniques of inference increase the confidence with which survey results can be accepted.

2   *Quota sample.* Whereas in the random sample the interviewer is given the details of the people selected for interview, with the quota sample the interviewer is provided with a check list of characteristics and instructed to interview a specified number of people with those characteristics. In filling the quota, the proportions will be laid down so that these reflect the proportions in the population as a whole, or in the proportions known from previous data to be of significance for the product or market which is the subject of the survey.

For example, let us say that a quota sample is being used for Arnold's survey of tableware. Let us imagine that Arnold's (or their research specialists) know that the purchase of this class of tableware is markedly correlated with socio-economic status and with age. That the 'young marrieds' do not figure prominently in this market, nor do those of lower social status. An analysis of current data may therefore lead to an individual interviewer being asked to interview 100 housewives according to the following classifications:

Age group	Social grade	Numbers		
15—24	ABC$_1$	10 } 15		
	C$_2$DE	5		
25—44	ABC$_1$	25 } 45	} 100	
	C$_2$DE	20		
45—65 and over	ABC$_1$	25 } 40		
	C$_2$DE	15		

(Note: The explanation for the social grade classification is provided in Chapter 4, Market segmentation.)

The advantages of this method of sampling are that surveys can be conducted more quickly and economically than with random sampling and there are no costly 'call-backs'. Moreover it is possible to use the method if a suitable sampling frame for random sampling does not exist. Against this, it is not theoretically strictly admissible to estimate the standard error and since the selection of respondents is left to the interviewer the method is open to bias in that the more enthusiastic and articulate respondents may be favoured for selection leaving the quota of interviews slanted in favour of this sub-population, with certain other key groups under-represented. However this danger can be overcome by adequate investigator briefing and supervision.

Sampling: concluding thoughts

This subject has been treated at some length in this chapter since it is at the root of the many facets of marketing research. Even so, only a bare outline is provided here and it is important for any student/intending practitioner of marketing to read more widely. Through such study, the reader will be able to appreciate that other forms of sampling, e.g.

- systematic random sampling
- stratified random sampling
- cluster sampling
- multi-stage sampling

have their place in marketing research. Moreover recourse is often made to *weighting* certain sub-groups of the sample so that the number of interviews is increased in these sub-groups in accordance with particular survey objectives.

The reader can do no better than consult the works of Chisnall, Crimp, and Proctor and Stone mentioned in the bibliography. Also, the Chapter on Sampling by Martin Collins in the *Consumer Market Research Handbook* edited by Worcester and Downham, is clear and interesting. Anyone seeking a good basic introduction to the subject will also find appropriate sections of TJ Hannagan's work helpful.

Finally, so that the reader will not be misled, it should be noted that although the quota sample does not fulfil the theoretical conditions for calculation of sampling error, nevertheless, as Martin Collins[18] points out:

In practice, however, sample estimates are useless without some statement of their accuracy and we tend to apply the same theory.

Here, the reader might easily remark 'what price scientific method?' The following points are important:

1   experience tends to demonstrate that the greater sources of opportunity for error occur more at the interview stage, or through ambiguous questions or in faulty processing of data, than in sampling error – therefore the advantages of quota sampling often outweigh the disadvantages;
2   since most marketing research work deals with broad trends, aggregates, averages etc, statistical perfection is not really being sought.

We shall return to this topic before the end of the Chapter.

The design of research surveys

It is important that the collection of marketing research data is preceded by a detailed *research design*, which has been defined by Robert Ferber[19] as:

a series of advanced decisions that, taken together, comprise a master plan or model for the conduct of the investigation.

Planning the design will call for answers to the questions set out in the sequence which follows.

1   *What is the problem?* This is not an easy question to answer. For example, it will not usually be enough to say 'declining sales'. Is this due to the product? its price? its distribution? its promotion? is the decline restricted to certain regions? or to certain products? It is necessary to be precise in order to shape the research design purposefully. If the internal reports sub-system cannot provide the answer, a preliminary investigation may be necessary.

2   *What specific data are necessary to assist in solving the problem?* Do these relate to market size? market share? competitors' sales? competitors' advertising expenditure? user motivations and buying behaviour? distributors' attitudes? etc. Once the data has been identified it must be recorded in an exact written statement which also identifies the format in which the data should be presented.

3   *What are the sources of such data?* What secondary data is available which bears on the problem? What gaps consequently exist upon which primary data has to be acquired;

4   *How should the required primary data be collected?* Who should be contacted? e.g. user demographics or other classifications; description of distributors (types and numbers); buyers in user industries (types and numbers). What detailed data should be gathered? e.g. buying behaviour? opinions? motives? purchasing policies? technical specifications etc. By what method(s) should it be collected? e.g. by survey method(s)? if so, by telephone? by mail? by personal interview? and/or by observation method(s)? e.g. by in-store viewing techniques? by television audience measurement? and/or by experimental method(s)? e.g. by test marketing? by market simulation techniques using computer analysis?

5   *What are the time and cost factors for this project?* What is the budget available? How does it relate to the costs of the proposed methods of data collection? How quickly is the data required? How does this relate to the proposed methodology?
(Note: again, this is a fundamental question and often time and cost factors act as constraints in formulating research design. A balance must be struck between reputable research and the danger of seeking increments of information whose cost is out of proportion to their value). (see further note on p. 102)

6   *Related to Question 5, who will conduct the research?* For example, if the organisation has its own marketing research department, will the research be conducted by it, or by specialist external agencies, or will the project be shared? If so, in what proportions? (This will enable field work to be planned and scheduled, personnel and other resources to be detailed, the project to be fully costed and authorised against a set time schedule).

7   *How will the data be analysed, tabulated and presented?* This is an extension of Stage 2 and clarifies how findings should be presented for the executives who will examine them and subsequently take action. Cross-tabulations of data may be specified at this, or a later stage – never forgetting that costs and relevance are factors to keep constantly in mind.

A number of terms appearing in the above outline call for explanation.

User demographics (Question 4)

Traditionally, consumer markets have been analysed in terms of such classifications as:

age, sex, socio-economic group, household size etc. These classifications do correlate with buying behaviour in some instances and are frequently used as broad, general classifiers in current research. However, Yankelovitch[20] and others have commented more recently on the weak relationships between consumers' buying behaviour and their socio economic status.

We shall examine these and other classifications in Chapter 4, Market segmentation.

Survey methods (Question 4)

(a)   *Telephone interviews.* These can be very effective, particularly if the interview is limited to simple, clearly worded questions, a drawback being the difficulty of obtaining information on the characteristics of respondents. It is an expensive method in the UK. A recent suggestion[21] is that the marketing research industry should be campaigning for a reduced rate for telephone research and lobbying the telecommunications authorities for better service (see also Chapter 5 on the vast increase in the number of UK telephone subscribers).

(b) *Mail survey methods.* These facilitate the conduct of wide-spread research at reasonably low cost. Frequently, however, they obtain low response and since the response may be unrepresentative of the total market, bias can thereby be introduced into the findings. Response rates would be better for specialised topics among respondents known, from previous data, to be interested in the topic (e.g. production control systems in a survey of factory managers). In order to increase response rates the mailed material may contain some incentive to reply and follow-up material is used or telephone contact is made with non-respondents.

(c) *Personal interviews* are the best method for obtaining good and representative response rates, with detailed information, but are clearly expensive and time consuming. This type of interview allows the field worker to modify the approach to allow for the personality of the respondent. Detailed questions (and answers) can be carefully explained, thus minimising misinterpretation. Even so, bias can be introduced through the personality of the interviewer, careless recording of answers etc, but careful initial briefing of interviewers and an adequate level of supervision 'in the field' – standards which any UK marketing executive would expect from a reputable research organisation – will markedly reduce these dangers.

Experimental methods (Question 4)

Test marketing. Since there are so many variables in marketing campaigns, the use of test marketing is based on the view that in the end information on sales volume, costs and profitability is best provided by trying it in the market place. The 'limited-area try-out' as it is sometimes called, may take place in a town, city or a commercial television region and broadly speaking the idea is to select a geographical area for its close similarity to the main market in terms of level of competition, availability of advertising media, distributive structure, characteristics of user population, adequacy of research facilities etc, and then to launch a marketing campaign scaled down to allow for the proportionate significance of the area in terms of market potential. To put it another way – the scale of effort in the test market, on all dimensions of marketing activity, will be in proportion to the planned marketing effort in the main marketing region when this is subsequently undertaken. In this way, forecasts of projected sales volume/return-on-

investment in the event of broad-scale marketing will be, hopefully, that much more reliable.

As may be discerned, the method would be particularly suitable
for testing the potential of new products.

Two approaches may be distinguished: 1 *the use of a single test
market*, e.g. for launching a new product, either for sales forecasting or to identify problems which may arise in subsequent marketing and 2 *matched-area testing*, where, in addition to the above
objectives it might be useful to test the outcome of variations
in one factor of marketing strategy (e.g. price), all other factors
being held constant.

Great care is needed in the selection of the test market(s) and
the controls to be applied to the conduct of the experiment,
not least in matching the scale of local promotional effort to
that of the projected (national) effort.

As Cannon[22] points out, the method has not been adopted here
with quite the same degree of enthusiasm as in the USA where
'the complexity of the market, its size and the costs involved
have created an environment in which the savings usually
outweigh the risks'. One of the risks that Cannon refers to in
this context is where the technology gap between products and
organisations is so small that competition may introduce a new
brand 'based at least in part on information obtained at the inno-
vator's expense'.

Time and cost factors (Question 5)

Much marketing research has to be carried out at speed, due to
the pace of change in the market and within the limitations of
affordable budgets. At this time, budgets are much tighter than
was the case up to the middle of the 1970s.

The implications of these points are:

(a) research companies should not recommend unnecessary
techniques;

(b) marketing executives should not seek over-elaborate information – the purpose of marketing research is to assist management in the decision-making process and therefore, effective
research is research that will 'just do'.

(c) research executives in marketing organisations and practitioners in research companies should resist the reflex reaction
which bids them to 'do a study', if intensive reanalysis of existing

data would be sufficient or at least provide a context for the development of useful hypotheses.

In an interesting reading on 'Research: The Ways of Academe and Business', Holbert[23] amusingly sums up the in-built professional tension between academic and business researchers. Since academic researchers can become tendentious and obsessive about the sophistication of their procedures this may result 'in articles centering more on methodology than meaning'. At the same time, 'academicians viewing the work of commercial researchers often wonder if the latter know their asymptotes from their elementals'.

The issue hinges on the concept of *balance*. Business researchers cannot afford to eschew the scientific approach but, as Jolson[24] points out, mathematical notation and statistical methodology are often allowed to dwarf the primary goals of marketing research, for the business researcher is not a number-gatherer but a member of a marketing team.

The objective of research that will 'just do' becomes more rather than less important when practitioners have to tailor the project and the methodology ever more carefully to match the budget.

In stating that the net value to be realised from any major primary research project is the marginal increase in the expected value of the decision, less the cost of the research, Jolson[25] adds that it can be expressed mathematically as follows:

$$V_o = (V_r - V_f) - C_r$$

where

V_o = The net value of the research project;
V_r = the expected value of the marketing decision when made with the aid of research;
V_f = the expected value of the marketing decision when made either without the benefit of research or with the benefit of secondary data only
C_r = the cost of research.

Although the formula assumes that V_r and V_f can be quantified, usually in money terms, this author includes Jolson's formula here because it expresses the issue of costs v. benefits much more eloquently than any collection of words can do.

When the student-reader becomes a marketing practitioner he will fully understand why the issue is so significant.

Who will conduct the research? (Question 6)

This question provides the opportunity to make some general comments on the organisation of marketing research.

Tom Hegedus[26] in a recent commentary upon the British scene made these points:

Comparatively few businesses are aware of what market research is all about or what it can do for them. Yet it should really be considered to be on the same level as other ingredients in the marketing mix, such as advertising, packaging and distribution.

The multinational conglomerates know what market research is all about, but small businesses need the same knowledge of marketing conditions as the big firms, even though it is on a smaller scale.

Therefore, only the very largest firms would have their own marketing research department and even they would doubtless relate to specialist agencies for assistance with the conduct of surveys since they could hardly afford to employ a large 'field force' of interviewers.

What is more usual, among the medium and large-sized firms that support and implement the marketing approach, is to designate responsibility for marketing research to an individual manager reporting to the head of marketing. Assisted perhaps by two or three personnel, this manager's department will provide data for decision-making based on analyses of the firm's internal records, and particularly sales records; it will conduct research in part or whole, which involves the acquisition and analysis of secondary data and it will be responsible for choice of, and liaison with, specialist agencies briefed to conduct survey work for the acquisition of primary data. The briefing of outside agencies together with monitoring of their activities calls for a high level of specialist knowledge and skill in the research manager, including familiarity with the techniques involved and a continuing grasp of developments in research methodology.

The table on p. 76 shows that UK organisations have an increasing acknowledgment of the value of marketing research. Yet in many organisations, this type of research function is not accorded the status it deserves. Writing in 1966 on 'The identity crisis of the market researcher' and quoting an international study ranging over nine countries, Rogers[27] reported that:

Frequently, marked anxiety prevailed between marketer and researcher ... Researchers claimed that marketers neither understand nor appreciate research; do not permit researchers to acquaint themselves with all the relevant aspects of the problem; do not provide adequate resources in expenditure or time for 'good research'; are disinclined to permit 'general research' essential for long-range planning...

One believes that there has been improvement since that time although this author recalls finding in the mid 1970s one large UK organisation with its own sizeable, self-contained and quite expert marketing research department in which the researchers had no forum for making presentations to senior management, even about such fundamentally important matters as product development!

Research is therefore quite useless unless the executive(s) concerned are given sufficient status to enable them to influence marketing policy. Moreover it is vitally important that research is not seen by top management as a fragmented, spasmodic function only to be activated when management perceives it has a problem. Marketing research must be seen as a continuing process, linked in a systematic fashion to decision making mechanisms through the type of information system which has now been made possible by developments in micro-computing and telecommunications. Intelligent managers can capitalise on such developments, even if they manage only small organisations.

The market research industry

In concluding this Chapter, it might be helpful to say something about the specialist organisations in the marketing research field, with emphasis on the current situation in the UK.

The measure of the UK's sophistication in this field can be gauged from a key publication, *The International Research Directory of market research organisations*. This is published jointly by The Market Research Society (of the UK) and the British Overseas Trade Board. It surveys marketing research in some 60 countries and in the short period between two recent editions the number of organisations listed had grown from 900 to 1100 providing 'compelling evidence of the extent of the resources engaged'. The student reader is advised to peruse the latest edition of the publication. Under the UK listing a large number of organisations are included, so that a wide range of research services is available to marketing organisations, including:

ad hoc consumer research, advertising research, attitude research, continuous consumer research, desk research, industrial research, international research, qualitative research, media research, omnibus research, packaging research, product testing and retail audits.

Further proof of the growth of the industry is demonstrated by the establishment of an increasing number of associations representing specific sectors, e.g.

IMRA representing industrial market researchers;
AURA representing buyers of research;
AQRP representing qualitative researchers;
AMSO representing the larger research agencies; and
ABMRC representing smaller research agencies.

The Account Planners Group, comprises researchers who work in advertising agencies. It is a significantly active organisation.

The professional body to which most marketing research practitioners belong is The Market Research Society of 15, Belgrave Square, London SW1X 8PF. The Society publishes a Code of Conduct to which its members (over 3000 at the beginning of the 1980s) and the members of the Industrial Marketing Research Association, agree to be bound. The contents of the Code have been described in the author's work *Introduction to Marketing* (pp. 217–219) and the conscientious student might refer to these or obtain a copy of the Code and examine its provisions carefully. The European Society for Opinion and Marketing Research (ESOMAR), Wamberg 37, 1083 CW Amsterdam, Netherlands, is another important organisation. Among other activities, it organises conferences and publishes valuable papers on research topics.

Self-assessment questions

1   What is meant by cybernetics? What relevance has it for the establishment of a marketing information system?
2   List the user needs that you think should be taken into account in the design of a marketing information system.
3   How could an internal reports system be used to monitor and control marketing operations?
4   Define marketing research. How does it differ from market research?

5 What are the characteristics of the scientific method? Relate this method to a marketing research project, outlining how the scientific approach influences the conduct of such a project in its various stages.

6 Write notes on the following:
primary data; desk research; continuous data; syndicated research; quantitative data; qualitative data; omnibus surveys; channel marketing information system.

7 What is the standard error of the estimate from a sample? What is meant by limits of confidence? Describe some of the ways in which bias may be introduced in a sample survey.

8 Outline how a research survey should be designed.

9 Describe the methods by which survey data may be collected.

10 How do the factors of costs and time affect the conduct of marketing research?

References

1 Ampère, A. M. *A handbook of management*, Thomas Kempner, ed, Harmondsworth, Middlesex, Penguin, 1977, p.110

2 Wiener, Norbert. *Cybernetics*, 2nd edn, MIT Press and J. Wiley, 1961

3 Brien, Richard H. and Stafford, James E. Marketing information systems: a new dimension for marketing research, *Journal of Marketing*, July 1968, p. 21

4 Kotler, Philip. *Principles of Marketing*, Englewood Cliffs, NJ, Prentice-Hall, 1980, p. 136

5 Oliver, Gordon. *Marketing Today*, London; Prentice-Hall International, 1980, p. 115

6 Kotler, Philip. *Principles of Marketing*, Englewood Cliffs, NJ, Prentice-Hall, 1980, p. 137

7 Ibid p. 136

8 Harper, Marion, Jr. A new profession to aid management, *Journal of Marketing*, January 1961, p. 1

9 Lockley, Lawrence C. History and development of marketing research, *Handbook of Marketing Research*, Robert Ferber, ed, New York, McGraw-Hill, 1974, p. 1

10 Committee on Definitions. *Marketing definitions; a glossary of marketing terms*, Chicago, American Marketing Association, 1960, pp. 16–17

11 International Chamber of Commerce and European Society for Opinion and Marketing Research. International code of marketing and social research practice, *Consumer Market Research Handbook* 2nd

edn, Robert M. Worcester and John Downham eds, New York, London, Van Nostrand Reinhold Company, 1978, p. 714

12 *Marketing Today*, p. 98

13 Twedt, Dik Warren (ed). *1978 Survey of Marketing Research*, Chicago, American Marketing Association, 1978, p. 41

14 Farbridge, Valerie. The push-button problem solvers of a new society, *Campaign*, London, 9 July 1982, p. 47

15 Schwartz, David J. *Marketing Today*, 3rd edn, New York, Harcourt Brace Jovanovich, 1981, pp. 57–58

16 The push-button problem solvers of a new society, *Campaign*, p. 47

17 Ibid

18 Collins, Martin. Sampling, *Consumer Market Research Handbook*, 2nd edn, Robert M. Worcester and John Downham eds, New York, London, Van Nostrand Reinhold Company, 1978, p. 83

19 Ferber, Robert et al, The design of research investigations, *Marketing Research Series*, No 1, Chicago, American Marketing Association, 1958, p. 5

20 Yankelovitch, Daniel. Market segmentation, *Consumer behaviour*, (Ehrenberg, A. S. C. and Pyatt, F. G. eds) London, Penguin, 1971, pp. 46–47

21 Hegedus, Tom. The death of the yes men? *Campaign*, London, 9 July 1982, p. 54

22 Cannon, Tom. *Basic marketing – principles and practice*, London, Holt, Rinehart and Winston, 1980, p. 172

23 Holbert, Neil Bruce. Research: the ways of academe and business, *Marketing management* Marvin L. Jolson, London, Collier Macmillan Publishers, 1978, p. 191

24 Ibid p. 191

25 Ibid p. 220

26 The death of the yes men? *Campaign*, p. 54

27 Rogers, K. The identity crisis of the market researcher, *Marketing research*, (Seibert, Joseph and Wills, Gordon, eds) Harmondsworth, Middlesex, Penguin, 1970, p. 157

4 MARKET SEGMENTATION

Objectives

For most organisations the 'market' usually means some specific group within a total population of individuals, industries or even countries. We are now about to examine some of the ways in which key groups can be identified and described, in order that the whole marketing effort is made that much more manageable and economic.

A number of ways in which individuals and groups can be so segmented are depicted in this Chapter – not only in terms of what people are, for instance, but also in terms of what they do – i.e. how they behave in the market-place.

Some approaches to segmentation in industrial marketing are also outlined.

Introduction

The rationale of segmentation

From what we have observed so far in this book, marketing is a process by which the organisation uses its resources to provide acceptable products or services for a market. Let us now consider what we mean by *market*. Quite simply it is a collection of:

1 individuals or organisations, with
2 specific needs and/or wants, and
3 adequate purchasing power and
4 the propensity to purchase.

We will not ponder on all the elements of this definition. If the reader thinks about them they are self-evident and require no explanation. Moreover, the above definition encompasses *consumer markets* (composed of individuals) and *industrial markets*, as well as *markets for services*.

Yet the approach to the market seldom means the direction of marketing effort to some total population of potential buyers for a class of product or a type of service. More usually, the process entails directing marketing effort at a *specific target group* within that total population. For example, the total market for ceramic tableware comprises potential buyers for each type of formulation of the product, including fine bone china, earthware and vitrified hotel ware. Within each product type there are a number of grades of quality, each with its own range of prices, and within those grades of quality there are a number of types of decoration, including lithographs, colour bands and lines, under-glaze prints, silk-screen prints etc, which result in further price sub-divisions. So that when we talk of the 'market' for ceramic tableware we are not speaking of a single undifferentiated market but of an aggregation of minority markets or sub-populations of buyers, with each sub-population requiring a particular type of tableware.

The individual organisation, such as Arnolds, will not usually attempt to cater for all these minority markets – although if the individual organisation is part of a conglomerate, the conglomerate may do so. At the level of the individual production unit, resources are finite: capital equipment, knowledge of raw materials and the level of skills of the labour supply are fixed factors, if only in the short term. Meeting the needs of the customer is therefore a question of *matching* these fixed factors to market opportunities. If the market so changes that the types of resources at the disposal of the supplier are obsolete, then the supplier has to re-invest in new capital equipment or diversify into other markets.

The philosophy of directing products and services at specific target groups is termed *market segmentation*. As Lunn[1] indicates, it is a philosophy which has gained a great deal of influence in the post-1945 period. Moreover, as people have become wealthier and as traditional values have changed, tastes and needs have widened and the structure of requirements in many markets has become increasingly differentiated. New products have therefore had to be developed which appealed to particular market segments, at least initially. It is the function of market research to identify those segments which permit the development of products and services with clear identities but which are, nevertheless, large enough to permit economical production and adequate returns to scale.

A caveat

Rising real incomes and the move away from traditional class-determined patterns of behaviour will further increase the significance of market segmentation. Having said that, there are instances where direction of marketing effort to the total market for the category of products is justified. For example:

1 the market may be so small that directing marketing effort to the total market may be the only profitable strategy;
2 heavy users may constitute such a considerable portion of the market that the obvious strategy is to concentrate on developing products for, and communicating with, these heavy users;
3 the organisation's product (its 'brand') may so dominate that market that its appeal is total – i.e. it elicits a positive response from all segments of the market and, therefore, there is little point in concentrating merely on one or two segments.

There considerations aside, however, the whole marketing effort becomes more manageable when some key group is identified as the target market. Products can be developed more effectively through closer attention to a more homogeneous group of potential buyers. When the group has been identified, marketing communications are often easier and more economical. Costly wastage of advertising expenditure (e.g. due to the overlapping of groups with neither the means nor the intention to buy) can be avoided.

The identification of appropriate market segments begins with such questions as:

1 Who buys?
2 Why do they buy?
3 How are their needs being satisfied?

Describing this approach to markets at the onset of its development, Wendell Smith[2] wrote:

Segmentation is based upon developments on the demand side of the market and represents a rational and more precise adjustment of product and marketing effort to consumer or user requirements.

To devise the strategy it is important to discover what characteristics of users (user classifications) best correlate with purchasing activity for the product or service in question. These classifications are termed the *segmentation variables*. The Section which follows describes some of the variables which have been established in the field of consumer goods.

Consumer products – types of segmentation

Demographic variables

The classification of users by such factors as:

1   age;
2   sex;
3   socio-economic group; and
4   family size

has been an important exercise traditionally. The descriptors in general use for the first three of these factors are set out below.

Age	Sex	Socio-economic group
15–24 years	Male	A
25–34	Female	B
35–44	(and	C₁
45–54	housewives)	C₂
55–64		D
65 and over		E

The classification 'socio-economic group' is based upon the occupation of the head of household and since the 1950s the stratification given below (and in its up-to-date form) has been the one widely adopted for research and other marketing activity.

These classifications are used in the UK's National Readership Survey (see Chapter 8) which is conducted under the direction of the Institute of Practitioners in Advertising (IPA) and are referred to by marketing and advertising executives, researchers, consultants and the like as the 'IPA definitions'.

There is no doubt that the *age* of users is an important classifier of market activity. As was illustrated in Chapter 2 (page 49) there is a world of difference between the *young adult market*

Social grade	Social status	Occupation of head of household	Approximate % of UK total population
A	Upper middle class	Higher managerial, administrative, professional	3%
B	Middle class	Intermediate managerial, administrative, professional	12%
C₁	Lower middle class	Supervisory or clerical and junior managerial, administrative, professional	23%
C₂	Skilled working class	Skilled manual workers	32%
D	Working class	Semi and unskilled manual workers	21%
E	Those at the lowest level of subsistence	State pensioners or widows (no other earners), casual or lowest grade workers	9%

with its heavy emphasis on the purchase of soft drinks, pop records and cassettes, transistor radios and cinema admissions and that of the *retired, elderly market* with its high level of demand for health care products, chiropody and other medical support services.

The *sex* classification is also important variable for segmentation. Health and hygiene products, including slimming aids; beauty products and services; the distribution and sale of magazines for female readers etc, are examples of some of the fields where this variable is highly relevant. And whilst the differences in the interests of men and women are becoming less marked than hitherto, the market for beer is predominantly a male market and angling and car maintenance do not as yet have many female adherents. Within the 'female' heading it is also usual to incorporate the sub-division *housewives* – that is, those responsible for household catering. The significance of such segmentation for food products, domestic cleaning products and other 'family budget' items is clear.

The socio-economic group (or social grade) which is based upon the occupation of head of household has not been without its critics. Its efficiency in circumscribing and predicting spending patterns has been questioned. Yankelovitch[3] writing in 1964, and Frank,[4] in 1967, have both commented on low correlations of socio-economic variables with buying behaviour. The well-known British researcher, Mark Abrams[5] writing in 1968 commented that people thrown together in the same occupation – income-groups may differ widely in their life styles depending on the size and composition of their families, their educational backgrounds, their cultural and recreational standards and behaviour and their age.

Nevertheless, socio-economic classifications have been found useful in describing the markets for such diverse products as motor cars, telephones and ground coffee, as well as for banking services. The variable continues to be used and may often be found to have significance. For example, a report published in 1979 on newspaper readership provided the surprising information that the largest decline in reading national dailies has been among the AB socio-economic group, with the trend at its smallest among the D group.

Occupational groupings do tell us something about disposable income and disposable income provides some guide as to what is bought (e.g. we would expect the ABs to constitute a highly significant part of the market for luxury goods). As Tony Lunn[6] says:

Demographic variables describe important aspects of people's circumstances which give rise to purchasing needs. They also act as moderators upon the translation of these needs into behaviour, e.g. a low income household may have expensive tastes but little prospect of indulging them.

Lunn also points out that demographic characteristics have been studied over a long period of time and that their relationships with other market factors such as media usage (e.g. newspapers read; TV viewing habits) have become well-known. He suggests that some of the criticism of demographic variables could be overcome by a more critical or imaginative treatment of demographic criteria – as illustrated by the *life-cycle concept* (see below).

Family size; family life cycle

Despite the pressures that have been put upon it of late, the family is still the basic social unit in our population structure and is, therefore, of intrinsic interest to marketing researchers. Obviously, the market for many products and services will be related to the number of dependants in the family (*family size*) and the stage which has been reached in family formation (*family life cycle*). The segmentation factors usually related to the life-cycle concept are shown below.

Young, single	Young couple, no children	Young couple, youngest child under 6	Young couple, youngest child 6 or more	Older couple with children 18+ at home	Older couple, no children at home	Older, single

Education

Education is often an important factor in buying behaviour, for quite aside from the fact that it is typically related to such factors as income and occupation, the type and length of education one receives often directly influences other aspects of one's life style including cultural and leisure interests. These in turn are related to the purchase of products and services. Dr Mark Abrams[7] concluded, from fieldwork conducted throughout the 1960s, that an analysis of newspaper readership in terms of educational background reveals differences which are often larger and more significant than analysis along the conventional lines of sex, age and socio-economic grade. Since that time, *terminal educational age* has been included among the respondent classifications in a great deal of consumer research. As Margaret Crimp[8] suggests, with the development of information technology and its influence on consumer habits and attitudes, the terminal educational age (TEA) classifier will become even more relevant in segmentation studies.

Ethnic, religious and national classifications

Misguidedly, we think of Great Britain as possessed of a homogeneous culture deriving from the fact that her people are white, Anglo-Saxon and protestant. And we hold to this view whilst conceding that the Welsh, the Scots and the Irish do have their eccentricities, of course. The truth is that Great Britain has always been a multi-cultural society and since 1945 the trend to greater cultural segmentation has been most marked. In 1981, for example, it was estimated[9] that whilst 95 per cent of Britain's population was classified as 'white', a further 1 per cent was classified as West Indian or Guyanese, 2 per cent Indian, Pakistani, or Bangladeshi and a further 1 per cent as 'other' or mixed ethnic origin. This 'other' category included an estimated 91 000 people of Chinese origin, 65 000 of African origin and 36 000 of Arab origin.

As this author has written in his earlier work *Introduction to Marketing*[10] such ethnic minorities as the Jews, the Irish and the later immigrants from the former Empire and Commonwealth countries are important and interesting sub-groups. Many of these groups have their own news media, their own entertainment facilities, their own dietary laws and their own cultural patterns – all factors of great significance to marketing organisations. Many of these groups also have their own retail outlets and the high level of self-employment among men of Indian, Pakistani or Bangladeshi origin has led to their noticeable incursion into Britain's more general retail businesses, particularly in the grocery trade.

Religious beliefs frequently have marketing significance not only with regard to the development of products, but also linked to the packaging and advertising of those products, particularly concerning the colours and symbols used. And while some purchasing differences often correlate with religious and cultural ideologies, others, though significant, are more difficult to explain. Van Tassel,[11] for example, points out that Negro families in the United States buy substantially more cooked cereals, corn meal, household insecticides, cream, rice, spaghetti and frozen vegetables than their white counterparts. The average Negro male apparently buys 77 per cent more pairs of shoes during his lifetime than the average white male and is prepared to pay more for them.

Ethnic and religious factors can therefore be of value in identifying differences in purchasing behaviour, not only for marketing to overseas countries where such factors predominate, but also for marketing to minority segments within larger markets.

As to national classifications, the textbooks and the business magazines provide countless examples of how products have to be developed or modified in order to suit national tastes. These national differences are not simply differences between developed and developing countries, for example. They frequently hold good for countries that are adjacent to each other and are at broadly the same stage of economic development. It is interesting that in the consumer goods field, the French are undoubtedly fashion conscious whilst the Germans have an inbred traditional taste and are particularly concerned with the durability of products. Paul Jenner[12] likewise reports that the Danes are fairly conservative, open to new designs but less susceptible to innovation for its own sake whereas the Finns are very design conscious and the requirement to 'look good' as well as to function effectively applies as much to capital goods as to consumer products. The importance of national classifications is further developed in Chapter 13 (International marketing).

Spatial (geographic) segmentation

It is sensible to plan marketing operations in phase with the way in which research data is made available – more of this later in the Chapter. For now, and for a start, we can say that the *region* is an important concept in this context, because:

1 a number of continuous research services provide data on a regional basis;
2 the independent television companies not only provide data on the composition of their audiences, region by region, (as does the BBC), they also provide information on wholesale and retail distribution (by product groups); patterns of expenditure and population trends within those regions;
3 the use of regional planning, for test marketing and for the extension of full-scale marketing activity, region by region, makes for better cost control and the minimising of risk.

The use of the Registrar General's Standard Regions (see the various publications of HM Government's Statistical Service) can form a suitable basis for the planning and control of marketing operations. As a start, statistics of population, recent changes in population and forecasted changes for the standard regions enable the marketing planner to establish a framework for operations and provide an early warning system for any requisite re-direction of marketing effort (in the UK for example, the recent history of population trends shows marked increases in the 'Outer South East', the 'Outer Metropolitan Area' and the 'East Anglia' regions).

Beyond this, an analysis of regional variations in the distribution of total household expenditure (as provided by the UK government's *Family Expenditure Survey*) may disclose significant information.Unhappily too, there are today significant differences in employment and prosperity levels within UK regions. In international marketing, regional variations are often of greater significance and we do not have to look very far afield to notice this, as witness the examples provided by Italy, Switzerland, West Germany and Belgium.

Finally, regional analysis often provides the first step in further important sub-divisions for marketing activity, such as countries and boroughs in the UK. In a country such as the USA, regional analysis becomes even more fruitful. It is worth noting, as a result of the declining farm population and the population increase in towns, cities and suburbs, that the US Federal government has established the *Standard Metropolitan Statistical Area (SMSA)* as a geographic market-data measurement unit. The SMSA is a county or group of contiguous counties with a minimum total population of at least 100 000. It must comprise a socially and economically integrated unit in which virtually all employment is non-agricultural. The SMSA may cross state lines and at its heart-centre should be a city, or two closely located cities with a total population of 50 000 minimum. Stanton[13] reports that at the end of the 1970s the ten largest SMSAs contained almost 25 per cent of the nation's total population. Even beyond this stratum, the US Government in 1975 designated 13 *Standard Consolidated Statistical Areas (SCSAs)*. These are former SMSAs that have so joined together that for all practical purposes they have become a single socio-economic unit. At the time of their designation, they accounted for 33.33 per cent of the US population, buying power and retail sales. The moral here is, for a small/ medium sized British export organisation, a single SCSA might constitute a huge, concentrated unit.

A Classification of Residential Neighbourhoods (ACORN)

A recent refinement of spatial segmentation has been developed in the UK by the CACI Market Analysis Division, of London. This is ACORN, a segmentation system which classifies consumers according to the type of residential area in which they live. ACORN is based on the published census statistics and it classifies districts and the households in them by the predominant housing conditions in those districts. The classification takes into

1981 ACORN profile, Great Britain

ACORN groups	1981 population	%
A Agricultural areas	1 811 485	3.4
B Modern family housing, higher incomes	8 667 137	16.2
C Older housing of intermediate status	9 420 477	17.6
D Poor quality older terraced housing	2 320 846	4.3
E Better-off council estates	6 976 570	13.0
F Less well-off council estates	5 032 657	9.4
G Poorest council estates	4 048 658	7.6
H Multi-racial areas	2 086 026	3.9
I High status non-family areas	2 248 207	4.2
J Affluent suburban housing	8 514 878	15.9
K Better-off retirement areas	2 041 338	3.8
U Unclassified	388 632	0.7

Reproduced by kind permission of CACI Market Analysis Division

account 40 different variables encompassing demographic, housing and employment characteristics. Applying cluster analysis, 38 different neighbourhood types are derived and these, in turn, aggregate to 11 neighbourhood groups. The 1981 ACORN Profile is set out in the table on p. 119. To give some indication of what lies behind these broad descriptions, the following extracts are reproduced from the CACI User's Guide for ACORN.

Group A: agricultural areas

This type of area contains the three per cent of the population living in communities which depend directly on farming for their livelihood. Generally these areas are too far from large towns to prove attractive to commuters.

Poor local job opportunities result in generally low household incomes and few chances for women to work. Housing conditions in many cases are also poor with a large proportion of tenants of tied cottages lacking basic amenities.

Low wages and the absence of retail competition result in somewhat unsophisticated consumer preferences and leisure is spent less through commercial outlets than in social activities and rural pursuits.

Group B: modern family housing, higher incomes

This type of area is populated primarily by young families living in modern houses, typically on small private estates in commuter villages or on the outskirts of large towns. The housing often suits the needs of people whose career advancement may depend on moving to a different part of the country or who may expect to move to a larger house in a more select neighbourhood as their real incomes rise.

Incomes, car ownership and educational attainment are all well above average in these areas and there is a tendency for people to travel considerable distances to work or shop. These factors, combining with rapid population growth, result in relatively weak community networks and a fairly high expenditure on consumer goods and family leisure activities.

One basic research application for ACORN is as a stratification variable in sample design – for it does provide a basis of ensuring geographical representativeness in a manner relevant to many markets. It can also indicate, on a basis of probabilities, where the brewery organisation, for example, might locate its public houses or the building society its branches. It clearly has value in organising and structuring the activities of a field sales force, and in *direct marketing* (see Chapter 7, Distribution planning).

The British Market Research Bureau Ltd, which co-operated with CACI in developing ACORN has written:[15]

ACORN has shown how widely different consumer behaviour can be in areas of apparently similar social status. Fashionable inner city areas such as Kensington, in London, and Edgbaston, in Birmingham, produce very different life style characteristics compared with high status suburban areas such as Northwood or Solihull. These differences result in widely different behavioural patterns, and hence product demand, for different types of high status area. At the other end of the scale, council estate dwellers in areas of economic decline such as London's dockland or the North East have for many product fields far less potential than council estate dwellers in growth areas such as Northampton or Milton Keynes. The differences in product potential can be mapped out for any area, of any shape or size, throughout Great Britain.

In his work *Introduction to Marketing*, this author, using data supplied by the British Market Research Bureau has provided an example[14] of the value of the ACORN classification when linked to the Bureau's own Target Group Index (TGI) which is described in the next Section. An element taken from the data table related to that example is as follows:

Neighbourhood type	AB social grade index	Wine heavy usage index
I	233	367
J	200	142

Source: *Acorn: A new Approach to marketing* The British Market Research Bureau Ltd, 1980

Here it can be seen that although the social grade profiles of the two areas are similar, there are marked differences in life style, as measured on the dimension of wine drinking.

Behavioural segmentation

Intelligent observation will reveal a straightforward, logical way of classifying consumers in terms of what they do. What they are like is important enough, particularly when devising advertising messages but what they do, in terms of usage of the product or service in question, has its special significance. Do they ever buy the product? Do they ever buy the brand? Do they frequently buy the product? Do they regularly buy the brand? If the brand is unobtainable, do they refuse all substitutes (i.e. how 'brand-loyal' are they)? Such questions, relating to consumption patterns, are sometimes termed *direct* or *market* classifiers, as opposed to the *indirect* classifiers, such as demography. This is not to suggest that indirect classifiers have no place, but that market classifiers do allow direct targeting of marketing activity, including media planning, as we shall see presently.

The *heavy-half* theory popularly attributed to D. W. Twedt[16] draws attention to the fact that in many product fields, 50 per cent of consumers will account for 80 per cent or more of consumption. Now this is not to say that light users or non users should be neglected, for they may provide the best prospects for future expansion. Nevertheless, *heaviness of buying* may well be the most simple, logical and profitable way of targetting market operations.

Some of the most effective data for behavioural segmentation is provided in the UK by the Target Group Index (TGI) of the British Market Research Bureau Ltd. The Index is a national product and media survey which collects information from 24 000 adults each year. The service is available on a subscription basis to advertisers, advertising agencies and media owners. TGI measures:

1   Heavy to light usage for over 2500 brands in more than 200 fast moving consumer product fields. Also, usage patterns in other fields are covered, including banking, building societies, airlines, holidays, cars, grocery and other retail outlets.
2   Media 'audiences' for approximately 150 newspapers and magazines, the weight of ITV viewing and half-hourly viewing behaviour for television, the weight of listening to commercial radio, exposure to 'outdoor' media (i.e. posters, etc) and the cinema.

By 1983, the Survey had been operating for 15 years. By directly linking brand and product data to readership, TV viewing and other aspects of media usage, it is of great value in media planning. TGI also produces evidence of the growth/decline of products and brands over the period since its inception. Changes in the demographic characteristics of product/brand consumers in this period are also available. The product fields and brands are analysed by:

- sex, age and class;
- standard regions and TV regions;
- household income;
- terminal educational age;
- marital status;
- years married and number of children

as well as readership habits, TV viewing and other media usage plus other classifications which may be thought appropriate.

TGI also provides a significantly useful measurement in the field of consumer appliances and durables. The 'decision maker' is identified, i.e. who made the purchase decision and whether that decision was made alone or with someone else.

In addition to the allocation of expenditure to media, such behavioural data are obviously valuable in determining where marketing opportunities lie. Also, the subscriber to the service obtains information on the users of competitors' brands as well as his own.

The above example must conclude this Section on behavioural segmentation but the conscientious student of marketing will seek, and find, other examples. He or she will also keep open a keen eye for further developments and methods. Nor is this the place to enter into a discussion of the relative benefits of indirect and direct classifiers, except to add that the value of behavioural segmentation was underlined by one speaker[17] at a 1980 seminar, whose paper was entitled: 'What else do we need except product usage?'

Psychographic segmentation

Psychological classifications

In the last twenty years or so, the standard repertoire of consumer classifications has been critically re-examined, based on the feeling that demographic classifications alone were inadequate for segmentation.

Advantage has been taken of the progress made in theoretical and applied psychology in the investigation of *personality*. Such inventories as the Cattell 16PF, emanating from the USA, and the inventory developed by Eysenck in the UK, are numbered among the techniques used to classify consumers along such dimensions as *introversion – extraversion* and *neuroticism – emotional stability*. This *a priori* approach, in which concepts and theories developed for quite different purposes have been taken over without clear hypotheses as to their probable value, has been disappointing – by and large. As Margaret Crimp has concluded:[18]

It was generally found that responses to standardised inventories did not correlate well with consumer behaviour, while the 'rather abstract relationships' established were of only marginal help when it came to making marketing decisions. *The fit was not good enough.*

From these disappointments stemmed the alternative *empirical* approaches devised by such UK researchers as J. A. Lunn.[19] Here, the basic idea is not to fit the consumer to a pre-determined set of classifications but to derive new classifications from a study of the consumer.

This *criterion group* approach begins by identifying groups with known different purchasing patterns. Next, the research method seeks to discover the psychological characteristics that differentiate such groups. Lunn's own research has established a repertoire of consumer personality scales, each of proven value in a number of product fields under examination. Some of the more general dimensions which have emerged include:

thrift
experimentalism
traditionalism

The thrift dimension was found to have two distinct facets:

economy mindedness, and
bargain seeking

Tony Lunn[20] explains the difference here as follows:

One way of putting the distinction is that whereas the economy-minded housewife abhors extravagance, the bargain-seeking woman may welcome it – but she looks for the cheapest shop in which to be extravagant.

Lunn also confirmed that the more economy-minded housewives tended to have lower socio-economics status than the bargain-seeking housewives, who were to be found among all social classes, and whereas the economy-minded did not come from any particular family size group, the bargain-seekers tended to come from larger households.

The import of this approach is that if experimentalism emerges as a key variable for a particular brand, then the marketing strategy would be so devised that the target group lies among the experimentalists. Samples of respondents for marketing research purposes (e.g. for product testing or advertising 'copy' testing) would be mainly drawn from this priority group. Similarly, if experimentalists could be shown to have particular viewing and reading habits (such data being collected from respondents in the same survey), then the planning for advertising and publicity campaigns would take this into account. (The reader should note the reference at the end of the chapter relating to an article by J. A. Lunn in which this approach to segmentation is clearly explained. Also, in addition to the a priori and empirical approaches to consumer behaviour, a third approach – the eclectic one, can be distinguished. Reference is made to it in Chapter 5, Characteristics of markets.)

'Life style' classifications

This approach is based on responses to questions on *activities, interests and opinions* (AIO). A typical survey known to the writer used some 230 life style statements for male respondents and a slightly larger number for females. The research interviewer seeks agreement or disagreement with the statement which may typically range over such topics as:

Likes	
Worry	Religion
Fashion	Friends and neighbours
Home	Social issues
Housework (for women)	Money
Men's interests (for men)	Jobs/unions
Food	Morals
Health/hygiene products	Smoking and drugs
	Attitudes to other countries, etc.

Within the interview, data are collected concerning the press readership, cinema-going, radio listening and television viewing of informants. Product usage data of the Target Group Index type are also obtained from informants, who are also analysed by such established classifications as age, sex, social grade, education, etc.

What results from such research is an extremely large bank of data which is subjected to sophisticated analytical techniques using the computer. These *data reduction techniques*, such as *cluster analysis*, are used to group informants so that each group or 'cluster' contains people who are similar to each other and different from the people in the other groups on the behavioural components measured – activities, interests and opinions.

The life style groupings produced are thought to be a useful supplement to standard data for such marketing activities as product planning and the design of advertising campaigns (particularly the 'creative' approach required).

A good example of this system of classifiers, based on clusters derived from a data bank of 15 000 interviews conducted in the UK over the period 1973–1981 are the MONITOR Value Groups of Taylor Nelson Associates Ltd. 158 scaled items have been used each year in a personal interview among 1500 respondents to measure 37 social trends. The Seven Value Groups produced by the MONITOR system are presented in the table on p. 128.

The main purpose behind the MONITOR system is to help companies respond to the general changes in values that are taking place (according to Dr Elizabeth Nelson, the Chairman of Taylor Nelson Associates). Such changes are valuable data inputs to an organisation's analysis of threats and opportunities (see Chapter 2). The Value Groups are therefore a by-product of the MONITOR system. They are an *indirect* method of classification but they have often been found to be of more use than demographics or simple attitude segmentation, both in terms of advertising content and new product development, for a knowledge of how values are changing over time can be very helpful to a marketing manager.

In concluding this Section on psychographic segmentation it might be useful to record the views of Michael Head[21], the market research manager of the H. J. Heinz Company. Relating his experiences of the use of psychographic classifications, he writes:

They can be helpful, particularly in fleshing out personality types to whom advertising campaigns, or packaging designs in particular, should be addressed. However, they must be related to particular buyer or user groups to be effective. Again they form a secondary classification system for describing those groups identified by the primary usage system.

Monitor value groups
(Size of groups based on population estimates for 16–64 year olds)

	Millions	
	1973–74	*1979–80*
1 *Self explorers* 'I am what I am.' Personal fulfilment through self-expression. Creative individuals seeking intellectual and emotional satisfaction.	4.4	4.7
2 *Social resisters* 'Society needs changing to my way to thinking.' Critics of the way Britain has developed although still patriotic and loyal. Active in local community and charitable causes.	4.3	4.2
3 *Experimentalists* 'I'll try it.' Fashion followers looking for novelty, fun and excitement. Ambivalent over social issues.	4.3	3.7
4 *Achievers/conspicuous consumers* 'Look at me!' Status conscious, acquisitive and emulative. Concerned with superficial appearance more than with inherent quality.	4.5	5.2
5 *Belongers* 'My family comes first.' A future-oriented, self-sacrificing, achievement-directed group. Few interests or concerns outside the home or workplace.	6.6	6.1
6 *Survivors* 'The working class is *my* class.' Conventional, conservative, chauvinistic. Rigid thinkers along sex/class stereotype lines.	4.9	4.6
7 *Aimless* 'I couldn't care less.' Social casualties – demoralised, goalless, apathetic. Blame their plight on convenient scapegoats. Without hope for the future.	2.3	2.8

Benefit segmentation

The question of discovering the causes of consumer behaviour rather than merely describing consumers led Russell Haley[22] to pioneer the concept of *benefit segmentation*. Haley reasoned that it is mistaken to assume that all consumers seek the same things from a product. An individual product is many things to many people. In Haley's own research into the toothpaste market he discovered that one segment bought toothpaste for its flavour, another for its effectiveness in preventing decay, yet another for its power in brightening teeth, etc.

Similarly one segment of the ceramic tableware market might buy the Arnold brand for its design attributes, another for its durability, another for the status it conveys upon the household, whilst a fourth segment may be conditioned by the belief that, at its price, it provides the best value for money.

Benefit segmentation is apparently favoured by a growing number of researchers since it produces reasons why certain brands are favoured, rather than merely describing the members of a particular segment.

The evaluation of brands and the levels of significance of various attributes is discovered by attitudinal research. Respondents are asked for their agreement/disagreement to a battery of questions which is centred upon the characteristics of the product group and the benefits being sought. The data is then subjected to the *factor analysis* technique of data reduction, with a cluster analysis programme subsequently being used to identify the segments which relate to the specific benefits sought.

British writer, Michael Thomas[23] states:

Studies have shown that benefit segmentation is a better determinant of consumer behaviour than several of the other approaches used to segment a market. Benefit segmentation directly facilitates product planning, positioning and advertising.

As Thomas explains, it is often the case that individual benefits are 'shared' by various segments, but the significant factor is the amount of importance each segment places on each benefit. This is the distinguishing characteristic of each segment.

Once the segments have been determined, further data – e.g. demographics and information on life style attributes, personality and product usage – are also collected on them. This enables a marketing strategy to be developed based on considerations of the volume/profit thought to be obtainable from the various segments and a product and advertising strategy based upon a comprehensive knowledge of the consumer.

Segmentation and interlacing

In concluding these Sections on consumer segmentation mention must be made of SAGACITY, a system of groupings recently introduced in Britain by Research Services Ltd.

According to this organisation, a classification system should ideally combine both descriptive features and predictive power. Thus, the direct classifiers, which are based on product usage, though superficially very attractive, have only a limited general utility. In other words, such information can be used as a classification system for a particular product, but it will have no predictive value for other products unless they are closely related to that particular product.

Demographic classifications, such as age and social grade, may now have lost much of the previous discriminating power due to profound changes in society, and also because they are often used as a single dimension. On behalf of Research Services Ltd, Pym Cornish[24] argues that when interlaced with other data, particularly that relating to life cycle and income level, this can produce highly discriminated population segments without abandoning the valuable role social grade has for many markets and media. The power of the computer, which so steadily reduces in relative cost, can generate complex classifications if they are found to have significance.

The fundamental basis for the SAGACITY group is that people have different aspirations and behaviour patterns as they move through their life cycle. Four main stages of the life cycle constitute the framework:

Total Adults 15+ (100%)

| The dependant stage (16%) | The pre-family stage (8%) | The family stage (36%) | The late stage (40%) |

The second and third levels of the groupings are related to the *income* and *occupational characteristics* of the individual or couple forming the household. The income breakdown is applied only at the family stage and the late stage, because of the relatively small sample sizes of the other two groups (dependant stage; pre-family stage), which makes subdivision unrealistic. Also, differences in disposable income are less marked and therefore less important in these earlier stages.

A twelve-cell segmentation of the adult population is produced by this approach and SAGACITY is often applied to the male and female populations separately. The twelve groups are shown below, with their descriptive notations and their size, expressed as a percentage of the total adult population.

SAGACITY groupings

Dependant, White (DW) 6 per cent
Mainly under 24s, living at home or full time student, where head of household is in an ABC1 occupation group.

Dependant, Blue (DB) 9 per cent
Mainly under 24s, living at home or full time student, where head of household is in a C2DE occupation group.

Pre-family, White (PFW) 4 per cent
Under 35s who have established their own household but have no children and where the head of household is in an ABC1 occupation group.

Pre-family, Blue (PFB) 4 per cent
Under 35s who have established their own household but have no children and where the head of household is in a C2DE occupation group.

Family, Better off, White (FW+) 6 per cent
Housewives and heads of household, under 65, with one or more children in the household, in the 'better off' income group and where the head of household is in an ABC1 occupation group. (65 per cent are AB).

Family, Better off, Blue (FB+) 9 per cent
Housewives and heads of household, under 65, with one or more children in the household, in the 'better off' income group and where the head of household is in a C2DE occupation group. (72 per cent are C2).

Family, Worse off, White (FW−) 8 per cent
Housewives and heads of household, under 65, with one or more

children in the household, in the 'worse off' income group and where the head of household is in an ABC1 occupation group. (72 per cent are C1).

Family, Worse off, Blue (FB−) 14 per cent
Housewives and heads of household, under 65, with one or more children in the household, in the 'worse off' income group and where the head of household is in a C2DE occupation group. (47 per cent DE).

Late, Better off, White (LW+) 5 per cent
Includes all adults whose children have left home or who are over 35 and childless, are in the 'better off' income group and where the head of household is in an ABC1 occupation group. (60 per cent are AB).

Late, Better off, Blue (LB+) 7 per cent
Includes all adults whose children have left home or who are over 35 and childless, are in the 'better off' income group and where the head of household is in a C2DE occupation group. (69 per cent are C2).

Late, Worse off, White (LW−) 9 per cent
Includes all adults whose children have left home or who are over 35 and childless, are in the 'worse off' income group and where the head of household is in an ABC1 occupation group. (71 per cent are C1).

Late, Worse off, Blue (LB−) 19 per cent
Includes all adults whose children have left home or who are over 35 and childless, are in the 'worse off' income group and where the head of household is in a C2DE occupation group. (70 per cent are DE).

The discriminatory or predictive power of SAGACITY is demonstrated by the indices in the table opposite.

In the first example, 10 per cent of all adults claimed to have taken a package holiday abroad in a previous 12 month period (index number 100). In the FB− and LB− groups, the comparative proportion falls to four per cent (index numbers 36 and 44). In the PFW and LW+ groups, the figure exceeds 20 per cent (index numbers 208 and 200 respectively). The returns for the other three items in the table also provide some interesting variations from the percentage figures for 'All Adults'.

Market penetration, all adults – by SAGACITY

All adults %	Index	Dependant		Pre-family		Family stage				Late stage			
		DW	DB	PFW	PFB	FW+	FB+	FW−	FB−	LW+	LB+	LW−	LB−
Package holiday taken abroad in last 12 months													
10.3	100	154	109	208	117	156	92	100	36	200	129	108	44
Owns cheque book													
52.9	100	105	57	169	114	171	111	146	73	162	91	132	46
Refrigerator acquired in past 2 years													
14.0	100	—	—	173	168	130	117	109	106	103	91	74	54
Moved home in past 2 years													
14.7	100	—	—	502	340	109	86	115	115	69	44	54	50

Source: ADMAP Publications Ltd, October 1981

Industrial segmentation

Much of the demand in industrial markets is derived, which is to say that a product, a component part, a sub-assembly, or a service, is required as a result of the demand for some other product or service. In order to estimate demand, the producer of industrial goods will therefore look to user industries. Some products or services do not pre-select any particular segment of user industries. Office equipment and supplies, industrial cleaning equipment, the installation and maintenance of internal telephone systems etc can quite logically be marketed to industries and organisations of all types. However, for most industrial products the market is not such a huge, undifferentiated one but is segmented into relatively small groups. The concept of segmentation is therefore as relevant in this context as it is in the field of consumer goods, although industrial segmentation is more difficult to apply.

There is a great deal of secondary research data on industrial markets. General government statistics (e.g. Annual Abstract of Statistics, Monthly Digest of Statistics, Census of Production etc), specialised statistics (e.g. Highway Statistics, Housing and Construction Statistics, Overseas Trade Statistics), data from the press and other publications (e.g. The Economist, The Financial Times, Kompass Register, Dun and Bradstreet's directories) and data available from professional, technical and other organisations (e.g. the CBI, the Industrial Marketing Research Association and the BIM), all help to provide a basis upon which knowledge of the structure and size of industrial markets can be developed. The Kluwer-Harrap Handbook[25] listed at the end of this chapter provides much information on data sources and a clear exposition of the methodology of industrial marketing research.

Although geographical segmentation is one basis for splitting a large heterogeneous market into appropriate sub-markets, and although there is some geographical concentration of particular types of industry in Britain, the more useful approach to segmentation is based on the product and the basis upon which production is analysed is the Standard Industrial Classification (SIC). The broad outline is that overall industry categories ('Orders', of which there are 27) are broken down into sub-groups ('Minimum List Headings', of which there are 181). Thus:

Order II Mining and Quarrying, comprises Minimum List Headings 101–109, as follows:

101 Coal Mining
102 Stone and slate quarrying
103 Chalk, clay, sand and gravel extraction
104 Petroleum and natural gas, etc

HM Government's *Business Monitors Production Series*, the *Service and Distributive Monitors* and the *Annual Census of Production Report* will provide the basic data for segmentation. Chisnall[26] points out some of the pitfalls in using the SIC breakdowns and the important use of tied indicators in deriving market size from published statistics.

Following Frank and his co-authors, Peter Fitzroy[27] points out that industrial segmentation can be approached in two stages.

1   The identification of macrosegments, based on such characteristics as:
●   size of customer
●   customer usage rate
●   application of the product
●   SIC category of customer
●   customer organisational structure
●   geographical location of customer
(and these bases, either singly or in combination, are common forms of industrial segmentation).

2   The sub-division of each macrosegment in terms of:
●   the structure, authority and methods of the buying centre
●   perceived importance of the purchase
●   whether first purchase or repeat purchase
●   relative importance of the determinants of the buying decision
●   loyalty and attitudes towards vendors.

An example of how marketing strategy can be devised from segmentation analysis is provided by the heading 'customer usage rate'. In the majority of UK markets, the pattern is for 80 per cent of industrial production to be attained by 20 per cent of the firms concerned (compare the 'heavy half' theory in consumer segmentation). The individual organisation must then decide whether to put in its marketing effort to these large firms or whether to cultivate the smaller firms, with their admittedly smaller market share, but which may well be neglected by competitors. Industrial marketing research supplies the basic data for decision making, to which must be applied considerations of the organisation's own size and resources in relation to competition. Thinking of the 'relative importance of the determinants of the buying decision', in the subdivision of macrosegments, provides another example. A good question here is *Who buys?* Is it the buyer – or is the buyer a provider of information and a mechanism for placing orders? Is it the production manager? Or the accountant? Or the research and development executives? What are the relative influences of the several people who figure in the typical industrial buying decision? Who does the salesman interview if it is not possible for him to be seen by these 'relevant others', what implications does this have for advertising and publicity policy?

Perhaps these questions will illustrate the importance of segmentation analysis.

Before leaving this necessarily brief section, it might be helpful to add that a significantly important data unit for the international marketing of industrial products is the *International Standard Industrial Classification (ISIC)*, devised by the United Nations Organisation. Its objective is to standardise statistics between nations so as to facilitate comparisons.

Endpiece

In this limited, but hopefully useful, chapter, the process of segmentation as an approach to marketing has been described and a number of examples of the way in which data are analysed for segmentation have been provided. The writer would like to add here that readers, many of whom will be on the threshold of careers in marketing, should keep closely abreast of developments in the field of user-classifications and their links with behaviour. In the whole field of marketing, there is no more fascinating, and potentially valuable, subject for study.

Having said that, we must pause to consider. Marketing is no mere intellectual exercise. It is about obtaining an adequate return-on-investment or achieving some similar criterion of efficiency in a non-profit organisation. So in considering possible segments as an entry to markets, we must also ask some questions about each segment. Firstly, *can it be measured?* As one writer has put it, the fact that potential users are characterised by moodiness may be interesting, but how far does it take you? Can the size of the market provided by a segment actually be measured?

Next, *how accessible is the segment?* Can it be reached through channels of distribution and/or advertising media, for example? A segment must be submitted to this test.

Thirdly, *how large is the segment?* Sufficiently large to make marketing efforts worthwhile? Ultimately, we can come down to segments of one, since every user is in some senses unique. The test therefore must be: what are the *volume: cost: profit relationships* of approaching the market by way of this particular segment?

Michael Thomas[28] adds a fourth test to questions such as these: *is the segment stable?* Can you predict its behaviour in the future? Obviously the dynamics of the market, denoted by its rates of change, must come in for consideration here. It is futile to develop a considered strategy to cultivate a segment if, when operations commence, the market has changed in the meantime.

Simon Majaro,[29] a shrewd observer of the marketing scene, makes a telling additional point:

A further pitfall is the fact that many marketers seek to 'cheat old age' of a declining product by simply differentiating it vis-à-vis a specific segment which in turn happens to be on the decline as well.

Two final observations:

1 In this Chapter we have been examining segmentation from the standpoint of *user typologies;* a related approach is to study products with a view to grouping them on the basis of their attributes, so as to find market 'gaps' useful for the strategy of *product differentiation* or *product positioning* – this aspect of segmentation is discussed in Chapter 6, Product planning.

2 The development of marketing strategies based on segmentation raises questions for the organisation of marketing activities – these are described in Chapter 12.

Self-assessment questions

1 What do you understand by the term market segmentation? Why has it gained influence in recent times?

2 What are the instances when it would be inadvisable to pursue a policy of market segmentation?

3 List the main demographic variables. Explain their use.

4 Describe some approaches to spatial (geographic) segmentation, with emphasis on any recent refinements of this type of classification.

5 What is the heavy-half theory? What are its implications for marketing strategy?

6 Distinguish between the a priori approach to psychological classification and the criterion group (or empirical) approach.

7 In what ways are life style groupings thought to be a useful supplement to standard market data.

8 Choose a product or service and outline how the concept of benefit segmentation might be applied to it.

9 Describe a classification system based on the interlacing of data.

10 Explain how the concept of segmentation is applied to the marketing of industrial products and services.

References

1 Lunn, Tony. Segmenting and constructing markets, *Consumer Market Research Handbook*, 2nd edn, (Robert M. Worcester and John Downham eds), New York, London, Van Nostrand Reinhold Company, 1978, p. 343

2 Smith, Wendell. Product differentiation and marketing segmentation as alternative marketing strategies, *Journal of Marketing*, (July 1956), p. 5

3 Yankelovitch, Daniel. *Consumer behaviour*, (Ehrenburg, A. S. C. and Pyatt, F. G. eds), London, Penguin, 1971, pp. 46–47

4 Frank, R. E. Socio-economic factors Reading 3 in *Consumer behaviour*, (Ehrenberg, A. S. C. and Pyatt, F. G. eds), London, Penguin, 1971, p. 36

5 Abrams, Mark. Some measurements of social stratification in Britain Chapter 6, *Social Stratification*, (Jackson, J. A., ed), Cambridge University Press, 1968

6 Lunn, Tony. *Consumer Market Research Handbook*, p. 349

7 Abrams, Mark. Education, social class and reading of newspapers and magazines, *IPA Occasional Papers*, London, Institute of Practitioners in Advertising (IPA), (i) January, 1966, (ii) July 1969

8 Crimp, Margaret. *The Marketing Research Process*, London, Prentice-Hall International, 1981, p. 99

9 HM Government Statistics frequently provide interesting information in this context. See, for example, *Social Trends*, Central Statistical Office (HMSO)

10 Frain, John. *Introduction to marketing*, 2nd edn, Plymouth, Macdonald and Evans, 1983, p. 97

11 Van Tassel, Charles E. Paper No. 27, *Dimensions of consumer behaviour*, (James U. McNeal, ed), New York, Appleton-Century-Crofts, 1969, pp. 304–5

12 Jenner, Paul. *Europe: an exporter's handbook*, London, Euromonitor Publications 1981, p. 67–8 and p. 93

13 Stanton, William J. *Fundamentals of marketing*, 6th edn 1981, New York, London, McGraw-Hill, p. 72

14 *Introduction to Marketing*, p. 107

15 The British Market Research Bureau, *Acorn: A new approach to marketing*, London, 1980

16 Twedt, Dik Warren. The concept of market segmentation, in *Handbook of modern marketing*, (Victor P. Buell and Carl Heyel, eds), New York, London; McGraw-Hill, 1970, p. 2–12

17 Hulks, Robert. As reported in *The marketing relevance of classification systems*, (by Brian Allt), London, ADMAP Publications, October 1981, p. 517

18 *The marketing research process*, p. 101

19 Lunn, J. A. Empirical techniques in consumer research, *Industrial Society – Social Sciences in Management*, (Denis Pym, ed), Harmondsworth; Penguin, 1968, p. 413

20 Ibid, p. 414

21 Head, Michael. *What do manufacturers want to know about people?* London, ADMAP Publications Ltd, November 1981, p. 582

22 Haley, Russell I. Benefit segmentation: a decision oriented research tool, *Journal of Marketing*, July 1968, pp. 30–35

23 Thomas, Michael. Market segmentation, *The Quarterly Review of Marketing*, Autumn, 1980, Cookham, Berks, Institute of Marketing, p. 26

24 Cornish, Pym. *Life cycle and income segmentation – SAGACITY*, London, ADMAP Publications Ltd, October 1981, pp. 522–26

25 Maclean, Ian (chief ed). *Handbook of industrial marketing and research*, Brentford, Middlesex, Kluwer Publishing Ltd, 1982

26 Chisnall, Peter M. *Effective industrial marketing*, London, Longman Group Limited, 1977, pp. 108–10

27 Fitzroy, Peter T. *Analytical methods for marketing management*, London, McGraw-Hill, 1976, pp. 125–27

28 Market segmentation, *The Quarterly Review of Marketing*, p. 27

29 Majaro, Simon. *Marketing in Perspective*, London, George Allen and Unwin, 1982, p. 33

5 THE CHARACTERISTICS OF MARKETS; CONSUMER BEHAVIOUR

Objectives

This Chapter puts even more emphasis on the frameworks for analysing markets. The characteristics of consumer markets are described in terms of some classifiers of proven significance – age, sex, geographical distribution, economic status, social mobility, educational attainment, spending patterns and so on. Various concepts of why people buy and how they attend to stimuli are considered, as well as such influences on behaviour as reference groups and social change.

A framework for the analysis of organisational markets is outlined, as are some of the insights obtained from studies of the organisational buying process.

Introduction

The analysis of markets

With approximately one third of the ground to be covered by this textbook now behind us, it would be helpful to reflect upon the plan of the route we are following. Chapter 1 defined marketing, traced its development and looked at it in action. Chapter 2 described the environmental influences on marketing activity and outlined the role of marketing management in developing a marketing mix to attain the objectives of the organisation. In Chapter 3 the importance of information for the planning and execution of marketing activity was explained. Some typical methods of marketing research were reported. Chapter 4 dealt with the strategy of segmentation; specific target groups within a total population are typically the subject for marketing operations. Some methods by which markets might be segmented were detailed.

In this chapter we are moving from specific market segments to markets 'in the round', for we shall be examining the *frameworks for analysing markets*. This is the step which accompanies (in some senses, precedes) the determination of target groups. Its importance will be affirmed if we look back to Chapter 3 (page 77) where, in the survey of marketing research activity, such objectives as:

- measurement of market potentials;
- determination of market characteristics; and
- analysis of market share;

occupied the first three places of importance in the list reviewed.

We cannot classify markets without first classifying the products we wish to introduce to those markets. It is usual to adopt the following categorisation:

1 *Rapid turnover consumer goods.* Goods manufactured for direct, immediate consumption, which are bought regularly and have a limited life (examples: food, drink, confectionery, tobacco).

2 *Durable consumer goods.* Goods manufactured for direct, immediate use but which are bought less frequently and are of much longer life (examples: television and radio sets, washing machines, video cassette records, home computers, motor cars).

3 *Industrial 'consumption' goods.* Products manufactured for use or transformation in the process of further production and which, because of their consequentially limited life, have a frequent purchase pattern (examples: chemicals, lubricants, cement, clay, sheet steel, plastics moulding powder).

4 *Industrial durable goods.* The machinery and equipment which is used in the production of further goods (examples: lathes, furnaces, grinding and milling machinery).

Organisations are classified in accordance with the goods they produce and the markets for those goods are classified as *consumer* or *industrial* markets. Of course, some organisations may operate in both types of market. Arnold Ceramics, for example, may be active in the consumer market with their fine tableware bought by housewives and in the industrial or *institutional* market with their heavier and more robust 'hotelware' which is used in factory canteens, hospitals and schools.

Beyond these classifications are the *markets for services*, which will be described later. In the following Sections bases for the analysis of consumer markets will be described and some thoughts will be provided on why people buy (*consumer behaviour*). The approach to the analysis of *organisational markets* then follows (organisational meaning industrial, agricultural and governmental markets).

The characteristics of consumer markets

A framework of analysis

Markets mean people, so the first important characteristic by which consumer markets are analysed is based on statistics of *population* and *population trends*. The table on page 143 provides some very general statistics on the UK population. Even at this first level of analysis, some important facts emerge. Note the comparative populations, population densities, and gross domestic product (per capita) of England, Wales, Scotland, Northern Ireland and the United Kingdom as a whole. Note the unemployment rate in Northern Ireland compared with that in England, the variations in average gross weekly earnings and, for all the countries, the significance of the service industries in the provision of employment. All of these very basic facts tell us something of significance for marketing operations.

If at the next stage we look at the *distribution of population*, in England and Wales, we have a clear idea of the significance of the size of regional populations. For the year 1981, the population statistics for the Standard regions of England and Wales were as follows:

	Thousands
North	3114
Yorkshire and Humberside	4907
East Midlands	3840
East Anglia	1895
South East	17027
Greater London	(6851)
South West	4363

West Midlands	**5181**
North West	**6460**
Wales	**2807**

Source: *Annual Abstract of Statistics* 1983 edition, Central Statistical Office.

Obviously, it is not possible to reproduce a large number of statistical tables here, but an analysis of population statistics would show that a third of Great Britain's people live in less than three per cent of its land area, i.e. in the eight major metropolitan areas of Greater London, Central Clydeside, Greater Manchester,

Table 5.1 General statistics of the UK population

	England	Wales	Scotland	Northern Ireland	United Kingdom
Population ('000, April 1981)	46 221	2 790	5 117	1 547	55 676
Area (sq km)	130 439	20 768	78 772	14 121	244 100
(sq miles)	50 363	8 018	30 414	5 452	94 247
Population density (persons per sq km, April 1981)	354	134	65	110	228
(persons per sq mile, April 1981)	915	343	168	284	591
Gross domestic product (£ per head, 1980)	3 431	2 937	3 229	2 518	3 363
Employees in employment ('000, mid-1981)	17 890	914	1 927	467	21 198
Percentage of employees in: (June 1981, provisional)					
agriculture, forestry and fishing	1.6	2.5	2.3	1.9	1.7
engineering and allied industries	13.5	10.5	10.4	8.0	12.9
all other manufacturing	15.6	15.8	15.0	16.2	15.6
construction	5.0	6.5	7.5	6.1	5.3
mining, quarrying, gas, electricity and water	3.0	6.2	3.4	2.3	3.2
service industries	61.3	58.6	61.5	66.0	61.3
Unemployment rate (per cent, June 1981)	10.6	13.9	13.5	18.0	11.1
Average gross weekly earnings (£, all full-time men, April 1981)	141.0	132.7	140.0	129.7	140.5
Identifiable public expenditure (£ per head, 1980–81)	1 339	1 759	1 696	1 946	–

Source: *Britain 1983 An Official Handbook*
Reproduced by kind permission of Her Majesty's Stationery Office

Merseyside, South Yorkshire, Tyne and Wear, the West Midlands and West Yorkshire. By contrast, much of Scotland and great areas of Wales, Northern Ireland and the central Pennines have very sparse populations. Similarly (in April 1981) very nearly 13 million people were living in the UK's 13 main urban districts (Greater London, Birmingham, Glasgow, Leeds, Sheffield, Liverpool, Bradford, Manchester, Edinburgh, Bristol, Coventry, Belfast and Cardiff).

The assistance to marketing strategy provided by successively deeper levels of geographical analysis has been explained in Chapter 4 and the significance of the UK's television areas will be described in Chapter 8. Trends in the distribution of population are also significant. In common with other developed countries, Britain has recently seen a movement of people away from the main centres of conurbations and into the surrounding suburbs. This trend, highlighted by the 1981 Census, clearly has implications for the siting of retail shops and other service organisations as we shall see in Chapter 7 (Distribution planning). The trend has been marked enough for Greater London, as recently as the mid 1960s the world's third city in terms of population, to descend to eleventh in magnitude on that rating. There has been a similar decline in the proportion of the population living in the majority of the metropolitan counties. The population of Scotland and the North of England has declined in the recent past, whilst the East Anglian region has gained population, as have the East Midlands and the South West. One factor in the increase of the East Anglian population has been its attractiveness for retired people. The south coast of England has gained population for the same reason.

Age distribution of the UK population

Geographical distribution is a 'jumping-off' point for analysis. The demand for many products and services is influenced by the age of the consumer. If we look at Chapter 2 (page 49) statistics were provided which demonstrate how the structure of the UK population is changing and changes in the demand for products and services are related to the profile of Britain's ageing population. Common sense will tell us that the purchases of certain categories of products are closely correlated with age groups: that baby food, toys, perambulators, push-chairs are related to the numbers of infants and toddlers in the population. The 'young marrieds' (age 20–35 perhaps) will be setting up home and in addition to purchasing on behalf of toddlers and infants will thus constitute the primary market for furniture, houses, bank and building society services, and 'economy' class cars. Those in the retirement age category will be heavy users of the products and services mentioned in Chapter 2. Beyond these population segments there are additional segments – schoolchildren, teenagers, the 'young' middle-aged, the older middle-aged. The demand for yet other types of goods and services will be markedly correlated to the numbers of people in these segments. Trends in the age distribution of the population may therefore greatly influence marketing strategy. The phenomenon of the ageing population is not restricted to Britain, of course. It is common to most developed countries. The author recently attended a conference on research related to the planning of higher education. The tables which follow were presented by a conference member from the United States and they should be examined in relation to each other. For median age the first chart shows the changing profile of the general population. The second chart shows that the median age of the non-white groups is markedly lower than that of the white population. Further data show that non-white groups exhibit a higher drop-out rate from advanced educational courses. Here is obviously much food for thought for educational planners.

Educational levels

This might be an appropriate point to say more on the classification of terminal educational age. Reference was made to it in the last Chapter, not only because of its influence on life style and ultimately, purchasing behaviour, but also for its relationship to media usage. What are the trends in this context? If we take just one indicator from HM Government Statistics[1] it will serve our purposes. In 1970, the number of full time students in further education was 391 000. In 1979, the comparable figure was 495 000: an increase of over 25 per cent in this comparatively short period.

Now in addition to the influences of education on consumer demand, outlined earlier, and giving rise as it does to an increased call for books and other published material; travel services; cul-

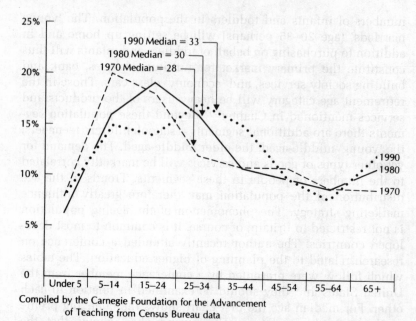

Compiled by the Carnegie Foundation for the Advancement
of Teaching from Census Bureau data

Fig. 5.1   *Median age of total population, 1970, 1980, 1990 (USA)*

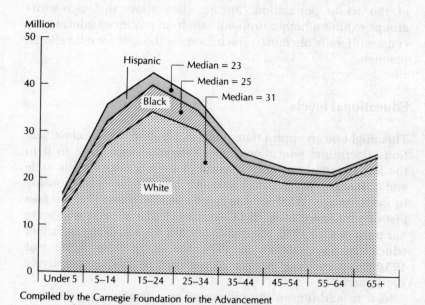

Compiled by the Carnegie Foundation for the Advancement
of Teaching from Census Bureau data

Fig. 5.2   *Age distribution by ethnic group 1980 (USA)*

tural pursuits; and an increased interest in museums and the arts, marketing organisations must bear in mind that an educated consumer is generally a more discriminating consumer. This means more attention to the *tactics* as well as the *strategy* of marketing, particularly concerning claims in advertising, standards of advertising presentation and, not least, product design and performance.

Trends in income and expenditure

A fundamental factor in *effective* demand is that users have the necessary incomes or access to credit — and the second is, of course, very much a concomitant of the first. At the primary level of analysis we have to fix the market concerned in the 'world table' of income levels, since the gap between the World's rich and poor is enormous. The UK belongs to the rich industrialised West, many of whose inhabitants belong to the high average annual income group of over US $5000. The average annual income for the inhabitants of Bangladesh is around US $90. Such figures need no elaboration. The OECD (Organisation for Economic Co-operation and Development) has reported that by 1980, the inhabitants of the rich, industrialised countries such as the United Kingdom were 'consuming' twice the quantity of goods and services they were in 1950. So that unlike the poor Bangladeshi, the wants of most UK consumers will not be centred on food and shelter, but on obtaining even better educational provision, better housing, better cars, better calculators and television sets. It is true, that like many other Western countries, Britain has felt the effects of the recent recession in world trade and has rising unemployment rates. In 1961, the UK had 346 000 registered unemployed. By 1971, the comparable figure was 792 000. By mid 1982, the total had become 2 985 000. Yet tragic as these figures are in human terms, they do not obscure the fact that for consumer goods and services, the UK is a rich market and one that gets richer.

For example, *total household disposable income* increased from £36 billion in 1971 to £159 billion in 1981. After allowing for inflation, this was an increase in real terms of 24 per cent.

The schematic (Fig. 5.3), in respect of a broadly similar time period, indicates how some of this real increase in disposable income was spent.

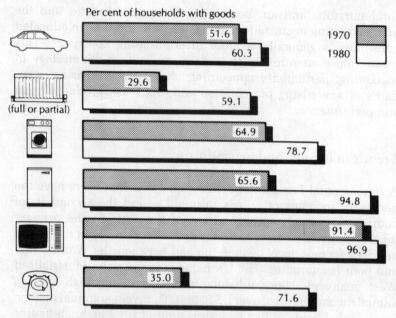

Per cent of households with goods

51.6   1970
60.3   1980

(full or partial)   29.6
59.1

64.9
78.7

65.6
94.8

91.4
96.9

35.0
71.6

Source: Britain 1983. An Official Handbook (HMSO)

Fig. 5.3   *Availability of certain durable goods*
Source: Britain 1983. An Official Handbook (HMSO)

The marketing executive is also interested in how increased real income influences spending patterns. The diagram opposite illustrates a point here.

These expenditure profiles show the *decreased* percentage expenditures on food, clothing and footwear; the *decreased* expenditure on tobacco (doubtless as a result of the 'smoking and health' issue, as well as HM Government's intervention on advertising) and the *increased* expenditures on housing and services. The effect of the oil price rises of the early 1970s are clearly an important element in the 40 per cent increase (on the 1971 average) in running costs of motor vehicles. This will undoubtedly have resulted in consequential reductions to other parts of consumers' expenditure. The importance of such trends in the consideration of marketing strategies will be evident to the reader.

It is beyond the scope of this Chapter to explore the matter in great detail, but the *distribution of incomes* is also a subject of great import to marketing practitioners. Some aspects of this issue ought to be mentioned here. Firstly, it is clear that since

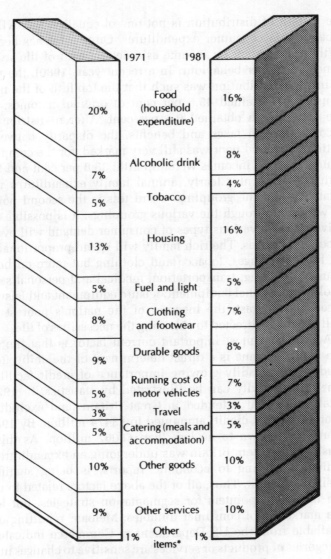

	1971	1981
Food (household expenditure)	20%	16%
Alcoholic drink	7%	8%
Tobacco	5%	4%
Housing	13%	16%
Fuel and light	5%	5%
Clothing and footwear	8%	7%
Durable goods	9%	8%
Running cost of motor vehicles	5%	7%
Travel	3%	3%
Catering (meals and accommodation)	5%	5%
Other goods	10%	10%
Other services	9%	10%
Other items*	1%	1%

*Consumers' expenditure abroad plus wages, salaries, etc paid by private non-profit-making bodies (apart from those in catering) plus capital consumption of assets owned by private non-profit-making bodies plus income in kind not included elsewhere minus expenditure by foreign tourists, etc in Britain.

Fig. 5.4   Components of consumers' expenditure in 1971 and 1981
Source: Britain 1983. An Official Handbook (HMSO)

the pattern of distribution is not one of equality, this will have a bearing on consumer expenditures. Quite a lot has been said in the last Chapter on income as a determinant of life style and hence consumer behaviour. In a recent year (1980), the pattern of income distribution was such that the top fifth of the nation's households obtained 45.5 per cent of *original* incomes, whilst the bottom fifth obtained 0.5 per cent. After re-distribution of income through taxes and benefits, the disparity between the nation's rich and poor was still very marked, for the comparative figures for final incomes were top fifth: 38.8 per cent and bottom fifth 6.8 per cent. Clearly, annual family expenditures will be related to income groupings – and this is the second point, for as we move through the various groupings, it is possible to perceive how the various types of consumer demand will evolve as income increases. The rich family will spend proportionally less on food, beverages, tobacco and clothing but more on housing, house furnishing, transportation, medical and personal services, books, educational equipment, leisure equipment and leisure services. By contrast, the incomes of the nation's poorest homes will be largely directed to obtaining the necessities of life.

A third and most important current factor is that the size of the family income is a direct determinant of the *ability to raise credit*. The steadily growing importance of credit facilities for marketing activity can be illustrated by statistics. In 1976, the total new credit extended in Great Britain (and excluding the charges for that credit) amounted to £3474 million. By 1981, the figure had grown to no less than £8067 million. As this book was being written, Britain was undergoing an expenditure boom which, according to economic reports, is being significantly fuelled by credit. Thus, all of the above factors related to income are important pointers for segmentation strategies, not least in the marketing of consumer durables. Meloan[2] reporting on data available from the US Department of Commerce indicates how categories of products or services are sensitive to changes in personal income. A 1 per cent change in disposable personal income relates to a 3 per cent increase in airline services and a 1.6 per cent increase in purchases of petrol and oil, but only a 0.4 per cent increase in purchases of shoes and a 0.6 per cent increase in men's and boy's clothing. Although these particular statistics are now somewhat dated, they are quoted here to illustrate the importance of such indicators for forecasting purposes. The topic of *tied indicators* will also be mentioned in the later Section on industrial marketing.

Market size and market share

We now have some impression of how to consider consumer markets 'in the round', of how to estimate the size and determine the characteristics of markets for particular classes of consumer products and services. The early pages of this Chapter emphasised the primacy of such research objectives as:

- the measurement of market potentials, and
- the analysis of market share.

To end this Section of our study, the following example will illustrate why this is so.

If we look at the lower curve in Fig. 5.5, we will note the steady rate of increase in sales obtained by our friends Arnold Ceramics.

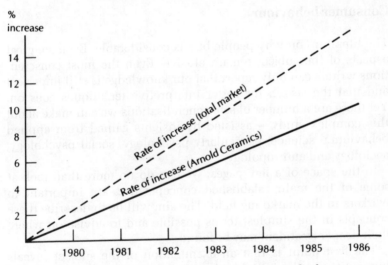

Fig. 5.5   *Arnold ceramics: rate of increase in volume of sales* (% per annum)

This appears to be satisfactory until we see that the curve above it indicates that the *total sales volume* being absorbed by the market is increasing at an even faster rate. Unless Arnold Ceramics improves its current rate of sales increase its very survival might be threatened, because the better sales performance of Arnold's competitors may well enable them to achieve lower production costs (by dint of increased production volume). If these lower costs are passed on to users in the shape of lower prices, this will further increase the rate of improvement in sales volume obtained by competitors, leaving Arnold Ceramics perilously placed.

The moral here is that no organisation can afford to relax in the comfort of a rising sales curve. This *might* be enough for the individual firm's success – but what is often much more important is the firm's *market share*, which in turn means that it should obtain an up-to-date assessment of *market size* – which is why the determination of such information often constitutes the objective for marketing research surveys.

So in looking at markets 'in the round', we must establish the numbers, characteristics and buying power of users.

At the next stage, we must try to discover why people buy.

Consumer behaviour

The literature on why people buy is considerable. Even so, great aspects of the subject remain elusive. Even the most conscientious writers can only report that our knowledge is still imperfect and that the search for better interpretive techniques goes on. Yet there are a number of safe generalisations we can make about this complex study – assisted by insights gained from applied behavioural science, particularly psychology, social psychology, sociology and anthropology.

In the space of a few pages, we can do no more than look at some of the main established concepts that are important to workers in the marketing field. The aim will be to describe these concepts in the simplest terms possible and to advise on where their deeper treatment may be found.

The first point is that an examination of the subject reveals two entities – *the individual consumer* (and particularly his or her psychological make-up) and *the environmental forces* influencing the individual consumer.

Boone and Kurtz[3] in stating that consumer behaviour is the outcome of both individual and environmental influences have expressed the belief in these terms:

$$B = f(P, E)$$

i.e. consumer behaviour (B) is a function (f) of the interaction of the personal influences of consumers (P) and the influences of environmental forces (E). We shall now examine some of the conventional ideas about both sets of influences.

Personal influences on consumer behaviour

The theory of *self-concept* is a useful starting point. The proposition is that how people see themselves – their self-concept – has a number of facets. The *real self* constitutes the objective view – what the person is really like. The *self-image* is how the individual sees himself and since 'no man can be a judge in his own case' this is likely to contain some element of distortion. The *mirror self* is how individuals think others see them whilst the *ideal self* is how the individual would like to be – the components of the ideal self-image serve as a set of behavioural objectives. In this sense, we are all striving towards the attainment of ideal self.

The implications for purchasing behaviour are not difficult to discern. When *The Times* newspaper advertises that it is read by 'top people' it is appealing to those whose ideal-self image is one of success and influence – be it in government, business, public service, the arts or whatever. The young boy who aspires to be an international footballer is likely to buy kit and equipment endorsed by 'star' players – the people the boy wishes to emulate. When a young lady is diffident about the dress she is considering, and asks herself 'is it really me'? she may perceive that wearing it will threaten her ideal-self image.

Maslow's hierarchy of pre-potent needs

Since marketing is to do with the satisfaction of human needs attention has been focused on the nature of needs. A need has been defined by one psychologist[4] as:

a condition marked by the feeling of lack or want of something, or of requiring the performance of some action.

Hence the need is seen as the first factor in a sequence leading to the purchase decision. The *need* generates the *motive*, or moving power, for the consumer to take action (i.e. the act of purchasing) so as to relieve the tension arising from the felt need.

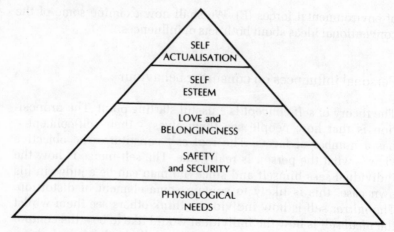

Fig. 5.6   *Abraham Maslow's hierarchy of pre-potent needs*

A model which has found some favour with the marketing fraternity with regard to consumer motivations is that based on Maslow's hierarchy of needs.

Writing in 1954[5] Maslow proposed that there are five distinct categories of need:

physiological – the needs to satisfy hunger, to obtain shelter and clothing;

safety – the need to protect oneself from physical harm, to obtain security and safety from accident and similar unexpected dangers;

love and 'belongingness' – the social needs, centred on the desire for acceptance, the needs for affiliation and acceptance;

esteem – the need for status, for a sense of achievement, for recognition and respect stemming from one's accomplishments;

self-actualisation – the need to realise one's full potential, to ensure that one's capacities and skills are being totally utilised.

Maslow argued that these needs are arranged in an order of importance – the lowest order needs being physiological and the highest or fifth-level category being based on self-actualisation. He also suggested that satisfied needs do not provide motivation and that the needs at the base of the pyramid must at least be partially satisfied before the next higher level need becomes important and a motivator of action (hence 'prepotent' in the description).

The practical implications of the theory are easy to describe.

First, it is easy to perceive how particular products and services are related to particular needs: food to the physiological category; life insurance to safety; fashions in dress and hairstyles and membership of particular groups and sub-cultures as being grounded in the social needs.

The second point relates to the possibility of the higher order needs emerging. In Bangladesh, for example, most activity will be motivated by physiological needs – to the business of staying alive. In western societies, on the other hand, there is very much more opportunity for self-actualisation, although the degree of opportunity will vary according to income level.

Maslow's ideas are well-known to marketing practitioners and we can observe marketing and advertising activity being undertaken with these ideas in mind. However, as with many other aspects of the study of human behaviour there are warning notes to sound. Robertson and Cooper[6] point out that despite its obvious appeal, Maslow's theory has not been well supported by empirical studies of its validity. Oliver[7] exhorts us to bear in mind that 'it is naïve to expect a direct causal relationship between motive and behaviour', that any item of behaviour might spring from multiple motives and that even if individuals are impelled by the same single motive their behaviours might be quite different.

Nevertheless, any review of consumer behaviour, however brief, has to include mention of Maslow's hierarchy.

Perception

A primary objective of marketing activity is to direct attention to the organisation's product or service. This it does through the stimuli, such as advertising messages, which are directed to target populations. Perception, in this context, means sense perception, a process in which the object recognised or identified is the object affecting a sense organ. Thus we can perceive by seeing, hearing, touching, tasting and smelling the object and marketing communication is brought about by affecting one or more of the sense organs by a stimulus object, usually a representation of the product and an accompanying promotional message. Of course, this is not the only information processed by the perceptual system. Other sources of relevant information may come from peer groups, consumer groups, family and friends.

Perhaps the most important point for marketers is that what is perceived is often different from what is there to be perceived: the percept, the mental product of the act of perceiving, must not be confused with the thing perceived.

Another way of expressing this is to say that perception derives from two interacting factors: (1) the properties of the stimulus object itself: the size, colour, shape of the product or the advertising message; (2) the manner in which the first factor is mediated by what the individual brings to the act of perceiving – not only his or her sense processes but also a complex amalgam of past experiences, aspirations, motivations and so forth. Thus in the introductory pages of this textbook, during the conversation with the television producer, the author was making this very point. The mind of the consumer is not a *tabula rasa*, a blank slate upon which the message sender is free to make his impression, for, through the process of mediation, people will have quite different perceptions of the same stimulus object.

A corollary of this is the process of *selective perception* – people do not necessarily perceive everything the organisation chooses to send them – they perceive only what they want to perceive. As was stated at the beginning of the conversation with the television producer, people tend to interpret information in a way that supports rather than challenges their own beliefs. People tend to hold on only to the information that fits their preconceptions.

At Christmas 1983, HM Government reputedly spent £750 000 on an advertising campaign to help curtail drunken driving. It was reported that in spite of the campaign one in four drivers independently surveyed stated their intention of driving a motor vehicle even if they knew they were over the legal limit of alcohol consumption. Quite rightly the finding gave rise to much heart-searching and anguish. The author felt this a telling example of selective perception at work.

Because of the filtration device incorporated within the perceptual mechanisms marketing men employ a variety of techniques to assist the attention-getting value of their communications: colour in a black and white newspaper; humour on the advertising hoarding; a large size advertisement or one in which the reader has to rearrange the message for it to make sense; the arresting opening in the television commercial. These are not fortuitous occurrences but a tactical way of penetrating the consumer's perceptual screen. Communications campaigns which detail the size and nature of the audience reached enabling a 'cost per thousand impressions' to be calculated are only at a low level of sophistication so far as marketing planning is concerned for in spite of all we do not yet know about consumer behaviour, we do know that what the advertiser may transmit is one thing but what the consumer perceives may be quite another.

Attitudes

Many of the studies of consumer behaviour are based upon a concept of *information processing* – that is, the consumer gathers information (from advertising stimuli, for example) which is then processed for the purposes of decision making. The processing comes about by the consumer *evaluating* the gathered information through his or her system of beliefs and attitudes. Attitude research, including attitude measurement, has therefore become an important part of marketing activity.

The psychologist Drever[8] defines *attitude* as:

A more or less stable set or disposition of opinion, interest or purpose, involving expectancy of a certain kind of experience, and readiness with an appropriate response; ...

We can see from this definition that an attitude reflects the tendency for a person to act or react in a certain manner when placed in particular situations and so attitudes must have relevance to the consistencies, and inconsistencies, to be observed in consumer behaviour.

A further point is that although *attitude* is an abstract concept: it cannot be observed directly nor can it always be measured, simply or directly, nevertheless we do know there is a pronounced *quantitative* aspect to attitudes – people hold them in various strengths.

Therefore, an organisation wishing to measure attitudes to its product, brand or service will usually become involved in research to:

1   *identify attitude dimensions*: usually by informal interviewing and/or group discussions, sometimes aided with projective pictures – the interviews being tape-recorded and subjected to a thorough content analysis;
2   *develop suitable measuring instruments*: attitude scaling methods being important here.

A well-known method of attitude scaling is the *semantic differential*, developed by Osgood.[9] It consists of a number of seven-point rating scales, with each extreme point of the scale being defined by an adjective or a descriptive phrase. Thus the scales being used for product image testing of a newspaper might include the following:

interesting	└─┴─┴─┴─┴─┴─┘	uninteresting
informative	└─┴─┴─┴─┴─┴─┘	uninformative
truthful	└─┴─┴─┴─┴─┴─┘	untruthful
appealing layout	└─┴─┴─┴─┴─┴─┘	unappealing layout
good value	└─┴─┴─┴─┴─┴─┘	poor value

The informant then rates the newspaper on each dimension by ticking one of the seven boxes (points) between the two extremes. A profile of the newspaper for that respondent can then be produced by linking the ratings so obtained. The implications for product development are clear enough. The averaged rankings of all informants in the sample surveyed becomes the generalised profile of the newspaper. This can be compared with the profiles obtained for other newspapers and with a profile of the ideal newspaper the attributes of which can be constructed using the same semantic differential technique. Thus favourable attributes of the research sponsor's own newspaper can be capitalised upon (e.g. in marketing communications) whilst the unfavourable ones can be modified so as to move the newspaper towards the ideal profile.

Of course such research, which Oliver[10] terms *attitude to object* research, whilst important, does not disclose the consumer's attitude to the act of buying a particular newspaper. Establishing the link between attitudes and behaviour is much more elusive. A variety of pressures bear on an individual in the behavioural situation. Sometimes they combine to reinforce or to deter an aspect of behaviour. Sometimes they conflict with each other to the extent that the resultant action can only be described as marginal. Much research has been done in the recent past to identify and measure the individual pressures. Significant contributions in this context have been made by British researcher Mary Tuck and in reporting this research, Oliver[11] indicates that financial constraints, demographic and socio-economic factors, expected stock levels at distributive outlets and the influence of other people who are significant to the buyer (the 'subjective norm') are all interrelated pressures that combine with attitudes to influence behaviour.

Much recent interest has been taken in the various forms of multivariate and taxonomic analysis in order to obtain from these data a fuller understanding and, ultimately perhaps, prediction of buying behaviour.

Learning

Interpreters of consumer behaviour have also been interested in the theory of learning, which may be described as the modification of a response following upon and emanating from experience of results. Research has entailed examination of the drives (or impulses) towards purchase behaviour; e.g. hunger, fear, pride, the urge to compete; the environmental cues directly related to response, such as advertising, point-of-sale display etc; and the responses of the individual to such cues and drives. Since response depends upon cues, drives and whether or not existing behaviour has become a habit, to a greater or lesser degree, learning theory may provide valuable information on brand preference and brand loyalty. Entrenched habit may, of course, inhibit 'new learning', that is, we may filter out advertising messages for competing brands. Yet another variable in the equation is expectations of the outcome resulting from particular responses ('if I buy this brand it may not be as nourishing as the one I usually buy'). Clearly the organisation will benefit from acquiring knowledge of the expectations that surround the possible purchase of its products.

Cognitive dissonance

In this brief review of consumer behaviour, as influenced by the psychology of the individual, we have concentrated on influences prior to purchase. Marketing activity must also take note of a post-purchase influence – that of cognitive dissonance. This is also notable from another standpoint, for although attitudes are decidedly resistant to change, attitudes sometimes change significantly after the purchase! The work of Leon Festinger[12] and his associates denotes the importance of suppliers staying concerned with the attitudes of users in the post-purchase stage because of the possible development of cognitive dissonance – a state of doubt, anxiety or uncertainty as to whether the correct decision has, in fact, been made.

This anxiety will typically accompany major purchase decisions such as house and car buying and will be accentuated if the item purchased is discovered to be faulty, albeit in minor ways, or if the attraction of alternatives is emphasised to the buyer (perhaps one of the most dangerous elements in such dissonance is the 'knowing friend').

The user will seek to reduce cognitive dissonance either by establishing confirmation that the decision was a sound one, by becoming a troublesome client seeking redress, including perhaps legal redress, or by disposing of the goods. Whilst the risk of such psychological disharmony is greater when the product is an expensive one, such as a consumer durable, it can arise with repeat-buying products (where it is clearly of added significance) as it can with the purchase of industrial goods.

As will be emphasised in the next Chapter, under the heading of the *total-product* concept, sound and reliable after-sales service is the powerful antidote to cognitive dissonance, as is any speedy and equitable system for dealing with post-purchase complaints and user requests for information and advice.

Reassurance advertising, in which the quality of the product and its significant features, the problems it overcomes, its economies etc, are emphasised, is also very important. Cognitive dissonance is important enough for the UK's Institute of Marketing to stress the assistance to be derived from after-sales service and reassurance advertising in a report[13] of the Institute's Construction Industry Marketing Group.

Environmental influences on consumer behaviour

It is well established that the behaviour of the individual has both an individual and a social aspect – in effect, that 'no man is an island'.

Research and observation of the market-place reveals that this is just as true of the development of consumer behaviour as of any other aspect of behaviour with which the social psychologist is concerned.

One of the primary influences here is that of the *human group* and its *norms* of behaviour: its socially sanctioned rules of conduct which represent the values held by the group and which the group itself enforces.

Think of the groups you belong to – the family group, the working group, the professional group, perhaps a student group. Each of these has its norms of behaviour, perhaps overtly expressed as the *code of practice* of the profession or 'understood', as in the work group, where one never 'lets down colleagues'.

The social system encompassed by the group is one of *roles* and *role relationships* and many products and services enable us to perform these roles. What are the concepts of the role of the mother within the family group, of the accountant within the professional group? Church groups, neighbourhood groups, friendship groups, all human groups to which we belong accord us status (our relative position in the group) and ascribe to us our roles (i.e. the expectations others have of us in that position). The food we buy and prepare, the clothes we wear, the equipment we use, the car we drive and the holidays we take may all, to some extent at least, be manifestations of group influence.

A corollary of this is *reference* group theory. Although the individual may be a member of such a group, membership is not a pre-condition for reference group influence, the reference group being the group to which the individual so aspires that it becomes a standard, a reference point for goals and behaviour. 'Pop stars', international athletes, the aristocracy, successful business executives, the 'caring' professions all constitute reference groups for some of us. The main implication for purchase behaviour is based on the level of visibility or conspicuousness of the product in question. If we refer to successful business executives for our standards, for example, then a motor car is a very appropriate product and the purchase of a Mercedes, not to say a Rolls-Royce, would very much fit our idealised perception. The purchase of relatively inconspicuous products such as foodstuffs would not (although many a child recognises the correlation between sporting success and the consumption of certain breakfast cereals). On the other hand, advertising for cosmetics often draws upon the influence of the reference group: 'the glamorous', 'the model girls'.

In the preceding Chapter mention has already been made of social class segmentation based on the IPA standard definitions which derive from the occupation of the head of household (see Chapter 4, page 112). In spite of the truism that occupational groupings do tell us something about disposable income and that disposable income provides some guide to products bought, housing lived in, type and level of education and 'value systems' adopted, doubts surround the use of the socio-economic classification as a dependable general correlate of consumer behaviour. Whilst many conclude that social class is still a very useful discriminator for sampling purposes and for data interpretation, others conclude that due to the way life is changing, the old established segmentation of individuals into white and blue collar groups is now a questionable way of projecting consumption patterns.

Therefore, whilst a long-term uniform system of social classification does have value in comparing trends over time (e.g. as to how the structure of youth unemployment, and hence buying power, correlates with social class through a time period – say 5 or 10 years), nevertheless one research practitioner, Clemens,[14] warns against over-valuing the current system. He argues that the 1972 Oxford Social Mobility Study, which pioneered a different form of classification may well have advantages for marketing.

The Oxford Social Mobility Classification, 1972

	Classes	
Service	I	Higher grade professionals, administrators, managers
	II	Lower grade professionals, administrators, managers
	III	Clerical, sales and rank and file service workers
Intermediate	IV	Small proprietors and self employed artisans, 'petty bourgeoisie'
	V	Lower grade technicians and foremen, 'aristocracy of labour'
	VI	Skilled manual workers in industry
Working	VII	Semi and unskilled manual workers in industry
	VIII	Agricultural workers and smallholders

The service class, shown above, broadly approximates to the AB socio-economic group of the IPA classifications, whilst working class partially covers the IPA's C_2DE grouping. The intermediate class, which includes the IPA C_1 grouping, and may be termed the new middle class is thought to be nearer the service (or AB) classification, in both incomes and life styles, than to the working class. Clemens hopes that experimental work might be done to assess the value of such a classification framework as a predictor of consumer behaviour. It might indeed be useful.

Some interesting propositions have been advanced on innovation and its implications for behaviour. Everett Rogers[15] in his 'Diffusion of innovation' suggests a typology of customers based on *adoption categories*. He suggests that perhaps 2.5 per cent of a user population might be classified as *innovators* – the economically venturesome, who are prepared to try something new – a new product, a new concept. Innovators are usually to be found in the higher income, higher social groups. At the other end of Rogers' scale are the *laggards*, some 16 per cent of the population, who are change resistant and lacking in imagination. Between these two groups are the *early adopters* (13.5 per cent and almost in the same class as the innovators) the *early majority* (34 per cent and with less 'leadership' than the previous two categories) and the *late majority* (also 34 per cent, and who are imitators but rather cautious). The statistically-minded reader will perceive that these percentages relate to the bell-shaped curve of a normal distribution.

In similar vein to Rogers, Katz and Lazarsfeld[16] suggest that within each human group there are a minority of trend setters or *opinion leaders*. Marketing information flows from the organisation to the opinion leader and from these leaders to the rest of the market. The opinion leader obtains self-actualisation by being 'first in the field' – with the colour television, the home computer, the video cassette etc. Hence the importance of this sub-population, not only for the 'launching' stages of new products, but also for their influence as opinion formers and word-of-mouth advocates. The views of opinion leaders carry much weight with the rest of the population and their advice is often sought.

Although these ideas on innovation and opinion leadership stand in need of empirical investigation and further development, the reader will doubtless perceive them, purely from a priori reasoning, as being significant elements in the environment influencing consumer behaviour.

It goes without saying that a group which has a marked influence on purchasing behaviour is the family. Clearly the norms established in one's original family have a marked influence on attitudes, beliefs and behaviour. Marriage provides the opportunity for the formation of a new family and the stages in the family life cycle which follow bring with them changes in the demand for products and services, including housing and domestic equipment. Roles and role relationships exert their influence as they do in any human group. *Role specialisation* is clearly related to the pattern of household decision-making. Engel, Kollatt and Blackwell[17] distinguish four role categories:

autonomic decisions are made individually by one or other of the married partners (e.g. on alcoholic beverages, certain types of tools and equipment);
husband dominant (e.g. on life insurance, car accessories, garden tools);
wife dominant (e.g. on food, children's clothing, kitchen ware, cleaning products), and
syncratic decisions are made jointly by the married partners (e.g. on housing, schooling, furniture, holiday plans and outside entertainments.)

Within the general pattern of family roles there are, of course, strands of continuing change. For example, in 1961 less than one in four of married women, with two or more dependent children, were in employment (either full-time or part-time). By 1971 the figure had risen to 35 per cent and by 1980 to approximately 50 per cent, with signs that the proportion was still increasing. This not only has implications for respective roles in the household and the extent to which advertising should be directed to one or other of the partners, Boone and Kurtz[18] also report that studies of family decision making have shown that working wives tend to exert more influence upon decision making than non-working wives. The influence of children on the purchase of certain products has also been well noted in the past by marketing organisations. The alacrity with which children have responded to developments in computing and informatics, in comparison with adult members of the family, suggests that this is an influence which will extend rather than contract in the future.

Mention of the family does focus attention upon the latter-day pressures upon the established pattern of family life and the significant increase in one parent families, single person households and the numbers of divorced couples. This fragmentation of society, which suggests that segmentation studies will become more rather than less important in the future is being accompanied by the increasing diversity of cultures, sub-cultures and minority interests. 'Culture' in this sense may be taken to mean 'shared orientations', an amalgam of values, attitudes, ideas and beliefs which plays its part in the shaping of behaviour, which changes from one generation to the next and includes consumer behaviour.

All of these trends can be incorporated into the general heading of *social change* and this exerts such a powerful influence on market behaviour (as witness the recent fashions for pine furniture, peasant style dress, eastern style dress, 'work clothes' style dress, such as jeans and donkey jackets) that a growing number of marketing organisations have concluded that the charting of social change will make them better prepared for the market places of the future.

The UK researchers Taylor Nelson Group Limited, operating through the *International Research Institute on Social Change* (RISC) have recently been able to isolate 23 common trends operating across Europe. These trends indicate, among other things, that:

1   fewer people are now motivated by security or status, more people are dominated by 'personal autonomy' – the desire for self-fulfilment and personal expression;
2   there is a movement to spontaneity and informality, a search for pleasure continuing to grow within many European countries and allied to this trend are increased desires for risk taking and a desire for 'a full rich life';
3   people are becoming much more open to other people's feelings and to their own emotions; people are more open to change;
4   as a reaction to rigid hierarchies and bigness, there is a rejection of manipulation, a greater awareness of insincerity and resistance to those institutions which are seen as manipulators.

Other trends revealed by the survey are an increased emphasis upon physical fitness, the search for novelty, an increased concern about the environment and an increased emphasis upon individuality.

Whilst such trends do not generally relate to the demand for products and services in a strict sense, they are powerful influences upon the composition of demand upon producers in both the private and the public sectors. They also demonstrate that the concept of national stereotypes which underlies a great deal of international marketing activity is becoming outmoded. The trends also have a special significance for the marketing of ideas, particularly political ideas and we shall return to this subject before the end of the Chapter.

This Section has attempted to set out some of the main strands of our present knowledge of consumer behaviour. The reader seeking deeper and more extensive information should refer to the books listed in the bibliography. The work of Foxall and the early chapters of Oliver have particular value. Further reading of the 'outline' type provided in this Chapter, supplemented in some instances by short, readable case histories can be found in the works of Boone and Kurtz, William Stanton and David Schwartz.

It can be seen from the outline provided by this Section that a great deal of thought and effort has been applied to the question of 'why people buy'. But, understandably perhaps, the approach has been one which looked at the *components* of behaviour and has therefore been fragmented, as a consequence. This raises the question of whether an attempt has been made to fit the components together into an interpretive theory of consumer behaviour. To put it slightly differently, it would seem from what has been said that a number of variables come together to influence purchasing behaviour, e.g.

1 *input variables* such as the elements of the marketing mix which act as stimuli in the decision making process;
2 *internal variables* 'provided' by the buyer, such as motives, attitudes, perception, personality – which may crudely be thought of as part of the internal mechanisms – the 'black box' – within which the input stimuli are processed;
3 *external variables* such as social class, culture, pressure of time on decision making and the financial status of the buyer which mediate the perceptions and other internal variables provided by the buyer;
4 *output variables* usually purchase decisions, decisions not to buy, formation of attitudes etc.

Have efforts been made then to construct models of buyer behaviour; to represent 'what goes on' and so better inform marketing decision making and to assist the *prediction of outcomes*? The answer is 'yes' but integrated models of buyer behaviour that can be used as fixed factors in developing managerial strategy are still some way off.

The reasons are that consumer buying processes are complex and comprise a multiplicity of *products*, brands, outlets, and degrees of risk; a multiplicity of *people* each with their individual value systems and psychological 'make-up' and a multiplicity of *external influences* and patterns of communication.

The models of this complex process are therefore complex in themselves and since they are not open to simple explanations and because they stand in need of further empirical testing, it is difficult for the practical business man to perceive their theoretical abstractions in terms of pragmatic value.

It is beyond the scope of this work to discuss these models in detail but it would perhaps be fair to say that a typical approach to such models is to see behaviour as based upon the interaction of the first three of the four variables mentioned on page 166. Other assumptions are that buying is a *problem-solving* process and that *learning* plays an important part in that consumers store a great deal of information based on past experience of products, services and brands so that much buying behaviour becomes routine and repetitive. Where the 'feedback loop' of experience produces negative impressions then the process of problem solving – the search for a better product, a better brand, begins again.

It is proper, indeed important, that work on the refinement of these models should continue. It is also important that the student should become acquainted with the work in this field of such influentials as Howard and Sheth,[19] Nicosia[20] and Engel, Kollatt and Blackwell.[21] The conscientious student should also keep abreast of developments. Since marketing is to do with the manipulation of those variables over which the organisation has control, it is important that aspiring executives can visualise the total behavioural process they are attempting to influence. The textbooks mentioned earlier will enable the reader to appreciate the existing approaches to modelling as will the work of Peter T. Fitzroy, which is also listed in the bibliography.

Characteristics of organisational markets

It has often been the rule in the past to lump together all marketing activity other than consumer marketing and title it *industrial marketing*. This artificially restricts non-consumer marketing to a role largely related to supplying goods and services to manufacturing industry. This cannot be correct when Britain's industrial sector accounted for only 32 per cent of total employment in 1980. It neglects the growth in employment which has been especially strong in the services sector, where financial and business services (insurance, banking, leasing and real estate) and hotel and catering services are so prominent. It neglects the agricultural market which, though engaging less than three per cent of Britain's employed labour force, produces nearly two thirds of its food, thanks to its high level of productivity. It overlooks the markets resulting from the transformation of Britain's energy position, the country having become self-sufficient in energy in net terms (Note: the output of the petroleum and natural gas industry amounted to £12 000 million in 1981, equivalent to almost six per cent of gross domestic product). The restrictive 'industrial marketing' label also encourages us to forget the important markets provided by central and local government, for despite the policy of the present UK government to encourage the private sector, the public sector of Britain's economy employs no less than 34 per cent of the work force.

It is therefore sounder to think in terms of organisational, rather than industrial marketing, as the partner to consumer marketing in the binary system of total marketing activity. Before dealing generally with other types of organisational market, an extra few words are warranted on the agricultural and governmental markets.

British agriculture is characterised by its high level of efficiency and productivity. Despite its small size in employment terms, the two thirds of Britain's food requirements it currently produces is a significant increase even on the 1960 figures when just under one half of the country's needs was being met by home production. Nearly 80 per cent of the land area is used for agriculture whilst the cool temperate climate and even distribution of rainfall ensure a long growing season. Innovation, efficient farming and an important and extensive research programme are continually increasing crop and other yields. Britain therefore provides highly lucrative markets for farm vehicles, farm machinery, fertilisers, other chemical products and animal feeding stuffs. Many of the suppliers to these markets are highly skilled in marketing. On the *output* side, agricultural products are marketed by private traders, producers' co-operatives and marketing boards, these latter being producers' organisations empowered by government to regulate the marketing of milk, wool and potatoes. A great deal of attention is paid to consumer interests in the marketing of Britain's agricultural produce – a panel has been established to advise the Minister of Agriculture, Fisheries and Food on marketing, there is strong emphasis on the role of co-operatives and there have been recent efforts by growers to improve the marketing of onions, carrots, dessert apples and lamb.

Government, both national and local, is an important customer to many of Britain's business organisations. Currently central and local government organisations account for some 19 per cent of gross domestic product. Substantial contracts for goods and services including plant, machinery, buildings, military equipment, drugs and pharmaceuticals, food products, cleaning materials, telecommunications equipment, office equipment, books and educational equipment, motor vehicles and textiles are frequently placed with private sector organisations by governmental bodies. Motorway construction, other public civil engineering projects and the exploitation of Britain's reserves of oil and natural gas also offer substantial opportunities to efficient business organisations.

Many firms are daunted by the size and complexity of the governmental markets, calling as they do for skill and speed at procedures for tendering. It is also true that the value of the average government contract makes for extremely keen competition among the tendering suppliers. Moreover, it is true that in addition to the price tendered for the contract, the reliability of the supplier on delivery promises and maintenance of quality, as well as the specifications and performance of the products and services offered and the effectiveness of after-sales service arrangements, are all carefully assessed. Nevertheless, the lists of 'approved suppliers' established by central and local government departments contain a multiplicity of firms large and small. Such firms typically discover that operating within the efficiency criteria of governmental markets improves their effectiveness in other markets.

The analysis of organisational markets

Having established the rationale for the term 'organisational marketing', let us now consider some of the main characteristics of such markets. In estimating demand we are interested in:

1   the type of organisations that typically buy the product or service;
2   the typical purchasing procedures used;
3   the motives and influences bearing upon the decision to buy.

We are concerned with *users*, as in consumer marketing, but whereas a household food product might have a potential market of 56 million users, even if we had a product of potential interest to all the industrial organisations in Britain (sole traders, partnership, 'private' and 'public' companies, public corporations) our total of potential contacts would be significantly less than three million. And as we saw in Chapter 4 the market is rarely so huge and undifferentiated – and, in fact, may in the case of a specialised product be restricted to a relatively small group of organisations – (200 or even less). The first distinguishing characteristic is therefore the *relatively small number of organisations* the average supplier will be dealing with, compared to the consumer market.

The next characteristic relates to *organisational* size and in the UK, as in the USA and other developed economies the pattern is for a large amount of output and employment to be accounted for by a relatively small number of firms.

Over 90 per cent of net output is attributable to the five largest companies in a large number of sectors, including: tobacco; cement; man-made fibres; margarine; surgical bandages; wheeled tractors; fertilisers; coke ovens and manufactured fuels. The following sectors – batteries; watches and clocks; industrial engines; cans and metal boxes; electronic computers and dyestuffs and pigments – are among those in which over 80 per cent of net output is attributable to the five largest companies.

Of course, in devising strategy, these data can be interpreted in either of two ways (1) to devote main marketing effort to these dominant organisations or (2) to specialise upon the smaller organisations which, in the aggregate, may amount to an extensive and lucrative market. Much will depend upon the size and geographical location of the supplier, the nature of the product or service and competition policy. All the marketing approach assumes is that strategy will be based upon recent and relevant data.

The third characteristic typically used to analyse organisational markets is that of *regional concentration*. Whilst some of Britain's industries are not clustered geographically (e.g. man-made fibres, electronics and pharmaceuticals), there are locational factors to be taken into account for a number of types of manufacture. The following list provides a brief illustration.

London: food and drink (especially brewing); instrument engineering; electrical and electronic engineering; clothing, furniture, printing.

South-Eastern counties/Thames valley:	pharmaceuticals, pumps, valves, compressors; instrument engineering, electronics; aerospace manufactures; timber, paper and plastics products.
North West:	food processing, textile machinery, chemicals, clothing, glass making, cotton and allied textiles.
West Midlands:	steel tubes, iron castings, non-ferrous metals, machine tools, motor vehicles, electrical engineering, carpets, pottery (with 80 per cent of UK's industry in Staffordshire), rubber production.
Yorkshire/Humberside:	cocoa, chocolate and confectionery; woollen and worsted goods, textile machinery, iron and steel; carpets, clothing and glass containers.
East Midlands:	steel tubes, iron castings, hosiery and knitted goods (over two-thirds of UK industry); footwear.

The list is in no sense complete, and in the case of many products it denotes a degree of, and not an absolute concentration. Nevertheless, the geography of a user industry can be an important characteristic and particularly for the small/medium sized supplier for whom a local or regional pattern of marketing would be more effective and economical than would an attempt to 'go national'.

The use of the *Standard Industrial Classification (SIC)* within the framework for analysis has been mentioned in Chapter 4. As already indicated, Chisnall sounds a warning note, reporting Maclean's view[22] that the statistical breakdowns provided by the SIC tend to be too wide for the analysis of *specific* industries (e.g. 'harvesting machinery', as distinct from 'barn machinery'). He also reports Maclean's idea of the way in which some gaps in statistical information might be remedied. For example, Maclean suggests that where a homogeneous industry classification is appropriate then a relationship might be established between the number employed in the industry and the usage rate of the product in question, e.g. oxygen consumption per employee in constructional steel work = 200 cubic feet, whereas in agricultural machinery it equals 10 cubic feet.

More will be said on the techniques of forecasting in Chapter 10 but the value of secondary research data in the demand characteristics of an organisational market are worth re-stating here. Some of the appropriate government statistical sources were mentioned in Chapter 4. In addition to the official statistical publications, each main department of HM Government has its own statistical division and it may be worthwhile contacting it to determine whether additional information is available and at what cost (which might be one way of augmenting the normal SIC levels of analysis). In addition valuable information is available from *trade sources* and *trade publications*. The British Plastics Federation and the Federation of British Rubber Manufacturers are among the trade associations which publish and distribute a great deal of information about their industries.

There are also a number of *subscription services* available. The Economist Intelligence Unit, which produces regular reports on countries and products, has been mentioned earlier in this volume. Surveys are also available from the National Trade Press Group (e.g. Chemical Data Surveys), *The Financial Times* and the Thomson Group on a subscription basis. International data are available from several sources (see Chapter 13) and Directories of Business Establishments, provided they are comprehensive, up-to-date and relevant are economical sources of data.

Allied to the demand characteristics of an organisational market is the question of *growth rates*. The recent history of the UK manufacturing output is that, after the 1973 rise in international oil prices, output fell but staged a gradual recovery from the mid 1970s to the end of the decade. Yet the rise was not constant for all sectors and was most marked in the chemical industry; the paper, printing and publishing industries; electronics; food processing and instrument engineering. The period between 1979 and 1981 saw another marked decline in output, due to the burgeoning costs of energy, with output stabilising by mid 1981.

A further characteristic hinges upon whether the market in question can be described as *vertical* or *horizontal*. Some simple illustrations will make this clear. Fig. 5.7 depicts the market for machinery used in producing ceramic tableware. Fig. 5.8 depicts the market for china clay. In a vertical market, the product is closely tailored to the needs of user industries and is supported by promotional and selling efforts of a highly technical nature. In the case of the machinery in the example, the UK market would

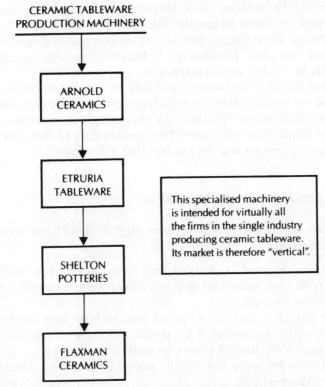

Fig. 5.7   The 'vertical' market for ceramic tableware machinery

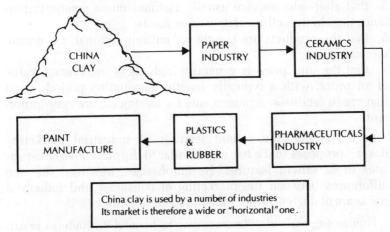

Fig. 5.8   The horizontal market for china clay

also be highly localised. In a horizontal market, the product is developed for broad usage and the marketing effort usually has wide industrial and geographical spread. Raw materials and other operating supplies (stationery, lubricants, cleaning products) typically have a horizontal market.

As was stated at the beginning of this Section, when estimating demand we are interested in who buys. Some of the characteristics described above will help in answering that question. Let us now think about the other two components of the problem – the *buying process* and the *motives* that influence it.

The organisational buying process

There are a number of apt truisms used in describing organisational markets:

1   that the demand is *derived* and therefore demand analysis begins with user industries and also incorporates a consideration of economic forecasts;
2   that though a particular market may be large in value terms it is typically concentrated by number of buyers; comparative importance of the buying points; geography or whatever;
3   that the products are much more complex and therefore require expert selling;
4   that there may be a large number of influences at work in purchasing decisions – that buying is a *group* process;
5   that after-sales service usually assumes much greater importance than in the selling of consumer goods;
6   that the products are bought for entirely rational, i.e. economic motives;
7   that the unit price is generally high, as is the average value of an order, with a typically lengthy negotiation period – and that credit facilities, arrangements for leasing etc are very important.

In describing 'the salient features of industrial marketing Baker[23] proposes that a list very similar to the one above encapsulates these salient features. He emphasises, however, that the differences between the marketing of consumer and industrial goods are of *degree*, rather than *kind* and he adds:

... undue emphasis of differences may be harmful if it induces practitioners in either field to neglect thought and practice in the other.

To understand why Baker holds this view let us take a hypothetical example. Consider the custom provided by an organisation
such as Arnold Ceramics. Typically, it purchases:

1   *Raw materials* (clays, felspar, quartz, ceramic colours)

2   *Product components* (e.g. blades and other fitments for its
ceramic handled cutlery)

3   *Capital equipment and installations* (e.g. production machinery, glazing apparatus, kilns etc)

4   *Ancillary equipment* (e.g. drying and storage racks, fork-lift
trucks, industrial vacuum cleaners, office equipment)

5   *Operating supplies* (e.g. lubricants, stationery, sponges, etc)
If we then classify the purchasing procedures used for these
five product categories, using some of the features of organisational markets previously listed, we arrive at Table 5.2 (Note: the
question of *motives* for purchasing is dealt with later in this
Chapter).

Crude and simplistic as these indicators are, they provide ample
support for the proposition that the apt truisms of marketing
to organisations should be treated with caution. A better axiom
would be to say 'it all depends on the product' (and hence, the
market). There is the qualification, of course, that the indicators
in Table 5.2 will need some adjustment depending on whether
the purchases were new as opposed to repeat purchases, particularly where a change of supplier was being contemplated.
Nevertheless, the argument still stands – the differences between
consumer and organisational marketing are usually differences
of degree rather than of kind.

Models of organisational buying behaviour

A number of models have been proposed in an attempt to integrate the many variables which influence the purchasing process
and the actual organisational buying decision.

The BUYGRID model was initially developed by Robinson and
others.[24] It is based on extensive empirical research by the Marketing Science Institute of America and was subsequently adopted

Table 5.2 Arnold Ceramics: some characteristics of the purchasing process

Type of product	Order contract value	Negotiation period	Group participation	After sales service	Need for expert selling
Raw materials	Medium	Short	No (Buyer and production manager)	Not too important	Not important
Product components	Medium	Short	No (Buyer and production manager)	Not too important	Not important
Capital equipment installations	Very high	Long	Yes (Minimum of 6 executives)	Very important	Very important
Ancillary equipment	Low to medium	Short	No	Fairly important	Not too important
Operating supplies	Typically low	Short	No	Not important	Not important

by that Institute. Robinson and his colleagues concluded that the buying process is an *eight stage* model which though broadly sequential might well have two or three of the stages occurring simultaneously. In addition to these 'Buyphases', there are within the model three categories of buying decision, termed 'Buyclasses' viz:

new task classes the most complex and difficult usually with several influences and decision makers involved;
modified rebuy classes which are more routine; and
straight rebuy classes in which decisions are relatively automatic.

Buy phases	Buy classes		
	New task	Modified rebuy	Straight rebuy
1 Anticipation or recognition of a problem			
2 Determination of characteristics and quantity of needed item			
3 Description of characteristics and quantity of needed item			
4 Search for and qualification of potential sources			
5 Acquisition and analysis of proposals			
6 Evaluation of proposals and selection of supplier(s)			
7 Selection of an order routine			
8 Performance feedback and evaluation			

Fig. 5.9   *The BUYGRID model of buying behaviour (Source: Marketing Science Institute)*

It is suggested that those situations occurring in the top left-hand portion of the grid are the most complex. The point is also made that as the decision making process develops through the various Buyphases so also does commitment on behalf of the purchaser, so that there is a diminishing prospect of other suppliers entering the negotiations. In his appraisal of the Buyphases and, in this context, Gordon Brand writes:

The suppliers who are involved at the early problem stages and who assist the purchasing organisation's technical staff in making up their minds can provide a far more persuasive quotation.

The question of group influence on organisational buying has been incorporated in the Fisher model[25] which is based on two factors: *product complexity* and *commercial uncertainty*.

Product complexity

		High	Low
Commercial uncertainty	High	Total involvement	Policy maker emphasis
	Low	Technologist emphasis	Buyer emphasis

Fig. 5.10   *The Fisher model: functional area involvement in the organisational buying process*

Note Product complexity refers to the perceived complexity from the buyer's stand point (variables here would include the technology of the product, newness of the product, degree of after-sales service, ease/difficulty of installation). Commercial uncertainty refers to the degree of business risk which the buying decision involves (and variables here include: size of investment, time span of commitment, potential effect on profit and ease of forecasting).

Some other important models are the detailed one developed by Sheth[26] and the integrated model of Webster and Wind.[27] Lehmann and O'Shaughnessy[28] influenced by the Fishbein model of choice behaviour, have conducted an empirical investigation of the *attributes involved in supplier choice*. These and other models of organisational buying behaviour are described in the work of Peter Fitzroy (see bibliography), whilst the works of Chisnall, and Oliver, also listed, provide valuable additional reading.

Self-assessment questions

1   How are products classified in order to classify markets?
2   Suggest a framework for the analysis of consumer markets.
3   Explain the significance of market size and market share.
4   What is the relevance of Maslow's hierarchy to marketing decision-making?

5 Define the following: selective perception; attitude; learning; cognitive dissonance; reference group theory.

6 Describe Rogers' typology of customers based on adoption categories.

7 Why are marketing organisations paying increasing attention to the charting of social change?

8 List the variables that come together to influence purchasing behaviour.

9 Suggest a framework for the analysis of organisational markets.

10 Discuss the proposition that the differences between the marketing of consumer and industrial goods are of degree rather than kind.

11 Outline some models of organisational buying behaviour.

References

1 Central Statistical Office. *Annual Abstract of Statistics*, Norwich, Her Majesty's Stationery Office, 1983, p. 99

2 Meloan, Taylor W. Analyzing markets for consumer goods, *Handbook of modern marketing*, (Buell Victor P. and Heyel Carl, eds), New York, McGraw-Hill, 1970, p. 2–23

3 Boone, Louis E. and Kurtz, David L. *Contemporary marketing*, 3rd edn, Hinsdale, Illinois, The Dryden Press, 1980, p. 105

4 Drever, James. *A dictionary of psychology*, (Rev. by H. Wallerstein), Harmondsworth, Middlesex, Penguin, 1971, p. 182

5 Maslow, A. H. *Motivation and personality*, New York, Harper, 1954

6 Robertson, Ivan T. and Cooper, Cary L. *Human behaviour in organisations*, Plymouth, Macdonald & Evans, 1983, p. 80

7 Oliver, Gordon. *Marketing today*, London, Prentice-Hall, 1980, p. 31

8 *A dictionary of psychology*, p. 23

9 Osgood, C. E. et al. *The measurement of meaning*, Urbana, University of Illinois Press, 1957

10 *Marketing today*, p. 24

11 Ibid., p. 26

12 Festinger, Leon. Cognitive dissonance, *Scientific American*, (October, 1962), New York, Scientific American Inc, pp. 93–102

13 Institute of Marketing. *Marketing in the construction industry*, (2nd report of the Working Party – Construction Industry Marketing Group), London, William Heinemann, 1974, p. 41

14 Clemens, John. Telephone interviewing as a discipline for classification systems, *Admap*, November 1981, London, ADMAP Publications, p. 575

15 Rogers, Everett M. and Shoemaker, F. Floyd. *Communication of innovations*, 2nd edn, New York, The Free Press, 1971
16 Katz, Elihu and Lazarsfeld, Paul. *Personal influence*, New York, The Free Press, 1955, p. 325
17 Engel, James F., Blackwell, Roger D. and Kollat, David T. *Consumer Behavior*, 3rd edn, Hinsdale, Illinois, Dryden Press, 1978, p. 152
18 *Contemporary marketing*, p. 123
19 Howard, John A. and Sheth, Jagdish N. *The theory of buyer behavior*, New York, John Wiley, 1969
20 Nicosia, Francesco M. *Consumer decision processes*, Englewood Cliffs, NJ, Prentice-Hall, 1966
21 *Consumer behaviour*.
22 Chisnall, Peter M. *Effective industrial marketing*, London, Longman, 1977, p. 109
23 Baker, Michael J. *Marketing – an introductory text*, 3rd edn, London, The Macmillan Press, 1979, p. 134
24 Robinson, P. J., Faris, C. W. and Wind, Y. The BUYGRID analytic framework for industrial buying situations, *Marketing: a Behavioural Analysis* (Peter M. Chisnall), Maidenhead, McGraw-Hill, 1975, p. 245
25 Fisher, L. *Industrial marketing*, 2nd edn, London, Business Books, 1976
26 Sheth, Jagdish N. A model of industrial buyer behaviour, *Journal of Marketing*, **37**, No. 4, October 1973
27 Webster, F. E. and Wind, Y. *Organizational buyer behavior*, Englewood Cliffs, NJ, Prentice-Hall, 1972
28 Lehmann, Donald R. and O'Shaughnessy, John. Difference in attribute importance for different industrial products, *Journal of Marketing*, April 1974, pp. 36–42

6 PLANNING THE PRODUCT OR SERVICE; THE 'TOTAL PRODUCT' CONCEPT; PRICE PLANNING

Objectives

The product is the foundation upon which all marketing effort is built and can be a service, an organisation, a personality or an idea, as well as a physical object. We are about to see that products are bought, as a rule, for what they will do and not for what they are. We shall look at some of the reasons underlying product success and failure and consider such concepts as the total product and the life cycle in relation to strategy.

Some ideas will be offered for systematic product planning and management and the importance of innovation will be stressed. Finally we shall consider why pricing is likely to become more rather than less important and see what such techniques as break-even analysis have to offer to price formulation.

Defining 'the product'

So far we have learned that those responsible for directing the organisation must review plans in the wider context of the environment, determining the size and nature of the organisation's activity in relation to the threats and opportunities that lie ahead, with special regard to the resources available. Marketing's contribution to the strategy is to match a mix of product, price, place and promotion to the requirements of the organisation's customers.

We can see from this why the product is so pre-eminent because it is the foundation upon which the marketing mix is constructed – without the product there is no need for the other elements.

Is it so difficult to define the product? The answer is that unless we bear three points in mind we might well arrive at an incomplete and inaccurate definition. The first point to bear in mind is that in some of the literature of marketing, the product is defined very broadly. The American Marketing Association would have it include not only various categories of physical objects, but also services, personalities, organisations and desires. On this definition, the entertainment provided by the local theatre, the candidate in the parliamentary election, the Outward Bound Trust and the desire to awaken interest in the plight of the world's wildlife are all products to be marketed. To this list we can add other products – e.g. places: tourist areas, or the new towns being established by the efforts of the various development corporations. So although in this Chapter we shall operate on the more restricted concept of product as being a physical object, before treating services and ideas separately in a later Section, the reader should be aware of the wider definitions which are often applied to the product (although if we remember Kotler's concept of meta-marketing in Chapter 1, these wider definitions should come as no surprise to us).

The second important point is that the product is rarely a simple concept. It is frequently much more than a collection of component parts and sub-assemblies, or the outcome of mixing together some raw materials. Very often it includes (a) accessories, (b) an installation service, (c) an operating manual, (d) a package, (e) a brand name or trade mark, (f) a user guarantee and (g) an undertaking that an adequate level of after-sales service will be available to the user as and when it is required. Even the most seemingly simple consumer product incorporates within its offering something more than a product of a given specification. There are additions – if only a package and a brand name. So we must be wary of abbreviated definitions. In fact, the complexity of the product offering has earned for itself the label of the *total product concept* and it has important implications, not least for pricing strategy, as we shall see later in this Chapter.

The third point to bear in mind is that products are bought not for what they are but for what they will do. The physical specification is only important in so far as it satisfies the wants of the customer. If the reader looks back to Chapter 1, it will be clear that this is why Levitt exhorts the organisation to ask itself 'what business are we in?' It follows that any preoccupation with the product that does not begin and end with the *want satisfaction* of the user is production orientation and not market orientation. In this connection, a good example is provided by Baker[1] who tells us that 'fitness for purpose' invariably ranks first among the criteria applied to industrial products by purchasing agents.

Moreover, want satisfaction does not stop at concrete, objective satisfactions, such as economy, speed, rate of output, ease of application or whatever. For as we saw in the last Chapter, psychological and social satisfactions are often extremely important too – people may buy a product because it satisfactorily relates to their self-image or to the norms of some significant group – such as the family or to their age group or professional group.

The reader is therefore invited to devise a definition of the product for himself, but in doing so, to bear in mind that 'the product' invariably means more than a mere physical object, that it is bought for want satisfaction and that this satisfaction has both tangible and intangible aspects.

Product success and failure

It seems that although there is pressure on most organisations to innovate (because of the rate of change in most markets) product innovation is nevertheless usually characterised by high failure rates. Examining the studies that have been made, together with the views of writers on the topic, the following reasons frequently appear:

1   insufficient attention was paid to analysing the market;
2   the product was defective in some way – e.g. quality, performance, user appeal etc;
3   the project of developing the product resulted in higher costs that had been anticipated – resulting in unattractive prices to the user, or insufficient profit contribution to the organisation;
4   the timing for the introduction of the product was faulty;
5   the strength and strategies of competitors were assessed insufficiently or inaccurately;
6   insufficient marketing effort was made to present and advertise the product effectively;
7   an inadequate level of sales force activity was devoted to the

product (and this problem has been increased recently, with the reduction in size of many sales forces);
8   the level of wholesale and retail distribution obtained proved insufficient (again, a problem on the increase as distributors have become more selective during economic recession).

In connection with point 3 above, it is worth adding Peter Kraushar's observation[2] that a new product project 'generates a momentum within a company which is difficult to stop and it is then looked at with rose-tinted spectacles'. In a clear and perceptive contribution to this subject, Baker[3] remarks on the apparent paradox of increasing pressure on organisations to inno-vate at a time when increasing costs of innovation and high failure rates may prove ruinous. Lest we become daunted by the difficul-ties, Baker nevertheless reminds us that:

1   while reports on the incidence of new product failures are commonplace, they are rarely based on 'hard evidence', and
2   there is no universal and simple definition of 'failure' and what may constitute failure to one organisation (e.g. failure to obtain a target rate of return on investment) may well be success to another.

Nevertheless, the risks are there and organisations would be happier if the failure rates, however defined, were reduced. Many marketing practitioners and writers would agree with Stanton[4] that some turn-around of this situation would be achieved if more organisations:

1   took practical steps to systematise their new product plan-ning;
2   made better use of marketing research in order to assess market needs and opportunities properly;
3   perfected methods to screen and evaluate products and ideas for products.

This Chapter will consider some of the actions which might be taken to attain these objectives.

The product life cycle

Consideration of the strategy of product development entails some description of the product life cycle, if only to sketch in for the reader an idea of historical background. The concept has been in vogue for a considerable part of the last three decades. Shakespeare wrote of the seven ages of man – from infancy to death, and the concept suggests that products, like humans, have a life cycle. Analysis of the sales performance of many products demonstrates, through time, relatively slow progress in the *introduction* stage, rapid increase in sales volume in the *growth* stage, a slackening of sales growth during the *maturity* stage, which precedes the *decline* stage, in which sales fall off at a highly significant rate. Fig. 6.1 illustrates the idea.

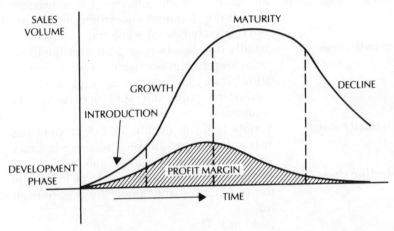

Fig. 6.1   The product life cycle

The proposition is that such knowledge about product behaviour facilitates a more informed approach to marketing strategy. To take promotion as one element of the marketing mix – this will not be based on a standard rate of expenditure throughout each of the stages. At the introduction stage, particularly in highly competitive markets, a disproportionately heavy expenditure is typically undertaken to launch the product – not least because the user must be 'educated' about its distinctive qualities. This *investment budget* strategy may well extend over a considerable period with profit 'pay back' being realised only when the product has become established and promotional support has been adjusted to more normal levels. By contrast, at the *decline* stage it may be decided to withdraw promotional support altogether, thus 'killing off' the product more quickly, in order that new and improved replacement products can be introduced from the firm's portfolio.

Similarly, the price may be experimental at the *introduction* stage and wide variations may exist between the product's price and those of its competitors. Price differences may still be significant at the *growth* stage but settling down to a pattern determined by the products seen to be market leaders. Price differences may be minimal at the *maturity* stage with an awakening of price competition in the *decline* stage as firms fight to retain their market share. Profit performance at these stages generally follows this pattern:

introduction stage low profits for the innovating firm because of high development and promotional costs and relatively low sales volume;

growth stage usually the stage of peak profits for the innovators despite the emergence of price competition from new entrants; unit costs of production falling and rapid increase in sales volume;

maturity stage profits begin to decline as the product has reached its mass market and there is fierce price and non-price competition;

decline stage further decline in profits, perhaps leading to the product's abandonment by the innovating firm.

(see Fig. 6.1)

It must also be remembered that although the life cycle concept may be thought of as a statement of general tendency, it is not a fixed and immutable law – the individual organisation does not have to accept the shape of the sales and profit curves in Fig. 6.1.

Imagine our friends Arnold Ceramics produce a tableware product in a 'true' porcelain body. Such a body composition is capable of a variety of uses – e.g. ceramic insulators, wall and floor tiles, ornamental ware. It is possible that by finding new uses for its porcelain, Arnolds could extend its life cycle as depicted in Fig. 6.2.

Similarly, when sales are declining, management may decide to abandon the product but it also may be able to adopt alternative strategies such as:

1 modification and/or improvement of the product itself;
2 modification and/or improvement of production techniques or marketing strategy;

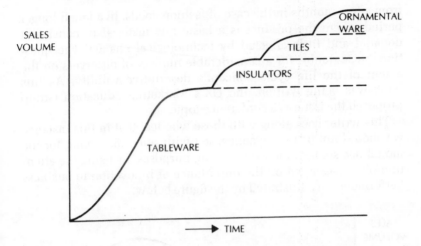

Fig. 6.2   A hypothetical life cycle for Arnolds' 'true' porcelain

3   rationalisation of the range of varieties of the product, if this will reduce costs or improve efficiency (a point to which we shall return later);
4   preservation of profitability during the decline by other cost reductions (e.g. scaling down of promotional support).

With regard to strategy 2 (above) it is interesting to see, from the list of primary causes of product failure set out earlier in this Chapter (p. 183), that far more causes of failure stem from the marketing mix than from the product itself.

Why at the beginning of this Section was mention made of the life cycle concept in terms of historical background? The answer is that, of late, the concept has been assailed for its lack of rigour. If the sales cycle is supposed to follow this generalised 'normal' curve, why is it that well-known brand names in certain product fields appear to sustain long-term growth without diffi-culty? This raises the question of the level at which we are attempting to describe the sales cycle – is it at the level of *product class* (e.g. ceramic tableware)? or *product form* (e.g. teaware)? or at the level of individual brands of teaware? One study,[5] in the ethical pharmaceutical field, suggests that at the brand level bino-mial and polynomial shaped curves are more typically the case than normal curves. Does decline in product class and product form necessarily mean that an otherwise healthy brand should be phased out? What is meant by *time*?... Surely this will vary from a few months in the case of fashion goods, to a much longer period where the product is a basic raw material in consistent demand and little affected by technological change. The questions raise doubts for a considerable number of observers on the extent of the life cycle concept's descriptive validity. As this book was being written, the UK's Marketing Education Group proposed the issue as a conference topic.

This writer goes along with those who feel that in this instance we should not be overly concerned with scientific rigour, for the model has some value for planning purposes, focusing the attention of management on the importance of innovation to business performance, as illustrated by the figure below.

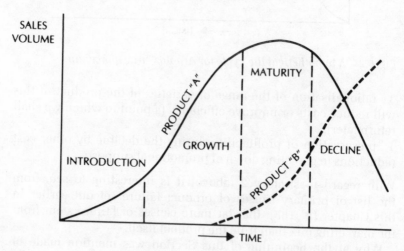

Fig. 6.3   *The product life cycle as an aid to planning*

Innovation: the creation of product ideas

Mention of innovation poses the question 'is it really necessary'? What is the justification for all the effort and expense? We need look no further than *information technology* if we are seeking an example of why organisations must 'innovate or perish'. Consider the influence of information technology on:

shops   with stock checking through point-of-sale terminals and hand-held terminals; lasers scanning bar codings and shoppers purchasing goods by means of magnetic cards;

schools   with computerised systems helping music educa-
             tion; microelectronics meeting the learning needs of
             retarded children; animated displays helping pupils
             with reading problems; the development of 'talking
             books' to help dyslexic children;

home   with video games; video telephones; cable television;
             personal home computers; control of television by
             the human voice (ideal for disabled people); automa-
             tic control of temperature and lighting;

workplace   with computerised typesetting; word processing;
             electronic message systems; teleconferencing sys-
             tems; automatic display and draughting systems;
             and the computerised co-ordination of 'families' of
             machine tools and robots.

It takes little imagination to conceive the vast changes being
fashioned in the markets for hundreds of products as a result
of information technology. And, moreover, just as technology
changes, people change too. In economies such as our own,
increasing purchasing power and an abundance of products means
more discriminating consumers since most people have long ful-
filled their basic wants. As Thorstein Veblen has suggested, it
is at this point that many have passed through their period of
conspicuous consumption to a phase of conspicuous undercon-
sumption where, in a condition of market satiation, they are more
critical of fads and fashions and more searching in their appraisal
of new products. It is now more than twenty years since Cyert
and March[6] in outlining their 'behavioural theory of the firm'
stated that the firm must be 'adaptively rational' in order to
respond to the internal and external constraints acting upon it.

Since that time, the external environment has quickened even
further the pace of its change. So the case for innovation brooks
no argument – as someone has said, operating an organisation
is like riding a bicycle – you either keep moving or fall down!

We have considered just two examples of the pressures to innovate. Changes in tastes and fashions, dramatic changes in raw
materials, energy and labour costs, the activity of competitors
and political changes giving rise to effects on taxation or imports
are other examples. So the individual organisation must be resilient and the first test of its resilience is its capacity to generate
new product ideas. Important sources here are:

- the organisation's own research and development efforts, par-

ticularly in technical, engineering and design research;
- marketing research sources, including ideas from consumer groups and distributors and the scrutiny of publications, market reports etc;
- the establishment of creative thinking and brainstorming groups which go beyond the inhibiting rules and patterns of analytical thinking and encourage participants to range far and wide in their mental approaches to problem solving and the generation of ideas; use being made here of *lateral thinking* and *synectics*;
- the examination of competitive products and other products from national and international sources, the question here being 'is there a better way of producing or marketing this product?'

Other important sources include *technology and product licensing* which can provide a significant source of new products and is an effective way of maintaining technological parity without heavy increases in research and development expenditures. *User complaints*, strange as it may seem, can also assist innovation. The marketing oriented organisation would not, in any event, shy away from complaints but turning them to positive objectives may well be a new idea for many. A study quoted by Adamson[7] in the National Consumer Council's booklet mentioned in the references section, suggests that a well organised department for handling complaints can attain an annual return on capital invested of more than 10 per cent.

No source of new product ideas should be discounted, for no organisation can have too many, particularly when the decay-curve of new product ideas is borne in mind. Boone and Kurtz,[8] for example, quote one survey which established that, following tests for commercialisation and other screening devices, of 58 ideas, less than two per cent resulted in successful products.

Mention of 'new' products again gives pause for thought. 'New' may mean truly unique – a product such as a power-belt that we could strap to our bodies and which would move us through the air to wherever we wanted to travel. In this sense, the motor car, the aeroplane and the computer were, at the initial stage, new products. Most new products are, however, developments or modifications of existing products and are usually the result of technological or market-derived improvements. Thus new products can be produced from modifications to the ingredients, durability, shape, size, weight, performance etc of existing products. Similarly, changes can be made to warranties, after-sales service, packaging, advertising etc and again we may be justified in talking of a 'new' product – but one point deserves special emphasis here – the *degree of success* of the 'new' product, whether it is intrinsically new or whether it is a product modification, will depend upon the degree to which real benefits for the user are produced. This cardinal principle was demonstrated by Project Sapho, a major study conducted at Sussex University, and any innovating organisation must keep the principle constantly to the forefront.

Talking of innovation also brings to mind the admonition contained in the ACARD (Advisory Committee on Applied Research and Development) report on 'Industrial Innovation'[9] which argued that poor performance in innovation was one of the key reasons for Britain's industrial decline. In this context innovation must be distinguished from invention. A naturally inventive nation, Britain is a world leader in this regard, being one of the few net exporters of patents and licences. Innovation is not the same thing, for it follows invention and is concerned with the introduction of the newly created idea to the market. The ACARD report suggested that Britain is 'woefully lacking in the marketing skills essential for successful innovation'. There are two important phases in the process of innovation:

1 the creation of a stock of creative ideas for product or process development or improvement;
2 the rigorous 'screening' and careful evaluation and selection of these ideas.

Some thoughts on point 1 have been given earlier in this Chapter. The second point will be developed in later pages.

A final observation; the organisational 'atmosphere' is crucial to successful innovation. Management should operate an 'open society' in which ideas from everyone – production workers, research personnel, salesmen etc – are welcome. Resistance to change is a powerful block to organisational progress. Change is often construed as a threat to status, job security, devaluation of a committed capital investment and so on. If the importance of the market is constantly emphasised, this will assist in the removal of barriers to change. In this regard, marketing executives can be powerful change-agents.

Planned obsolescence

So called 'marketing' activities sometimes generate ill-will through what is known as planned obsolescence. The layman, urged on by crusading journalists, takes this to mean marginal changes to the style and outline features of a product which yield no improvement or additional benefits but only serve to render last year's model out of date. The charge laid at the organisation's door, particularly in the consumer durables market, is that the addition of mere fripperies, usually termed 'style changes', are really part of a plan to artificially induce an early replacement market so as to increase profits.

The moral of the story is that the organisation should ask itself 'is this really new?' 'New' is an overworked word in advertising and is used to propagate the idea of 'new exciting ingredients', 'breakthroughs' and 'startling discoveries' which yield nothing of lasting benefit to the user and debase promotional messages for nothing more than the ceaseless exploitation of a hollow brightness.

The organisation which genuinely believes in the marketing approach will use the word 'new' when it has something genui-nely new to announce – a technological improvement, a new safety feature, a new process which, hopefully, makes for more economical use of scarce, not to say finite, raw materials, energy and other resources.

The diffusion of innovations

A consideration that is economically significant for the introduc-tion of new products is knowledge of the diffusion process. Seg-mentation studies demonstrate that locating first buyers of new products – the 'experimentalists' or 'early adopters' can be a rew-arding process. This is not necessarily an easy process for although some general characteristics are pertinent – early adopters tend to be young, affluent, of high social status, of higher job and geo-graphical mobility than other groups, nevertheless early adopters of one product or service are not necessarily early adopters of other products or services. However, investigations by Everett Rogers[10] and others have resulted in the identification of five categories of purchasers categorised by *relative time of adoption*:

- innovators ($2\frac{1}{2}$ per cent)
- early adopters ($13\frac{1}{2}$ per cent)
- early majority (34 per cent)
- late majority (34 per cent)
- laggards (16 per cent)

The adoption of a product or service by the 'first purchasers' can be a useful guide to its eventual success, the more so since this sub-population often acts as the opinion leader for other groups, who seek its advice and are influenced by its attitudes. The organisation has to bear in mind that the chances of adoption increase in proportion to the benefits provided by the new product or service – the greater the benefit (economy, improved performance, ease of use etc) the faster the rate of adoption. The product or service must also be compatible with the values and expectations of the first purchasing group. The simpler the product and the easier the benefits are communicable or observable, the faster the adoption rate. Baker[11] points out the value of applying this concept to the marketing of *industrial* products. He suggests that while many innovating organisations concentrate their efforts on the market leaders, their purposes might be better served by identifying the early industrial buyers and concentrating initial sales efforts on these.

Brand names and trade marks

Branding, in its original sense, was the burning of a mark into the flesh of a person or animal with a hot iron. As we saw in Chapter 1 from the days of the winning of the wild frontier 'branding' has passed into the American vocabulary of marketing and has since become generally adopted wherever marketing is practised. Two important connotations arise from the term brand:

1   *identity*   the slave, the thief, the army deserter was branded to identify him; and

2   *ownership*   cattle were branded so as signify that they belonged to a specific ranch.

Today, branding is employed for less gruesome purposes but the connotations of *identity* and *ownership* still apply. An organisation brands its product or service by using a name, term, stylised form of lettering, symbol, picture or some combination of these in order to identify its product or service and to establish its ownership. With regard to ownership, when the brand is listed in a register maintained by the UK's Comptroller-General of Patents, Design and Trade Marks, this 'registration gives the proprietor the exclusive right to the use of the trade mark in connection with the goods in respect of which it is registered, and any invasion of this, as by another using a mark the same or so similar as to be likely to confuse, is an infringement, actionable for an injunction, damages, or an account of profits'.[12] Thus we can see that the term *trademark* is, in essence, a legal term and denotes a brand which, through registration, has been given legal protection. Unregistered brands, if and where they exist, are not protected against infringement although an action for 'passing off' is available to the injured party. To complete this introduction to the terminology, the brand name consists of that part of the brand or trade mark – be it words, letters and/or numbers – that can be vocalised. Thus the brand of a particular type of gravy powder incorporates a name and a symbol – a picture of two children delighted by the gravy's aroma. The brand name is 'Bisto'.

The organisation which brands its output is committed to promoting the brand(s) and to maintaining the quality of the product or service in question. A manufacturer would set out, usually through the cumulative, repetitive force of advertising, to establish the identity of his brand in the mind of the user who, finding that the product is all that was claimed for it, maintains a loyalty to that brand so preferring it that it is insisted upon in preference to all others. Product quality is fundamental to *brand loyalty* for the advertiser has identified his product and if the user is subsequently disappointed then it is the brand owner's sales, not competitors', which suffer. In a market which is not characterised by brand loyalty, there is usually a significant level of *brand switching*.

The tactics of branding vary. An organisation may market its products or services using one brand name – examples here are 'Hertz' and 'Avis', in the car rentals field and 'Heinz' in foodstuffs. This is known as *multiproduct branding* and using the name of the organisation itself supplies the brand identification. Linked to the family brand, there is usually identification for the particular product; thus we speak of the Ford 'Escort' and the Datsun 'Cherry'. Under the 'Kellogg' and 'Cadbury' family names there are subordinate identities for a host of individual products. In contrast to multiproduct branding, is the approach in which the organisation markets a number of products each with their own individual brand. Here, the brand and not the organisation is emphasised in promotion – as with 'Bisto' and the many other brands emanating from RHM Foods Ltd, and 'Tide' and the many other detergents marketed by Procter and Gamble, the approach being one of *multibrand products*.

The characteristics of good brand names would merit a Chapter on its own. Suffice it to say that 'distinctiveness' is the primary requirement, not only from a commercial standpoint (where ease of recognition is a must) but also for legal reasons (this attribute having much to do with suitability for registration). The name must be easy to remember and to pronounce: it makes no sense to spend a deal of promotional money if the consumer is embarrassed or uncertain about how to ask for the product. Where the name can evoke the qualities being claimed for the product or suggest its ease-of-use or whatever, then this is a bonus. 'Ready Brek' and 'Instant Whip' convey the advertiser's message, 'Frigidaire' is an effective name for equipment to refrigerate dairy products, as are 'Electrolux' for high quality electrical products, 'Limmits' for a slimming aid, 'Hardura' for floor coverings and 'Band-Aid' for an adhesive bandage. The ultimate goal of every proprietor might well be for the brand name itself to become so institutionalised that it becomes a substitute word for its action in use – as with 'Hoovering' for the process of vacuum cleaning. The international advertising agency, Saatchi and Saatchi Company plc have demonstrated how effective branding, linked to good products and powerful promotion, can produce successful results over a remarkable span of time (see below).

UK Brand Leader 1933	Position at January 1984
Hovis, Bread	No 1
Stork, Margarine	No 1
Kellogg's, Cornflakes	No 1
Cadbury's, Chocolate	No 1
Rowntree's, Pastilles	No 1
Schweppes, Mixers	No 1
Brooke Bond, Tea	No 1
Colgate, Toothpaste	No 1
Johnson's, Floor Polish	No 1
Kodak, Film	No 1
Ever Ready, Batteries	No 1
Gillette, Razors	No 1
Hoover, Vacuum Cleaners	No 1

'Own-label' products

As we shall see in the next Chapter, the last quarter-century has seen a marked concentration of retailer buying power. Organisations such as Sainsbury's, Tesco, and Marks and Spencer, by imposing a standard assortment of products upon their branch networks and concentrating the buying power of these networks, have been able to secure the fullest discounts from suppliers and pass these on to the consumers in the shape of lower prices – a prime factor underlying their phenomenal growth. It has been a logical step for these organisations then to develop their 'own-label' products. This has enabled manufacturers to obtain the economies of large-scale production without having to bear heavy promotional costs of launching products into mass markets – a daunting expense, particularly for small/medium sized organisations. Larger manufacturers have usually found it possible and profitable not only to adopt a composite strategy of marketing some of their production under their established brands but also to provide for the retailers' 'own-label' market at the same time. A situation has thus emerged where many hundred of manufacturers have been directing some or all of their production to the market under the Woolworth 'Winfield' label, the Marks and Spencer 'St Michael' label, or the family brand of 'Sainsbury', 'Tesco' etc. The initial appeal to the consumer was through lower prices than manufacturers' nationally advertised brands and although the buying public may at first have been circumspect and doubtful about the quality of such products, user experience coupled with market-standing of such organisations as Sainsbury's, Marks and Spencer and others has long since dispelled the doubts and fears.

The Taylor Nelson Group has been monitoring attitudes to brands for over 10 years. The writer is indebted to Dr Elizabeth Nelson, the Group's Chairman, for her permission to reproduce some of the research findings here. For example:

1   the image of (manufacturers') national branded products has declined in recent years, whilst confidence in (retailers') own label brands has increased significantly;
2   certain notions held in the early 1970s, e.g. that the AB socioeconomic group, highly rational consumers, were the main own-label customers, were now suspect at best (it was found that all own-label products appealed across the various socio-economic groups, with a bias towards the C_1C_2 groups, if anything);

3   as an extension of 2, the belief that the appeal of own-label is based on lower prices is also suspect, for the Group has emphasised from the beginning the statistical correlation between consumer scepticism (linked to a growing concern about the honesty of big business) and predisposition to buy own-label (in the early 1970s, retailers were not perceived by consumers as 'big business', so much as 'the shop around the corner');

4   it is incorrect to conceive of a total own-label category in which all own-labels are alike, this category differing from the national brand category, for the fact is that some own-labels (e.g. Sainsbury) have increased in favourability while others (e.g. Co-op) have decreased. In the consumer's mind, own-label is more diversified and complex than in the past;

5   that whereas as recently as 1981 shoppers had a much higher acceptance of own-label brands for some product groups (e.g. flour, jam and biscuits) than for other groups (e.g. tea, coffee, cereals) there is an increasing trend towards own-label even for product groups in which acceptance is currently quite low;

6   the Group's research suggests that whilst there is a growing body of consumers who are prepared to pay more for quality products, there appears to be at the same time another body of consumers for whom price is the main, and often the only criterion. The Group therefore asks whether the market is polarising into two types of consumer and whether the manufacturers should address themselves to the former group, which will respond to brands which communicate quality and a 'positioning' strategy which strongly projects an individual brand image. (Despite these comments, the report concedes that the *leading* brands in many markets have maintained their share, as indicated earlier in this Chapter, p. 195).

Generics

A phenomenon of the late 1970s has been that a number of supermarket chains have introduced products with no more than a simple description on their containers of the type of product contained therein. The AC Nielsen Company describes these *generics* as follows:

generic labelled products are distinguishable by their basic and plain packaging. Primary emphasis is given to the contents rather than a distinguishing brand or retail chain name. Fine print, usually at the bottom or on the back of the pack, identifies the distributor and gives any legally required information[13].

By means of the *Nielsen Store Observation Service* it surveyed the location of generic labelled products within retail stores and also examined the price differentials between generic, own-label and major branded items. Such product groups as washing-up liquid, vegetable oils, canned dog food and cat food, marmalade, tea bags and instant coffee were among the total of 15 groups surveyed. Neilsen state that in Great Britain, whilst the main characteristic of generics – emphasis on contents – still holds good, the range of generics on offer is principally identifiable by store group; the yellow packaging of the Fine Fare range, for example. The survey was conducted within five store groups: Carrefour, Fine Fare, International, Presto and Tesco. Its findings were:

1   there were diverse policies on location within the store – whereas in some groups (Carrefour, International) the generics were grouped with similar branded products all round the store, in others (Fine Fare) generic labelled products were placed in separate 'generic only' areas, as well as with product groups;
2   price levels for generics are some 40 per cent below brand leaders and approximately 20 per cent below own-label.

Quoting from their own recent study in the United States, the Nielsen Organisation adds that in 1978–79, the initial growth in generics was at the expense of the own-label sector, whereas in 1980–81 the continued growth came proportionately from branded products and own-label. With regard to Great Britain, AC Nielsen conclude that it is unlikely that generics will have any effect on market size and that they will most probably expand at the expense of both branded and own-label products.

Packaging, labelling

Packaging is the term applied to the immediate outer container of the product and packages come in a variety of materials, sizes and forms – jars, bottles, boxes, tubes, cans, drums etc and the product within has often been pre-measured, pre-sorted or pre-weighed by mechanical means, as the final stage in a mass production process.

It is clear that the package has basic utilitarian functions to perform – protection of the contents against breakage, corrosion, leakage, dampness and other climatic or atmospheric hazards. Allied to this the package must be easy for the user to handle, open, close, store, dispense from and dispose of. Distributors must find it easy to stock and display as well as economical of space if it is to be acceptable to them. Other functional aspects that add to the package's effectiveness are that it should be of appropriate weight and shape for it to be carried and, if possible, should allow the contents to be seen. There is a supplementary bonus to the consumer if the package can be re-used in some way, e.g. as a storage jar, and an equal bonus to the manufacturer whose advertising message is seen for as long as the package is being re-used.

In addition to the many utilitarian functions of packaging, some of which have just been described, packaging is a marketing tool. In this context, the 'good' package can make a substantial contribution to sales appeal and sales volume – the 'bad' package militates against them. There are at least three aspects to the marketing role of packaging:

1 the necessity for the package to *identify the product* so precisely and unmistakably that competitive products cannot be substituted for it;
2 the requirement that the package, through its shape, size, colour, materials, design etc projects powerfully the *product image* the supplier is trying to convey – whether this be beauty, quality, economy, dignity, happiness, or some combination of these or other product attributes (this aspect requires the package to be carefully co-ordinated with the supplier's advertising);
3 the importance of the function of the package as a *silent salesman*, particularly where the method of retailing is self-service or self-selection – here the designer of the package must take note of the visual effect produced en masse by the shelf displays of the product itself and also its visibility and impact in relation to that of competitors' packaging.

Perhaps no other area of marketing has come in for such criticism as packaging. Typical criticisms have been that it uses up far too big a proportion of our scarce resources; that often the amount spent on packaging exceeds the intrinsic value of the product itself; that packaging can be used to deceive the customer, suggesting that far greater amounts of the contents are contained in the package than subsequently proves to be the case;

that some types of packaging can be dangerous (e.g. aerosol cans) and an environmental hazard (e.g. the plastic detergent bottle that cannot be recycled).

The answer to these criticisms is that notwithstanding the legitimacy of the outcry against such excesses, marketing in its correct and best sense, puts consumer interests to the forefront and is not a mechanism for deceit. But there is a moral tale here for marketing organisations, which is to maintain a sense of balance on expenditures whilst not neglecting the necessary importance of the several functions of packaging within the marketing campaigns. Two anecdotes might usefully serve to illustrate the importance of packaging. The first concerns the Marks and Spencer organisation which is nothing if not user-oriented. Its entry into the quality food market has been distinctly successful. Typical of the care it takes on the customer's behalf relates to the packaging of a cream meringue which retailed in 1983 at 17 pence. The package, in clear plastic, incorporated shoulders to hold the meringue in place so that even if the package was turned over, the cream of the meringue would not smudge the lid.

The second story is based on the author's own experience. Some years ago, whilst conducting a survey into the actual and potential role of the applied psychologist in marketing and marketing research, he visited the marketing services department of a large manufacturer of packages and packaging material. The organisation had an interested, supportive attitude to psychology and psychologists and had, in fact, recently asked consultant psychologists to appraise those research techniques which could assist in optimising the performance of packaging on many dimensions: functional, visual, aesthetic, psychological, informative and communicative. Their report contained detailed information on:

the properties of stimuli individuals attend to, and methods of measuring these; the functional, perceptual and emotional aspects of packaging and their influence on attitudes; the ergonomic aspects of package design, including the use of the hands and the strength of forces required to lift, open and close packages in terms of turning moments, leverages etc, the psychological factors underlying the functional aspects of packaging; aesthetic, cultural and product-linked factors in design; an appraisal of appropriate research techniques (including projective techniques, use of the tachistoscope and discrimination testing).

The author retains the clear impression he gained during that visit which was that while some past criticism of packaging activities may have been justified, a great deal of it was inaccurate and unjustified. Packaging is an important process from which the user can derive great benefits and sound marketing practice must devote the proper, high level of attention to it.

Labelling

Perhaps the word 'label' is now a little out-of-date for the stick-on type label is now frequently incorporated into the package design, particularly so on plastic containers. The label is that part of the package providing details of the brand name, manufacturer's name and address, size of the product and where appropriate, details of the product's composition and instructions for its use. Where the product is perishable, date stamping is also frequently incorporated within the label: the 'use before (date)' panel.

The design of the label must be fully in phase with the desired image of the product; in fact, it is the part of the package which carries the whole of the identification/promotion functions described earlier in the Chapter. The marketing organisation must also keep in mind the legal requirements relating to the contents of the label. In the UK, the Trade Descriptions Acts of 1968 and 1972 (concerning false trade descriptions), the Weights and Measures Acts of 1963 and 1979 and the Price Marking (Bargain Offers) Order of 1979 are some of the relevant statutes.

Note. The design of packaging for overseas markets poses additional problems. The topic is further dealt with in Chapter 13.

Product planning and management

New product development

The case for new product ideas having been made, it might be helpful to describe some techniques which can be applied to the genesis of new products.

In Chapter 5, mention was made of Osgood's semantic differential scales. Though the technique has met with criticism, it has nevertheless proved popular with and been widely used by the marketing fraternity. Osgood developed the technique in order to investigate the meaning certain concepts had for people ('coloured people', 'the American nation' etc). The figure below depicts its use for the image testing of newspapers and shows two competitive papers (A and B) compared (for the relevant group of users) with an 'ideal' paper (C).

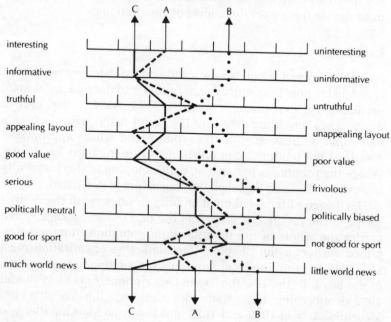

Fig. 6.4 *Product images of newspapers using the semantic differential technique*

Its popularity as a technique stems from its speed in administration. It is a standardised method for identifying the multiplicity of factors which make up the brand image; it is easily repeatable and it avoids stereotyped responses whilst providing a comprehensive picture of the image of the brand. It has also been used to test the company image, the advertising image and the profile of the consumers of the product group. In most marketing research, five point rather than seven point scales are used, being easier for both interviewer and respondent and presumably sacrificing little in the way of validity. Careful induction of interviewers on the use of the scales is important as are the phrases or adjectives used to define the ends of the scales – these are usually derived from qualitative research (using the Kelly repertory grid technique, see below, for example). As can be deduced from the profiles shown in Fig. 6.4 the semantic differential can assist product modifications (through attention to weak points in the individual brand's profile) and product development (e.g. the introduction of a newspaper proximate to the ideal profile). Whilst it might be thought that respondents would use the extreme points of favourable attributes in order to describe their ideal brand, according to Mindak[14] this is not really the case in practice.

Because it is dangerous in attitude research for the researcher to assume that he knows what attributes are relevant and how best to express them, unstructured exploratory interviews in such research have more recently been supplemented by such techniques as the repertory grid. Strictly, it is much more than a technique and historically it emerged as a testing procedure attached to a highly developed and formal theoretical framework called *personal construct theory* which was published by an American psychologist, G. A. Kelly. Since Kelly's personal construct theory is a statement containing a fundamental postulate and eleven corollaries, there is not the space to discuss it here. Let us just say that Kelly's actual definition of a construct is as follows:

a construct is a way in which two things are alike and by the same token different from a third.

This has led to the 'triads' technique which is used in a highly structured test situation and employs a strict stimulus-response procedure. Staying with the example of newspapers, the 'brand names' (of newspapers) are presented to respondents in sets of three with the question: 'in what important way are any two of these alike and in that way different from the third?' Mention has been made of the approach in relation to the semantic differential, and it could also be used in a *gap analysis* approach. The grid could be used on a sample of readers to establish the 'dimensions' of the product. The attributes thus evolved would undergo factor analysis and then be matched against existing, new or even imaginary ('ideal') newspapers by means of a brand/attitude survey. The information which emerged could then be used to construct a multi-dimensional model which related both attributes and brands. To take a simple example, a three-dimensional version in the newspaper field might appear as depicted in Fig. 6.5.

Note. The attributes in the model are merely for the purposes of illustration and are purely speculative. The writer has no particular grounds for believing that they are important, or even relevant, as characteristics which satisfy reader requirements.

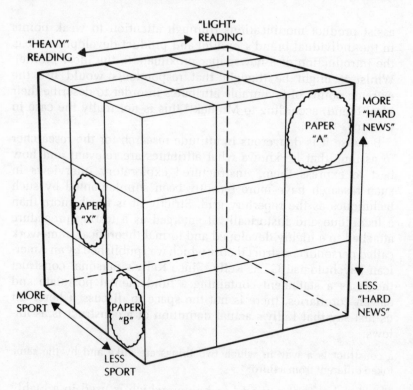

Fig. 6.5   Gap analysis: newspapers

Paper A which has a great deal of light reading, quite a lot of 'hard news' and relatively little sport in its editorial make-up has quite a considerable market, according to sales figures. This is also true of paper B, which has an editorial policy slanted to 'heavy' reading, although not so much 'hard news' (as distinct from news comment) and not very much sport. Meanwhile, there appears to be a market for paper X, a 'heavy', with not so much hard news as paper A, but with rather more sport than either paper A or paper B.

Such an approach can be very useful for charting attitudinal constructs. Finding market gaps by such a method could be helpful both for *testing* new product ideas and for *generating* new product ideas in areas of unfulfilled needs.

Value analysis and engineering

Value analysis is a technique which applies the approaches of method study to the design of products. Value analysis, as a technique, scrutinises all the elements of cost of an existing product in order to determine:

1   whether elements of cost can be reduced, or eliminated, without impairment of functional and quality requirements;
or
2   whether functional and quality requirements can be improved at the existing level of costs.

When this comparison of costs with functions is applied to new products in the development or prototype stage, the technique is referred to as value engineering.

It might be thought a somewhat superfluous technique since the value/cost quotient is something to which designers should pay close attention anyway but, according to its originator, Lawrence D. Miles, reductions of 15 per cent to 25 per cent in manufacturing costs have quite commonly been achieved as a result of the application of value analysis. Its success rate is such that it is obligatory for many government contracts, particularly in the United States. It has also to be remembered that the constant development of new materials and new processes of production provide an opportunity for the application of value analysis, even when the cost/value quotient has been rigorously attended to in the original design.

The incorporation of a supplier's technical representative within a team drawn from the cost accounting, production, design and purchasing functions of a customer organisation enables the supplier's representative to act virtually as an assistant buyer for the customer, thereby strengthening the possibility of obtaining business. Value analysis can thus be a powerful tool for the salesman.

Not surprisingly, a procedure which objectively examines the function of products, materials, components, sub-assemblies, etc, considers their cost, derives alternatives and evaluates these will have its greatest application in the mass production process of standardised items so that a fractional saving per unit of production may result in very large total savings. The approach can be used for industrial and consumer products. In the industrial field, for example, an organisation supplying Arnold Ceramics with production or drying equipment might, through the application of value engineering, devise a product with an increased life-span, or which minimises energy costs in use. In the consumer goods field, an organisation might produce a consumer durable with brazed, rather than soldered assemblies, thereby reducing the price to the consumer whilst maintaining performance standards. Where a supplier is examining the existing products or processes of a potential customer and proposes an important development, then this for the supplier will be a new product though it arises from the context of the client's existing production. Perhaps it is for this reason that some authorities use the terms value analysis and value engineering interchangeably whereas others have differentiated between them.

Systematic new product planning

Earlier in this Chapter, the point was made that the failure rate for new products could be considerably reduced if organisations took practical steps to systematise their new product planning. New product development should follow this planning sequence:

1 the generation of new ideas;
2 the screening of those ideas;
3 an analysis of shortlisted ideas for their technical and economic feasibility;
4 market analysis (and possibly test marketing);
5 further product/marketing modifications, as necessary;
6 market introduction (full scale);
7 monitoring and evaluation of marketing performance.

Lengthy and detailed tomes have been written about the process, frequently accompanied by models of immense elaboration. The reader wishing to acquire expertise in this regard has a rich variety of sources and should not exclude an examination of such techniques as PERT (Programme Evaluation and Review Technique) and CPA (Critical Path Analysis) from his review. This volume can only provide a brief treatment of a detailed field, but the author suggests that the seven stages listed above contain the heart of the matter. We now consider each of these stages in their turn.

1 *Generation of new product ideas.* A number of important sources are listed earlier in this Chapter (pp. 189–190).

2 *Screening of new product ideas.* There are at least two factors of importance here:

(a) *compatibility of the idea with organisational objectives* e.g. growth and return-on-investment targets (*Note:* only considered in broad terms at this stage), and non-profit objectives (e.g. market and organisational 'image', environmental considerations)

(b) *compatibility of the idea with user needs, wants, preferences etc* here, very often, techniques of *concept testing* are employed in which users have the idea explained to them by means of pictures, drawings, mock-up samples, 'concept boards', models or photographs (particularly for consumer durables). The reactions of individual users and/or discussion groups will identify those ideas worthy of further study.

3 *Technical and economic feasibility.* Typical considerations are:

(a) *technical:* is the idea compatible with existing technical expertise? with existing skills of workers? if not, what training is necessary? are the necessary raw materials available? if imports are required, are they available? is the necessary manufacturing equipment available? if imported machinery is required, is the supply position feasible? is the technology available to develop the product?

(b) *economic:* what investment (if any) will be required in equipment/technology/training? what are the likely fixed and variable costs of production? what appears to be the unit price of the product from this pattern of costs? how does this price relate to competitive prices? would the suggested unit price be satisfactory to the user for the specification offered? what is the likely demand for the product at the tentative price? (here, perhaps with the use of mathematical models, a number of price:volume studies may be conducted); what contributions to organisational growth and profit targets emanate from the suggested price/volume relationships?

In addition to these questions there may well be legal issues to consider including patent and trade mark registration; and legislative requirements on health and safety, the product formulation, additives etc.

The answers to the questions under these headings will determine whether it is worth proceeding with the development of prototype products and perhaps small-batch production so that more formal marketing research can be conducted at the next stage.

4   *Marketing analysis/test marketing.* Distribution through selected outlets (perhaps utilising the computer models of key distributors) or limited area 'try-outs' (test marketing) may be appropriate here. The objective at this stage is to obtain a detailed quantitative assessment of user acceptability and potential return-on-investment of the proposed new product. The product and the marketing strategy, i.e. all the elements in the marketing mix, are now under examination. Where these variables are being tested, the 'paired comparison' approach may be appropriate (e.g. price may be varied in two identical test markets with all other factors held constant). When test-marketing is employed the time to conduct the test and the technological uniqueness of the product must have been previously considered, in case competitors, having notice of the new product, quickly duplicate it and move to full-scale marketing before the originator does.

5   *Product/marketing review.* The design and technical/economic elements of the proposed product and the marketing strategy are then reviewed in the light of what has been learned at Stage 4. The feasibility of the entire plan is considered and the necessary changes are made to the product and/or to marketing and production planning if the marketing analysis at Stage 4 points to the necessity for this. At this point, the final decision is made on whether to market the product on a commercial scale.

6   *Commercialisation.* The full-scale marketing programme is put into effect.

7   *Monitoring and evaluation.* The 'performance' of the product and the entire marketing programme are continuously monitored and adjusted where necessary and if possible. It is only at this stage that the ultimate future of the product and its contribution to organisational objectives can be assessed. Where an investment budget procedure has been adopted (i.e. a disproportionately high early promotional expenditure is undertaken in order to launch the product) this will be carefully monitored. Consequential

adjustments to the marketing strategy may also be called for as a result of the reactions of competitors.

> An approach such as that outlined above will better assist the organisation to develop and market products for which there is adequate demand; which are environmentally, legally and socially acceptable; which are in phase with the organisation's production, financial, marketing and management capabilities; which coalesce with the organisation's image and fulfil its objectives.

Product strategy and management

New products are part of what is termed the organisation's *product mix*, which is the full range of products offered for sale. The product mix has two dimensions – breadth and depth. Arnold Ceramics, for example, might decide to produce a range of teaware as well as dinnerware, and to add to this ornamental ware (e.g. vases, figurines, jardinières) and perhaps advertising ware (i.e. ware bought by breweries and other firms – jugs, coasters, whisky barrels – for sales promotion purposes). Such decisions relate to the breadth of its product mix – to the number of product lines carried.

Within each of these product lines, decisions have to be made upon the assortments offered, e.g. how many shapes of dinnerware? how many styles of decoration within each shape, e.g. under-glaze and on-glaze, lithographs, band and line etc? how many colours/designs within each style of decoration? The decisions to be made here relate to the depth of the product mix.

Product strategy in its primary aspect has to do with the breadth and depth of the product mix. Other strategic decisions may be called for on whether to expand the product mix (as witness the multiple organisations traditionally retailing clothing, e.g. Marks and Spencer, British Home Stores, which have now added food, books, house-plants etc to their 'mix'). The strategy of *product positioning* frequently calls for a deal of management attention. Typical questions are: how shall we market this product in relation to (1) competition? (2) other products in our own range? A shoe manufacturer may have to decide whether to move into synthetic materials in order to compete with low-priced foreign imports or whether to position his output away from this type of competition, utilise only the best quality leathers and develop a reputation for high quality and good design through a related emphasis on styling and presentation.

The issue of product positioning is very often connected with such longer-term considerations as whether to *trade up* or *trade down*. Profit and non-profit objectives often figure in the decisions here. In an attempt to differentiate itself from competition, a manufacturer of photocopying equipment may add small low-priced copiers to its range with the ultimate objective of trading away from competitors and specialising in the lower priced corner of the market where, it is considered, the organisation is better placed to counter competition. This is a trading down strategy based on profit objectives. A supplier of medium-priced watches may decide to add high-priced, precision watches to his range in the ultimate hope of developing an institutional image of high quality. This is a trading-up policy and stems from a mixture of profit and non-profit objectives, no doubt.

Managements frequently have to face decisions on whether to rationalise the product mix. There is an insistent pressure for the product range to expand; the tendency is almost as concrete as a law of the physical sciences! The firm sees the opportunity for increased sales by producing accessories to the main product. Sales representatives and distributors encourage production in 'another size', 'another colour' or 'another material'. Often this is all to the good, particularly where fixed costs have been reco-vered and the extra production makes a more than proportionate return on outlay. With dangerous frequency, however, the net result is not to expand sales, so much as to extend a static volume of sales over an increased product mix, with a consequent reduc-tion in the average sales per product. When this happens, costs increase through uneconomical production runs, and possibly split deliveries, as the firm attempts to cope with 'out-of-stock' situations which result from too large a product mix for current production capacity.

When this occurs a situation may be disclosed where a large proportion of the firm's output is responsible for a small propor-tion of sales or profits or both, whilst a relatively small proportion of output is responsible for most of the sales/profits. The shorth-and notation for this condition is known as the '80/20 rule' (because 20 per cent of the mix may be bringing in 80 per cent of the sales volume/profits and vice versa). When this happens management may adopt a rationalisation strategy, dispensing with the unprofitable products and marketing a 'leaner' but more effective range. It is important to ensure that such a strategy does not justifiably alienate distributors or so alter the distribution of manufacturing overheads that hitherto profitable products now become unprofitable. Also, arrangements may well be made to sub-contract either the marketing or the production of the products contributing to the flatulence of the product mix. This enables the organisation to continue to offer the less profitable products but to improve their profitability by decentralising their production or marketing.

Another way of analysing product strategy is to examine the *product-market* relationship. Some organisations produce a single product and market it to all customers with a single marketing mix. This *undifferentiated marketing* approach typically utilises mass distribution and mass advertising with a broad, general promotional appeal. Whilst it might be difficult to find many examples today, the approach was very popular in the early days of mass production (as with Henry Ford's Model 'T' motor car). A differentiated marketing approach is one in which a number of products are marketed by the same firm, each one being directed to its individual segment of the market and utilising its own particular marketing mix. A *concentrated marketing* approach is one in which the organisation's total marketing activity is focussed upon a single segment of the market.

Finally, mention must be made of the distinction between *product development* and *market development*, since both strategies might usefully be pursued in the search for growth. Consider the manufacturer of electrical porcelain products; the insulators, for example, that are used by the electricity supply industry. The search for, and introduction of, new types of porcelain insulator would constitute a strategy of product development. If the manufacturer wished to guard against reliance on the vagaries of a single market, he might pursue a market development strategy. Because of the chemical composition and the heat treatment required by 'true' porcelain products, they are highly resistant to devitrification ('crazing'). Accelerated weather-tests would probably demonstrate the material to be highly suitable for the production of architectural tiles for cladding the exteriors of domestic and commercial buildings. Such a market development strategy would have discovered a new use for the manufacturer's basic product.

The planning of services

As we saw in the last Chapter, economic well-being, rising standards of living and increased leisure time generate a phenomenal growth in the demand for services. *Personal services* (hairdressing, tailoring, counselling), *professional services* (legal, commercial, medical), *general services* (entertainment, sport, information), *business services* (transport, cleaning, consultancy) etc, all benefit from this rapid increase in demand. If the suppliers of services are to trade profitably and to withstand the competition that buoyant markets inevitably attract, then their need for market analysis is just as pronounced as if they were selling a product. They have to understand how trends in population and income affect the need for their services, what particular market segments they can best cultivate, what user needs and expectations they should aim to satisfy, the price/value dimension typically employed by consumers and the co-ordinates of buying behaviour including personality factors, peer group influences or whatever.

Moreover, the development of new services and the improvement of existing services, in the user's terms, is as salient to success with services as it is with products. The service organisation must decide upon the characteristics of the services to be offered, the width and depth of the services mix, the positioning of the individual service in relation to competition and to other services in the total services mix and, not least, what support the service will be given (e.g. by advertising, branding, warranties etc). The term planning at the head of this Section is used as in *product planning* and perhaps the most interesting and lively way the planning of services may be described is to provide a few examples.

Library services

It is interesting that public spending cuts and the depletion of library funding have forced a growing number of Britain's librarians to think carefully about the services they are trying to provide. By 1982, for example, the British Library had funded 25 research projects into the use of data terminals in public libraries. The new technology is developing support for libraries in countless new ways. Businessmen, professional people, local authority executives and elected representives are using and supporting data services to an increasing degree.

Some radical thinkers in the field do not believe this goes far enough. They believe that the local libraries should be doing more to inform the communities they serve about de-industrialisation, unemployment, social decline and that they should offer community groups adequate facilities (rooms, typewriters, pamphlets) so that re-education can begin.

There is a touching story of a Manchester librarian who noticed that every day at a certain time a group of women assembled at a bus-stop. She invited them into the library to shelter from the rain and discovered that they were all mothers of handicapped children waiting for the bus that returned them from a special school. She offered them a room in the library and volunteered to obtain specialist books for them. The mothers began to use these facilities, set up a self-help group, invited specialist speakers to their sessions and studied the medical tests on the nature of their childrens' handicaps. It is said that these beginnings helped to transform Manchester's policy and provision for mentally handicapped children.

The same librarian, who has now moved on to Derbyshire, has been examining the informational needs of rural areas. The mobile libraries which visit these areas now carry an official from the Social Services department. In addition to being able to obtain books, the relatively isolated users can obtain advice on rates, housing, legal services and similar matters.

This is a striking example of marketing in action. Sometimes the practitioners neither know it nor describe it as marketing, but marketing it is, though it may be termed 'outreach', 'diversification', 'expansion' or 'policy change'.

Education Services

Many readers of this volume will be studying marketing at a College, Polytechnic or University. They have at first hand a striking illustration of how the 'services mix' is being adapted to changing market forces. This is not only to do with the new courses developed for the new technologies, for the unemployed and for the re-training of older workers. With reductions in funding from central and local government many establishments of further and higher education increasingly resort to 'self-help' in order to maintain adequate levels of equipment, consumables, teaching and educational support staff. They are achieving this with a positive, entrepreneurical outlook and a heightened awareness of market forces. Income-earning courses developed for local industry, the Manpower Services Commission, trade associations and the professions are one means by which job security can be safeguarded and depreciating equipment, buildings and other assets can be replaced.

The case study by James E. Lynch[15] which is mentioned in the references at the end of this Chapter provides, as Lynch claims 'a telling practical illustration of how the marketing concept can be applied by a non-profit organisation'.

Hertford College, Oxford is one of the 28 Colleges of that University and is among the smallest, least well-endowed financially with, until recently, a largely undistinguished academic record.

The case study outlines how, with a dispassionate analysis of its own competitive standing, new objectives were devised, new market segments were cultivated, the needs of a potential target market were identified and new policies on student entry were implemented. The result of the strategy has been a marked improvement in the College's reputation and academic standing, both within and beyond the University. The reader would benefit from reading this case-study but, as Lynch points out 'the Principal and Fellows have never consciously considered that what they were doing was "marketing", this is largely a question of semantics – not unlike Molière's Monsieur Jourdain in *Le Bourgeois Gentilhomme*, who was amazed to find that all his life he had been speaking "prose" without realising it'.

Insurance Services

Insurance companies have shown some sensitivity to market needs in the recent past with policies to provide a mixture of types of insurance (accident-fire-life etc. within the one policy) and increased 'accessibility' for the user through the medium of vending machines, department stores and motoring organisations.

Insurance has usually been described in the literature as an 'intangible' but this writer would not agree with this for, like many services (e.g. restaurant services), it is a mixture of a product and a service. The service is the insurance cover provided in return for the premiums paid – the product, which evidences the service (and is therefore an intrinsic part of the service mix), is the policy. It is now evident that the more marketing oriented of the companies recognise that the legal jargon in most policies proves dauntingly impenetrable so that when some clients sign the policy they are not so sure of the benefits to which they are entitled and may even suspect that the forest of 'heretofores' and 'notwithstandings' could well assist the insurer to avoid honouring the policy.

Unintelligible English is now beginning to disappear from policy documents. General Accident was the first UK Company to devise an easily understood policy for motor insurance. With Phoenix Assurance, the same company was a joint first in the introduction of a simple 'home' policy. In October 1982, the General Accident Company launched the country's first plain English life assurance policy. General Accident has aimed at 'a level of understanding that the popular daily newspaper reader would be comfortable with'.[16] The system is based upon the work of American philologist, Dr Rudolph Flesch. Another example of marketing in action!

Travel services

The reader will be aware of the heavy promotional expenditures undertaken by travel agents, and travel companies operating in the holiday/tourism markets. One would like to say that it is all one aspect of practical marketing in its fullest and best sense. However, the brochures produced by a minority of travel organisations do not constitute honest and objective promotional literature based on sensitivity to user needs. They would be better classified as a branch of romantic fiction!

This observation aside, however, there is a great deal of practice in the field which constitutes good marketing. After a family holiday in Switzerland a few years ago, the author received a detailed questionnaire from the travel company involved seeking data on the composition of the family group and reactions to the travel arrangements made in the UK, on the Continent and for the crossing to the Continent. Responses were sought concerning the hotels used en route and in Switzerland, the menus and services provided, the amenities available in the chosen resort. The questionnaire invited suggestions for improvement of the services and there was ample space to add any complaints. The information obtained by the organisation would obviously be of value in the planning and development of its travel services.

Nor is this research-based approach confined to Western countries. The following year, the family holiday was taken in Eastern Europe. The writer was pleasantly surprised to receive at the end of the holiday, a questionnaire from the organisation responsible for the country's tourism. It was designed so as to obtain a great deal of user reaction to the country's hotels, tourist amenities and travel facilities.

Hopefully, enough has been provided here for the reader to deduce how the marketing approach assists the planning of services.

The marketing of ideas

The work of the International Research Institute on Social Change (RISC) has been mentioned in Chapter 5. The Institute has been able to identify a large number of social trends now developing in Europe. The writer is indebted to the UK partner in RISC, the Taylor Nelson Group, for permission to reproduce the Chart on p. 217 which depicts very many of these trends. A report on these trends prepared by Dr Elizabeth Nelson[17] observes that: 'Many of our rigid and rather outdated institutions have failed to respond' to the social dynamic that the countries of Western Europe now share. Dr Nelson points out that the gap between the needs of the citizen and the inability of institutions to respond is especially noticeable in the political sphere. In France, for example, the survey established that the majority of the population were not in favour of their new political system and they expressed considerable misgivings about the future. An extract from the data tables in shown below.

%

I strongly support the new
politics.....................

I envisage a promising future   5.2

I support the new politics....
but I am a bit worried about
the future   24.6

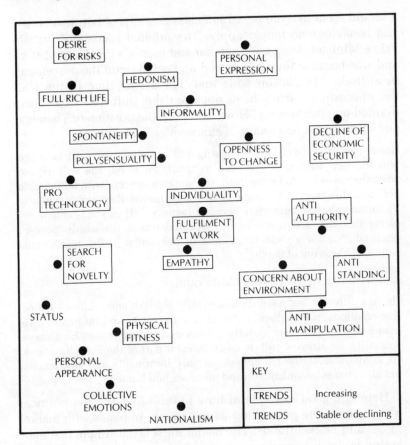

Fig. 6.6 *RISC map of social trends*

I am more in favour of the new politics than I was a year ago: I think things are developing well	5.2
I am in favour of the new politics but I am disappointed with what is happening	22.9
I was reserved about the new politics, now I am quite opposed	11.1
I think with the new politics France is heading for disaster	18.7

It would seem that the post 1945 classifications of political views and behaviour no longer apply. The original success of British Prime Minister, Margaret Thatcher and France's President Mitterand was because they recognised and acted upon the movement in attitudes. Dr Nelson adds that 'For a long time in the UK, the opposition parties have not seen the shift and have been divided on how to react.' Now, however, the position of Thatcher and Mitterand is less secure. Thus, on Mrs Thatcher:

Her appeal is certainly to risk taking and individualism, and here she taps the new values. She is seen to speak her mind, she will expose what she considers to be the truth, she shows a concern with honourable policies. However, in her appeals to status, materialism and apparently Victorian values of aggressive competitiveness... Here she is communicating in outmoded ways. In her repeated use of the words 'power', 'succeed', 'compete', 'efficiency' and in her denial of the autonomous values... she is out of touch.

and with regard to President Mitterand:

He taps different, but nevertheless equally old fashioned values – collective emotions, nationalism, a denial of spontaneity and informality. He comes across as a very orderly person and authoritarian. He stresses solidarity, he stresses culture as an integral part of the French outlook. He conveys austerity. He misses not only informality and spontaneity, but also misses hedonism, fun and pleasure, and humour.

Here is a good example of how ideas – in this case, political ideas – are being propagated which are out of phase with market forces and market trends. The reader must be clear here that marketing is not being advanced as a device to manipulate electorates. What is being clearly implied in Dr Nelson's paper is that leaders must show a proper sensitivity to changes in the views and attitudes of those they seek to govern.

It is not difficult to discern how ideas can be effectively marketed. The reader is invited to try this for himself as a pencil-and-paper exercise. Health care, protection of the environment and other socially-beneficial causes would prove interesting.

Price planning

Introduction: pricing decisions in context

Kotler[18] reminds us that price is the one element of the marketing mix that creates sales revenues and that the other elements (product, place, promotion) are costs. Because it is so important, it might be supposed that marketing executives have become skilled at setting prices, but Kotler says this is not so and lists these common faults:

1   organisations are too inward-looking, concentrating too much on the costing approach to pricing, and paying insufficient attention to the demand function and to the psychology of the buyer;
2   prices are not revised with sufficient frequency to reflect changed conditions in the market place, nor are they varied enough to reflect the differences in product specifications and market segments;
3   prices are often set without regard for the other elements in the marketing mix: because of its place in the marketing strategy pricing must be approached with regard for its influence on product, place and promotion.

Baker[19] expresses his disappointment at the frequent lack of a 'creative pricing policy' which takes account of external as well as internal variables. He writes of rudimentary formulae based on 'rule of thumb' approaches leading to 'mechanical' decisions which overlook the dynamic nature of markets. Such an approach is unlikely to have clear and logical links with overall objectives.

Yet pricing is becoming more not less important, not least because of world-wide inflation and surging raw material costs which have tended to reduce the significance of 'non-price competition' as an approach to strategy.

Good pricing practice will include proper consideration of the following:

1   the cause and effect relationship of prices with other elements in the marketing 'mix';
2   external constraints on prices – including Government economic measures and legislative control (when appropriate) and the reactions of competitors, distributors and suppliers;
3   the influence of price on demand; the elasticity of demand as it influences cost : volume : profit relationships;
4   the relationship of price to the product life cycle;
5   the relationship of price for the individual product to the requirements of the total product portfolio and hence, ultimately, to organisational objectives;
6   the fact that pricing strategy will be at least as much influenced by the market and by competition as by cost;

7 the fact that future trends in costs, demand and competition must be woven into the pricing strategy and the pricing policy must be adapted to changes in market conditions;

8 the aim, wherever possible, to incorporate market research and other management techniques as an aid to pricing.

Price and the marketing mix

With regard to point 1 in the above list, in the early pages of this Chapter reference was made to the *total product concept*. It is manifestly important for the user to understand fully what is being offered in exchange for the price. A product or a service certainly, but frequently there is also a warranty, an installation service, a maintenance service, a commitment to train the customer's staff in the selling or the operation of the product or service. The customer can invariably claim to find a cheaper source of supply, but the question from the supplier must then be 'are you comparing like with like?' Only when the customer is fully informed about the *total product* can he judge the 'price/value' dimension. Price, of itself, cannot be the criterion – 'value for money' is the basis on which judgment should be made. The CBI has recently suggested that if British organisations laid more stress on the total product concept, they would be more successful in export markets (where quality and reliability are often rated more importantly than price).

Earlier, the point was made that products are bought not so much for what they are, but for what they will do. This has more than one dimension. Firstly there are the *physical* attributes – the characteristics (size, colour, weight, design etc), quality, performance standards – and the higher the price the better the possible specification. The product will also possess psychological attributes – images of dignity, exclusivity, durability may be evoked through packaging, branding, presentation, advertising copy, distribution policy – and may be just as important to the buyer as the physical attributes. The *perceived value* approach to pricing emphasises the buyer's perception of value as being more influential than the mere totality of the seller's costs and this perception has psychological as well as physical dimensions.

Finally, the links between price and the elements of place and promotion are evident enough. The higher the price, the greater the opportunity to support distributors – through increased margins, quantity discounts and selling support; the higher the price the greater the possibility of increased budgets for advertising, publicity, sales promotion and salesmen's salaries and commissions.

Price and the organisational image

The individual price decision should be taken with reference to overall objectives. Where the image to be cultivated is one of 'value for money', the emphasis will be on pricing lower than competition. Where a quality image is being cultivated, a high-level pricing approach is usually necessary to cover the costs of the extra research and development that may be required and the costs of high quality raw materials, packaging and presentation and highly skilled labour.

Pricing and external constraints

Organisations are rarely free agents in setting prices. Government policy on prices and incomes (when it is being pursued), on monopolies and mergers and on price-fixing agreements deemed contrary to the public interest, are all important influences on pricing policy. The rise of consumerism and increased government intervention on product performance and product safety frequently act as further influences. Such statutes as the Consumer Credit Act 1974 and the Price Marking (Bargain Offers) Order 1979, are examples of legislative intervention in this field.

Price: demand relationships

On page 222 are two typically downward sloping demand curves. Where a change in price results in a less than proportional change in quantity sold, demand is said to be *inelastic* (Fig. 6.7). Where a change in price results in a more than proportional change in sales volume, demand is said to be *elastic* (Fig. 6.8). Where demand is elastic pricing will be an important area for management decision-making: a great deal of prior thought must be given to price changes. To obtain a foothold in highly competitive markets, an *investment-budget* approach, incorporating low prices, may be

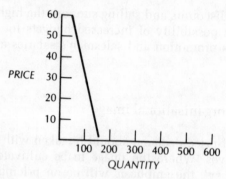

Fig. 6.7 Inelastic demand curve

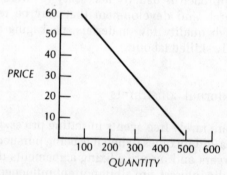

Fig. 6.8 Elastic demand curve

necessary in order to gain a foothold, with prices being revised upwards as (hopefully) brand loyalty develops. Where demand is inelastic, product-differentiation and other forms of non-price competition become more appropriate. Where different, even dissimilar, substitutes can be seen to compete against the product in question (toughened glass, plastics, and even paper, compete with ceramics in the tableware market) there is said to be *cross-elasticity of demand*. Pricing strategy, and competition, must then be considered in the context of total supply to the market and not simply that of an individual industry.

Price and the product life cycle

If the yearly accounts of our friends at Arnold Ceramics were examined, we would see that within the total cost of their operations, various *types* of costs can be discerned. Thus:

- costs of the labour employed in the production process;
- costs of the raw materials 'consumed' in production;
- costs of the fuel used in the kilns to fire (i.e. bake) the table-ware.

Such costs are called *variable costs* because, quite simply, they vary with the volume of output.

We would see that there are other costs that are obviously not directly related to the scale of output – e.g. rent and rates, interest on loans, the cost of buildings and equipment, the cost of insuring these, the cost of administrative, managerial and main-tenance staff. These are described as *fixed costs*; not fixed in amount from period to period but fixed in the sense that Arnolds must provide for them *regardless of the volume of output*. (Note that we talked above of an accounting period of one year – an important point, because in the *long run*, as opposed to the *short run*, all costs will vary with changes in the level of output.)

The price structure for an individual product is the sum of:

the variable costs of its production +
the apportionment of fixed costs +
the 'mark-up', or desired balance over cost

The 'mark-up' need not be rigidly fixed for the entire life cycle of the product. At the introduction stage, *market share* may be preferred to *profitability* and the customary mark-up may be reduced (see p. 228). If the product is well into the maturity stage, the mark-up may be fixed so as to yield the largest balance over cost – a way of financing new products even if it means an earlier demise for the mature product.

Price and the product portfolio

Individual products and services are usually part of a collection of products and services – a product mix or a product range. It follows that the approach to pricing an individual product cannot be taken in isolation – its effect upon or contribution to the overall objectives of the organisation must be assessed. 'The long-term target rate of return-on-investment of x per cent' may be the primary objective. If an examination of the sales: volume: profit performance of the existing portfolio of products shows a number of products operating at or near the *break-even point* (see p. 228) in order to attract sales volume and ensure high-level utilisation of plant capacity then a new product may be deliberately priced so that it becomes a 'high yielder' in return-on-investment. For example, marketing research may demonstrate that at three possible selling prices for a product, e.g. 100, 110 and 120, the respective sales volumes are likely to be 5000; 4800 and 4700 units. The 100 price seems appealing since it generates the highest volume but since there are already enough sales-gathering products in the range then the 120 price would be chosen if an analysis of the fixed and variable costs of producing and selling 4700 indicated the highest level of return-on-investment.

Mention of marketing research leads to the additional point that no matter how sophisticated and experienced the marketing organisation is, no one can really say, short of full-scale marketing, what the exact relationship between price and sales volume is likely to be. Test marketing, if properly conducted, can be of help. Consumer panels and attitude research are also of value, given the same provisos about the quality of research. Techniques of *sensitivity analysis* using computer modelling techniques can also give a guide as to the influence of price changes on volume. The writer has found that canvassing the opinions of distributors and sales personnel can also be helpful. The writer has used the computer analysis of a large retail organisation in order to forecast the likely demand for a new product from that organisation (the model was based on a pilot distribution of a small-batch of production to a pre-determined number of the 'multiple' retailer's branches). By 'grossing up' the volume on the pilot study, the writer was then able to make a quite accurate forecast of the first year's sales from all customers. Managerial judgment is always required, but sound data to inform that judgment should be carefully gathered from whatever source is available.

Pricing strategy and the market

Within the markets for most products and services a single price, or *price-band* (i.e. a narrow range of prices) becomes established in the user's mind as being synonymous with 'value for money'. This price or price-band is often referred to as the price *confi-*

dence-level and the supplier must bear in mind that it may be as fatal to his prospects to be below it as to be above it (users may suspect that a 'low' price indicates a low level of quality). So the supplier must make a dispassionate analysis of the advantages of his own product vis-à-vis competition, his organisational size and power to influence events in the market, the size of the promotional budget for market-entry and any other factors that bear on the situation. The issue for resolution is, should the new supplier be a *price maker* or a *price taker*? To be a price maker one needs to be able to tell a credible story – about a new technological discovery, a new production process (that improves quality, reduces costs etc) – something that will realistically allow for a bold policy of specialisation on price, no matter what the established price situation is. Most products, however, are 'old friends in new forms' and the new supplier to the market has usually to be a price taker – taking the confidence level very much into account. In assessing the organisation's strengths against competition, indirect competition may pose as big a problem as direct competition. Life styles change, as we have seen earlier from the Taylor-Nelson studies. One of that organisation's surveys revealed that the traditional English breakfast is on the decline and that more people are going without breakfast altogether (40 million fewer breakfasts were eaten in 1982 than in 1980). So when the bacon producer is reviewing his pricing strategy he must not only do this with direct competitors in mind but with the realisation that yoghurts, fruit juices or the single piece of toast are now replacing his product in a nation which is becoming increasingly health-conscious but which also seems to have less time for formal meals.

In assessing change and its implications for pricing, due attention must be given to how internal and external factors – costs, competitive activity, user attitudes, the composition of demand – are likely to change over time. Dynamic pricing policies, which adapt to changed conditions, will ensure that the organisation capitalises on market opportunity. Just as the organisation has often to take the long view on prices, as with the investment budget, this thinking may have to be applied to its *production capacity* over the longer term; will it be able to supply the expected volume efficiently, and what are the 'break points' in volume which will necessitate extra plant and equipment or the working of additional shifts and what influence will this have on pricing strategy?

Pricing objectives and pricing policies

Marketing is all to do with attaining objectives. The setting of objectives applies as much to price as it does to the other elements in the marketing mix. We can safely assume that, as a result of translating organisational objectives into marketing objectives, translating these into pricing objectives, there are quite a number of possibilities. Some typical pricing objectives are considered below.

1 *The attainment of a percentage profit on sales, or a target rate of return on investment.* The first of these is a rate of profit and is a function of a number of variables including price, product mix, production costs, marketing and administrative costs and, of course, sales volume. The second (return-on-investment) is the turnover of assets employed or the rate at which each invested £1 is generating sales pounds; it is a calculation based on the assets employed in relation to sales volume during a particular time period. It is the rate of utilisation of assets − plant and equipment, inventories, receivables and cash − and is independent of costs or profit. With a percentage profit on sales of 10 per cent (i.e. profit rate 10 per cent), the return on investment is calculated as follows:

$$\frac{\text{£ net profit}}{\text{£ sales}} \times \frac{\text{£ sales}}{\text{£ investment}} = \frac{\text{£ net profit}}{\text{£ investment (assets employed)}}$$

(rate of profit)   (turnover)   (return-on-investment)

$$\frac{\text{£}100\,000}{\text{£}1\,000\,000} \times \frac{\text{£}1\,000\,000}{\text{£}666\,666} = \frac{\text{£}100\,000}{\text{£}666\,666} = 15\%$$

$$10\% \times \qquad\qquad 1.5 = \qquad\qquad 15\%$$

Thus with a profit rate of 10 per cent and an asset turnover of 1.5 a return on investment of 15 per cent is produced. To improve the return-on-investment the organisation could attempt to increase the profit rate, the turnover rate or both. Any of these moves could well have implications for pricing policy.

2 *Profit maximisation.* In this context, we are discussing the maximisation of long-term profitability rather than short-run pro-

fits. There is, in any case, reducing opportunity to maximise short-run profits these days. The rapid diffusion of technological change, the presence of substitutes for most products, the role of government as watchdog on prices and restrictive practices all make this approach less and less of a prospect. New suppliers are quickly attracted to markets in which good returns are in prospect and where demand temporarily exceeds supply. Even if the product is so startlingly novel it commands a very high introductory price, a number of factors combine to make short-run profit maximisation socially undesirable. Increasingly articulate, well-organised consumer groups and consumer publications are there to remind organisations of this.

The usual approach is to pursue *long-term profitability* and frequently an investment budget policy is the key to this. In launching a new product the organisation may be prepared to budget for financial loss (say in the first year), to subsequently 'break-even' (i.e. to equalise revenue and costs, perhaps in the second year) and to move into profitability at the next stage (e.g. year 3). The budgetted profit in the third year should ideally recoup the loss in the first year and show some balance over total costs for the three-stage period – which is termed the *payback period*. This period can be lengthy in highly competitive markets, hence the need to base pricing policies upon adequate and competent research.

The second point to make is that organisations do not invariably seek profitability for every individual product or service. They may, and often do, regard profit targets as corporate goals in the sense that the *range of products as a whole* should attain the profit targets. This will allow for some products to be offered as *loss-leaders* in order to generate goodwill and, hopefully, sales-support for more significantly profitable products. (Office equipment manufacturers frequently market office machinery at especially 'keen' prices in order to obtain good returns on consumable items – e.g. paper used in photocopiers.)

3 *Equalisation of competition.* In markets for highly standardised products there is often a *price-leader* whom it is impossible to undersell because of the returns to scale such an organisation enjoys. Since there is little opportunity for product differentiation the strategy may be to equalise the prices of the market-leader, around which other supplying firms will also have based their prices. Operating at this confidence-level of prices,

the organisation will then adjust its production and marketing operations so as to obtain the best possible return on its investment.

4 *Maintenance or increase of market share.* Where the market is expanding and the organisation is already earning a reasonable rate of return, the pricing strategy might well be to maintain or to increase market share. Through continuous research services, market share can be monitored quite well, the important factor being the organisation's trend line compared to the trend line of the total market.

Break-even analysis

In utilising the methods of setting prices, marketing practitioners have become well acquainted with the technique of break-even analysis. It is a useful aid in determining the range within which the price of a projected new product would have to fall for its introduction to be financially justified. Let us look at the process in three stages.

We have talked about the nature of fixed and variable costs on p. 223. The reader will remember that while variable costs related directly to the volume of output, fixed costs are those costs that must be provided for regardless of how much is actually produced. Though this is admittedly a short-run tendency, it is conceptually sound enough to use in approaches to pricing.

Arnold Ceramics are considering the introduction of a new 21 piece set of good quality tableware with an attractive floral decoration which will be named 'Diana'. It is oven-proof, microwave proof and has all the other standard hallmarks of good quality. The range of possible prices extends from £45 to £60 per teaset, this being the 'final' price to the user. (i.e. the recommended retail selling price). Arnolds intend to use wholesale organisations as the major marketing channel, but will also supply multiple retail organisations on a direct basis. Allowing for the usual trade discounts, Arnolds price to the trade is 40 per cent of the recommended retail selling price. Preliminary costings indicate that the 'Diana' teaset could be marketed at £50 to the user which would mean an ex-Arnold price of £20 per teaset.

Figure 6.9 is a break-even chart representing the pattern of costs, revenue, profits and losses at this £20 unit price. We see,

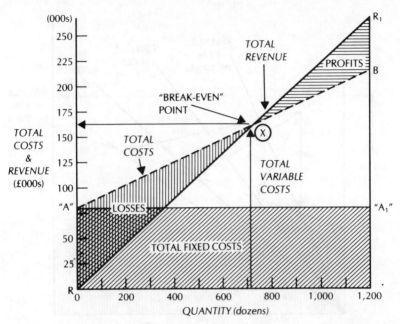

Fig. 6.9   Break-even chart. Ceramic 21-piece teasets at an ex Arnold price of £20 per teaset

for example, that the total fixed costs, represented by line AA₁ are £80 000. (note that whether the output is nil or 1200 dozen teasets, these costs remain the same, hence the line AA₁ is horizontal). Variable costs increase as production gets under way. The line AB illustrates this increase, the total variable costs being represented by the area ABA₁, and total costs by the whole area under the line AB. The trend in total sales revenue is represented by the line RR₁ and where this line intersects line AB is the break-even point (X). The appropriate values for X on the scales are:

Quantity: 720 dozen teasets,
Equalisation of total costs and total revenue at £168 000.

Below a sales turnover of £168 000, Arnolds will be making losses (see area RAX) but will move into profit above this turnover (area XR₁B).

We did say earlier that the confidence-level of prices established in the market for a teaset of the 'Diana' type and quality extended from £45 to £60 per set, at retail.

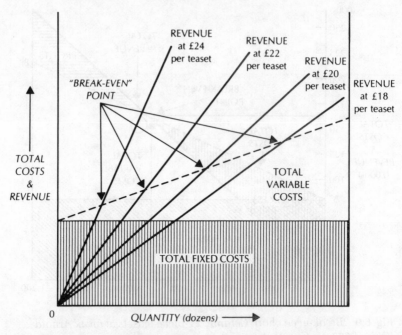

Fig. 6.10   *A consideration of costs, revenue, volume and profit relationships at four ex-Arnold prices for the 'Diana' 21 piece teaset*

The four predominant prices within this range are as follows:

recommended retail selling price	price from Arnold Ceramics (40% rsp)
£60	£24
£55	£22
£50	£20
£45	£18

Figure 6.10 shows the break-even charts resulting from an analysis of the fixed and variable costs emanating from the production and marketing of the teaset at each of these four prices (net to Arnolds). The chart depicts how the most appropriate price may be determined from the revenue and quantity data appropriate to each of these break-even points.

Although break-even analysis is well-known in marketing circles it does have limitations. The most fundamental is that it is essentially a 'laboratory' method, using the cost-plus approach, and taking no account of the realities of the market. It is one thing to say that 'we will break even at sales of 700 dozen teasets',

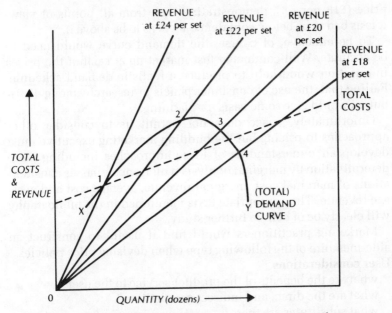

Fig. 6.11   Maximising profit through considerations of break-even analysis and the total demand curve

but what guarantee is there that they will be sold. In a dynamic market, with a significant amount of competition it would be foolish to guarantee anything. At the beginning of this Section it was said that we would look at the process in three stages. Fig. 6.9 demonstrates how the technique is used for a single price and Fig. 6.10 how it can be used over a range of prices for comparison purposes. Fig. 6.11 is meant to convey how, with marketing research data, it can be used to take the realities of the market into account. XY is the demand curve which shows *total* revenues obtainable at each of the four prices mentioned in the previous figure (Fig. 6.10). (The reader will note that the shape of the curve is different from the usual demand curve, which slopes downward and to the right, see Figs. 6.7 & 6.8. The reason for this is that the curve in Fig. 6.11 depicts *total* revenues, whereas the more usual Figs. 6.7 & 6.8 depict *average* revenues.)

It can be seen that the price of £22 per set is the one at which the balance of revenue over cost is maximised since at point 2, the demand curve is at the greatest vertical distance above the total cost curve. Arnolds would actually make a loss at the lowest price (£18 per set), demonstrating that, from all points of view, it is as bad to be below confidence-level as to be above it.

To be effective, of course, the demand curve would need to be accurate. Well-conducted test marketing at each of the prices in question woud help to produce a realistic demand schedule. Failing that, the use of consumer panels or research among distributors would give some basis for planning.

Unfortunately, space does not permit us to consider other approaches to pricing but the budding marketing executive must develop an understanding of these approaches including price determination by *marginal analysis* which encompasses considerations of marginal cost, marginal revenue, average cost and average revenue. The appropriate texts mentioned in the bibliography will clearly be of help in further study.

Marketing practitioners would find it useful to construct an aide-memoire of the following type when devising price policies.

User considerations

what are the benefits of the product/service to the user?
what are the direct and indirect competition?
what substitutes are there?
what is the price confidence-level?
what are the typical buying motives and actual/potential psychological appeals – hence, possibilities of non-price competition?

Organisational considerations

current and anticipated costs of production?
ratio of expected volume: plant capacity?
cost: volume relationships?
break-even points at alternative prices? price: demand relationships?
contribution to fixed costs? profit targets?

Market information

what is the actual/target market share for the product or service, compared to competition? proposed price(s): competitors' prices?
what does direct and indirect competition provide by way of a *total product*, i.e. warranties, after-sales service, packaging etc?
would the appropriate policy be one of price-making or price-taking (see page 225)
what are the prevailing methods of physical distribution?
what marketing channels are typically used?

what are the trade margins and discounts available at various stages in the marketing channels?

are there changes in the pattern of distribution?

if so, what implications do they have for pricing policy?

what are competitors' policies with regard to marketing communications, trade and promotional support, sales force deployment and call-cycles, the granting of exclusive sales rights?

Additional considerations

is there any legislation in force which affects price policies, e.g. concerning monopolies and restrictive practices; methods of quoting prices; the granting of credit and hire purchase facilities; maintenance of minimum quality standards, health and safety standards?

what considerations, other than price, influence the marketing of the product/service, e.g. the need to reduce 'seasonality' and even out demand on production resources, the desirability of 'rounding out' the range to improve service to users and distributors?

The reader will be able to assess what other questions might be added to this aide-memoire as we move through the succeeding chapters of this book.

Self-assessment questions

1 Discuss the statement: 'the product is rarely a simple concept', with reference to its significance for marketing practitioners.

2 What are the main reasons underlying the high failure rates of new products?

3 Why is it claimed that knowledge of the product life cycle makes for a more informed approach to marketing strategy?

4 List some of the important sources of ideas for new products.

5 Why is knowledge of the diffusion process significant for the introduction of new products?

6 What's in a brand name?

7 Prepare notes on the following: own-label products; generics; gap analysis; value analysis; product positioning; the 80/20 rule; perceived value.

8 Suggest a sequence for planning the development of new products.

9 What, in your view, are the similarities and differences

between the marketing of products and the marketing of (a) services and (b) ideas?

10 Devise a list of the factors which must be considered in competent pricing practice.

11 Describe some typical pricing objectives.

12 Explain the uses and limitations of break-even analysis in the setting of prices.

References

1 Baker, Michael J. Developing and launching a new industrial product, *Marketing Handbook* ed. Michael Rines, 2nd edn, Aldershot, Gower, 1981, p. 144
2 Kraushar, Peter. Ibid. p. 132
3 Baker, Michael J. Ibid. pp. 145–146
4 Stanton, William J. *Fundamentals of marketing*, 6th edn, New York, Mc Graw-Hill, 1981, p. 173
5 Cox, W. E. Product life cycles as marketing models, *Journal of Business*, (October 1967), **40** pp. 375–384
6 Cyert, Richard M. and March, James G. A behavioural theory of the firm, *Writers on Organisations*, Pugh, Hickson and Hinings, 3rd edn, Harmondsworth, Middlesex, Penguin, 1983, p. 107–113
7 Adamson, David. *Consumers in business*, London, National Consumer Council, 1982
8 Boone, Louis E. and Kurtz, David L. *Contemporary marketing* 3rd edn, Hinsdale, Illinois, The Dryden Press, 1980, p. 170
9 Advisory Committee on Applied Research and Development (ACARD). Innovation is not Britain's strong suit, by Tom Cannon *The Guardian*, 14 March 1980
10 Rogers, Everett M. and Shoemaker, Floyd F. *Communication of innovations*, New York, The Free Press, 1971, p. 182
11 Baker, Michael J. Developing and launching a new industrial product, *Marketing Handbook*, pp. 152–153
12 Walker, David M. *The Oxford companion to law*, Oxford, Oxford University Press, 1980, p. 1228
13 A C Nielsen Co. Ltd. A marketing research study, *Generics – a first look*, Cookham: The Institute of Marketing, *The Quarterly Review of Marketing*, (April 1983) pp. 28–30
14 Mindak, William A. Fitting the semantic differential to the marketing problem *Dimensions of consumer behaviour*, James U. McNeal, ed, 2nd edn, New York, Appleton-Century-Crofts, 1969, p. 34
15 Lynch, James E. *Hertford College, Oxford: a case study in non-profit marketing*, University of Bradford Management Centre. See also: How an ugly college gets beautiful results. *The Sunday Times*, 26 August 1976

16 Dibben, Margaret. Ungobbledegook, *The Guardian*, 9 October 1982
17 Nelson, Elizabeth H. Extract from a draft paper *The needs of the citizen in a fragmented society*, (in private possession of this author)
18 Kotler, Philip. *Principles of marketing*, 2nd edn, Englewood Cliffs, NJ, Prentice-Hall, 1983, p. 317
19 Baker, Michael J. *Marketing – an introductory text*, 3rd edn, London, The Macmillan Press, 1979, pp. 230–231

7 THE 'PLACE ELEMENT' –PLANNING DISTRIBUTION

> **Objectives**
>
> 'Being in the right place at the right time' has a great deal to do with marketing success and failure. This Chapter describes the processes of physical distribution and marketing channel activity emphasising the depth of attention an effective marketing manager extends to them.
>
> The changing patterns of distribution for both industrial and consumer products are described and their links with distribution policy are demonstrated.
>
> Dealer co-operation and support are hard-won objectives. The final part of the Chapter makes some suggestions to help.

Introduction

The distribution function – definitions and objectives

In the last Chapter we saw something of what is involved in getting the product 'right', in the dual sense of being right for the user and right in terms of its contribution to objectives – profit objectives usually. The function of distribution is usually described as one of ensuring that the right product we speak of becomes available to the user: 'in the right place and at the right time'.

Therefore, the 'place' element in the marketing mix really has two dimensions:

1 *utility of place:* which means making a product or service available at *a location convenient to the user* (and not at the supplier's factory or his distribution depot, both of which may be far away from the user);

2 *utility of time:* which means ensuring that the product or service is available to the user *when* it is required.

Examples of both of these utilities are very easily visualised. The truck manufacturer requires tyres *at the place* where he assembles the trucks. They are of little use to him in the tyre manufacturer's warehouse. Similarly, the business executive who has ordered a light-weight suit for his summer schedule of visits to customers requires it *at the time* he is setting out to make his calls. It will be of little use to him if it is delivered in November.

Arranging these time and place utilities is the role of the distribution function. The function itself has two elements:

1   physical distribution, and
2   marketing channel activity.

The first element encompasses such activities as transportation, warehousing, inventory control, and (in some organisations) packaging, packing and order-processing.

The second element comprises the selection, use and support of intermediaries such as wholesalers, retailers, agents, brokers and others. In many cases, the task of the physical distribution element is to deliver goods promptly, economically and safely to the second element, the marketing channels, although on some occasions (particulary with industrial goods) delivery is made direct to the user.

It should be mentioned that, often in large organisations, physical distribution also encompasses the *inward* movement of products and materials to the point of manufacture, as well as the *outward* movement of finished products to customers. There are clear advantages in adopting this approach, not least in ensuring a high level of utilisation of transport fleets on both outward and return journeys. A separate department, physical distribution is established within the organisation under the control of a physical distribution manager who may be (but is usually not) subordinate to the marketing manager. The process of physical distribution is, however, of great relevance to the marketing manager. The Centre for Physical Distribution Management, established in 1970 under the aegis of the British Institute of Management (BIM), defines the aim of physical distribution management (PDM) as follows:

to achieve the highest possible measure of efficiency in the physical distribution activity. That efficiency can be measured in two ways: cost, and quality of service. These are, in turn, interdependent, since the higher the level of service, the greater is the cost. PDM is essentially a matter of co-ordination – both internally as between its constituent activities, and externally with marketing, production and purchasing so as to ensure the best overall balance in the interests of the company as a whole.[1]

Note the word *cost*, because organisation costs are directly related to its return-on-investment. The definition embraces the objective of *quality of service*, which could be alternatively expressed as 'user orientation'. Finally, the definition makes it clear that PDM is essentially a matter of co-ordination ... in the interests of the company as a whole: this is the organisational integration we also speak of in the broad concept we have come to know as marketing.

Thus we are able to see a distinct affinity between the aims of physical distribution management and the three strands of the marketing concept, viz:

- user orientation;
- adequacy of return-on-investment;
- organisational integration.

The approach here is not concerned so much with whether the marketing manager actually controls the physical distribution function, but in illustrating its importance to his own task and to establish why he should have a marked influence upon its activities. The above definition is very valuable in setting out how the function and the concept are so closely related. In our next Section we will examine the physical distribution function as it should be viewed by a marketing manager.

Physical distribution

According to the Institute of Directors[2], the function of physical distribution accounts for more than one fifth of the United Kingdom's gross national product, and whilst 'costs' vary from industry to industry, total distribution costs are seldom less than seven per cent of sale price, and usually very much more.

The Institute also points out that physical distribution costs contain some elements which are likely to inflate at a faster rate than the other costs of manufacturers. The labour intensity of present warehousing methods, the dependence of current transport systems on fossil fuels which are so high in price and the ever-increasing capital costs of maintaining adequate stock levels are some of the factors here. Recent research[3] indicates that total distribution costs seem set to inflate at a rate which is 50 per cent greater than the projected rise in other industrial costs and that between 1978 and 1990, the freight transport element of distribution cost would increase from an average of 5.5 per cent to an average of 7.4 per cent of retail sales price. Moreover, Philip

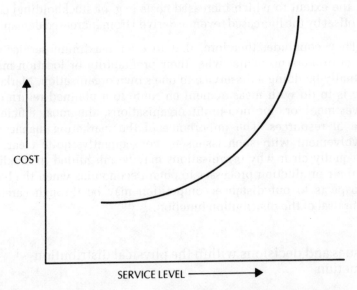

Fig. 7.1   *Costs increase exponentially as the level of service improves*

Winrow[4] is of the opinion that this pressure on costs will increase in the future, for:

The manufacturer will be continually faced with extending his product range, without increasing investment in inventories, at the same time providing an increasingly higher level of service in order to retain a market share.

The relationship between 'level of service' (which may be defined as the percentage of occasions the product is available to the customer when and where he wants it) and costs, hence return-on-investment, is quite a dramatic one as Fig. 7.1 shows.

As the level of service improves, costs increase not in a linear fashion, but exponentially. Christopher, Walters and Wills[5] express the view that it is beyond the 70–80 per cent level of service that the associated costs increase by far more than is proportional. They suggest that management must therefore be very clear about:

1   the level of service which is currently being provided;
2   the manner in which the level of demand is influenced by the level of service;
3   the incremental costs of improving the level of service;
4   the extent to which increased costs (e.g. of stockholding) can be offset by the increased revenue derived from increased demand.

They conclude, therefore, that to offer maximum service to all customers no matter what their profitability or location may actually be doing a disservice to one's own organisation. Marketing is to do with measurement en route to a planned return on investment or, for non-profit organisations, the most efficient use of resources. The importance of the marketing manager's involvement with such issues is, consequently, quite clear. It is equally clear why organisations may be misguided in looking to their production processes to obtain economies when the best prospects to out distance competition may be through careful appraisal of the distribution function.

Issues and decisions within the physical distribution function

It is impossible to maximise the level of customer service and, at the same time, minimise physical distribution costs. Management decision-making in this area has to do with finding the best balance between variables which are often opposed to each other, the 'best balance' being the one which will provide an effective level of service and also help to meet organisational objectives (e.g. return-on-investment). How are variables 'opposed to each other'? Let us look at some examples.

1   *Choice of transport.* The supplier usually has the following options:

rail transport; road haulage; canal transport; coastal transport; air freight; postal deliveries; parcels and small freight delivery services.

With regard to road haulage, he must make the choice of whether to own and operate his own fleet of vehicles or whether to utilise contract hire vehicles. Alternatively he could send his consignments via a road haulage operator paying carriage charges on each individual consignment.

Now each of these transport modes has its advantages: there is, for example, the flexibility of road transport; the accessibility to dock systems that canal transport provides when the loading port handles barge traffic; the speed of air freight. But all of these modes give rise to different costs and usually, the more the advantages, the greater the costs. Choice of transport methods involves consideration of a number of factors, including:

- any special requests made by the customer;
- the required speed of transit (i..e. delivery lead-time);
- the nature of the journey;
- the volume/weight/value of the consignment;
- the physical nature of the goods;
- the freight, packing and insurance costs which would be incurred by the various transport options.

Another crucial factor, rarely found in check-lists such as the one above, is the quality of service offered by the carrier; the degree of understanding, co-operation and flexibility which, in turn, will have such a great bearing on the supplier's own success.

The supplier can also choose a combination of two or more modes, as in export movements, where the rail trunking of road vehicles (using the 'kangaroo' trailer method) provides both the high speed of rail transport and the flexibility of road transport in the 'through' carriage of consignments. The choice of transport for a single consignment is often quite complex. Where the whole volume of required movements within a given time period (usually a financial year) is under review, the examination of all the variables is extremely complex and a great deal will also depend upon the accuracy of the organisation's sales forecasts.

2 *Inventory policy.* The opposition between the variables relating to stock levels is another area where management decisions must try to achieve a satisfactory balance. The sales manager will take one view as to what satisfactory stock levels should be. But this view may not be shared by the financial manager or the production manager. Fig. 7.2 attempts to represent these opposing views schematically.

The schematic is an over-simplification, of course. The production manager, for example, may be lured by the quantity discounts

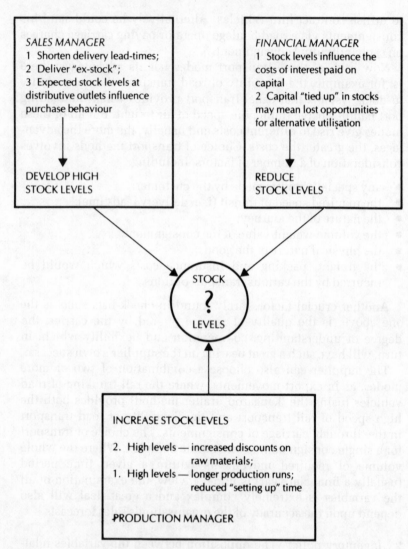

Fig. 7.2   What should the stock levels be?

that high stock-levels make possible on the purchase of raw materials. This will benefit his production budgets. Against this, of course, he must weigh the cost of the space taken up by high stock levels. Space taken up by stock will also ultimately affect the flow of production. So the problem is even more complex than Fig. 7.2 depicts.

The role of the marketing manager

By looking at two issues in physical distribution – choice of transport mode and stock control – we can perceive that here is an important but complex function in which the optimal solution is unlikely to be achieved by guesswork and experience ('we've always done it this way'). What then are the implications for the marketing manager?

The first essential is for him to recognise the nature and complexity of physical distribution issues. It would be an abrogation of responsibility for him to say 'I leave such matters to the transport manager, he's very shrewd.' In the first place, transportation cannot be exclusively the interest of the transport manager. Techniques of transport raise important questions of sales policy, e.g. how far can sales representatives be motivated to increase order quantities in order to take advantage of containerisation or some other type of unit load? They raise important points of design policy – the marketing team might ask itself 'how many more products could we fit into the 8 × 8 foot container module by some modification to shape, and if we modified the shape, would this affect demand?'

In making judgments on transport methods, transport managers are usually preoccupied with freight rates. Yet the freight cost element is merely one cost among many for any method of transportation. Accurate comparison between methods entails taking into account items additional to the freight rate, including warehousing costs, interest on capital, insurance premiums and packing costs. Let us look at a very simple example.

Transport cost comparison

Arnold Ceramics 'Diana' tableware:
initial consignment

	London – Zurich		
	Sea	Trailer	Air
Packing	£1100	£330	£300
Delivery to (air)port (1 lorry)	100	–	90
Freight and port charges	220	400	320
Insurance	126	122	126
c.i.f. Zurich totals	£1546	£852	£836

(*Note.* local delivery charges; customs clearance and duties; local taxes; extra, as appropriate)

The above calculation relates to a consignment of the new 'Diana' tableware being despatched by Arnolds to a department store in Zurich. It can be seen that although the normal surface movement by sea offers the lowest freight rate, the total c.i.f. cost is practically double the costs of the alternative methods, of which air freight is marginally the cheaper. This calculation is not untypical and it is frequently the case that where air freight, for example, is more costly from the standpoint of freight charges its use may still be justified on the basis of overall economy.

Air freight movements usually entail lower packing and insurance charges (because of reduced transit time). The lower lead (i.e. transit) time of this method also means less interest on capital for the supplier – another item which would be taken into account by a comprehensive total distribution cost analysis. So here is a calculation based on a particular consignment illustrating that a particular transport mode offers the least-cost method of sending goods to a particular market. But what is the situation concerning the *total sales volume* which is predicted for a market and how does the costs situation alter above and below that volume?

Imagine, for example, that a manufacturer of engineering components has established a warehouse in Western Europe in order to provide an intensively good service to a number of customers operating mass-assembly plants there. He is now considering alternative methods of servicing his customers, as indicated in the following total distribution cost (TDC) analysis approach:

1   *Method A.* By sea ex UK→ to Brussels warehouse→ to customers' assembly plants by road.

2   *Method B.* By Air freight ex UK→ direct to customers' assembly plant (i.e. by local delivery ex airports)

The starting point for TDC analysis here is to classify all the data on the distributive costs of both methods as fixed or variable, fixed costs being those costs which would still have to be allocated to distribution even if there were no engineering components in the pipeline (in jargon terms: at zero throughput). The analysis might be structured as follows:

Method A (sea/Brussels warehouse/road)

(a) *Freight costs of transportation* classified as variable costs

(b) *Warehousing costs* classified as partially fixed/partially variable (e.g. fixed costs – costs of occupation, local rent, rates etc; depreciation of fixtures, fittings, stock handling machinery, delivery vehicles)

(c) *Interest on stocks held* classified as partially fixed/partially variable (e.g. the interest on the minimum allowable stock level may be used for calculation purposes as the fixed element).

Method B (Air freight and local delivery to customers)

There is clearly a much lower element of fixed costs by this method. There are no warehouse occupancy costs and the minimum allowable stock levels in the UK can be lower because the lower lead time of air freight requires a lower level of 'buffer' stock.

Let us assume that when the classification of cost data is completed, the analysis appears thus:

		Fixed costs	Variable costs
(A)	Sea/Brussels warehouse/road	35%	65%
(B)	Air freight and local delivery	20%	80%

and the construction of a cross-over chart appears thus:

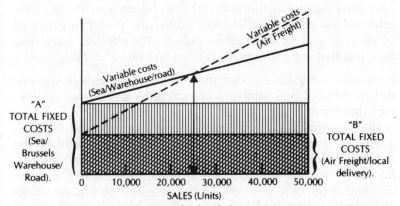

Fig. 7.3   Comparison of two methods of physical distribution – the TDC analysis approach

From this chart it can be seen that until a break-point in sales volume of 25 000 units is reached, it is uneconomical for the supplier to have a warehouse in Brussels. Obviously, if a volume break-point can be established for each transport method to each market it serves, the firm can alter its method of moving goods to a market according to how and when the volume of business transacted with a market, or group of markets, expands.

TDC analysis can be criticised on the grounds that it is an 'ideal method' and on the grounds of the work that it entails. Certainly it calls for more information on distribution costs than most firms possess but if marketing is to do with measurement then many physical distribution decisions are too complex and too far reaching, not least because of their effect on selling prices, to be left to the transport manager. In fact, from the exercise just outlined it can be seen how important an influence on distribution decisions is the task of sales forecasting and the marketing manager must ensure that it is closely integrated with such decisions. Distribution budgets must be prepared, with projected sales for each market, as the starting point. Where the organisation markets a large range of products, the calculations for such analyses may permissibly be based on *average* values and weights, without too great an effect on the quality of decision making.

Concluding thoughts

This brief outline of the physical distribution system will have achieved its objective if it has enabled the reader to gauge its complexity and its potential contribution to effective marketing. It is clear that any rigorous study must take into account:

marketing variables e.g. demand forecasts; analyses of volume/weight/value of consignments; typical order sizes; required delivery times; nature of products;
production variables e.g. unit costs of production; costs and availability of raw materials, component parts, sub-assemblies etc; required delivery times for raw materials and components etc;
financial variables e.g. interest on capital invested (e.g. in vehicles and depots); interest on capital necessary to finance stocks and goods in transit; discounts available for bulk purchases of raw materials, components and other supplies;
transport variables e.g. information on the costs and benefits of various modes of transport (road, rail, air freight etc); nature of journeys, including road network and traffic density information; transport conditions, climate and geography in overseas countries; packing and packaging methods including the economies of palletisation and the unit load; location and suitability of

inland customs depots, free port facilities and Freightliner terminals etc.

The marketing manager cannot be expert in all the details of
physical distribution. The study of one element – warehousing
– has now become a field for the expert, calling as it does for
knowledge of design, automation and mechanisation; the technology of movement of goods; space, labour and energy costs and
the design and performance of work horses, e.g. counterbalanced
lift trucks; electrical trucks; i.c.e. trucks and lateral stacking
trucks. Yet it is fair to say that the marketing manager must
fully understand the nature of the physical distribution function,
recognise it calls for high-quality decision making, realise that
this cannot be delegated to managers with a narrower functional
perspective and acquire knowledge of the techniques to assist
decision-making. Operational research techniques, assisted in
their application by the computer, are now frequently used to
identify the relationship between the variables in a distribution
system. Models of these systems are constructed which enable
deductions to be drawn and the sensitivity of the model to various values of the variables to be investigated. Typical applications relate to the optimum location of depots, the route
scheduling of vehicles and the optimum stock levels in factories
and depots.

The effective marketing manager must be familiar with such
techniques and with their widening range of applications. (Note.
More is said about the physical distribution function in Chapter
13 – International marketing.)

Marketing channels

Marketing channel policy, the second element of the distribution
policy entails the selection, use and support of intermediaries
(such as retailers, wholesalers, brokers, agents and merchants)
as a general rule. In some cases, and particularly so in the case
of industrial products, the marketing channel is direct to the
user. In this Section we shall consider the types of intermediary
organisations typically active in the marketing of products; we
shall then outline how the pattern of distribution has changed
since 1945 and finally we shall examine how decisions on channel
policy are made.

Retail organisations

The main functions of the retailer are these:

1 to purchase products in reasonably large quantities from manufacturers and wholesalers and to break these down into smaller quantities appropriate for the consumer (the word 'retailler' in French means to cut again);
2 where appropriate, to provide credit and after-sales service;
3 to advise the consumer on the quality, specifications and performance of products;
4 to act as a liaison between the consumer and the manufacturer;
5 in some instances, and particularly for grocery products, to pre-prepare the products for sale – as with cheese, meat, bacon etc.

The main types of retail organisation are listed below.

Independents

Officially described as retail organisations with less than 10 branches, the majority are small one-branch family businesses of the corner-shop type providing a good local service. Prominent in the grocery trade they still comprise approximately 80 per cent of Britain's outlets but currently account for about 40 per cent of total retail sales volume whereas in 1950 their share was 62 per cent.

Multiples

These are retail organisations with ten or more branches. Originally 'multiple' denoted a chain of similar shops with identical store design, layout and stock display, each selling a limited, cohesive range of products, e.g. books; chemists' goods; cameras and optical equipment; electrical goods; footwear. By concentrating their buying power through centralised stocking and promotional policies, thus securing the fullest discounts from the manufacturers and operating on narrow profit margins with high turnover products they have been extremely successful in the last three decades and are prominent in the field of own-label products. Latterly, they have widened their previously limited ranges of products and should now perhaps be described as *speciality* chain stores, to distinguish from *variety* chain stores.

Variety chain stores

The 1971 Census of Distribution (now superseded by the 'Annual Retail Inquiry') defines variety and general household stores as 'variety' or 'bazaar' stores selling a very wide range of goods usually displayed in trays or racks for selection by customers. 'General household' stores are defined as shops selling a varied range of household goods but which cannot be appropriately classified as 'departments'. Their sales of at least two of the following product groups – furniture and floor coverings; radios, electrical goods and hardware; clothing, soft furnishings and household textiles – must each amount to not less than 20 per cent of total turnover. FW Woolworth, with over 1000 UK branches, is prominent in this group. The Woolworth chain, like a number of others is, on the strict definition given above, also a multiple. As we shall see in the next Chapter, such organisations account for a significant proportion of UK advertising expenditure. They are also prominent in the own-label field commissioning supplies from a large number of manufacturers for their house brand.

Department stores

By definition, these employ 25 or more persons and sell a wide range of goods including a significant amount of clothing and household goods. The definition also extends to prescribed proportions of sales in certain product categories, including men's and boy's wear; women's, girls' and children's wear, footwear, furniture, radio and electrical goods, food, drapery goods, leather goods and household textiles.

There are about 800 department stores in the UK, many of them belonging to large groups (e.g. John Lewis Partnership, Debenhams, House of Fraser), which again constitutes them as multiples in the strict sense. Their share of total UK retail trade is a fairly constant 5 per cent.

The initial method of trading, as devised by Aristide Bouçicaut at his Bon Marché store in Paris, is that of several departments or 'shops within a shop'. The 'shops within a shop' concept has an added dimension now that many manufacturers sell their own products (e.g. jewellery, cosmetics) by way of *leased departments* in these stores.

Department stores typically occupy large central sites in urban areas, and by advertising their 'sales' and other events concentrate on attracting customers to the store from the large 'catchments' they serve. Unlike the real multiples, they offer a high level of personal service, including credit, delivery, restaurant, hairdressing and theatre booking services. A number of the stores (e.g. Harrods; Selfridges of London; Macys of New York; Galeries Lafayette of Paris) have become international institutions.

The consumer cooperative movement

The guiding principles of the organisation – open membership, democratic control (one man, one vote) and profit sharing for members related to their purchases, as established by the *Rochdale Pioneers* in 1844, are still in evidence – although price-cutting and dividend stamps redeemable for cash have replaced the old-style dividend distribution.

Today, the UK's cooperative retail societies own more than 12 000 retail outlets, a bank and an insurance organisation. They also jointly own the Cooperative Wholesale Society (CWS), one of the largest food manufacturing and wholesaling organisations in Europe.

Despite the ownership of more grocery outlets than all the other multiples combined, the Movement's share of total retail trade has gradually declined in the post-war period (from 12 per cent in 1957 to approximately 7 per cent today). In contrast to the position in some European countries, where the consumer cooperative movement is quite strong, the market position of the UK movement has been eroded by the dynamism of the multiple organisations, and particularly the grocery chains (Tesco, Sainsbury etc).

Mail order organisations

There are a number of types:

1   the small-scale operator, offering one or a few products, through the 'Postal shopping' section in newspapers and magazines;

2   the 'postal service' section of department stores;

3   the large-scale wholesaler-retailer organisation, offering goods direct to the public by way of an illustrated catalogue, orders being obtained by post or through commission agents.

The last-named type of organisation dominates the mail-order trade and includes such well-known names as Great Universal Stores (GUS), Freemans and Littlewoods.

In addition, recent years have seen the significant growth of *direct marketing*. This is really an extension of method 1 above and is primarily conducted by direct-response advertising in the colour supplements of the national quality Sunday newspapers. The magazines of the credit-card companies (e.g. Barclaycard) are also an important avenue of contact with the more affluent consumers which manufacturers and wholesale organisations are seeking to reach by the direct-marketing method. Books and records; pottery, glass and cutlery; watches, medals and electronic products are prominent in this rapidly expanding sector of distribution. Prominent names emerging in the formative years of direct marketing have been Scotcade, Kaleidoscope (a subsidiary of the W. H. Smith organisation) and Post Haste (owned by the Burtons tailoring multiple).

The mail order trade as a whole has grown markedly in the last 30 years. No doubt, the increased number of working wives has been a significant factor here. In 1950, the method accounted for a mere one per cent of total UK retail trade. Currently, this share is approximately five per cent. In the early to mid 1970s, according to Thomas[6], catalogue sales grew by 152 per cent and involved 15 million customers.

Franchising

In this type of retail operation, the franchiser provides the goodwill, which attaches to his name or 'institutional image'; the product to be sold; financial facilities (usually by way of a proportion of the venture capital required); and consultancy services on such matters as location of premises, management and financial control of the business. For his part, the franchisee provides most, if not all, of the venture capital and enters into an agreement to purchase his supplies exclusively from the franchiser.

The system, which has gained a noticeable foothold in Britain, in recent years, has been used successfully in the catering field (e.g. Wimpy; Kentucky Fried Chicken), and in cleaning services and soft drinks.

Other types of retail distribution

Market stalls, mobile shops, kiosks, vending machines and home selling all play a small but significant part in the total pattern of UK retail distribution. Avon Cosmetics and Tupperware are significant in home selling, a field in which the personal service and advice offered by the agent is an important factor.

The new dynamics of retailing

In the post-1945 period, the British consumers have had more money to spend and a wider range of goods from which to choose. They have become more discriminating in their choice, as a consequence. Private cars and improved transport systems have extended the catchment area of retail units, enabling them to become larger. The provision of adequate, trouble-free parking facilities has long been of prime importance (a factor which has militated against the growth of centrally sited department stores and has assisted in the development of out-of-town shopping centres). Full employment and high labour costs have increased the importance within distribution of such labour saving techniques as self-service and payment at the 'check-out' point. The result of these trends is that, what have been described as the new dynamics of retailing, are now well established in Britain. These new dynamics are summarised below.

Supermarkets: these are self-service outlets with a minimum selling area of 4000 square feet, having three or more check-out points and offering a full range of foodstuffs and household requisites.

Hypermarkets: are stores of at least 50 000 square feet of selling space, all on a single level, offering a very wide range of products, both food and non-food, with self-service retailing, 15 or more check-out points and free car-parking space at least three times the size of the selling space.

Superstores: these are stores of at least 20 000 to 30 000 square feet of selling space, on a single level, with a wide range of food and non-food products, 10 to 20 check-out points and free car parking facilities of one to three times the area of the selling space.

Discount stores: are stores based on the selling of branded goods at prices well below manufacturers' recommended retail selling prices. Little or no provision is made for customer services or facilities and 'self-service' is the operating method (the Argos and Comet organisations are now well-known in the UK).

Voluntary groups and chains: these are cooperative organisations which aim to develop and maintain the competitiveness of whole-

salers and retailers through bulk-buying and the adoption of operating efficiency techniques. Mace, V.G., Spar, Vivo and Wavy Line
are examples of these organisations. They are now said to account
for over 50 per cent of 'independent' grocery trading. Nu-Mark
is an important group in the chemists' field. Voluntary associations are also prominent in the hardware and textile trades.

A number of these new dynamic ideas originated in the USA,
although the Spar voluntary group organisation, the forerunner
of its type, began in Holland. In Europe, since 1945, West Germany, Switzerland, Holland and the Scandinavian countries have
developed the sophisticated distribution systems which have
appeared in the UK. The new dynamics have appeared in Belgium,
France, Austria and Italy at a somewhat slower pace. Greece, Por-
tugal, Spain, Turkey and Jugoslavia still have relatively unsophisticated systems (see Chapter 13 International marketing).

The wholesale trade

In relation to the manufacturer and the retailer, the main functions of the wholesaler are as follows:

1 to share the financial risk, by purchasing in advance of active
demand;
2 to stock the product in locations convenient for the distribution process;
3 to break down 'bulk' consignments from the manufacturer into
consignments appropriate to retailer needs;
4 to maintain a team of sales representatives to book orders
and provide advice to retailers;
5 to provide a two-way flow of information between manufacturer and retailer, thus assisting the marketing of current products and the development of new products;
6 through the purchasing and storage function, and the granting
of credit, to even out fluctuations in the supply of, demand for,
and price of, the product.

Historically, the wholesale trades in Great Britain have been
active in such fields as grocery and provisions; fruit and vegetables; clothing and textiles; hardware and electrical goods; building materials; agricultural supplies; and some types of industrial
materials and machinery. Toys, gifts and fancy goods, ceramics
and jewellery are other product groups where the wholesaler is

an important intermediary. Some wholesale organisations may
also perform retail functions – as in the field of building materials,
garden machinery and garden requisites – such wholesalers having
a consumer and a trade (i.e. retailer) section.

With the decline of the independents, the wholesaler has been
under great economic pressure, especially in the grocery trade
where the multiple organisations have made great inroads into
the market share of the small shops. As may be imagined, the
wholesaling of food products is a low profit margin, high sales
volume operation. In the last ten years, as is typical in a highly
developed economy, the total demand for food products has been
relatively static. This trend and the decline in importance of their
traditional customer, the independent shopkeeper, has seen wholesalers working on a net profit margin of around one per cent of
turnover! The breakdown of the food wholesalers' profit margin
is reckoned to be as follows:

Gross margin (on turnover)	9%
Handling and distribution costs (as % of turnover)	4.5%
Administration, selling, depreciation and other costs (as % of turnover)	3.5%
Net margin (on turnover)	1.0%

To defend their position, wholesalers have developed *cash and
carry* operations (in which small retailers buy goods at the lowest
prices for cash, arranging their own transport of these from the
wholesale warehouses). Another important measure has been the
development of wholesaler-inspired *voluntary groups*. In these,
retail members undertake to purchase a large proportion of their
requirements from the group wholesaler in return for:
1 lower prices
2 assistance from the wholesaler to improve retail stock-turn
through advertising, advice on shop layout, utilisation of capital
and other measures to improve efficiency.

Although many observers of the distributive scene have been
sounding the death knell of the wholesaler for at least three
decades, he has proved remarkably resilient. In many instances,
this has been achieved by flexibility, by increasing operating efficiency (e.g. through closing old and badly sited warehouses and
constructing new single-storey depots) and by the application
of mechanical handling techniques.

Other institutions and specialists

Brokers and commission agents

These intermediaries do not take title or physical possession of products, but negotiate their sale in return for a 'brokerage' or commission on the value of the transaction. Commission agents are frequently employed by organisations entering international markets.

Produce or commodity markets and exchanges

These provide physical facilities in which buyers and sellers can make contact. The commodities traded in are graded and their prices are fixed. Market reports are also issued. The London rubber, tea and coffee exchanges are examples of this type of institution.

Merchants

These organisations, many of them substantial, take title to and, frequently, physical possession of, the goods in which they trade. Many UK merchants are members of the British Export Houses Association.

Other facilitating institutions

These include transport organisations, credit information bureaux, chambers of commerce and forwarding agents. All of them play some role in the distribution of products, e.g. carriage; documentation; and information on the creditworthiness of potential distributors. The 'groupage' services of forwarding agents often enable small exporters to enjoy the benefits of containerisation and other economies.

Vertical integration

Although it is generally the case that distribution is a process carried out by intermediary organisations, the recent past has provided many examples of vertical integration, in which the manufacturing and distribution processes have been linked up under the same ownership and control. Where producers market their output through their own retail outlets, their control over distribution is total and they reap all the benefits of being in close contact with the user. Against these benefits must be measured the high costs of such a policy. The United Kingdom provides numerous examples of vertical integration, both forward (i.e. beginning in manufacturing and moving forward into distribution) and backward (i.e. beginning in distribution and moving backward into the manufacturing process). The Marley Tile Company and Boots the Chemists are good examples of forward integration. The best-known example of backward integration is the Marks and Spencer organisation. Another is the WH Smith organisation, originally a bookseller and now a publisher in its own right.

Manufacturers such as Avon Cosmetics and the Kleen-e-ze Brush Company provide additional examples of forward integration although their contact with the user is at the doorstep and not in the retail shop. Although door-to-door selling is not extensive in Britain both of these companies have long employed the method successfully.

The changing pattern of distribution

The efficiency and level of concentration of a country's distribution system is directly linked to the country's living standards and the purchasing power of its population. The measure of a country's industrialisation and the productivity of its industry will give a good indication of how concentrated, or sophisticated, its distributive channels prove to be.

High purchasing power and the greater availability of mass-produced consumer goods is usually accompanied by a concentration of retail sales through fewer and larger outlets. There is accompanying pressure on the small shopkeeper who, in turn, will converge defensively with wholesalers and other retailers in order to survive.

High labour costs and a high level of employment increase the importance to distribution of labour-saving techniques. Soon the new dynamics of retailing – self-service outlets, voluntary groups, surburban shopping centres, as well as cash-and-carry wholesale units and an increased level of mail order trading – begin to appear on the North American pattern. A number of aspects of the UK's changed pattern of distribution have already been mentioned. Let us now look at the phenomenon in a little more detail. In 1950, multiple organisations accounted for 19 per cent of total UK retail trade. By 1966 this had increased to 29 per cent, Mail order firms increased their share from 1 per cent to 4 per cent in the same period, and the variety chain stores from 2 per cent to 4 per cent. The department stores marked time at 5 per cent throughout the period, but the proportion accounted for by the independents declined from 62 per cent to 50 per cent and the share of the co-operative stores reduced from 11 per cent to 9 per cent.

The process of concentration slowed to some extent in the 1970s but proof that it still continued was provided by the UK Government's SDA/25 Business Monitor which showed that whereas in 1971 there were 368 222 retail businesses in existence, by 1977 the number had shrunk to 262 443. The casualties were almost exclusively among the corner shops (i.e. the independents) and nowhere were these more beleaguered than in the grocery field where, by 1975, just over 380 buying points were responsible for more than 80 per cent of total turnover. Statistics available from the AC Nielsen Company show that the independents' share of UK grocery sales fell graphically in the period 1971–78, a 42.5 per cent share in the former year being reduced to 33.1 per cent in 1978. The comparative figures for the multiples showed an increase of 9 per cent (1971: 44.3 per cent; 1978: 53.3 per cent). Table 7.1 demonstrates the comparative importance of the independents and the multiples over a wide range of products in the year 1980. It also emphasises how marked has been the decline of the independents, both overall and in certain product groups, particularly food and drink.

The trends are easily enough explained. In the grocery field, for instance, it was no longer necessary by 1950 for the retailer to prepare the goods for sale. Mass production techniques ensured the goods came pre-weighed and pre-packed. The standing of the retailer was no longer necessary to guarantee product quality. The guarantee now came through the branding and advertising activities of the manufacturer. The multiple organisations had become able to secure the fullest discounts from manufacturers by imposing a standard assortment on their branches and combining the requirements of all branches into large orders. The newly emerging dynamism of the multiples increased pressure for the abolition of *resale price maintenance* and when this was virtually

Table 7.1 Commodity sales and other receipts (a), 1980: percentage distribution between forms of organisation

Commodity or service sold	All businesses	Single outlet retailers 1 outlet	Small multiple retailers 2–9 outlets	Large multiple retailers 10–99 outlets	100 or more outlets	
	%	%	%	%	%	
TOTAL TURNOVER	100.0	31.0	14.4	17.7	36.9	
Receipts from sales of goods through retail outlets and by special forms of trading	100.0	31.0	14.4	17.7	36.9	
1 Groceries and provisions	100.0	20.9	7.1	21.5	50.5	1
2 Fresh fruit and vegetables	100.0	42.2	17.7	12.1	28.0	2
3 Fresh milk and cream	100.0	26.4	10.9	32.2	30.5	3
4 Carcase meat and home-made sausages	100.0	39.8	18.4	12.7	29.1	4
5 Fresh fish, poultry and game	100.0	34.6	13.6	9.4	42.4	5
6 Bakery products	100.0	24.0	17.3	20.6	38.1	6
7 Alcoholic drinks	100.0	16.7	9.0	17.7	56.6	7
8 Chocolate and sugar confectionery	100.0	47.9	8.9	8.6	34.6	8
9 Tobacco and smokers' requisites	100.0	42.5	11.9	12.4	33.2	9
10 Newspapers and periodicals	100.0	61.2	13.1	6.2	19.5	10
11 Drugs, medicines, toilet preparations etc	100.0	31.9	16.4	10.4	41.3	11
12 Men's and boys' wear	100.0	23.8	17.7	20.7	37.8	12
13 Women's, girls', children's and infants' wear	100.0	30.3	15.4	19.2	35.1	13
14 Footwear	100.0	21.3	11.1	15.3	52.3	14
15 Travel goods, handbags etc	100.0	24.5	18.9	12.1	44.5	15
16 Carpets, carpeting and rugs	100.0	38.6	22.8	25.9	12.6	16
17 Household textiles and soft furnishings	100.0	38.0	17.6	21.6	22.7	17
18 Furniture and floor coverings	100.0	30.8	20.5	34.3	14.4	18
19 Radio, television and electrical goods	100.0	22.9	15.0	15.1	47.0	19
20 Hardware, china and glassware	100.0	36.9	16.9	14.0	32.3	20

21 Do-it-yourself and decorators' supplies	100.0	25.3	18.0	27.5	29.2	21
22 Lawnmowers	100.0	43.2	22.9	15.3	18.6	22
23 Musical instruments and goods, records and tapes	100.0	29.9	24.4	12.8	32.8	23
24 Antiques, works of art, prints etc	100.0	76.7	19.1	0.6	3.6	24
25 Novelties, souvenirs, gifts etc	100.0	49.1	27.3	9.1	14.5	25
26 Motor and motor-cycle parts and accessories	100.0	23.4	7.6	26.6	42.4	26
27 Books, stationery and office supplies	100.0	38.8	22.2	10.3	28.7	27
28 Photographic and optical goods	100.0	28.6	21.2	10.4	39.7	28
29 Jewellery, silverware, watches and clocks	100.0	41.2	22.7	18.4	17.7	29
30 Sports goods, toys, games and camping equipment	100.0	47.0	23.8	11.7	17.6	30
31 Cycles, perambulators and nursery furniture	100.0	51.9	20.8	5.8	21.5	31
32 Cut flowers, plants and garden sundries	100.0	53.8	27.2	5.7	13.3	32
33 Other new goods	100.0	28.3	13.2	15.7	42.8	33
34 Second-hand goods (except antiques etc)	100.0	63.2	18.0	3.7	15.1	34
35 Footwear repairs	100.0	18.2	6.7	14.9	60.1	35
36 Other repairs	100.0	39.4	15.0	12.3	33.3	36
37 Radio and television hire	100.0	10.5	7.1	17.7	64.7	37
38 Other hire	100.0	23.3	29.5	11.9	35.3	38
39 Any other receipts	100.0	13.6	13.4	32.9	40.1	39
Sales through central offices and warehouses	100.0	15.5	45.8	35.5	3.1	

(a) Inclusive of VAT

Source: SDA 25 Business Monitor. 1980 Retailing HMSO

brought about by the *Restrictive Trade Practices Act, 1956* and the *Resale Prices Act, 1964,* the way was open to the multiples to expand their trade still further by cutting prices.

Now while the passing of many small shops can be regretted in *social* terms, not least because of their value to the old and to young mothers, particularly in rural areas, these were *economic* trends of great significance to marketing executives and had to be taken into account for planning purposes. Moreover, even in social terms, the small shop was becoming less relevant for some sectors of the population. The increasing numbers of working wives meant more consumers with less time for shopping and the conversational, 'personal' approach of the corner shop. For a growing number of consumers, the shop counter was becoming a barrier to trade.

In addition to the proportion of total sales being achieved by types of outlet, there has been a noticeable pattern of diversification of the products handled by types of outlet. Mention has been made in Chapter 3 of the development of significant turnover in food and books by what were traditionally textile and clothing multiples. Confectionery is now sold in wine stores, cakes and biscuits in garden centres and a host of products, including food, fancy goods and gardening requisites, in garages. Furniture and carpets are now being extensively sold through supermarket-type operations and recently one of the largest UK firms in this sector, Harris Queensway, announced a joint venture marketing carpets, furniture and electrical goods within the branches of Debenhams, the department store group. Today tyres are not bought through garages so much as through the branches of multiple 'tyre and exhaust' firms which have emerged in the recent past. Boots, the chemists, has diversified so much in the last 25 years that it is now perhaps more accurately described as a department store group than as a firm of multiple chemists.

Changes in industrial markets

These trends have not been confined to consumer goods. The increasing complexity of modern technology, as it affects production systems, has increased the scale of requisite investment and hence the optimum size of production units. The last quarter of a century has seen many mergers and acquisitions in the production sector as a consequence. This has meant that in a large number of industrial markets, the pattern has been that 80 per cent of an industry's output has originated from 20 per cent of its firms, with the remaining 80 per cent of the firms each contributing a relatively small share. This 80/20 rule trend in the markets for both industrial and consumer goods has had important implications for other elements of the marketing mix and particularly for the numbers and structuring of sales forces as we shall see later. Of course, the emergence of conglomerates (e.g. British Leyland) in the production sector has not been trouble-free, particularly in industrial relations. The policy of the present UK Government is to dismantle these conglomerates where they lie in the public sector and to return them to the private sector. This trend, together with the general policy of encouragements for small businesses may see some reversal of the 80/20 tendency. It will be interesting to see how the pattern develops for it is certain that such changes will continue to be important influences on marketing practice. Today the question is not 'is there a changing pattern of distribution?' but 'how is distribution changing and what is the pace of the change?'

Marketing channel policy

The selection of marketing channels for the business organisation entails striving for a balance between achieving time and place utilities for the user and an adequate return-on-investment for the firm. The firm must therefore make an adequate assessment of the costs and benefits of alternative channel policies. The first influence upon channel selection is the product.

Rapid turnover consumer products

Food, drink, tobacco, confectionery, are usually made available through a wide variety of outlets – supermarkets; department stores; specialist food, confectionery and tobacconist shops; garages; the village stores; sub post-offices etc.

Durable consumer products

Motor cars, washing machines, TV sets, videos, usually require specialist outlets such as car dealer showrooms and radio and electrical shops, where both technical advice and after-sales service is available to the user. However, an increasing volume of electrical goods is now being sold through the *discount-house* type of operation where the user foregoes after-sales service in exchange for the lowest possible price.

Industrial consumption products

Chemicals, lubricants, cement, clay, stationery etc, are distributed in a variety of ways. If detailed specifications and close control of composition, quality and performance are called for by the user, as is the case with many raw materials, the manufacturer may distribute direct to the user. On the other hand, operating supplies such as lubricants and engineering supplies (bolts, nuts, rivets, valves, pipe-fittings etc) usually reach the user via merchants and engineering suppliers. The merchant supplying lubricants may, in fact, distribute both to end-users and other sub-distributors, supplying at the same time small tools, cleaning material for tanks and drains and other 'maintenance' supplies.

Industrial durable products

Lathes, grinding mills, furnaces, machine tools, main-frame computers etc, are invariably distributed direct to the user. Distribution typically follows a lengthy negotiation period in which details of the specification and performance of the required equipment are exchanged between the supplier and the user. The result is often a purpose-built product installed by the maker on the user's premises, frequently as a result of a tender for the contract, with a continuing high-level of after-sales service provided as a part of that contract.

Other examples of the product's influence on the channel can be provided.

1 Perishables must be marketed whilst they are fresh, therefore middlemen must be few. On the other hand, wholesalers figure very prominently in the distribution of canned foodstuffs.
2 Products that have a high unit value (e.g. furniture) are usually sold direct to the retailer. This method entails proportionately higher packing, transport, selling, administrative and storage costs per product and hence a high selling price, but the nature of the product will usually bear such a price.
3 If the product has a high rate of retail turnover, where replacement stocks must be readily to hand, wholesale organisations

in appropriate locations may obviate the high costs necessary for the manufacturer to establish his own network of depots.

4   A high-quality 'exclusive' product, such as an expensive perfume or high priced jewellery, must be distributed to the type of outlet capable of attracting appropriate clientele and fostering the necessary level of appeal for the product, e.g. a similarly exclusive department store or jewellery store.

The second important influence upon channel selection is the *user*. The marketing organisation must make some estimate of the *size of the market* and if published data is available, so much the better. Questions on the geographical extent of the market, the number of actual and potential users of the product or service and how these are dispersed through the geographical area of the market have to be answered. The answers will provide the basis for initial thinking on channel policy. An important factor for consideration concerns *user expectations*. As we saw in Chapter 3 (Marketing research) expected stock levels at distributive outlets constitute part of the subjective norm, one of the influences on purchase behaviour. Here again there is scope for consideration of costs: benefits bearing in mind the admonition (see page 239) that costs increase exponentially as the level of service improves. It is for this reason that Christopher, Walters and Wills[7] advise that management must be clear about the factors already set out on page 240.

The third influence on channel policy is the *company* itself. What is its size, in absolute and comparative terms? Is it so small, for instance, that rather than set up a distribution network it might be more profitable to approach a large multiple organisation and offer its production capacity for the manufacture of the multiple's own brand merchandise? On the other hand, the company may be so large that it is economically justified in setting up its own branch offices throughout the market rather than rely on intermediaries to provide the intensively good service, and perhaps the after-sales service, that is required. In fact, if we look at the following schematic, which represents many of the channels for the distribution of industrial products, we can perceive that choice will be influenced not only by the nature of the product, but also by the size of the supplying organisation.

A fourth factor in devising channel policy is the consideration of the *prevailing method of distribution*. There are no absolutes, of course, when we consider how competitors distribute their

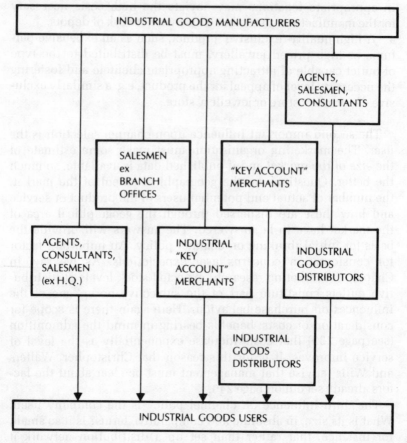

Fig. 7.4   *Some marketing channels (and types of sales organisation) for industrial products*

products (i.e. the prevailing method). Wholesalers may be so entrenched in the distribution network that it might be foolhardy to attempt to divert business from them. It may be clear that the mutiple organisations have become so preponderantly important that a prevailing method which is based upon their significance is the only logical policy to pursue. On the other hand, the newcomer might well decide that there is a marketing initiative to be gained by departing from the prevailing method. For example, where a market has a concentrated distribution system the newcomer may see that the independents are being neglected in consequence. He may decide that although the independents, for example, may have only 10 per cent of total retail sales, by adopting a bold policy of specialisation in favour of the independents he can secure 33⅓ per cent of their custom, which may constitute handsome volume sales for the newcomer. This again relates to the size of the organisation and what constitutes worthwhile sales volume. An alert appraisal of the changing pattern of distribution may indicate that certain outlets are diversifying into new product lines – the example of the expanding range being retailed by garages in the UK has been mentioned earlier. There may be marketing opportunity in a channel policy which focuses attention and effort on such diversification.

The fifth factor is the bearing that channel policy will have on the other elements of the marketing mix. Its influence on price is a cardinal factor. It is highly likely that there will be an established confidence-level – a price or narrow range of prices at which the user has come to regard comparable products as being of good value for money (the price/value dimension). The supplier must consider the effect that alternative channel policies have on the final price. Short channels (e.g. direct to the user, or via the retailer to the user) mean less provision for distributors' mark-ups (i.e. gross profit margins) but usually a marked increase in administration, packing and transport costs. Longer channels (e.g. with one or more wholesale intermediaries) usually mean lower administrative and transport costs but more provision for distributors' margins. Also, where there is a sales tax which is levied each time the goods change ownership, its cumulative effect on the final price may necessitate using the shortest possible channels. So it is a question of balancing the influence of channel choice on price and of examining the relationship between price and sales volume with its consequent effect on return on investment to the marketing organisation.

Short channels bring the organisation closer to the user, with all the benefits this implies and also enable it to exercise more control over the way the products are displayed and sold. Here, we must remember the effect on the promotion element of the mix. Often the manufacturer must do more than merely supply the product. He must arrange for its advertising and sales promotion in order to pull his products through the distributive network. The longer the channel the more necessary it is for him to do this, for the more danger there is that his sales message will lose its impact in transmission. Support at point-of-sale using dispensers, showcards and other presentation material becomes of great importance. The publishers of this textbook are extremely efficient at obtaining point-of-sale impact for their publications and the reader can judge this for himself when he next visits any of the UK's major bookshops.

The question of control over selling is clearly related to marketing success or failure. As we have seen, one solution is for the manufacturer to move directly into retailing if there is sufficient finance for the venture. Another is to lease space from the retailer on a shop-within-a-store basis, a method traditionally favoured by a number of cosmetics manufacturers. In both instances, the manufacturer controls the stock, can apply his merchandising expertise and can energetically promote the lines with the greatest turnover potential.

A good example of the supplier's control over selling through involvement in the distribution function comes from the field of paperback books. Although books of this type on popular themes – romance, science fiction, biography etc – have an enormous potential market, they do not sell particularly well in the traditional bookshop (65 per cent of the UK population never visit a bookshop). Websters Publications, facing the same problem as the manufacturer who wishes to improve the retailing efficiency of his products, own a 75 per cent share of Bookwise Service, a national wholesaling organisation which provides an in-store merchandising service that distributes titles selected from UK paperback publishers through an extensive range of retail outlets including supermarket chains, newsagents and branches of the Woolworth organisation. Space is provided on a rent-free basis by the retailer, who buys the stock and obtains $33\frac{1}{3}$ per cent discount from the retail selling price. Bookwise is responsible for keeping the stands continuously stocked and generating sales turnover through strategically locating the stands and arranging appealing displays. The method has enabled Bookwise to quadruple its volume turnover over a four year period in the recent past, and it now has such a significant share of the UK paperback market that its bulk buying policy enables it to obtain larger discounts from publishers, who benefit from longer print runs. The retailers also benefit – firstly by being able to offer a more integrated service (and this particularly applies to newsagents) and secondly by securing a return from floor space which was previously under-utilised.

To summarise what has been said so far the key influences on channel policy are: the product; the market (its size, geographical extent etc); the organisation (and particularly its size). Additionally, factors for consideration are; 1 the prevailing method of distribution; 2 any actual or potential changes in the method of distribution and 3 the influence that channel policy will have on other elements in the marketing mix, e.g. price and promotion.

There are several other points to make with regard to channel policy. These are now explained.

1   It is not invariably the case that a manufacturer will choose one marketing channel to the exclusion of all others. Let us imagine for example that there are a number of wholesalers who might serve Arnold Ceramics well in the distribution of their medium-priced tableware but that these wholesalers mainly serve the smaller china and glass retail outlets. Arnolds might establish a policy whereby large retail organisations (e.g. multiples, large department stores) capable of purchasing substantial quantities, will be designated as 'key accounts' and supplied direct. Now it may well be that certain other china and glass retailers are capable of large purchases from time to time. Arnolds might agree to supply these direct whenever they can purchase a *minimum value consignment*. Thus Arnolds have three channels, in effect; direct to key accounts; direct to category A retailers purchasing a stipulated minimum value and also via wholesalers to category A retailers; and thirdly via wholesalers to category B retailers who would never, ordinarily, buy in sufficient quantity to justify dealing direct with Arnolds. Another point, of course, is that all retailers would be free to use wholesalers whenever it suited them (e.g. for emergency orders; to supply matching items).

It is also conceivable that where a manufacturer produces two or more grades of the same product he may establish a policy based on the use of two or more channels. A manufacturer of ladies' fashions might sell an exclusively modelled, expensive version of the range on a direct basis to high-class department stores and fashion shops. He might also manufacture a cheaper range designed for a mass market, distributed via the wholesale trade which decides where best it should be retailed. This policy of *dual distribution* would be based on the careful consideration of costs and profitability so as to optimise the use of his production facilities in combination with a proper regard for user needs and interests. The required numbers, locations, levels and types of distributors are then established bearing these criteria in mind.

Figure 7.5 demonstrates how several channels could be used to distribute a range of products. Let us imagine that Arnold

Ceramics have developed a range of ornamental ware (e.g. jardinières, posy bowls, ashtrays, figurines, miniature teasets and reproductions of cartoon characters, manufactured under licence). Such a range would merit wide distribution. Certainly, restricting it to pottery and glass outlets would doubtless curtail sales.

Figure 7.5 represents a distribution policy designed to cater for the several segments which make up the total market for the range.

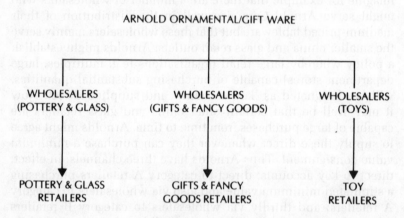

Fig. 7.5   *Multi-channel policy for the distribution of Arnold ornamental ware*

2   The second supplementary point is that the nature of the product will determine the nature of supplementary services which must be provided and these cannot be dispensed with (barring price reductions) – they must happen somewhere within the chain of distribution. If the retailer is not weighing the goods and preparing them for sale then the manufacturer must pre-weigh and pre-prepare them. If the distributor is not willing or able to provide an adequate level of after-sales service, the manufacturer must then set up his own service organisation. These services add value to the product, but they also add costs. What is important is to ensure that wherever the service is provided, there is a sufficient margin of gross profit to cover the costs involved. Conversely, the manufacturer must ensure that where a margin is allowed to distributors to cover supplementary services, these are, in fact, provided. As one experienced business-

man put it: 'We only allow trade margins for roles which we don't ourselves perform.'

3 Elaborating on point 2, the student of marketing must bear in mind that the interests of manufacturers and distributors do not necessarily coincide and that often it is a daunting enough task to find distributors willing to handle new products let alone provide supplementary services for them. In practice a negotiated consensus is arrived at as to who shall perform which function and the best way to ensure dealer co-operation is to make the distributor want to handle the products. This raises the question of dealer support, i.e. the help the manufacturer will give to ensure that the distributor can show an adequate return on the investment made in the goods.

In addition to products and services that are acceptable to users, distributors are entitled to:

(a) trade margins, discounts and credit policies which provide them with an adequate return for their role in sharing risk and arranging distribution;

(b) the reliability of their supplier on delivery promises and the maintenance of quality standards;

(c) reasonable policies with regard to the stipulated size of orders and an adequate marketing opportunity to liquidate their own investment in such order quantities (e.g. through territorial franchises, where appropriate);

(d) where applicable, assistance with stock-turn, through advertising support, assistance with trade exhibitions and the provision of sales promotional materials (leaflets, catalogues, manuals) and retail display materials etc;

(e) suitable support in arranging for an adequate level of after-sales service (including the training of distributors' personnel) and an effective system for dealing with complaints.

Heading (a) above listing trade margins, discounts etc, is an important element in support for distributors. These are now described.

Distributor's margin

This is the amount added to the product's price by the distributor in order to cover the distributor's costs and yield him a profit on his investment. For example, in the case of the Arnold ornamental ware it might be usual for the wholesaler to add a gross margin or mark up of 33⅓ per cent to the manufacturer's price to him and for the retailer to add 50 per cent on the price from the wholesaler. Such a price structure then makes for a retail selling price which is double that of Arnolds price to the wholesaler according to the following calculation:

	Product price
ex Manufacturer (e.g. Arnolds), say	100
Wholesale mark-up on cost (33⅓%)	33.3
Price to retail ex wholesaler	133.3
Retail mark-up on cost (50%)	66.6
Retail selling price	200

(*Note.* this simple outline takes no account of sales taxes, e.g. VAT, which may or may not be applicable from time to time and according to the type of product).

The margin or mark-up may alternatively be expressed as a discount from the selling price, e.g. 33⅓ per cent on cost price = 25 per cent discount on selling price in the above example ($\frac{33}{133} \times \frac{100}{1}$ = 25 per cent). Frequently, the distributors' margin is set out as a discount.

It is customary for the distributors' discount or mark-up to be related to a minimum quantity consignment or a minimum value order, e.g. 'the 30 per cent wholesale discount will be based on orders of not less than 10 packs'.

Quantity discounts

As an inducement for distributors to carry stocks above the stipulated minimum quantities, and particularly in advance of advertising campaigns, the manufacturer may offer additional discounts (e.g. 2½ per cent; 5 per cent) for the purchase of stocks at fixed levels above the qualifying minimum for normal distributors' discounts. Alternatively, the discounts may be set out on a scale ascending with order values;

e.g.

Minimum order (no. of packs)	Discount from recommended retail selling price
10	30%
11–19	$31\frac{1}{4}$%
20–29	$32\frac{1}{2}$%
30–39	35%
40–49	$37\frac{1}{2}$%
50 or more	40%

(The manufacturer would be able to offer these increased discounts if his calculations demonstrated that economies in packing, transport, stockholding, administration and/or increasing returns to scale of production made them possible.)

Settlement discounts

The marketing organisation must carefully calculate the influence that cash flow has on the cost of raising short-term finance from its own bankers. The company's normal payment terms frequently contain some inducement for traders to settle their accounts within a reasonable time, e.g. '$3\frac{3}{4}$ per cent discount for settlement within 28 days of the date of invoice'. According to its requirements to increase cash flow it may offer further inducements, e.g. '5 per cent discount for settlement within 28 days of date of invoice; $7\frac{1}{2}$ discount for settlement within 14 days of date of invoice'.

Other distributors' allowances

Where offered, these usually consist of discounts or allowances for retail displays, joint ventures at exhibitions, shared costs of local advertising etc and may be in cash (i.e. as deductions from invoices) or kind (e.g. additional quantities of the product).

(Note. Students frequently describe distributors' margins or discounts as 'profit.' The latter can only be calculated after the subtraction of distributors costs (e.g. cost of goods purchased; warehousing, packing, stock control and handling costs; carriage outwards; selling, advertising expenses; office salaries and order processing costs) from the revenue produced by the margin.

Self-assessment questions

1   Describe the two elements in the distribution function.
2   What is the relationship between physical distribution management and the marketing concept?
3   What factors influence the level of service?
4   Discuss the role of the marketing manager in relation to (a) choice of transport mode and (b) stock control.
5   What are the functions of the wholesale trade?
6   What is: franchising? direct marketing? groupage? vertical integration? the subjective norm? dual distribution?
7   Explain the significance of a changing pattern of distribution for marketing policy.
8   How does the product influence marketing channel policy?
9   What are the main elements in an adequate strategy for dealer support?
10   Define: distributors' margins; quantity discounts; settlement discounts; distributors' allowances.

References

1 The Centre for Physical Distribution Management. *Handbook of physical distribution management* (ed. Felix Wentworth) 2nd edn, Farnborough, Gower Publishing, 1981, p. 4
2 Institute of Directors. *The Director's guide to storage, handling, freight and distribution* London, Institute of Directors, 1980, p. 11
3 The Centre for Physical Distribution Management. Ibid. p. 11
4 Winrow, Philip. Physical distribution, *Marketing Handbook* (ed. Michael Rines), 2nd edn, Aldershot, Gower Publishing, 1981 p. 315
5 Christopher, Martin, Walters, David and Wills, Gordon. *Introduction to marketing* 3rd edn, Bradford, MCB Publications, 1978, p. 97
6 Thomas, S. Evelyn. (revd. L. B. Curzon) *Commerce – its theory and practice* 11th edn, London, Cassell, 1979 p. 328
7 *Introduction to marketing* p. 97

8 PLANNING MARKETING COMMUNICATIONS

Objectives

Is advertising 'wasteful, unethical and misleading'? Not if the campaign is carefully planned, balancing all the elements skilfully and honestly, is the message of this Chapter.

The characteristics, atmosphere, quantitative coverage and costs of the various communications media are recounted, together with some propositions for their selection and use.

An outline of advertising agency services and personnel is provided together with a representation of some of the processes involved in media planning and budgetting.

Introduction

We now come to the fourth component of the marketing mix – *promotion* in the 4Ps shorthand, customarily described as *marketing communication*. A major element of this activity, advertising, has drawn a great deal of adverse criticism for being 'wasteful', 'unethical', 'misleading'. In its own small way, this Chapter hopes to deal with these and other criticisms, admitting that in some cases they have been justified. We have all seen advertisements that infringe good taste, that are production oriented in that creative people have been more concerned with impressing their professional brotherhood than with persuading the market to take some course of action. We have also been misled on occasions in that the product or service involved did not live up to the promise of the advertisement.

Yet these advertisements are, on any reasonable assessment, very much in the minority of most people's experience of marketing communication and are certainly not the marketing way of doing things.

The objectives of marketing communications

The first requirement of marketing communication is that it is related to objectives. Organisational objectives, discussed in Chapter 2, give rise to marketing objectives and from these we derive the objectives of marketing communications. Therefore, contrary to what the critics would have us believe, marketing communications are planned, not unplanned. If they were unplanned they could not, on the definitions set out in this book, be marketing communications. To give an illustration of how objectives relate to each other, the organisational objective may well be:

In the next financial year our objective will be to increase the rate of return on investment by two per cent.

A marketing objective related to this may be:

To introduce the new range of 'Diana' branded tableware and to gain a five per cent share of the market in the next financial year.

The consequent marketing communications objective (first stage) may be:

To develop recognition for the new range within 50 per cent of the user groups described in this schedule, in the regions described in this schedule.

Alternatively, the marketing objective may be to increase the sales of a particular brand of pastry mix by means of a special offer. The marketing communications objective may be to convey information about the special offer and to ensure that at least 30 per cent of target households (subsequently described) obtain the coupon connected with the offer.

Aside from introducing new products or increasing the sales of existing products a particular campaign may be based on any one of a number of objectives. For example:

1　a manufacturer of industrial equipment may wish to obtain enquiries which will then be followed up by his technical representatives;

2　a supplier of a telephone cleaning service may wish to reach people not usually accessible to his sales force (e.g. company managing directors);

3　a manufacturer of DIY products may wish to improve dealer relations, with the secondary objective of improving/increasing the displays of his products;

4   a retail organisation may wish to announce the opening of
its first branches in a market abroad;
5   an oil company, in order to build goodwill and to further its
market standing, may wish to tell the public of its exploration
operations in the North Sea. Or it may wish to inform its shareholders of its selective investment and rationalisation programmes, including its diversification into chemicals, natural gas
and animal husbandry.

Each of these cases relates to the objectives of a profit organisation but the same holds good for non-profit organisations:

1   a Government department announcing a new issue of National
Savings Certificates, or the details of a new job-release scheme
designed to mitigate the effects of unemployment;
2   a charitable organisation providing aid to Third World countries (e.g. Oxfam, War on Want);
3   a church wishing to explain its system of beliefs (as does the
Roman Catholic church from time to time).

All undertake marketing communications in pursuit of objec-
tive(s). The communications campaign is then *planned* with
those objective(s) in mind.
When the objectives are being devised there is parallel consideration of the factors that will influence the strategy to be adopted.
The factors are these:

1   the nature of user wants, including any significant behavioural/
attitudinal constructs;
2   the nature of any trends in public outlook which may affect
user wants (e.g. research by the Taylor Nelson Group indicates
that the British are becoming more health-conscious and have
less time for formal meals, particularly breakfast – both factors
of significance in the marketing of cereals);
3   the characteristics/performance of the product or service, particularly where this will assist in the development of a specific
identity for the product, service or the communications message
(the 'unique selling proposition');
4   the financial and other resources available for the communications campaign;
5   the type and extent of competitive activity, when applicable;
6   the method by which the product or service is typically distributed and purchased.

From these preliminary comments it can be seen that, as with all objectives, the formulation of marketing communications objectives hinges on the responses to the four questions:

Where are we going? – (a goal or target)
How will we get there? – (to be achieved by a specific strategy)
When will we get there? – (within a specified time)
How will we know when we have arrived? – (using a means of measurement and monitoring progress).

The elements of marketing communications

Within what is commonly called the communications mix there are four elements:

advertising,
sales promotion,
publicity,
personal selling.

Communications activity consists of using these elements in a planned, balanced and systematic way in order to achieve objectives. It is not the case that all four elements will be used in every campaign but this is the general rule in the marketing of consumer goods. Personal selling is usually carried out by a team of representatives employed by the organisation. The functions of the team are (a) to obtain orders for the product or service, (b) to receive, as well as to give marketing information (since the contribution of the sales team to marketing research is often invaluable) and (c) to support, and integrate with, the other elements of the communications mix.

Personal selling is dealt with in detail in Chapter 9. As to the other three communications elements we must first of all define them.

1   *Advertising* consists of the purchase and use of space in newspapers, magazines or outdoor locations or the purchase and use of time on radio and television, by an identified sponsor, for the promotion of goods, services or ideas.

2   *Sales promotion* usually complements the organisation's advertising, personal selling efforts and publicity and includes those activities designed to encourage user-purchase at point-

of-sale and dealer effectiveness, e.g. in-store displays, demonstrations, and exhibitions. Expenditure on premium offers, competitions etc, is also normally included under this heading.

3 *Publicity* which can usually be taken to mean the creation of a favourable atmosphere in which selling can be done by means of 'free' publicity, e.g. editorial articles in newspapers and magazines, or programmes on radio and television in which the organisation and/or its personalities, products, processes and discoveries receive favourable mention.

Note The author has set out above what he believes to be an acceptable consensus based on current practice – the reader should be warned, however, that laymen, authors and practitioners often have their own definitions; 'publicity' is occasionally taken to encompass all the above activities.

In relation to these definitions it is also important to mention the role of *public relations* which is 'concerned with maintaining good communications between an organisation and its various 'publics'.[1] In addition to its customers, these 'publics' include its employees, shareholders, suppliers, citizens of the local community, departments of central and local government and trade unions. The role of public relations is not only to maintain and establish understanding and goodwill for the organisation's products or services, but also for its activities and operating policies. It may wish to build a new factory, merge with or acquire other organisations, defend its manufacturing processes against an anti-pollution lobby, explain its position in some dispute with a trade union, or it may have secured a large contract. In each of these cases it may approach the appropriate communications media (national newspapers, television, technical press etc) so that its story can be told. It will not pay for the editorial coverage or the transmission time obtained – the items being put forward are hopefully newsworthy in themselves – and will therefore have no control over the content of the communication. So it can be seen that public relations is not only concerned with communicating for marketing purposes but also for the broader purpose of developing a favourable corporate image among its many publics. Norman Hart,[2] a well-known writer and practitioner in marketing communications, points out (with regard to public relations in a general sense as opposed to its role in the marketing mix) that consideration must be given to an extensive range of items for their potential contribution to the corporate image.

The range extends from letterheads and correspondence, switch-board efficiency, the appearance of salesmen and the packaging of products to the standards portrayed by the organisation's advertising and publicity in its many forms.

The field of public relations also includes *press relations*, which attempts to serve the same range of organisational objectives by obtaining good editorial coverage, exclusively through the medium of the press. The preparation of materials (e.g. press releases, photography, videotapes etc) for dissemination to the media is usually done through, or with the guidance of, advertising agencies or public relations consultants, whose functions are explained later in the Chapter.

The media of marketing communications

The *medium* is the vehicle, or method, chosen to transmit the communication, and we must firstly distinguish between *above-the-line* and *below-the-line* media. The above-the-line media are those which pay a commission to the advertising agencies on the business they place on behalf of their clients, the manufac-turers and other marketing organisations on whose behalf the communications campaigns are being conducted. The above-the-line media comprise the press, television, outdoor and transport media, radio and the cinema. The below-the-line media comprise such media as exhibitions, direct mail and point-of-sale display. The advertising agencies are not reimbursed by way of commis-sion from media owners for the development of below-the-line media, but by way of fees which the agencies negotiate direct with their clients, the advertisers – (Note. the role of the advertis-ing agency and its sources of revenue are discussed on pages 291–294).

Current total annual UK advertising expenditure on above-the-line media is in excess of £4000 million (the comparable figure for 1980 being £2555 million). Apart from anything else, the cur-rent figure, which is the highest ever, proves that advertisers are maintaining their expenditures in real terms and this despite the recent economic recession and the slump in the *classified* advertising field due to unemployment levels.

Classified advertising comprises small lineage advertisements in simple typesetting, and is not distinctly different from the normal editorial make-up of the publication. The advertisements

Table 8.1   UK advertising expenditure by media

Media	Percentage of total expenditure		
	1982	1983	1984
National newspapers	16.5	16.3	16.7
Regional newspapers*	23.6	22.8	22.7
Magazines and periodicals	6.7	6.3	6.2
Trade and technical press	7.9	7.7	7.7
Directories†	4.0	4.3	4.5
Press production costs	4.8	5.1	5.3
(Total)			
Press	63.5	62.5	63.1
Television	29.7	31.0	30.7
Poster and transport	4.0	3.8	3.7
Cinema	0.6	0.4	0.4
Radio	2.2	2.3	2.1
Total expenditure	100.0	100.0	100.0
	(£3126 million)	(£3579 million)	(£4055 million)

* Including free sheets (i.e. papers distributed door-to-door and free to the user)
† Including Yellow Pages.

are usually grouped into appropriate sections, e.g. 'articles for sale'; 'motor vehicles'; 'situations vacant'. *Display* advertising, as its name implies, incorporates an element of design or 'display' – an illustration, a stylised form of lettering etc. The display advertisement is much larger than the typical classified advertisement and may well occupy a whole page or a considerable proportion of a page.

The comparative importance of the various above-the-line media can be gauged from the following analysis of total UK advertising expenditure, which has been compiled by the author with the assistance of the UK's Advertising Association. Table 8.1 sets out the proportions of total expenditure attracted by the various media, whilst Table 8.2 shows the proportion of display advertising which went to the same media in the time period 1980–1982. The footnote to this table provides the figures for total expenditure on display advertising in the years 1983 and 1984 (appended for comparison).

These figures show that although the press is by far the most dominant medium it has lost a little ground to television in recent years. Principally, this has been due to the reduction of classified advertising of employment vacancies in the regional press (where

Table 8.2   UK display advertising expenditure by media

Media	Percentage of total expenditure		
	1980	1981	1982
Press	52	50	49
Television	38	40	41
Poster and transport	6	6	6
Cinema	1	1	1
Radio	3	3	3
Total expenditure	100	100	100
	(£1970 million)	(£2207 million)	(£2437 million)

Note: Total UK display advertising expenditure amounted to £2779 million in 1983 and £3119 million in 1984.

traditionally it is the source of up to half of the advertising revenue). The recent widespread emergence of *freesheets* (by October 1982 there were 470 in the UK) has also attracted a great deal of advertising which was previously the province of the regional press. The high cost effectiveness of the freesheets is now enabling them to attract national as well as local advertisers and in a recent single year these newcomers increased their total advertising revenue by as much as 25 per cent (£105 million).

In order to complete this preliminary examination of the advertising media it might be helpful to say something about the *type* of advertising attracted by the main media. On a continuous basis this is monitored by *Media Expenditure Analysis Limited* (MEAL). In the calendar year 1983, the ten product groups for which highest gross television and press display advertising expenditure was recorded by MEAL were as follows:

1   Departmental/retail stores
2   Motor cars
3   Chocolate/confectionery
4   Government departments and Service recruitment
5   Chain grocery and cooperative stores
6   Building Societies
7   Cigarettes
8   Joint-stock banks
9   Lager
10   Records, cassettes, cartridges

Source: Media Expenditure Analysis Ltd (calculated at rate-card rates)

The analysis indicates the importance of advertising to the services sector of the economy (retail organisations, banks, building societies and departments of government). This is somewhat at variance with the impressions seemingly held by the critics of advertising who consider it largely a business of persuading people to buy 'products they don't want'. It is interesting that washing powders and other detergents, which have previously come in for a deal of the odium directed at advertising, do not even appear in the 'top ten' product groups.

The selection and use of communications media

We said on page 276 that the second question to be asked in formulating communications objectives is: – *how will we get there?* which involves devising a specific strategy. The strategy usually involves the selection and use of the media (both above- and below-the-line) in an appropriately balanced mix called the *campaign plan.* The selection of which media to use, in what proportions and for what role depends upon the advertiser's budget and a consideration of:

  the characteristics;
  the atmosphere;
  the quantitative coverage; and
  the cost

of the media available. The next section says something about each of these criteria for choice.

Media characteristics

These are the attributes of the media in question. They may make available to the advertiser the opportunity to use sound, colour, movement or a particular printing process. They may enable him to use lengthy advertising 'copy' or to ensure constant repetition of a simple selling message or perhaps to remind the user, when she is next at the shops, of the advertising previously seen in another advertising medium. The brief description of media characteristics which follows may make this clearer.

The press

The term press covers an extensive range of publications including national newspapers, regional newspapers and magazines. Britain is unique in that it has both daily and Sunday newspapers that are national, (i.e. simultaneously available everywhere in the United Kingdom) that have very large circulations, and are therefore very useful for mass marketing. Since they are *news-papers*, readers come to them looking for news and they are therefore considered to be a good medium in which to introduce new products.

Depending upon their writing style, the features material they publish, their type of layout and their political viewpoints, national newspapers are divided into 'populars' (*Daily Mirror, Sun* etc) and 'qualities' (e.g. *The Daily Telegraph, The Times, Guardian*). Another characteristic of national newspapers is their flexibility in that being a mass medium they can be used to appeal to both sexes, all age groups and all socio-economic groups and yet their stratification into populars and qualities enables the advertiser to 'skew' his message to certain segments of the total population if his objectives so dictate. Flexibility also extends to size, for advertisements may be classified or display, and if display may range from a few column inches of space to a whole page. Colour facilities are also available in a number of national newspapers within the make-up of the paper itself or through the colour supplements. By the Spring of 1982 there were no fewer than six of these colour magazines in the markets covered by national Sunday newspapers when the *Mail on Sunday* launched its magazine to join the well-established supplements of *The Observer, The Sunday Times* and *The Sunday Telegraph.*

We can see from data earlier in the Chapter that, in spite of recent difficulties, regional newspapers are an even bigger medium than the nationals. As many as four homes in every five read a local newspaper on an average day and because of its very high editorial content of local interest, it is thought by some to be more carefully read than the national press. Being so rooted a feature of the local community it has great significance for local advertisers. The salience of classified advertising to the regional press has already been commented upon. One writer, Owen-Browne,[3] believes that the classifieds are more important to some readers of the local press than its news or editorial content. Approximately 20 million copies of regional newspapers are published daily and the titles range from the *Yorkshire Post*, a quality newspaper of virtually national standing, to the large number of evening and weekly newspapers circulating in Britain's cities, towns and other well defined local areas. Although the freesheets have attracted national as well as local advertising, the main function of the regional press is to serve the local advertiser.

Magazines can be divided into clearly defined groups. The general interest magazines – such as *Radio Times*, *Punch*, *Ideal Home* and *Reader's Digest* – can be categorised with national newspapers in that they are frequently used for national advertising campaigns. Special interest magazines, such as *Amateur Gardening*, *Amateur Photographer*, *The Angling Times* and *Motor* also circulate nationally but cover highly particularised markets, especially those related to hobby and leisure interests, and can therefore be categorised differently from the general interest magazines. In the special interest field the advertisements are certainly read as closely and carefully as the editorial features and most of the titles give excellent coverage of their markets.

Trade, technical and professional magazines constitute the third important group. Each of these is aimed at a special category of reader – a manufacturer, retailer, accountant, architect, engineer, medical practitioner etc, and the professional journals attain virtual full coverage of their market since membership subscriptions are often devised to cover the printing and distribution costs of the monthly journal. Two particularly important roles can be distinguished for this category:

1   the use of trade journals to announce to retailers news of forthcoming national advertising to users, thus inducing retailers to stock up in advance;
2   the use of technical and professional journals to introduce news of new products, processes, developments etc, particularly where the professional concerned has an important influence on the purchase and use of the product – as would an architect with a building material or a doctor with a pharmaceutical product.

Finally, in addition to the freesheets mentioned earlier, there are giveaway magazines, such as *High Life* (published by British Airways) and the *Barclaycard* magazine which are useful for advertising relatively expensive products (jewellery, leather goods etc) to the higher-income groups.

Television

Television viewing is the most popular leisure pastime in Britain. The average viewing time per person is almost 24 hours per week. As the table in Chapter 5 shows, virtually everyone in this country has access to a television set (and over two homes in every five have two or more sets). So again, we are talking of a mass medium and one which provides the advertiser with powerful features: sound, movement, colour, the ability to demonstrate products and to develop brand identities, or 'personalities', for products or services, by means of the musical jingle or some other appropriate creative approach.

Although undoubtedly a mass medium, it is flexible in that campaigns can be initiated on a regional basis and extended region by region, towards national coverage and as the budget allows. (There are two commercial channels in operation; the second, Channel 4, began broadcasting in November 1982. Fifteen television programme companies hold the contracts to provide programmes in the 14 independent television regions and a further contract was awarded to another company to provide early morning commercial television from the beginning of 1983. The companies operate on a commercial basis and derive their revenues from the sale of advertising time.)

As can be seen from the table on page 280, television is an important medium for advertising services as well as products. Currently savings and investment, air travel, retailing and government advertising figure prominently in the medium. This is in contrast to its early days when such consumable products as petrol, soap, beer and food products dominated the 'breaks' for advertising. In the 25 year history of commercial television, the social grade composition of its audience has been biased towards the C_2DE sector but with the growing proportion of cultural and minority interest programmes on the commercial network, particularly with the advent of Channel 4, there will doubtless be some realignment of the ABC_1 audience which previously favoured the BBC channels (and watched less television than the C_2DE segment). An important segment in the commercial television audience are the nation's large families with young children.

Poster and transport media

There are approximately 180 000 poster sites throughout the UK. The products which predominate (e.g. petrol, food, drink and

travel) are those for which the sales message can be briefly con-
veyed, because the main function of poster (and transport) media
is to remind potential users of the product or service when they
are at or near the point-of-sale. For this reason, these media are
often referred to in campaign planning as 'support' media whose
role is to remind the user of the advertising in other media (e.g.
press, television) where the 'reasoned selling argument' was set
out at greater length. The reminder function usually confines
itself to a simple statement, a short slogan, or merely the brand
name and illustration of the product or service, the story being
told within a glance, since the viewing opportunity is such a
cursory one. A traditional difficulty for intending poster advertisers has been the fragmented nature of the industry in which
small family-run businesses with control of sites in single towns
or counties, rather than nationally, were a dominant feature.
Rationalisation has reduced the number of contractors from 700
(in the 1960s period) to currently about 70. The British Posters
consortium was formed by the major companies in order to offer
advertisers a more balanced selection of sites – in terms of both
location and size – than individual contractors could usually provide for themselves. These pre-selected campaigns or 'packages',
comprising approximately one third of the total sites available,
guaranteed the advertiser a given weight of coverage for national-
/regional/or local marketing. During 1983, however, the Monopolies and Mergers Commission ruled the consortium's monopoly
of poster sites against the public interest and enforced the wind-
ing-up of the consortium. At the present time, the major contractors (e.g. Mills and Allen; London and Provincial) are seeking to
conclude chartering arrangements with other contractors so that
these packages of sites – either nationally or by television region
– remain available to advertisers. Reverting to the characteristics
of the medium itself, an especially important feature is the opportunity it provides to use an extremely wide range of colours to
good effect.

   In addition to poster sites, facilities for advertising are available
on the 2300 stations of British Rail. The facilities of the London
Underground system also constitute a key feature of transport
advertising and, nationally, facilities are also available on more
than 21 000 buses. Advertisers are also able to commission the
painting of a complete bus to their own design (though the facility
is restricted to one such bus per route and to one product or
service per area).

Despite the reminder role of most poster and transport advertising it is possible to use these media for a 'primary' national campaign. However, the sales message must be capable of very brief treatment and, in the main, the approach has been used by large organisations able to dominate the media for at least some space of time (e.g. three months or more).

Radio

Although only a small medium in expenditure terms, there is no shortage of facilities for the advertiser. In addition to Radio Luxembourg, a station of long standing, 37 independent stations, distributed throughout Britain, had been established by 1983 with another 32 independent stations due to be established. This means that local commercial stations designed to serve large urban areas such as London (Capital Radio), Manchester (Radio Piccadilly) and Glasgow (Radio Clyde) are now being joined by other stations designed to serve smaller local areas such as Preston/Blackpool (Red Rose Radio), Bury St Edmunds (Saxon Radio), Swindon/West Wiltshire (Wiltshire Radio) and Hereford/Worcestershire (Radio Wyvern).

It is generally a support medium and its audience comprises the following broad segments:

housewives, during the hours of daytime broadcasting;
young adults, during evening broadcasting;
motorists, during the morning and evening traffic rush hour periods.

With the extension of the commercial network strong growth in its revenues has been forecast in some quarters. However, according to *The Financial Times*:

The main problem faced by commercial stations... is the reluctance of the major advertising agencies and their substantial consumer goods clients to use radio.[4]

Among the reasons advanced for this, are:

1 the lack of national – or until recently – proper regional coverage;
2 the reluctance of the best creative agency staff to commit themselves to campaigns worth only a few hundred pounds (see page 303 for some indication of costs).

In response to these criticisms, the commercial stations have formed regional airtime selling groups enabling advertisers to buy time for roughly the same geographical areas as the independent television network. The largest and most successful of the commercial companies, Capital Radio, has initiated a Radio Advertisement of the Month award to encourage creativity in the production of radio advertisements. Although it is likely to remain a relatively small support medium the alert student of marketing would do well to watch developments in this field.

Cinema

As the figures earlier in the Chapter show, the cinema is a very small medium in terms of absolute expenditure, attracting a fairly constant one per cent of the UK's display advertising expenditure. However, it is an important medium for reaching the young adult market for products and services, with soft drinks, confectionery, cosmetics, health and beauty services and the services of banks and building societies being well suited to it. It is also an important medium for the local retailers, with products for the 'prospective marrieds' and the 'young marrieds' (carpets, furniture, TV etc) figuring prominently in the medium.

Having said this, the medium's general importance has markedly declined in the post-1945 period, with cinema-going, hitherto a national pastime, being so adversely affected by the advent of television (less than one third of the 5000 cinemas operating at the end of the Second World War remain in business). Nevertheless the medium's distinctly important characteristics – colour, sound, the large screen, the 'captive' audience are important attributes and its particular 'atmosphere' of romance and escapism undoubtedly assists the marketing of some products. Advertising time is available through slides (used mainly by local organisations) and 30 second and 60 second films. Screening costs are relatively cheap (see details of campaign costs later in this Chapter) but it must be remembered that production costs for the film itself and for the prints to be made available at each cinema are a very significant item.

The characteristics of below-the-line media

These are briefly summarised below.

Exhibitions

Participation in exhibitions enables the product to be displayed, operated, tested, dismantled, adjusted etc and this means the medium is of great value, particularly in industrial marketing. In addition to the demonstration of products, for the purpose of selling, exhibitions enable the advertiser to conduct research into market potential; to find new agents and distributors; to support existing distributors where the exhibition is one which provides the supplier with contact with consumers; and to introduce new products, services and concepts. It will be gathered from this that the medium is particularly important in international marketing and HM Government's assistance to exporters in this regard is referred to in Chapter 13.

There are a bewildering variety of exhibitions including international fairs; national consumer goods exhibitions (e.g. the UK's Ideal Home exhibition); trade exhibitions directed towards wholesalers and retailers (e.g. the UK's Gifts and Fancy Goods Fair; the Toy Fair); technical exhibitions for manufacturing users (e.g. The Machine Tools Exhibition) and the local exhibitions organised by county and borough councils and chambers of commerce (e.g. the Northampton Enterprise Show). Information to enable the advertiser to judge the suitability of particular exhibitions is available from the *Exhibition Bulletin* (a monthly publication), the Association of Exhibition Organisers (AEO) and the Incorporated Society of British Advertising (ISBA). The latter organisation publishes valuable material on exhibitions and exhibiting. Many exhibition organisers provide data via the Audit Bureau of Circulations' Exhibition Data Form (EDF), but as McDermott[5] points out this should be supplemented by independent survey information on audience quality and reactions and opinions. This should be requested of the organiser, together with projected attendances at forthcoming exhibitions and how these will be verified.

There are about 60 towns and cities in Britain well equipped with exhibition facilities. Prominent among the most modern are:

National Exhibition Centre (Birmingham)
Wembley Conference Centre ⎫
Barbican Centre   ⎪
Earls Court   ⎬ (London)
Olympia   ⎪
Wembley Arena   ⎭

Brighton Centre (Sussex)
Harrogate Centre (North Yorkshire).

As important as the design of the exhibition stand, its position
in the exhibition site relative to the 'traffic' of visitors and the
knowledge and efficiency of selling staff, is that a speedy and
efficient system for processing orders and enquiries is established.
The quality of the 'follow-up' work often determines the ultimate
value of exhibition participation.

Direct mail

With direct mail it is possible to reach a target market, or a segment of a market, with a minimum of 'overlap'. It is important
that the details of the market are comprehensively documented
and that these details are up-to-date. Where the marketing organisation can exercise a finite judgment on the nature of the market
– it may be the membership of the medical profession, the legal
profession, the manufacturers of aircraft instrumentation or baby
carriages – then direct mail is a very suitable and relatively inexpensive medium. The products that are particularly suitable for
direct mail advertising have this well-defined market, are novel
in concept, are interesting to write about and have a high profit
margin (although they must constitute good value for money).
Where the product is light, and easily transportable in relation
to its value, it also becomes very suitable for selling by mail (*direct
marketing*). The organisation's own customers constitute a most
suitable basic *mailing list* and there are a number of specialist
organisations which can provide from their existing data mailing
lists suitable in a general sense or for particular objectives (e.g.
the introduction of a new product). It must be for the advertiser
to judge the value of the list provided by a specialist organisation,
the criteria here being whether the list is comprehensive and
up-to-date (a significant number of 'not known' returns raising
doubts on the latter criterion). In addition to providing these
lists the specialist houses will, for additional fees, undertake the
whole direct mail campaign including the design of brochures,
price-lists, letters etc and the mailing involved. Since the presentation of the direct mail communication is all-important, it is
in any event necessary that all the elements have a professional
appearance (some insurance against consignment to the waste-
paper basket). In addition to the introduction of new products,

direct mail is often used for a number of purposes: in order to obtain interviews for salesmen; to announce price-changes to users and distributors; to ensure that all industrial buyers have copies of the latest catalogue; to announce the development of a new accessory to be used in conjunction with the main equipment and for market research purposes (the author recently received a questionnaire on the behaviour and suitability of a recently-purchased motor car: the responses would undoubtedly assist the manufacturer in his further development of the model).

Recent developments in computing and word-processing will further assist in the use of this medium for many marketing purposes.

Point-of-sale display

We are dealing here with what is frequently called *merchandising material* – anything at or near the point-of-sale which is designed to assist purchase. Such material typically comprises showcards, window-stickers, mobiles, illuminated displays, crowners, leaflets, booklets etc. The campaigns for products which are often bought on impulse (e.g. confectionery) usually incorporate sizeable expenditure on point-of-sale display. The design of the material should incorporate the key elements of the advertising in the other media utilised for the campaign. Thus the slogan, illustration or brand symbol will obtain cumulative, repetitive force through being featured on the point-of-sale display and the purchaser is reminded of the advertising which has gone before. Point-of-sale material is often linked to sales promotion schemes, e.g. coupon offers, banded packs, consumer competitions, and it has become part of the changing role of the salesman of fast-moving consumer goods to become a *merchandiser*, i.e. to be responsible for the erection and maintenance of this material in retail premises (where there is now keen competition for locations of high store traffic and visibility).

It is fashionable to criticise the money spent on point-of-sale display as more evidence of marketing 'waste'. However, its reminder function can do much to ensure the productivity of expenditure in other media. This means that its design must be integrated with the other parts of the campaign in a precise and unmistakable way. Moreover, a little ingenuity can assist economy – the author has in the past 'unitised' exhibition displays in UK and international markets, by means of a series of illuminated display cases. These have subsequently been used in large department stores for point-of-sale display purposes and their 'allocation' has been related to the negotiation of 'minimum quantity' contracts.

The role of point-of-sale display is well enough appreciated by anyone with even rudimentary knowledge of the advertising/purchasing process. When retail distribution is carried out through supermarkets and other outlets where the material is not acceptable then the product's packaging is focused on and a great deal of attention is devoted to its design, both individually and en masse, with the rest of the campaign ensuring the instant recognition of the package, hence the product.

The advertising agency

As outlined earlier in this chapter the operations of marketing communication must be aligned with settled objectives, which stem from marketing objectives which derive, in turn, from the general objectives of the organisation. At this stage, the typical questions are:

1   How much should we spend and over what time period?
2   What is the appropriate balance of expenditure on advertising, sales promotion, publicity and personal selling?
3   What are the most appropriate promotional media?
4   What is the most appropriate creative approach?

Although all four components of the promotional mix must be totally integrated, personal selling is usually treated separately for budgetary purposes. Campaign planning typically concentrates on the other three components. Some large organisations have their own advertising department, under the control of a senior executive (e.g. advertising manager) or brand manager who assumes responsibility for the total marketing of a product or group of products, including promotion. Oliver[6] notes the growing trend for all aspects of advertising planning to take place within what were hitherto client companies of advertising agencies. Nevertheless, the agencies still feature dominantly in the:

1   planning of promotional campaigns;
2   creation of advertisements;
3   liaison with media owners (e.g. newspaper proprietors, commercial television companies);

4   arranging for the advertisements to appear;
5   checking that they did appear in accordance with the contracts;
6   paying the bills for the advertising and other services provided
for the client.

In addition, the typical agency can offer to the client, or commission on the client's behalf, advice on marketing, packaging and
display, exhibition design and layout, marketing research and
numerous other services. In fact, the advertising agencies have
been prime movers in the appreciation and acceptance of the
marketing concept in the UK, having frequently had to demonstrate to client companies that in order to spend advertising
money wisely it was important for the clients to develop a professional approach to marketing.

If the reader consults any current edition of BRAD (*British Rate
and Data* – an important UK guide to media costs and therefore
a fundamental publication for media buyers) the medium invariably incorporates details of the Agency Commission. For the commercial television companies this is 15 per cent of the value of
the business placed with them but there is some variation within
the press publications, e.g.

> *Daily Express; Daily Mirror; Daily Mail*, 15%
> *Radio Times* (weekly), 15%
> *TV Times* (weekly), 25%
> *Good Housekeeping* (monthly), 15%
> *Woman's Own; Woman's Realm* (weekly), 15%
> *Times Educational Supplement* (weekly), 12.5%
> *Melody Maker* (weekly), 10%
> *Time Out* (weekly), 10%
> *Popular Caravan* (weekly), 10%
> *Canoeing* (monthly), 5%

The Institute of Practitioners in Advertising (IPA) is the organisation which represents the interests of the UK agencies and is
very much concerned with the professional standards of advertising. The Institute's member agencies (275 in 1983) and its 1600
personal members (1983 figures) are subject to strict professional
standards, not only as prescribed by the codes of practice governing the content of advertisements, but also for financial integrity
and good business conduct. Only those agencies capable of providing full advertising services and who are able to satisfy the IPA

Council as to their professional competence are admitted as members. According to the Institute's 1983 Annual Report, member-agencies were then responsible for a total advertising investment of more than £2500 million, which represented 85–90 per cent of all UK advertising placed by UK advertising agencies. Through networks of branch offices and 'associates' overseas many member-agencies are also active internationally on behalf of UK client organisations (see also Chapter 13 on advertising overseas).

Agency remuneration

The criterion of the agency's financial integrity (see above) is an important feature of the IPA's Codes of Practice because once the advertisement has been placed with them it is to the agency and not the advertiser that the media owners look for payment. In this sense, the word agency is a misnomer, for the agencies are, in the legal sense, principals on the contract for the purchase of advertising space or time. In essence, there are two contracts – one between the advertiser and the agency and a second between the agency and the media owner. (Note An interesting summary of the evolution of the advertising agency, with comment on the historical significance of the word 'agent', is provided by Brian MacCabe – see reference at the end of this Chapter.) So the clear interest of the media owners in the financial reliability of the agencies can be well enough understood.

Agency income derives from the agency commission obtained from the media owners and additional fees negotiated with the advertiser. According to a report at the end of the 1970s, agency income as a percentage of turnover handled was estimated to be approximately 16 per cent, 70 per cent of income by way of commission and 30 per cent by fees. The use of above-the-line media generates the commission income for the agency, while the agency will agree fees from its client for the development and production of the below-the-line media. Marketing research, public relations activities and package design are some of the other services for which fees might be negotiated. The large agencies may well be able to provide public relations and packaging/display specialists from within their own organisation. Otherwise they will negotiate with a creative group or a PR consultant on behalf of the client, obtaining a supplementary fee for their services.

Again, the product in question (e.g. an air compressor) may logically require the use of technical periodicals paying no more than 10 per cent commission to the agency. In such a case, the agency may negotiate a supplementary service fee from the client so as to realise some overall requisite percentage return on turnover (and as has been stated earlier, the current average is 16 per cent). Let us now consider how agencies operate on behalf of the advertiser.

Agency personnel

The following specialist personnel are usually at the disposal of the advertiser:

1   *Marketing Research Group* which comprises personnel well-versed in primary and secondary research. The Agency 'library' or information department typically contains a great deal of published data on markets and media. If the Research Group does not devise and conduct field surveys from its own resources, it will commission a marketing research organisation (e.g. Aske Research Limited; Attwood Statistics Limited) and be responsible for its briefing, liaison during fieldwork and interpretation of its results to the client.

2   *Marketing Group*, alternatively described as 'Planning' in some agencies, the personnel comprise experienced marketing practitioners able to advise clients on overall marketing strategy, including the development and pricing of products and services, distribution and marketing communication. Dependent on the size of the agency there may be a number of groups, serving particular clients or groups of clients, under the control of the agency's marketing director.

3   *Client Service Group* which may also be described as the 'Account Control' or 'Account Management' Group. Under an account director, the personnel here comprise account executives or account managers. In this context, the client organisation is 'the account'. Each account executive is a 'contact man' or link between client and agency. His role is to acquire direct and comprehensive knowledge of the client organisation, its products, processes, market performance etc. He confers with the client's

marketing and senior management on its marketing objectives, its communications problems and the size of the budget available. He subsequently reports these facts to his account director or account control group, as appropriate. It is as a result of discussions within this group, based on the client's 'facts book' that briefs are prepared for the creative group (or department) and the media department.

4 *Creative department*. The personnel here comprise *copywriters* and *visualisers* (who create the words and pictures for the advertisements), and specialists in television production, typography etc. This department has been described as the 'heart of the agency'[7] for so very much depends upon the creative quality of the campaigns it devises. In large agencies, groups of copywriters may be responsible to a *copy chief*. Similarly, the work of visualisers may be overseen by an *art director*. The department is usually in touch with a number of external agencies specialising in the production of finished artwork, photography, and television films. It is part of the department's stock-in-trade to know how the agency's resources can be supplemented by good value external creative talent. Research is usually on hand to guide the creative people on user motivations for the product or service in question – but this is the starting point for the group's own creative 'sparkle'.

5 *Media department*. Here there are two basic functions: (a) that of *media planning*, which means dealing with media strategy, the determination of the required expenditure (the *media budget*) and how this will be apportioned to the media (b) that of *media buying*; the buyers collaborating with the *planners* on the development and implementation of the media plan. With their knowledge of media costs and availability the buyers test the feasibility of the media proposals, negotiate with media owners on costs, discounts etc, and actually purchase the space and time when the media plan has been approved. The media planner is the link between the department, the client, the account executives and other agency personnel and working groups.

Depending on the structure of the agency, the department may have its own *media research group*, comprising specialists in the analysis of data on media coverage and user profiles.

6 *Production department*. This contains specialists in print pro-

duction and the production of radio, television and cinema advertising. These specialists are responsible for the high quality execution of the ideas produced by the creative group. Whereas the external production organisations are still important, MacCabe[8] reports on the growing trend for advertising agencies to take on much of the work of the externals including the selection of casts, choice of locations, design of sets etc for television and cinema advertisements.

7   *Traffic control.* This important department is responsible for monitoring the progress of the advertisements in their various stages of planning and production so that artwork, films, copy etc all reach the media in good time for the transmission or press date. Because of the enormous volume of advertisement traffic generated by an agency, the personnel of this department must constantly be checking on the progress of all the various individual jobs on hand. They must also ensure that the timetable of each campaign is adhered to, with changes of advertisement being made as originally agreed by the client.

These then are the main groups to be found in the average agency. They may not always be titled as such and in the smaller agencies some of the functions described above may be grouped together in a single department (or be the responsibility of a single person!). Nevertheless, they do give a good guide to agency structure and personnel. Depending on the size of the agency, other functions represented may relate to *public relations*, the *design of promotional material* and advisory services on the *development of new products*. Of course, since the agency is also a business organisation itself it will also employ *financial and administrative staff* engaged in the general operation of the business.

Campaign planning

This is a two-stage process, consisting of:

1   determining the size of the budget available;
2   determining where, when and for what purposes the budget should be spent (the allocation of planned expenditure to media).

There then follows the *control* process, intended to ensure that the budget is spent according to the agreed plan.

Fixing the budget

This must be of sufficient size to accomplish the job expected of it. The major proportion of the budget must be large enough to support advertising of an adequate type, size and continuity and there should also be an adequate contingency reserve to permit adjustments in advertising volume as problems emerge or opportunities arise.

It is one thing to say 'fix the budget'. It is another to do it accurately. This decision has been described as one of the most difficult in the whole spectrum of marketing activity. The problem is grounded in the fact that management cannot predict the exact effect of this type of expenditure on the attainment of communication goals, which are usually to increase sales volume. Were it possible to predict how sales volume would vary in response to variations in volume of advertising the problem would not be so complex. In consequence, investigations reveal the use of a variety of methods of varying levels of logicality. Some of the main ones are now described.

1   *The arbitrary figure.* A specific sum is set aside each year, perhaps corrected for inflation. For example, the advertiser may say to the agency 'We spend around £100 000 each year, whatever happens'. The relationship of expenditure to sales volume or profit is not considered, beyond a crude assessment that within a given profit performance such an arbitrary sum is *affordable*. This is the antithesis of the marketing approach, it treats advertising expenditure as a *cost*, rather nebulous in nature but seemingly unavoidable, rather than as an *investment* designed to produce a *return*. Because no attempt is made at *measurement*, it is impossible to state whether the sum is too large or too little. It will only be a 'correct' figure by miracle.

2   *The percentage of sales method.* Here the appropriation is calculated as a percentage of past sales or anticipated future sales. The past sales basis takes no account of the dynamic nature of markets and too low a budget may deprive the firm of capitalising on some market opportunity. In this respect, calculating on the basis of expected future sales has greater realism. The percentage adopted is determined in relation to the product – in the food, drug and fashion industries the quantity and quality of advertising may be the most important factor in influencing sales, whereas

a staple raw material in consistent industrial demand may require only a low percentage of advertising support. The approach is simple, which may account for its popularity, but has little else to commend it. For one thing, it assumes that expenditure should be a function of sales rather than vice versa. In consequence a contraction in sales volume may result in a reduction in expenditure at a time when increased expenditure may be a necessary strategy to halt the decline. Again, the method may be based on the average percentage expenditure currently in vogue in the industry or product group. This only serves to illustrate how the method ignores the particular problems of the individual organisation. Consider the following:

Brand	Market share	Money value (£)	Advertising expenditure as % of sales (based on industry average)	Advertising appropriation (£)
A	40%	£20 000 000	5%	£1 000 000
B	10%	£5 000 000	5%	£250 000

Assume that brand B must expand its sales in order to be profitable. Further assume that expansion can only be achieved by taking sales from brand A (i.e. the market is a static one). A daunting task for brand B with only one quarter of brand A's advertising expenditure!

3 *Level of competitors' expenditure.* With this approach, the firm is becoming less introverted; it is looking outside of itself to what happens in the market. Through the syndicated research services available from AC Nielsen and MEAL it is possible for some advertisers to learn what share of the market is being obtained by competitors for what share of advertising expenditure. Where such services are not available, some estimate has to be made. It is no bad thing to know what competitors are spending, particularly in industries where there is a marked positive correlation between the share of the industry's advertising expenditure and the share of its sales. In fact, in some industries it may be the case that technology and the pressures of competition have reduced or virtually obliterated the significance of all the other factors that influence sales. As a *factor* in the calculations, competitive expenditure has its importance, but to discover it in order to equalise it is wrong. In many industries,

technologies and competition do not force standardisation. Each organisation is unique. It has its own product qualities, its own greater or lesser support from distributors, its own size and quality of sales force, its own pricing strategy and, not least, the greater or lesser *quality* of its own advertising. In short, each has its own marketing problems and opportunities, hence its own objectives and one of these should be to lead competition and not to follow it.

4 *The margin remaining method.* This relates the expenditure to required profit performance in that the total of production costs plus marketing costs plus the desired profit performance is subtracted from anticipated sales revenue. The margin remaining then becomes the budget available for promotion. Unfortunately, this rather mechanistic approach has its drawbacks too. Firstly, there is no guarantee that the margin remaining will be sufficient to generate the anticipated revenue. Once again, expenditure has become a function of sales revenue, rather than the other way around. When sales volume is expending, more is available for advertising and it may not in fact be needed. Conversely, in a declining market, approved expenditure will be reduced at a time when it may well be needed. As someone succinctly put it: 'One doesn't know whether one is trying to crack a nut with a sledge-hammer or empty a river with a sponge'.

5 *The task method.* Observers of the marketing scene and practitioners in the field seem agreed that, given our present incomplete knowledge of how advertising 'works', the task method of determining the budget is perhaps the most commendable one available to us. Firstly there is a careful examination and statement of what the campaign is intended to achieve: the objectives are set. Then a strategy for achieving the objectives is devised after a careful review of all the alternatives. The plan which emerges is costed and if it appears to be affordable then the sum arrived at becomes the appropriation. If the calculated costs seem beyond the resources of the organisation then the plan is modified, perhaps with a similar modification of the objectives. If after further consideration it appears to be worthwhile then the revised plan and budget are adopted. The task method attempts to realistically assess what can be accomplished within the resources of the firm and whether these anticipated results adequately serve the broader objectives of its marketing activity. A survey by the

British Institute of Management[9] reported that about 20 per cent of responding firms used the method and it is to be hoped that more organisations will find that this structured approach appeals to them.

These then are summaries of the more common approaches to fixing the budget but they need not be used in isolation of each other. In practice some combination of methods may be employed. One eminent British practitioner, Dr Simon Broadbent, suggests that the decision hinges on the answers to four questions:

1   What can the product afford?
2   What is the advertising task (related to agreed objectives)?
3   What are competitors spending?
4   What have we learned from previous years? (including the response of the market to changes in expenditure levels; consumer attitudes and brand loyalty; the growth or contraction of the market; reaction to competitive products etc).

He suggests that approaching the problem from different directions whilst producing different answers will clarify for the organisation the framework within which a reasonable answer lies.

Research can improve the quality of decision making, of course. Test marketing campaigns in comparable areas in which all variables other than advertising expenditure are held constant may be a way of isolating the effect of advertising in particular circumstances and thus producing 'benchmarks' for budget calculations. A danger here is unjustified confidence in what is only a 'still' in a moving picture, since markets are rarely the same year by year. Experiments continue with sensitivity analysis, using the computer, where such inputs as advertising expenditure are varied and the effect on outcomes is examined. These techniques depend upon credible models of market behaviour, which may necessarily be of immense elaboration. For his part, Broadbent has found such studies 'usually the least relevant'. In the meantime, the search and the debates continue.

The media plan

When members of the client services group, the creative group and the media department, plus any relevant others, meet in the agency to plan the client's campaign, the basis for their discussions will be the *media brief*. Some of the details typically incorporated in the brief are now summarised.

The objectives of the campaign

Some examples were given at the beginning of the Chapter. The group may be considering the introduction of a new product such as a new *History of the World* in twelve volumes from a mail order publishing house; or increasing the sales of an existing product (e.g. by developing the brand value of a personal and small business computer, so that users specify it and no other brand); or to given information on some aspect of the client's policy (e.g. the view of an employer on a current strike; a statement to shareholders on why they should resist a takeover bid). A variety of objectives requiring a variety of strategies.

The product or service

The nature of the product exercises a major influence on the promotional mix. A complex technical product with novel features will require emphasis on personal selling and a media plan incorporating advertising in the technical press and market 'education' through exhibitions and public relations activities. A mass-produced food product, with national distribution, heavily bought by mothers of young children will probably make use of television, women's magazines and the campaign may incorporate dealer contests, self-liquidating premium offers, store demonstrations and wide use of sales promotion material (signs, showcards, window-stickers and booklets).

The stage in the product life cycle is another important aspect. At the introductory stage, primary demand must be stimulated – potential users have to be 'sold' on the benefits of video cassette recorders before selective demand (i.e. for a particular brand) is stimulated at the growth stage. Intense competition at its maturity may force the seller of a mass-distributed convenience product to significantly expand advertising prior to a substantial reduction in promotional effort at the decline stage.

The packaging, pricing, unique selling features, sales history and promotional history of the product or service are also carefully considered as is the nature and extent of competition.

The nature of the market

The ultimate users must be described as precisely as possible in terms of age, sex, social grades, special interests, or some other relevant characteristic (e.g. innovators, early adopters) or by type of manufacture; size of organisation; exporting activity; size of household; ownership of consumer durables: whatever criterion for segmentation is appropriate.

The geographical extent of the market is also important. Advertising, in contrast to personal selling, becomes more economical as the market broadens geographically and numerically. The regional dispersion of the market and of current sales (if any) has to be examined so that an effective geographical spread of advertising, which takes account of any weak areas, or opportunities for expansion, can be devised.

The nature of the secondary market must also be thought about. These may be distributors, in which case the nature of distribution channels (direct to manufacturers; direct to consumers by mail order, advertiser's own showrooms or retail outlets; to consumers via retailers; to consumers via wholesalers and retailers) and the required weight of trade advertising and promotions has to be judged. The secondary market may consist of relevant third parties (e.g. doctors in the case of a new patent medicine; architects in the case of a new building material) and coverage must be planned for these important sources of influence.

Reverting to consumers, some data will be sought on such behavioural aspects as attitudes, brand loyalty, cognitive dissonance and characteristics of reference groups, if this is available and pertinent.

Either under this heading, or when considering the product or service, the nature of the after-market (if appropriate) will also be debated. Where products require after-sales service, the user will need to be informed about the guarantees, warranties, spares availability and the provision of after-sales service. There may be need to deploy some expenditure to operating manuals, user journals and the formation of a 'user club'. Public relations, which generates editorial features on 'satisfied users' is a valuable counter to post-purchase dissonance.

The budget

Some of the main approaches to fixing this have been discussed earlier in this Section. Certainly the size of the budget and its contingency reserve will be a major element in devising the media plan. Advertising is not cheap (which is not the same thing as saying it is not value for money). By way of illustration, here are some details of costs extracted from the May 1984 issue of BRAD:

The Daily Telegraph: full page (Monday to Friday)	£19 500 per insertion
half page (Monday to Friday)	£10 500 per insertion
The Financial Times: full page	£14 784 per insertion
Thames Television: 30 second spot (5.40 pm–10.40 pm)	£10 360 per spot
Anglia Television:	£7000 per 30 second spot
Granada Television:	£14 000 per 30 second spot
TV AM:	£4800 per 30 second spot
National 16 sheet poster campaign: months of October and November (9 regions)	£106 250 per month
Bus shelter four sheet poster campaign: 'Superweight' 6 days (10 000 sites)	£140 000 in total
Capital Radio 30 second spots: 15 over one weekend	£2685 in total

There is the concept of the 'threshold' in budgets, in that appropriations must reach a threshold before particular media plans become realistic. The decision whether to use television advertising on a national basis obviously requires this kind of consideration. Certainly advertisers with modest budgets might be best advised to build up advertising coverage region by region before 'going national'. The small advertiser very quickly learns that the sponsorship of a major sporting event or feature advertising at sporting events is only for those with large appropriations!

Timing and the timetable

There is the question of the time period over which the budget will be employed (three months, six months, one year) for together with the budget available this will greatly influence the affordable coverage of the target market (as a rule, the cost of a medium will rise in proportion to the coverage it provides) and the frequency with which the advertisements are repeated during a campaign. Most campaign plans seek to balance coverage and frequency at the optimal level affordable.

Another consideration is whether there is any seasonality in the sales of the product. Should the advertising be spread evenly thoughout the campaign or used in 'bursts'? Are there any seasons (e.g. Christmas, Easter) or days of the week which require extra advertising weight?

As to the timetable of the campaign, when is it due to start and finish? What amount of production time is required for artwork, films etc? When must firm bookings be made with the media? What are the cancellation and copy dates? Do these considerations rule out the use of any particular medium?

The objectives of the campaign may influence its phasing. For the introduction of a new product, a disproportionately heavy volume of advertising may be necessary to ensure that the product makes its mark with potential customers. A twelve-month campaign may be so phased that 50 per cent of the budget is allocated to the first four months so as to give the new product an adequate 'voice'. Such a media brief, considered by the agency personnel chosen to work on the campaign, will lead to formulation of ideas for a suitable creative approach and the evaluation of media, in terms of their characteristics, 'atmosphere', quantitative coverage and cost, leading to recommendations for a media plan.

The creative approach will be significantly influenced by the nature of the product. Technical explanation of the product in use with full visual treatment may be necessary. Perhaps a prosaic product in everyday use (e.g. dog food) may need to be treated humorously in a television cartoon so as to invest it with a 'personality'. The desirable brand image may be one of restraint and dignity (expensive after-dinner chocolates) or of escapism and romance (a popularly priced cosmetic). The attributes of advertising in colour may be important, either directly (for the newest shades of paint) or subjectively (to convey the 'magic' of holidays in 'sunny Spain'). The theme of competitors' advertising may give the clue as to how the client's product may best acquire its own special identity (if competitors use cartoon characters to extol the benefits of their dog foods, the agency may suggest a 'live action' commercial at the kennels of a noted dog-breeder who will endorse the client's product as the number one choice).

At this stage, the agency must consider carefully what is known about user behaviour and informational needs. Agency personnel will be guided by published data including any experimental methods such as test marketing which may have been used on the client's behalf before the main campaign.

Media evaluation consists of:

1   examination of the characteristics, atmosphere, quantitative coverage and cost of the various media against the budget available and the requirements of the campaign as revealed by the media brief;

2   which medium (or media) will carry the main weight of advertising; the primary media, and which will be used as support media. For example, for a new brand of non-alcoholic beer it may be decided to use television as the primary medium with posters in support to remind purchasers when they are next near to the supermarkets and wine stores. (A useful creative approach might be to use endorsement by a well-known sportsman for 'a refreshing drink with none of the dangers of alcohol').

3   the balance of expenditure between the primary and the support media, the size of the spaces or time spots to be purchased in the first and later stages of the campaign, bearing in mind the need for an adequate balance between the required impact (particularly important for new products) and the necessary degree of repetition. The manner in which above-the-line media should be integrated with the use of below-the-line media (if appropriate) will also be judged carefully at this point. Contrary to popular belief, point-of-sale display material, competitions, premium offers, 'celebrity' appearances and sponsorship activities are not meaningless fripperies lumped into campaigns by advertisers with too much money to spend. Where they are used, their use is planned in order to serve communication and marketing objectives.

Media characteristics comprise the facilities each medium makes available to the advertiser, e.g. the size of advertisement made feasible; the possibility of colour; sound; movement; the quality of print or sound reproduction; the flexibility of the medium (the ability to book, cancel or change advertising in some way, at short notice); the 'length of life' of a medium (television is a transient medium; a monthly magazine may be read over several months); the influence of the medium with groups other than the user (e.g. distributors, company directors as well as buyers); the facility to repeat advertisements; the extent of duplication arising from the use of more than one medium (e.g. the extent to which readers of one newspaper also read another).

Some words of explanation here – despite what has been said earlier about impact and repetition – they are not necessarily opposites.

Some media (e.g. television and radio) gain impact by means of repetition. Nevertheless it is often the case that advertisements of a large size (to gain impact) can only be obtained by reducing the frequency (i.e. repetition) of the advertisements, because the size of the budget demands that a balance be struck. Duplication may be an economical way of obtaining this repetition but there may be instances where it is thought to be wasteful and is therefore avoided. Every campaign is different.

Media atmosphere depends on a combination of a number of factors. These include the type of people using the medium (the cinema is mainly patronised by the young adult sector of the population – its atmosphere is youthful, romantic, escapist; *The Times* newspaper is read by the affluent and the influential – its editorial atmosphere, though it has changed slightly in the recent past, is dignified and authoritative). The conditions under which the medium is used are also an important determinant of its atmosphere; many morning and evening newspapers are read by people who are rushed and preoccupied. Editorial matter must be presented as briefly and succinctly as possible for the busy commuter. This atmosphere of urgency – reflected in the paper's content and make-up is one that may work either for or against the objectives of a particular advertisement. The atmosphere of the colour supplement to a Sunday newspaper is different again, as is the atmosphere of television. Subjective though it is, assessment of the atmosphere a medium provides is an important determinant of its suitability. A good appreciation of atmosphere is provided in the work of Anthony Swindells,[10] published some years ago but still helpful.

Media coverage and costs. In Chapter 3 (Marketing research), the work of the Broadcasters' Audience Research Board (BARB) Ltd in monitoring the composition and size of the UK audience for television was described, as was the Target Group Index (TGI) survey of the British Market Research Bureau (BMRB) which relates the purchasing habits of target markets to their media usage. The output of both of these services constitute important source data for media planning. Below are details of some of the other significant services with regard to coverage.

1   *The Audit Bureau of Circulations (ABC)* which provides independently audited details of the circulation of press publications.
The attested circulation figures (i.e. the number of copies of each
issue distributed) contained in the ABC certificate also indicates
the number of copies issued free or sold at less than normal trade
terms. Similarly, the Post Office will provide certificates of post-
ing for certain technical journals. Although circulation statistics
say nothing about the type of recipient buying the publication,
it is sometimes implicit in the journal's title (e.g. *Amateur Gar-
dener*) and it is frequently provided by the publisher via the ABC
supervised Media Data Form.

Circulation is, of course, only the first step in the measurement
of the audience for advertising for which the readership figures
are of far greater significance, particularly since the number of
readers per copy varies greatly with the type of publication (national
daily newspapers have about three readers per copy on average
whilst for some of the 'glossy' monthly magazines the comparable
figure is 20 or more, although this latter figure may be accumulated over several months and later readers – the secondary readership – may be people of different economic and social
backgrounds from the primary readers; the difference between
the doctor's wife and the patients in the waiting room, perhaps).
Nevertheless, two salient questions for the advertiser are:

how many people read my advertisements?

what type of people are they?

2   *The National Readership Survey*, sponsored by the Joint
Industry Committee for National Readership Surveys (JICNARS),
which represents the interests of media owners, advertising agencies and advertisers, provides a very detailed analysis of the
readership of over 100 major consumer press publications. The
readership data is classified according to age, sex, socio-economic
group, Registrar-General's regions, ITV regions, 'special categories' (e.g. petrol buyers) and exposure to other media (commercial
television, radio, cinema). In addition, a broad description of the
readership of local newspapers is also provided. The survey's
reports are issued twice each year covering January to December
of each calendar year and July (of one year) to June (of the following
year). The raw data upon which the reports are based is obtained
from a yearly sample of 28 500 adults.

With regard to the minor media, the National Readership Survey categorises the population with regard to their radio-listening

and cinema-going habits. A Joint Industry Committee for Radio Audience Surveys (JICRAR) has been established to oversee research into radio-listening habits and Radio Luxembourg produces its own research data (based on a twenty-four hour recall method). In addition to the data on cinema-going contained in the National Readership Survey, HM Government produces statistics on cinema admissions. The Joint Industry Committee for Poster Audience Surveys (JICPAS) oversees surveys used to measure the movement by the population past poster sites and to indicate the number of opportunities to see particular posters.

3   *British Rate and Data (BRAD)*. As has been mentioned earlier, this is the periodical which contains up-to-date information on media costs (see examples on page 303) and along with such publications as the National Readership Survey and the Target Group Index, it is a fundamental source of data for media evaluation and planning. It should be part of the development of every student of marketing to become familar with these documents (a copy of BRAD is usually available at the local reference library) and to conduct their own exercises in media planning (based perhaps on imaginary examples) using the data that they contain.

Media owners also publish rate cards and data on page traffic of their publications (intended to support the scale of charges for advertisements in the different parts of the publication). They also publish their own survey reports from time to time, based on ad hoc research and while the data they contain is of value in evaluating candidate publications, it is obviously intended to portray their own particular medium in the most favourable light.

Media schedule building

It is impossible to describe in detail here the complex and often lengthy processes undertaken in the Agency to prepare a media plan for the client. The reader is referred to the references Section at the end of this Chapter for further reading. Also, the 'Communications research' section of Margaret Crimp's *The marketing research process* (see Bibliography) provides many an insight into this activity.

What might be added in this work is that if the reader was a fly on the wall of the Agency, he would hear a discussion making much use of such terms as:

market weight a numerical weight applied to some part of the target market according to its assessed importance relative to other parts of the target market;

cost per thousand the cost of reaching each one thousand persons in the target market. For example, assume the target market is the ABC socio-economic group. A publication has one million readers in this group. An advertisement of appropriate size in the publication costs £5000. The cost per thousand is £5. (£5000/1000 (000's) = £5);

tvrs (television ratings) the size of the audience for television advertising is calculated in television ratings, each rating being equal to one per cent of the potential viewing category;

reach this is equivalent to coverage and is the percentage of the target market which will have at least one *opportunity to see (ots)* the advertising;

response function this is a set of numbers which denotes the relative value to the advertiser of an individual in the target population receiving one, two, three etc... advertising impressions (*cumulative response function*). The *additional response function* is the added value given by each separate, additional impression. The *value to the advertiser* depends upon the objectives of each separate campaign, e.g. whether the objective is to provide each of a large number of different people a small number of opportunities to see the advertising (as appropriate to a mass-produced product bought on impulse) or a smaller number of people an opportunity to see the advertising much more frequently (appropriate to a relatively complex product bought after long deliberation).

Before the media schedule is completed and presented to the client for appraisal there will also be consideration of whether the budget will allow for research to evaluate the effects of the campaign and the reaction of the target market to the advertisements.

Self-assessment questions

1 What factors typically influence the strategies of communications campaigns?

2   Define (a) advertising, (b) sales promotion, (c) publicity.

3   Distinguish between above-the-line and below-the-line media.

4   What are the 'characteristics', 'atmosphere', 'coverage' and 'cost' of advertising media? How are they considered in a campaign plan?

5   Write notes on the following: public relations; classified advertising; display advertising; quality newspapers; transportation media; exhibition data; direct marketing.

6   What are the functions usually carried out by advertising agencies?

7   How is an advertising agency remunerated, as a rule?

8   Prepare an organisation chart denoting the key departments of an advertising agency.

9   Outline the duties of the various departments identified at (8) and describe how their work is co-ordinated.

10   Describe the main methods of fixing the communications budget.

11   What are the details typically incorporated in a media brief?

12   How are media evaluated?

13   What is: BARB? ABC? JICNARS? JICRAR? BRAD?

14   Explain the terms usually employed in media schedule building.

References

1 Hart, Norman. Public Relations, *Marketing handbook*, ed Michael Rines, 2nd edn, Aldershot, Gower Publishing, 1981, p. 227

2 Ibid. pp. 227–228

3 Owen-Browne, Colin. Media, *The practice of advertising*, eds Norman Hart and James O'Connor, London, William Heinemann, 1978, p. 60

4 Churchill, David. Advertising in the 80's, *The Financial Times Survey*, 29 October 1982, p. 16

5 McDermott, Harry. Exhibitions, *Marketing handbook*, p. 291

6 Oliver, Gordon. *Marketing today*, London; Prentice-Hall, 1980, p. 229

7 Broadbent, Simon. *Spending advertising money*, 3rd edn, London, Business Books, 1979, p. 144

8 MacCabe, Brian F. The advertising agency, *The practice of advertising*, p. 48

9 British Institute of Management. BIM survey Marketing organisation in British industry, (Information summary 148), reported in *Marketing: an introductory text*, Michael J. Baker, 3rd edn, London, The Macmillan Press, 1979, p. 314

10 Swindells, Anthony. *Advertising media and campaign planning*, London, Butterworth, 1966, pp. 39–50

9 THE ORGANISATION AND CONTROL OF SELLING OPERATIONS

Objectives

Selling is next described – but, unsurprisingly in a marketing textbook, not so much as a process in itself, more as an element in a communications strategy related to organisational objectives.

Therefore the managerial role in the quality and the cost effectiveness of the selling effort forms the substance of this Chapter.

The techniques of conducting sales interviews are valuable study material, but they belong in other types of textbook. The selection, recruitment, deployment, motivation and evaluation of salesmen are our preoccupations here.

The personal selling function

In spite of the importance of marketing research, product development, sound pricing and well devised advertising, the success of the marketing campaign usually depends on the outcome of the interaction between the salesman and the prospective customer. Someone was once prompted to remark: 'Nothing happens until somebody sells something'. Certainly the extent to which an organisation's sales force is selling, or failing to sell, has a great bearing on its very existence. And that picture is largely unchanged despite the company mergers and acquisitions of recent years (resulting in reduced numbers of retail outlets) and the development of computer-based communications systems between supplying and customer organisations. In fact, for many organisations it would still be true to say that the personal selling budget is the largest single element in marketing expenditure, though this has to be qualified according to the nature of the product.

Yet the negative stereotype of the salesman, as someone high in persuasive power and low in integrity, persists, certainly in the British psyche. The reasons are understandable and stem from the period when many companies adopted a sales-oriented strategy, attempting to sell their production-oriented output through the use of high-pressure salesmanship reinforced by advertising. As a result of glib persuasion, too many people for selling's own good were left with products they neither needed nor could afford. Jolson[1] adds another reason for selling's bad name. He believes that while both advertising and selling have been criticised, the ill-effects of unethical personal selling have been the more damaging and he suggests that while advertising is more structured, with the 'company story' being told in the 'company way', the salesperson is less controllable, with some salesmen using exaggeration and occasional misrepresentations in order to obtain the sale.

We have to be clear. The unethical were never more than a small minority. But they have done damage to the commercial process out of all proportion to their numbers. Although the misconceptions about selling (and hence marketing) persist, one hopes and indeed believes, that they are less widespread than hitherto. This belief is grounded in two reasons:

1 the rise of *consumerism*, and the legislation it has impelled, make nefarious practices that much more difficult;
2 the rise of the marketing concept, which demands a more structured approach to the selling process, views it as one element in the communications mix, requires it to be fully integrated with other elements in the mix and establishes its operating policies and procedures in relation to *organisational objectives* – the basis on which the success or failure of the selling function is evaluated.

It is this second reason we shall be considering in this Chapter.

Organisational objectives

Enough has already been said of organisational objectives for us to recognise that their establishment gives rise to a *hierarchy of objectives*, in which the objectives of all the departments (production, finance, marketing, personnel etc) can be linked together in a *means-end chain*; the final objective or end of one department, becomes the means by which the next department in the flow of operations can achieve *its* objective.

Diagrammatically, we could represent the establishment of *personal selling objectives* as shown in Fig. 9.1:

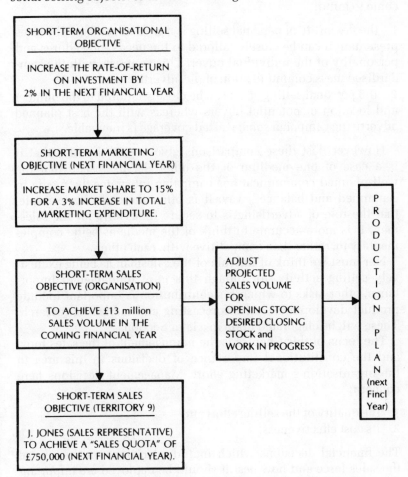

Fig. 9.1   *The relationship between organisational, marketing and personal selling objectives*

Hence the production plan to be followed is directly related to the personal selling objectives of John Jones, salesman, and his colleagues in the sales force.

So the place of personal selling in the communications mix, the amount of selling effort and the cost of that effort relative to the other means of communications (advertising, promotion, publicity) must be carefully planned and monitored. But what special premiums are there to charge to personal selling, bearing in mind its comparatively high cost? Two points immediately come to mind:

1   the *flexibility* of personal selling is a great advantage. The sales presentation can be closely tailored to the needs, procedures and personality of the individual buyer. This contrasts with the standardised mass communication of the advertisement;
2   the personal selling effort can be closely tailored to the number and location of potential buyers whereas with the best planned advertising campaign *some* wasted coverage is inevitable.

However, lest these comparisons give rise to the idea that it is a case of one medium or the other, let us restate that the well-planned communications campaign integrates the media in a planned and balanced way. It is often the case, for example, that the role of advertising is to secure interviews for the salesmen. It is more accurate to think of the media as being complementary to, rather than competitive with, each other.

Nor must we think of the role of the salesman as being exclusively selling activity, for though this is of fundamental importance, other tasks to which his contribution is important include product development, sales forecasting and marketing research. These will be elaborated upon in a later Section.

The focus of this Chapter is the *management* of the sales force and the constitutional importance of decisions in this area to the organisation's marketing effort. Management decisions here concern:

1   the quality of the selling effort and
2   its cost effectiveness.

The financial decisions which include decisions on the size of the sales force and how best it should be deployed are important enough – cost effectiveness is a key criterion of marketing standards. No less important is the quality of sales force activity. This calls for sound recruitment, selection and training procedures and adequate systems for rewarding effort. There are also key tasks of 'man management': the motivation and morale of the sales force is of great consequence. Here we must bear in mind that the salesman is more often than not working alone and since he occupies a *boundary role*, having to cope with demands from his own organisation and his customers which are often diverse and even conflicting, his job can be particularly stressful. Some thoughts on quality and cost effectiveness are set out in succeeding Sections. As a prelude to these, the Section which follows looks a little deeper into the selling role.

The diversity of selling

Most people tend to lump together all manner of selling roles under the general title of 'selling'. Yet if we pause to think about selling, we are immediately struck by the wide diversity of roles it encompasses and the marked differences in the tasks of each of these roles. A number of these roles are now briefly considered.

1 *Roundsman selling* The primary task is to deliver the goods door-to-door. Milk and other groceries are the commodities usually handled. The driver of the mobile shop visiting our village is just that and selling is his secondary role, but is not without importance.

2 *Retail store/showroom selling* The customer comes to the salesman and therefore these positions are sometimes referred to as *inside order takers*. The role includes skilled diagnosis of customer needs and effective presentation of the goods on offer thus 'assisting the buyer to buy'. Sales training is therefore required. The best organisations provide it. Where it is lacking, as is often the case, it is most noticeable and is an important contributor to selling's bad name!

3 *External selling* Incorporated in this heading are a number of selling roles, all of which entail going out to the customer in order to obtain orders. Within this very broad heading let us consider how the nature of the sales role is influenced by the product involved.

(a) *Rapid turnover consumer goods.* Most products which are mass-marketed are heavily branded and advertised. Food, drink and confectionery are typical product groups. The salesman requires little or no product knowledge. His selling role encompasses advice to distributors on forthcoming advertising campaigns, perhaps the arrangement of displays and other point-of-sale material, the taking of orders and possibly the checking of stock levels and the collection of cash. This sector of selling has seen recent reductions in the size of sales forces, as retail outlets have become fewer and larger and, as Cannon[2] points out, high interest rates have forced companies to look increasingly to the salesmen for debt collection. This inevitably restrains their selling activity, if only to a degree.

(b) *Consumer durable goods.* Here again, the salesman has an important task in maximising the effectiveness of the advertising campaign. Product knowledge is of some importance, however, since distributors will expect to be able to converse with sales personnel who are well versed in the technical details of the motor vehicles, washing machines and stereo equipment they are selling. This not only matters for the sake of the sales presentation but also for dealing with complaints from both the distributors and users.

(c) *Industrial consumption goods.* Some products in this group are standardised in composition and use (e.g. cement, lubricants, office supplies) and detailed product knowledge is not important. For very many products in this category, however, the reverse is the case and the salesman's product knowledge is very much part of his 'stock in trade' particularly if the products are to be used within the manufacture of the buyer's own products. In this context, the representative becomes as much an adviser or consultant as a salesman. He must gather adequate knowledge of the client's products and processes so that customer needs can be effectively diagnosed and the type of raw material, component or sub-assembly best fitted to client needs can be recommended.

(d) *Industrial durable products.* Usually before products in this category are purchased there is a lengthy consultation period. Many sources of supply are considered and those seeming most suitable may be asked to submit formal tenders. Scrutiny of alternatives may entail detailed assessment of technical specifications; product costs; installation and after-sales service costs (if applicable); data of output rates; usage of energy; compliance with technical, safety and other standards; facilities for the training of operatives; provision of warranties/user guarantees etc.

The salesman may well have entered selling through some related technology and possess graduate or equivalent status. Such knowledge and training may be fundamental to an adequate comprehension of his own products, competing products and the processes and needs of potential clients. The salesman's technical expertise often enables him to become a 'co-opted member' of the potential client's research and product development team – an important factor in determining the identity of the eventual supplier! Salesmen in this field very often co-ordinate a team of designers, production executives, financial, technical and other personnel in order to meet the requirements of potential customers.

Mention has been made earlier of the stresses of the salesman's boundary role. In their paper 'Reactions to Role Conflict: The Case of the Industrial Salesman', Walker, Churchill and Ford[3] write:

The industrial salesman's role-set includes a large number of diverse individuals. Hundreds of different customers each expect him to satisfy their particular needs and requirements. In addition, people in numerous departments within his own firm rely on him for the execution of company policies in dealings with customers and for the ultimate success of the firm's revenue producing efforts. All of these people hold definite beliefs about how the salesman should perform his job and they all pressure him to conform to their expectations.

(e) *Systems selling*. The 'systems concept' applied to selling can offer the supplier a competitive advantage by virtue of a closer relationship with the customer. In essence, the concept simplifies the customer's job in that instead of having to locate and negotiate with several suppliers in order to purchase a machine, its tools, controls, consumables and other supplies, the customer is able to purchase the complete, integrated *package* of hardware, services, operator training etc needed to perform a particular function or solve a particular problem. The idea is not new. Business machines have long been sold with the related 'paperwork' – returns, cards, forms, tapes etc. Computer selling encompasses the conduct of systems analyses and feasibility studies and the subsequent provision of hardware, software, training programmes and after-sales service. The concept has gained momentum through the accelerating pace of technological change. For example, not many companies possess a sufficient number of technically expert construction and engineering personnel to deal with the many suppliers involved in the construction and operation of an automated warehouse. Much less would they be able to bring together the building configuration, its environmental controls and the related products and services into a logical, co-ordinated system, involving the activities of numerous supply sources, so as to provide an effective warehousing/material handling operation.

The spread of the marketing concept, as well as technological change, has seen the emergence of the capable systems supplier who can produce a complete power distribution system; build a hospital or a large office complex or design, engineer, build, test and maintain a sophisticated manufacturing system.

Needless to say, the 'salesman' in this context operates as a member of an appropriately qualified project team developing a multi-skilled approach to the analysis and solution of a complex problem.

4 *Telephone selling.* Aside from its indispensability to other types of selling, the telephone has been effectively used for direct selling to both business organisations and consumers. Advertising space and time; photographic and interior decorating services; frozen foods and other grocery items are typical of the items sold by this method. It can be a low cost, effective method of sales communication. The personnel employed to sell by telephone must have an aptitude for the job which incorporates courtesy, good manners and must be trained in the techniques required to make a presentation in a relatively brief but interesting way.

In addition to the selling roles just described, the term 'salesman' is also used to cover what might more properly be called 'sales support' personnel. Examples here are to be found in:

(a) *Missionary selling.* A cosmetics manufacturer may send beauty consultants/demonstrators into the premises of retail customers in order to assist in the introduction of a new product.

(b) *Detail selling.* A pharmaceuticals manufacturer, having succeeded in placing stocks of his products with wholesale and retail chemists, creates a demand for these products by employing a detail selling team to call on doctors in order to provide details of research and development of particular drugs in the range, their composition, dosage, advantages etc.

5 *Services selling.* In very nearly all of the above examples we have been considering the sale of *tangible products.* The sale of

intangibles – such services as insurance, banking and credit, travel, consultancy, design and advertising – comprises a highly significant sector and one which assumes increasing significance with the further development of the service economy.

Although this field incorporates different levels of complexity, the selling role is an 'expert' one not only requiring qualifications and experience in the service being offered but also training in the determination of actual and potential customers and the pre-approach investigation of client needs.

These examples give some indication of the wide variety of selling roles. In the next Section let us consider the role and responsibilities of managing the selling effort.

The role of sales management

In the Sections which now follow an attempt will be made to summarise the role of the sales manager. The process would provide enough detail, of itself, to fill a sizeable textbook (and there are many of these about). We can therefore only examine the subject here in outline, though it is hoped that the outline will be valuable.

First, the organisation's manpower requirements must be linked to its objectives and sales force manpower is a part of the organisation's manpower. It follows then that from the marketing plan (designed to achieve organisational objectives) the sales manager will reach agreement with the marketing manager upon:

1   required recruitment levels for the sales force;
2   adequate planning for resignations, retirements, redundancies etc so that these are foreseen and, where necessary, handled as humanely as possible, allowing sufficient time for re-deployment and re-training, where appropriate;
3   required levels of activity and expenditures for training;
4   the establishment of career development programmes, where appropriate (e.g. salesman – senior ('key account') salesman – area manager etc.)
5   the assessment, monitoring and control of selling costs, and particularly where these relate to the introduction of new products or services;
6   projected changes in working methods, methods of remuner-

ation etc including, if necessary, negotiations with staff representatives and trade unions;

7   the provision of sufficient equipment (sample cases, video films, sales literature, motor vehicles etc), accommodation (including branch offices, service depots, showrooms) and support personnel (technicians, clerical and computer staff, demonstrators) to enable the sales targets to be achieved.

Fitting the man to the job

In the author's opinion, the tasks within the role just outlined can be very satisfactorily considered if we adopt the *fmj-fjm model* of the author's own mentor, Professor Alec Rodger, the eminent occupational psychologist, of the University of London. Though Rodger proposed the model for all types of workers, we consider here its application to selling.

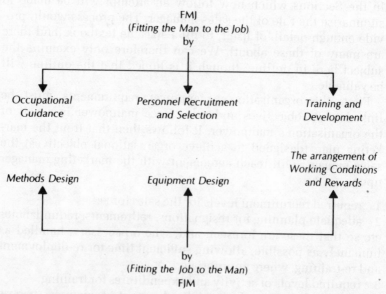

Fig. 9.2   *The 'FMJ-FJM' framework (adapted with acknowledgements to Professor Alec Rodger)*

We now consider each of these elements in the framework.

1   *Occupational guidance.* A managerial prerequisite is, of course, the suitability of the applicants from which to select but

since occupational guidance is not usually a responsibility of the sales manager, it will not detain us here. It must be said, however, that if more people were given guidance as to their aptitude for selling before they entered it, there might be a lot less frustration and disappointment.

2   *Recruitment.* These are some of the main sources for sales personnel:

(a) advertisements in newspapers, magazines, trade and professional journals;

(b) enquiries to technical and business colleges;

(c) business associates and customers;

(d) present employees;

(e) contacts in professional, social and voluntary organisations;

(f) enquiries to suppliers;

(g) job centres and employment bureaux;

(h) via chambers of commerce and trade associations;

(i) via advisory and consultancy organisations specialising in sales personnel recruitment

A useful guide to the comparative value of different sources can sometimes be gained from analysing data on salesmen presently employed. A major UK distributor of cameras and optical equipment discovered that all the *successful* salesmen had previously been employed in retail selling of these products. Many of the poorer performers lacked this experience. The distributor's own customers became an important source of recruitment.

3   *Selection.* Effective selection means that management must be very clear about what the selling job entails. The list of the various types of sales role in the previous Section indicate the wide diversity of tasks that might be included under the general title of selling.

The first step in effective selection consists of a *job analysis* – a careful examination of all the elements involved in the job. This analysis can then be set out in a written statement called a *job description*. From this job description it is then possible to devise a *job specification*.

According to Professor Alec Rodger, a job specification should provide the answers to the following questions:

(a) What does the worker have to do in the job?

(b) How, where, with what and with whom does the worker do the job and how is the worker rewarded?

(c)   What are the 'requirements' of the job?

This last heading requires some elaboration. Rodger believed that the most important criterion in selection relates to the broad objective of the employee's *satisfactoriness* to his or her employer and this criterion is, therefore, the performance of a role that has been described clearly, comprehensively and with emphasis on the *difficulties* and *distates* commonly experienced by those who undertake the role.

The difficulties in the job are those tasks which people find hard to do well.

The distastes are those aspects which people find irksome.

Now these may overlap, but essentially and initially they must be looked at separately for it is possible to find aspects of a job which are:

(a)   *difficult but not distasteful*: the job may be 'challenging' – for example, prospecting for new business or introducing a new product or service may require a great deal in the way of physical and mental effort but the salesman enjoys it;

(b)   *distasteful but not difficult*: routine repeat selling tasks or collecting cash or completing report forms may require little in the way of effort but the salesman may find such tasks dull or boring.

The importance of focusing attention on the difficulties and distastes of the selling job is that the job specification will then produce a clear picture of: the *capacities (and skills)* needed to overcome the difficulties and the *inclinations (and attitudes)* needed to overcome the distastes.

The selection process then becomes one of *matching* an applicant with the capacities (i.e. what the applicant is capable of doing) and the inclinations (i.e. what the applicant wants or would be willing to do) to the difficulties and distastes of the job, so that these may be overcome.

Such a process aims at providing the selector with a simple but scientifically defensible assessment system. In the job specification, of course, it is the required capacities and inclinations that must be emphasised and not the difficulties and distastes for there is otherwise some danger of discouraging candidates!

The job specification for a salesman would therefore contain the following components, as a rule:

Job title: e.g. 'divisional sales representative'; 'sales engineer'.

Objectives of the job: a short statement setting out the fundamental responsibilities of the job and the capacities and inclinations required to discharge these successfully, e.g. a 'positive entrepreneurial approach', 'technical training to graduate level', 'at least five years experience of tendering for such contracts' are examples of specific capacities; inclinations might be expressed as 'willingness to assist with point-of-sale demonstrations' or 'readiness to submit formal reports on market opportunities'.

Details of the salesman's immediate superior: e.g. area manager, sales supervisor (i.e. the line management relationship).

Other executives/departments for which duties are performed: these are the 'staff' relationships and may extend to tasks on behalf of the advertising department, the credit controller, the marketing research executive etc.

Specific responsibilities: including the types of customers to be serviced/contacted; average daily call rates; methods of placing orders; submission of reports and maintenance of records (company documentation; customer records; expenses records; journey plans etc); discretion to grant special terms/discounts; allowable expense levels.

Details of the territory to be covered

(Note: The job specification may or may not include details of the basis for the salesman's remuneration, but this would certainly be incorporated in the *contract of employment*.)

It is also important to bear in mind that the job specification is useful for a variety of activities associated with the selection process. These include:

the drafting of advertisements;

the preparation of application forms;

the preparation of information 'handouts';

the preparation of interview record forms;

the preparation of progress report forms.

Finally, a useful sequence for the selection process might be as follows:

(a) preparation of job specification;

(b) preparation of a concisely informative advertisement which brings out the capacities and inclinations required;

(c) placing of advertisement in appropriate media;

(d) despatch to enquirers a copy of the job specification and an application form so designed that it provides preliminary information on the applicant with regard to the difficulties and distastes of the job;

(e) Assessment of candidates for interview and preparation of short-list (or conduct first-stage interviews where appropriate – e.g. as for senior positions in the sales force);

(f) Interview candidates and administer any *relevant* tests (e.g. aptitude, achievement, personality and interest tests);

(g) Notification of selection decision to all candidates;

(h) Annotation of unsuccessful but promising candidates for possible future reference.

4 *Training and Development.* Throughout the whole of this Chapter, the organisation and control of selling operations based on a structured, integrated approach grounded in the market concept, has been emphasised. So it is with the training and development function. The content of a training programme and the methods of training depend on the job specification. Fig. 9.3 is an attempt to depict diagrammatically the conceptual approach to the training programme. To elaborate on each step in the process:

(a) *The job specification:* this details the objectives of the job, its specific responsibilities, its place in the organisation structure etc.

(b) *Task analysis:* what specific tasks does the job specification imply? the man selling complex industrial durables will have a vastly different range of tasks from the salesman in the retail store;

(c) *Knowledge and skill requirements:* these derive from an analysis which determines the knowledge and skills required to perform the specific tasks: the pre-approach investigation; the merchandising function (where appropriate); the diagnosis of customer needs; organisational and administrative tasks etc.

(d) *Trainee entry capabilities:* these set out what minimal level of knowledge and skill the salesman is required to possess in order to enter the training programme, e.g. level of educational attainment (GCE A levels; Graduate Engineer status; B/.TEC Higher Diploma); technical/sales experience; minimum age etc;

(e) *Specification of training requirements:* knowing the trainee's capabilities now and knowing what level of skills and knowledge he must acquire in order to perform the job effectively enables the training organisation to specify the content of the training programme. Most programmes cover the following three areas;

(i) company products or services; policies and practices;

(ii) the diagnosis of customer needs and customer products

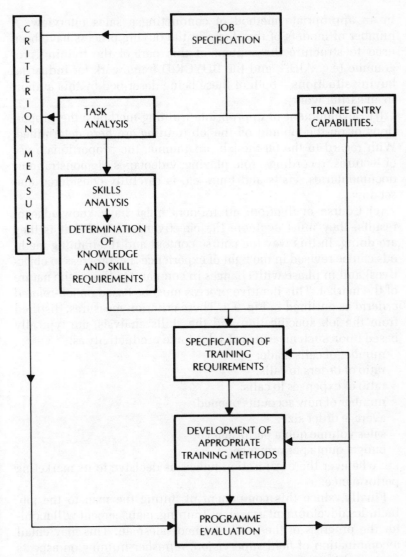

Fig. 9.3 A framework for the design of the sales training programme

and market knowledge relating to competitive products
and competitive activity;
(iii) the techniques of the selling process.

With regard to (iii), in addition to techniques of pre-approach
investigation and interview planning, the trainee will be schooled

in an appropriate method of conducting a sales interview. A number of models of the stages in the buying process have been used to structure the content of this part of the training programme (e.g. AIDA, and the BUYGRID framework for industrial buying situations – both of these being described by this author[4] in an earlier work).

(f) *Development of appropriate training methods:* the proportions of on-the-job and off-the-job training are here determined. With regard to the off-the-job programme, the proportionate use of lectures, recordings, role playing, videotapes, demonstrations, documentaries, visits and tours etc is carefully considered and set down.

(g) *Course evaluation:* all trainers must have knowledge of results, they must *evaluate* the effectiveness of what it is they are doing. In this way the course content and the training methods can be revised in the light of experience (i.e. progress to objectives) and in phase with changes in company policy or the nature of the market. This iterative process must be based on *job-related criteria* as outlined in Fig. 9.3. These criterion measures, distilled from the job specification and the skills analysis, are typically based upon such measures of sales-force productivity as:

 number of calls made;
 ratio of orders to calls;
 ratio of expenses to calls;
 number of new accounts opened;
 average order size;
 sales volume quota performance;
 budget quota performance,

i.e. whatever the organisation judges as decisive to its marketing performance.

Finally, since this component of 'fitting the man to the job' includes development as well as training, management will monitor the progress of the newly trained salesman. This may entail a combination of *field supervision, refresher training* on aspects of the selling process, and *product and technical briefings* conducted periodically to ensure that the salesman is abreast of new products and processes both from his own firm and from those of competitors. Personnel development will have two main objectives:

(i) to maintain the effectiveness of the salesman in his current role and

(ii) to provide a career development programme, where appro-

priate, in which sales personnel are prepared for increased levels
of responsibility (key account salesman → area manager → sales
manager etc).

In the latter respect close attention may be paid, via a *performance appraisal* system, to the results obtained by the salesman
pro rata to mutually agreed objectives (e.g. increased sales
volume; improved call rates; an increased level of responsibility;
a broader marketing research role).

Fitting the job to the man

According to Alec Rodger, the second side of the FMJ-FJM model
comprises these elements:

Methods design;
Equipment design;
The arrangement of working conditions and rewards.

In adapting the Rodgerian approach to the management of personal selling, we have to be a little liberal in our interpretation.
Methods design assuredly contains such tactical variables as the
sales presentation; sales reports and administrative procedures;
methods of prospecting for new business etc, which will be provided for by the training and development component on the
FMJ side of the model. But methods design on the FJM side incorporates important *strategic variables* – such as the size of the
sales force and how it should be deployed. Therefore, in talking
of methods design we shall now consider such managerial problems as:

1 'how many salesmen should we employ?'
2 'how should assignments be allocated to them?'

Therefore, we are discussing the design of methods by which the
total personal selling function might be organised and controlled
in pursuit of marketing objectives. This, in turn, presupposes that
robust conclusions have already been reached on:

1 the marketing communications mix, the integration of its
components (advertising, publicity, personal selling etc) and the
affordable budget for each component;
2 the relation of budgets involved to the profit, or other objectives, of the organisation.

The size of the sales force

As Oliver[5] points out, for most sales managers the size factor must be taken as given, since they are working with an established sales force. However in terms of the potential offered by the market, and its changes through time, one would not know whether by taking the number of salesmen as given one was trying to crack a nut with a sledgehammer or empty a river with a sponge. This is why Oliver regards such a standpoint as 'clearly myopic'.

The marginality approach

As readers acquainted with economic theory will know, the principle of marginality provides a powerful analytical tool for a manager wishing to optimise anything.

Thus, the size of the sales force is at the optimum when the extra revenue achieved by increasing the sales force size by one salesman (the 'marginal' salesman) is just balanced by the cost of employing that salesman (marginal cost). In other words, at the optimum, the *incremental* or *marginal* effect of a change in the controllable variable (salesmen) is equal to the change in the criterion variable (sales revenue). Below the optimum it would be to the advantage of the firm to increase the size of the sales force (marginal effect is positive) but above the optimum, the opposite is true.

To put it another way, imagine that a consideration of sales force expansion produced the following figures:

Additional sales from the employment of one further salesman £300 000
Additional fixed costs of the employment of one further salesman £50 000
Let us assume that the variable costs on this additional volume amount to 80 per cent
The contribution to overheads is therefore 20 per cent
The break-even point on this additional salesman

$$= \frac{\text{fixed costs}}{\text{contribution}} = \frac{£50\,000}{.20} = £250\,000$$

The break-even point = £250 000 and the projected incremental sales = £300 000, i.e. £50 000 above the break-even point.

On this additional £50 000 turnover, variable costs (80 per cent) = £40 000

Contribution to profit (20 per cent) = £10 000 which represents a 20 per cent return on the additional investment of £50 000 in fixed costs.

In other words, in this example, we note the value of using a comparative rate of return on assets employed as a method of evaluating the investment opportunity provided by the employment of an additional salesman.

Speaking to a conference of the British Institute of Management in London nearly two decades ago, Dr Arnold Corbin[6] pointed out that in adopting the marketing concept as a basic philosophy for operating a business such considerations should prevail. In effect, the business must ask itself whether the same £50 000 invested in some alternative might not produce a higher rate of return.

The difficulty with these approaches is, of course, the accuracy with which the marginal revenue can be calculated but in organisations with a sound knowledge of their markets, enabling them to assess the likely effect on sales of additional selling effort, some reasonable approximations may be possible.

The work-load approach

This can best be illustrated by an example. Imagine an organisation is producing an industrial consumable product, such as a raw material in consistent use by a number of manufacturing industries. It has established that no fewer than 20 000 organisations in the UK use the product in their operations.

At the first stage, it must grade the customers (usually in terms of the customers' size and therefore potential buying power) e.g.

	Estimated sales pa	No of UK firms
Type A	more than £50 000	1 000
B	£25 000 to £50 000	3 000
C	£10 000 to £24 999	5 000
D	less than £10 000	11 000
	Total	20 000

Then it must allocate each grade of customer a *call frequency*, and here we will assume that the service element in selling the product is such that the larger the buying potential the higher the required frequency of call.

Type A 12 calls pa (× 1000 firms)   = 12 000 calls
     B   6   (× 3000 firms)   = 18 000
     C   3   (× 5000 firms)   = 15 000
     D   1   (× 11 000 firms) = 11 000
                    Total Calls pa   = 56 000

So we can see that the UK market, serviced with the required regularity, imposes a yearly workload on the organisation as a whole of 56 000 calls

The organisation must now consider the *average daily call rate* of the salesmen. This will depend upon a number of variables including the complexity of the product, the geographical dispersion of user firms, the number of personnel to be seen (e.g. production, technical, design and buying executives) and the associated administrative and maintenance tasks to be performed, if such considerations apply. The word 'average' is very important here, for if the customer has a complex problem, or an intended use for the raw material which requires extended discussion with the salesman, this can markedly affect the call rate. Let us assume that the organisation establishes what it considers an equitable average at 10 per day. Assume each salesman, with appropriate allowances for holidays, area sales meetings, head office meetings, conferences, exhibitions and sales training, is calling directly on customers for 40 weeks in each year. This enables him to make 2000 calls per annum (40 weeks × 5 days per week × 10 calls per day).

To cover the market provided by the UK, therefore, requires a team of 28 salesmen (56 000 ÷ 2000). This number may be marginally adjusted in order to provide cover for sickness, salesmen under training etc and will require some additions, no doubt, for regional and national management. However, this will depend on a number of factors, not least, the profitability of the product and the nature of sales force costs. It should be added that the tendency currently is to economise sales force costs wherever and whenever possible.

Allocation of territories

Having decided on the number of salesmen it will employ, the organisation must now decide how best to allocate their assignments. The example which has been outlined assumes that the number, type, size and location of actual and potential customers is known.

Developing territories with as near as possible an equal work-load then becomes a question of grouping these customers together, block by block, bearing in mind the required number of calls on each type of customer, until an annual territorial work-load of 2000 calls is reached.

This is one way. It is not the only way. The approach outlined does have the merits of incorporating *potential*, as well as *established* sales volume. It is clear, therefore, that the sum of the projected sales from each territory will equal the projected sales force contribution to the organisation's *projected market share* (i.e. total sales volume) for the forthcoming period (usually a financial year).

An alternative approach for fixing an equitable work-load for each salesman is to do this on the basis of anticipated sales turnover from established customers and add to it a mutually agreed measure of time for the cultivation of new business, related to the sales potential of each allotted territory.

The objectives of management in designing territories are:

(a) to maximise coverage of the potential provided by the market at an affordable cost;

(b) to provide each salesman with a territorial work-load which is felt fair in terms of work-load and sales opportunity (as someone once said: 'salesmen have to be happy in order to produce').

Evidence that these aims are not easy to achieve is provided by John O'Shaughnessy[7] who in applying work study techniques to field sales force operations discovered, in one study, a disparity of 1:6 in territorial work-loads. In another study, during a one week period, and analysing 500 observations on each of four salesmen (i.e. 2000 observations in all), he discovered that actual selling time amounted to only 22 per cent of total time. In this same study, as much as 35 per cent of total time was spent driving around the territory.

One can imagine, of course, that with certain products and markets (e.g. the farm market) this might be a reasonable state of affairs. Management must determine the *acceptable standards* for the market in which it operates. To do this, it must have access to an adequate data base. Decisions can be no better than the data on which they are framed and the data base for territorial design will be an important sub-system within the marketing information system. The raw data for this sub-system can be quarried from published statistics on: the retail trade; the population; government expenditure; employment and earnings; building and construction; energy; the census of production; agriculture; transport; communications – whatever are germane to the organisation's products and markets.

Computer-based salesman reporting and analysis systems when matched with such national and regional statistics enable management to make rational decisions on territorial design, sales force size etc. Salesman allocation models using a market grid approach have been utilised by collecting and manipulating such data. This area is one which again amply demonstrates that 'marketing is to do with measurement'. Such planning-oriented systems leave room for important subjective judgment, even so. For example, management may have to evaluate which type of salesman (with respect to age, personality, technical or educational background) might be most productively deployed to which types of territory (or buyers).

Methods design will also call for continuing managerial surveillance on the changing pattern of distribution. In the industrial field, for instance, mergers and acquisitions among user companies may affect territorial assignments, as may any planned diversifications or technological developments within user companies. Changing patterns within retail distribution (e.g. continued growth of the multiples at the expense of the independents) may make some outlets unprofitable for direct servicing. This may require adjustments in call rates or the referral of these outlets to wholesalers.

Equipment design

This aspect of fitting the job to the man may seem, at first glance, to have little direct relevance to the selling function. Further thoughts will clarify, however, that this element of the sales administrator's responsibility has an important bearing on the effectiveness of the sales team.

The issue goes beyond the mere design of sample cases and the provision of appropriate vehicles. Where equipment is being demonstrated by the salesman it follows that its design must lend itself to a word-and-action perfect presentation. The economic availability of video cassettes now enables the salesman to advance convincing proof of the firm's size, organisational layout, production processes, quality control, or whatever is judged to be decisively important. Resources allocated to the making of good quality video films can reap useful returns, particularly where complex technical points have to be explained.

The design of display stands, dispensers and other point-of-sale material must provide for easy assembly and siting by salesmen and must take into account the pressure on floor, window and shelf-space in retail outlets.

Similarly, the design of exhibition stands, showrooms and display areas must be *user-friendly*. The author recalls an exhibition design which consisted of several display cases, illuminated and wired in sequence. These were subsequently used by the sales force, in individual lots, for use in key retail outlets. They proved a decided incentive in obtaining sizeable orders.

Again, where a maintenance function is undertaken by the sales representative, as may be the case with office equipment, a unitised interior design which enables the salesman to locate the fault, plug in a replacement sub-assembly and return the defective sub-assembly to the service depot for detailed examination makes the best use of the salesman's time and is appreciated by customers.

This aspect is one where the value of a little extra thought can be easily overlooked.

Working conditions and rewards

A cardinal element in this aspect of the model will be the fixing of salesmen's remuneration. The level and type of remuneration will be related to the proportion of the marketing communications budget allocated to the personal selling function. This will in turn be markedly influenced by the nature of the product and the market as briefly indicated in Fig. 9.4 below.

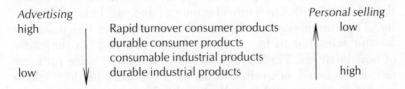

Fig. 9.4 *Proportions of the communications budget: type of product*

The Figure expresses broad truisms and the individual organisation will find its own particular place along these continua, but
in essence the combinations range from proportionately high
expenditure on advertising and low expenditure of personal selling – as in the case of confectionery or food products, to proportionately low advertising expenditure and high sales force
expenditure for complex plant and capital equipment.

From the total sum available for the operation of a sales force
an appropriate measure of selling expenses will be budgetted for,
the balance being taken up principally by salesmen's remuneration. The main methods of remuneration are summarised below
and again, it can be seen that the method chosen will largely
be determined by the class of product.

Salary only

This method is particularly suitable for complex industrial equipment, plant installations and systems selling where a lengthy
period of negotiation, technical advice etc precedes the making
of a contract. Used alone, the absence of an incentive for the
salesman to be constantly looking for increased sales is seen to
be a drawback. However, it could be argued that this latter
approach is an inappropriate one since manufacturing organisations do not re-equip every day. Moreover it is difficult to isolate
the value of the salesman's input when he is often supported
by a team of technical, financial and production personnel in
negotiating new business. It is a popular method within the
industrial equipment field and minimises friction and jealousy
among other staff. It is also easy to operate and provides the
firm with a precise calculation of its direct sales costs.

Salary + Commission; Salary + Bonus

Both of these methods are popular with salesmen and their
employers. The salary element, if at an adequate level, provides
the salesman with a measure of economic and psychological security. The commission or bonus element provides the incentive
for the salesman to be constantly 'up and doing' in the cause
of new business. The bonus may be on profits, or sales turnover
or cash received, according to needs of the company (e.g. where
salesmen are required to collect cash). The commission may be
paid on a sliding scale (e.g. increasing in rate as sales volume

increases or, what is not so defensible, decreasing in rate as sales volume increases). Differential commissions can also be paid according to the type of products sold. For some of the reasons outlined, the method can be difficult to operate, particularly if the qualifications for earning commission are complex.

Commission only

This is said to provide the finest incentive of all and should be especially attractive to the confident salesman. There is theoretically no limit to earning power, so the salesman should leave no stone unturned in order to gain orders. It is not a popular method, however, and where it is successful can cause disaffection and jealousy among other staff. Equally important, in the quest for sales, after-sales service and other customer support may be skimped or neglected by the salesman. Moreover, a poor business climate may result in economic distress for the salesman, with lowering of confidence and high turnover of staff.

Beyond these basic methods of remuneration there are a number of ways in which group effort may be rewarded, key account salesmen may be remunerated and other incentives for effort may be provided. These other incentives frequently take the form of prizes in cash or kind presented at sales conferences. Competition among salesmen is stimulated by the publication of league tables on 'progress to quota'.

The *sales quota* is a negotiated sales figure to be achieved for a given period (per month; per year) and is based upon the sales potential of the allocated territory.

As has been indicated on page 326, the productivity of the salesman can be evaluated by a number of criterion measures; calls made, orders taken, sales volume obtained, quota performance (on both sales and expenses), and any of these measures can be adapted in relation to the incentive element within the package of remuneration.

Working conditions

In addition to decisions on the type and level of remuneration management must design the general conditions of employment so that, while within cost and profit objectives, they act as a stimulus to recruitment. Thus the type of car provided, the company pension scheme, help with relocation and educational assistance, must all bear comparison with the employment conditions of competitors and help to attract good personnel. A balance must be struck between providing the employee with a social status fitted to his role in the organisation and not so 'featherbedding' him that the incentive to look for increased sales is stifled. Rather like the soldier in the sentry-box, he must be made comfortable but not too comfortable!

The evaluation of the salesman

Criterion measures can relate to the input of the salesman (average daily call rate; average daily mileage; monthly expenses as a proportion of expenses budget) and to his output (number of orders taken; number of new accounts opened; sales by product groups; sales by customer type etc).

Both the input and output criteria are measured quantitatively by reference to the established standards that have been devised to assist the firm to achieve its objectives.

However, management will also be interested in the following questions:

1 How co-operative, imaginative and resilient is he?
2 How is he regarded by his customers?
3 How is he regarded by his area manager and his colleagues?
4 How well does he know the company, its policies and its products and how well does he present these?
5 Is he decisive? Is he logical in his approach to problems?
6 Is he loyal?
7 Is he of good appearance and good health?
8 To what extent does he take a broad (i.e. marketing) standpoint in dealing with issues and what research contribution does he make?
9 Related to 8 what is the quality of his report-writing?

The answers to these questions provide some qualitative measures by which the salesman can be judged and, along with the quantitative measures, they make for a balanced evaluation of performance. The qualitative measures will have added significance when members of the sales team are being considered for allocation to key accounts or for promotion to supervisory roles.

In this context, one is reminded of the *motivation-hygiene theory* of Frederick Herzberg. A professor of psychology, Herzberg[8] evolved his theory from a survey of engineers and accountants who were asked to remember occasions when they felt exceptionally good or exceptionally bad about their jobs. Herzberg and his colleagues then investigated the underlying bases for the different sets of feelings.

Herzberg concluded that such factors as company policy, pay, security and working conditions – the *hygiene* or *maintenance* factors – would, if judged to be inadequate, ineffective or absent, cause job dissatisfaction, but would not of themselves cause job satisfaction. The satisfaction in work was provided by the *motivator* or *growth* factors of achievement, recognition, advancement and responsibility.

Thus, the executive responsible for motivating salesmen should bear in mind that lack of 'hygiene' will produce disease but hygiene of itself will not produce good health. A sales team that is 'healthy', in the sense that it is well-motivated, highly energetic and loyal, will be one in which as much creative energy as possible is liberated and where those capable of assuming broader responsibilities are given ample opportunity for personal and professional growth. Sales force supervision becomes more than mere mechanistic totting-up of calls made, orders obtained etc. Sales volume is important but so is the sense of psychological well-being from being appreciated for one's current efforts and being motivated to fulfil one's highest potential. The marketing concept with its emphasis on the contribution of the sales force to organisational objectives and the opportunity for salesmen to enact a key research and promotional function provides excellent opportunities for job enrichment.

Robertson and Chase[9] have suggested that much of the writing on the selling process, with its conglomeration of 'techniques', 'rules' and 'principles' is both incomplete and contradictory. They believe a more comprehensive analysis of the process is provided by viewing it as an *open system*; part of a given environment in which inputs, in the shape of salesmen, customers and technology, are transformed to specified outputs, with information being fed back from the outputs and the environment being searched for information which can be used in the next sales encounter. Again, this indicates a satisfactorily broad view of the selling role.

It was Arnold Corbin,[10] in typically thoughtful fashion, who proposed some years ago that companies might usefully consider evaluating salesmen in terms of the rate of return they produce on the company's investment in their territories. In other words, if salesmen were failing to attain their sales quota they were providing an inadequate return on the cash, receivables, inventory and promotion being invested in their territories. *Sales territory return on investment analysis* has not become a general basis on which salesmen are rewarded but the philosophy serves to underline the marketing responsibilities of the sales force.

Of course, the marketing responsibilities of the sales force are even more highly developed in the export field. In foreign markets, the salesman's role is one in which he is usually deeply involved in the marketing research function, touching upon such matters as the recruitment of sales agents, product and pricing strategy and the supervision of communications campaigns. Documentary and financial procedures, packaging and packing, transport and credit policies are all heavily influenced by the salesman. This role has been described at some length by the author[11] in an earlier work and reference is made to it at the end of this Chapter.

The sales function in a changing economic climate

The role of the salesman has been changing for the last two or three decades. Despite the reduction in the size of sales forces (stemming from changing patterns of distribution, concentration of buying power and the soaring costs of energy) the importance of the sales function has never been questioned, so much so that we were forced to conclude that: 'the salesman isn't dead, he's different'. The reference here was that with the growth of advertising, the salesman was becoming less of a seller and more of a merchandiser.

Today the changes continue and some would say 'What future for the salesman if buying power continues to concentrate and the client's computer will order from the supplier's computer in such a way as to optimise return on investment?' The answer is, of course, that the concentration process will never be total for people are not economic ciphers. Moreover, consumerism and anti-monopolies legislation will set limits to such growth so there will be more key accounts appointments and a call for more highly-skilled, professional selling but the sales force, as such, is hardly likely to become extinct.

Other changes continue, of course. The shortage of strategic raw materials means that the salesman is called upon to assist the organisation in the allocation of its supplies. The energy crisis and other factors that stoke inflation have seen the salesman called upon to a marked extent to interpret and justify to customers what appears to be a never-ending spiral of price-rises. On both counts – of shortages and of price rises – direct contact by the sales force has done a great deal to maintain customer goodwill. On both counts, too, the salesman has been increasingly cast as an 'assistant buyer', advising the customer how best he can maintain his business with the help of modified or substitute products.

Notwithstanding these changes, the role of the sales force is a durable one and it will continue to be the case that 'nothing happens until somebody sells something'. And managing a sales force well will continue to mean communicating well – which implies a readiness to listen as well as to exhort.

Self-assessment questions

1 Demonstrate the relationship of organisational, marketing and personal selling objectives.
2 What are the special advantages of personal selling?
3 Describe the variety of selling roles.
4 What is Rodger's 'fmj–fjm' model? How would you apply it as a sales manager?
5 Prepare notes which show how you would devise a sales training programme.
6 What is meant by the following terms: job specification; task analysis; programme evaluation; criterion measures; performance appraisal?
7 Describe some approaches to determine the size of a sales force.
8 What are the methods usually considered in fixing the remuneration of salesmen?

References

1 Jolson, Marvin A. *Marketing management* London, Collier Macmillan, 1978, p. 549
2 Cannon, Tom. *Basic marketing – principles and practice*, London, Holt, Rinehart and Winston, 1980, p. 243

3 Walker, Orville C. Jr, Churchill, Gilbert A. Jr, Ford, Neil M. Reactions to role conflict: the case of the industrial salesman, *Marketing management and administrative action*, (S. H. Britt and H. W. Boyd, Jr), 4th edn, Tokyo, McGraw Hill Kogakusha, 1978, pp. 367–375
4 Frain, John. *Introduction to marketing*, 2nd edn, Plymouth, Macdonald & Evans, 1983, pp. 179–180
5 Oliver, Gordon. *Marketing today*, London, Prentice-Hall, 1980, p. 235
6 Corbin, Arnold. *Implementing the marketing concept*, London, British Institute of Management, 1966, pp. 52–54
7 O'Shaughnessy, John. *Work study applied to a sales force*, London, British Institute of Management, 1965
8 Herzberg, Frederick. The motivation–hygiene theory, *Organization theory – selected readings*, (ed. D. S. Pugh) Harmondsworth, Middlesex, Penguin, 1983, pp. 324–344
9 Robertson, Thomas S. and Chase, Richard B. *Personal selling – a two-way process*, in Jolson (see reference 1), p. 550
10 *Implementing the marketing concept*, pp. 54–57
11 *Introduction to marketing*, pp. 184–187

10   SALES FORECASTING

> **Objectives**
> The sales forecast can be likened to a map which will help
> to guide the organisation through its next planning period.
> The objectives of this Chapter are:
> (a) to describe the influence of the forecast on all the
> organisation's operations;
> (b) to describe the types of forecast and the roles and
> responsibilities of those engaged in forecasting;
> (c) to introduce some of the forecasting methods commonly
> employed, including the quantitative and qualitative
> techniques generally used;
> (d) to say something of forecasting for new products.
>   Towards the end of the Chapter, something is added on
> the use of the computer in sales forecasting.

The status and purpose of sales forecasting

A businessman planning a working visit to a foreign country,
one previously unknown to his firm, would begin by acquiring
a map. This would enable routes to be studied and alternatives
weighed against considerations of time and cost. The map would
be the key to sound planning and decision making about the
work schedule.

Marketing is all about sound planning and decision making
and each financial year is to some extent a journey into the
unknown. The map by which the organisation's activity is guided
is the *sales forecast*.

Sales forecasting is properly regarded as a part of the marketing
research function relying as it does on the systematic analysis
of data both internal and external to the organisation. Such data

includes statistics of the firm's immediate past performance by products and markets, the results of the firm's own commissioned research into market trends and opportunities and environmental data, particularly that which indicates marketing threats or opportunities likely to arise from changing economic, social, political and legislative forces.

In this book, the author has separated sales forecasting from marketing research (Chapter 3) in order to relate it more closely to marketing planning, which is described in the next Chapter. The place of sales forecasting within marketing research is, however, well settled and the relationship should be self-evident to the reader.

A *sales forecast* may be defined as a estimate of the sales which will hopefully be obtained during some specified future period of time (usually one year) and based upon specified resource inputs.

Mention of the resource inputs having been specified suggests that the plan has already been formulated and this might raise the query 'which comes first; the plan or the forecast?' In practice, forecasting takes place in a context of broad goals – the objectives of the organisation – which may be taken as given. Linked to these goals, the forecaster must make certain assumptions about the resources (plant and equipment, raw materials, manpower and finance) which will be available in the period under review. In fact, the forecaster may be asked to introduce a range of levels of resources into his calculations so that the range of forecasts then emerging can be compared with the overall goals, and the forecast best suited to these goals can then be adopted. This approach is particularly suited, for example, to forecasting the sales of new products. Therefore, it is this chicken and egg situation of planning and forecasting which Willsmer[1] doubtless has in mind when he says: 'Forecasts shape plans and plans shape forecasts'. Once a particular forecast has been agreed it then becomes the key factor in the monitoring and control of all the organisation's revenues – cash flows, purchasing, production, marketing and sales activities and the budgetted expenditure allocated to these activities. All business organisations must therefore forecast, since forecasting is a major function in planning and budgetting. Even the executive who claims he has never formally undertaken any forecasting activity cannot possibly operate a business unless he makes some estimate about the future even if his estimate is one of 'no change' (a barely realistic

conclusion in the present climate). Similarly, the non-profit organisation lays claim to its resources based on its forecast of level
of activity for the next period.

Marketing, as we know, has to do with an adequate return
on-investment for the business organisation. That return will be
derived from realistic company planning accompanied by adequate management controls and business budgets. A sales forecast which can be employed with reasonable confidence provides
the basis for the planning and the controls. To understand why
Schwartz[2] believes that the sales forecast is the most important
operational procedure undertaken by a business, Fig. 10.1 shows
some of the operations within the major functions of the business
that are governed by the sales forecast.

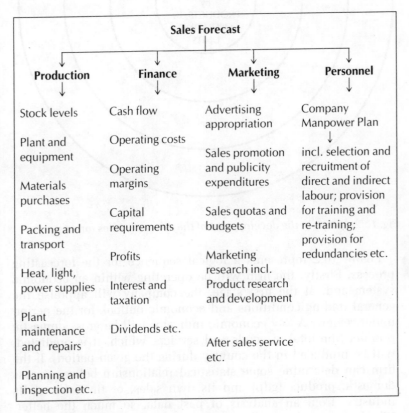

Fig. 10.1 *The influence of the sales forecast on organisational
operations*

Steps in the forecasting process

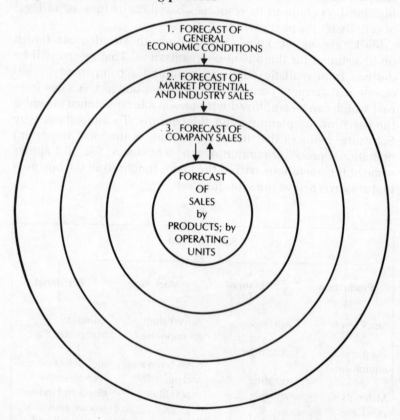

Fig. 10.2   *Steps in the development of the company sales forecast*

Figure 10.2 represents a logical sequence for the forecasting process. Firstly, the firm will be operating within an economic system and, at the first stage, the company will appraise the general trading conditions and economic outlook for the period under review. A key economic indicator will be *gross domestic product* (the total of goods and services which, it is predicted, will be produced in the country during the given period). If the firm can determine some statistical relationship between gross domestic product (gdp) and its own sales, or the sales of its industry, from an analysis of past data, so much the better. Whether or not gdp can be used as a *tied indicator*, its projected size will markedly affect business confidence and hence the economic atmosphere in which the firm will be operating. Unless the company is very large, with its own experts in economic forecasting, it will use the forecasts of such organisations, in the UK, as:

London Business School
National Institute of Social and Economic Research
Cambridge Econometrics
Henley Centre for Forecasting
Phillips and Drew
Society of Business Economists

and others, whose forecasts of annual percentage growth in gross domestic product; inflation rate and balance of payments position are widely published and commented upon in newspapers and professional journals. In addition to these consultancies, the UK clearing banks and government and quasi-governmental organisations (e.g. the Treasury, the CBI) are important secondary sources of such information. In addition to these broad economic indicators, trends in employment, world trade, industrial production, manufacturers' and distributors' stocks, raw material prices, bank loans and share prices are all useful barometers of the broad economic environment. Indeed, any one of these might be tied to the sales prospects of the individual firm in a very specific way. For example, one of the broad economic indicators is the value of new orders for the construction industry. If our friends at Arnold Ceramics are manufacturing ceramic tiles for kitchens and bathrooms they will be particularly interested in this indicator and especially in the projected figure for new housing starts.

The next stage in the process will be to forecast the size of the *potential market* in which the firm is engaged and the anticipated *sales volume* of the industry, of which the firm is a member. The first figure (market potential) is a measure of the maximum amount that could be sold with maximum possible marketing expenditures and effort within a given external environment. The anticipated industry sales will be an estimate of lesser magnitude than market potential since not all firms involved will be deploying maximum possible resources and effort to their marketing activity. Forecasting at this stage must be based, needless to say, on comprehensive knowledge of the industry's market(s) and the manner in which economic variables influence its sales. Again, selected economic indicators may be very useful in predicting sales for broad classifications of products, as outlined below:

Consumer products
population: age distribution;
consumers' expenditure;
family expenditure survey:
households and their
expenditure; index of retail
prices; average weekly and
hourly earnings; average
weekly hours; retail trade;
index numbers of value and
volume; hire purchase debt;
personal saving; etc.

Industrial products
index of industrial production;
manufacturers' sales of selected
product groups; output
statistics, e.g. energy; iron and
steel; industrial materials;
building and construction;
engineering industries, etc.;
bank loans by industry group;
investment expenditures and
intentions, etc.

Central to a realistic assessment of industry sales will be a consideration of environmental change and its relationship to industry prospects. The dramatic rise in oil prices during the 1970s had a depressant effect on the sale of large automobiles but increased the sales of a range of products designed to save energy (e.g. small cars, double glazing, insulating materials, etc.).

As we see from Fig. 10.2, the third stage in the process is to forecast the total volume of sales that can be attained by the individual firm under the expected environmental conditions for the period under review. We have seen that market potential is the theoretical upper limit of industry sales, with the forecast of actual industry sales as a somewhat lesser figure. If it is not too confusing we might think of this last figure as *actual market size* – the total sales that will eventuate based on the planned efforts of all firms in the industry. The individual firm must now forecast its market share – or company sales volume – which it expects will result from a given level of planned resource inputs, including marketing effort.

At the first stage of analysis, the firm will know from past experience whether there is a clear relationship between industry sales and its own sales. Where the firm belongs to an active and relatively sophisticated industry or trade association reliable data on industry sales may well be available for the calculation to be made with some confidence. Also, where the firm operates in more than one industry, then its anticipated proportion of sales must be calculated for each industry and aggregated to form the total of the firm's sales.

Reverting to Fig. 10.2 it can be seen from the direction of the arrows within the concentric circles that a 'top-down' approach to forecasting has been followed: the economy – the industry – the firm. At the level of the firm, however, the arrows move in two directions – from the 'top down' through a study of external data, but also from the 'bottom up' through a study of internal data relating to products (or product groups) and/or operating units (e.g. sales subsidiaries, branch factories or branch retail outlets). The objective is to reconcile the top-down forecast with the bottom up forecast and where these are widely disparate to re-examine both and arrive at an agreed forecast from which budgetted expenditure may be fixed and operational plans put into effect.

The internal analysis will consider levels and trends in: sales (products); sales (territories/markets); sales (calendar: monthly, quarterly, yearly).

An examination of the data will then be adjusted for: introduction of new products; ratio of planned marketing effort (e.g. communications budget; planned selling activity).

The forecasts initially produced may need modification taking into account such factors as:

the profit earning capacity of the various products;
the production capacity of the business;
the marketing and administrative costs implied by the forecast;
the financial requirements of the programme (e.g. considerations of cash flow; cost of bank borrowing, etc).

At that stage, the implications of the forecast for a planned and adequate return on investment can be evaluated.

The internal sales forecasting process will also take into account the elasticity of demand for individual products (i.e. the relationship between price and sales volume) and the stages in the product life-cycle each has reached. Where new products are to be marketed, the results from consumer panels and test marketing as well as the views of sales executives, salesmen and key distributors will be closely studied.

This is an outline of the forecasting process; one in which a variety of techniques is typically employed. These may range from simple statistical techniques for trend extension to sophisticated econometric models. They also include a number of qualitative techniques which allow for the inclusion of attitudes and opinions from inside and outside the organisation. Some of the techniques are described later in the Chapter. To all of them, the vital ingredient of executive judgment must be applied.

Types of forecast

What form should the company forecast take? What period should it cover? How frequently should it be revised? The answer to these and similar questions, e.g. to do with the detail and accuracy of the forecast, is quite simply: 'it all depends'. The purpose for which the forecast is required will determine the time period and the degree of detail. The size and nature of the organisation is another important influence.

Broadly speaking, the *short-term* forecast covers a period of one to three or six months ahead and relates very much to *tactical* decision making – on stock levels, production schedules, transport planning, buying schedules and short-term borrowing. Such forecasts are typically prepared in great detail by products, markets, sales regions, etc. and are reviewed on a monthly basis with adjustments being made as actual sales pro rata to forecast are monitored. This would certainly be the case with several consumer markets, but as Wilson[3] points out, the short-term forecast in industrial markets might extend to three years. Hence, 'it all depends'. The short-term forecast might be considered by many organisations to include the one year forecast, although it might be seen as a *medium-term* forecast (a description covering the period from one to five years) in other organisations. All organisations prepare one year forecasts. Where sales are seasonal, both the peak-selling and slack periods are therefore covered by the forecast. The forecast thus aligns itself with the yearly financial profit plan and is of primary importance in budgetting for expenditure and revenues, the planning of marketing expenditures, manpower levels, the mobilisation of working capital and provisions for taxation. The forecast will be reviewed at monthly or quarterly intervals and as with the shorter term forecast (one to three months or one to six months) it must be as accurate as is realistically possible since the ultimate financial results will be markedly influenced by the short-term forecast.

It has been said that the only certain thing that can be said of a sales forecast is that it will be wrong. This does not detract from the value of forecasting as a planning tool nor is it meant to deter the forecaster in his quest for accuracy. What it does highlight is the need for constant review of actuals:forecast, particularly where many factors influence sales. It should also be added in this context that the more forecasting the organisation does, the more likely it is to develop its accuracy.

On the question of whether the forecasting approach should be one of optimism or pessimism, the answer is neither. Objectivity is the keynote. Excessive optimism may mean that working capital is tied up in unsold stock. Undue caution may mean a lower than possible return on investment through failing to capitalise on market opportunity.

Medium-term forecasting (e.g. from two to five years) enables the organisation to plan its capital expenditure, its longer term marketing strategy, its research and development programmes, its management development and its policies of mergers and acquisitions through the length of the typical business cycle. This period is the one usually required to bring new plant, equipment and production processes into commission and to bring new products through the various technical feasibility and market testing stages to commercialisation. Long-range forecasts extend beyond five years and relate even more closely to programmes of replacement for production processes, plant, equipment and products (many of which will have completed their life cycle). This is the stage at which company objectives, including its visionary objectives, come under review. Obviously less detail is required for both medium-term and long-term forecasts and a high level of accuracy is not so important and is, in fact, difficult to attain (but this is not to say that the forecasting process is any less skilled).

With regard to longer term forecasting, mention should be made of *technological forecasting*. This is a branch of forecasting which attempts to predict the impact of technological change on both products and services, and upon processes and methods in customer industries. The wider social and economic implications of changing technology also come within its purview. More is said of technological forecasting towards the end of this Chapter.

Forecasting: roles and responsibilities

Who does the forecasting? Who should be responsible for it? To answer the second question first, if the organisation believes in the marketing approach and is seriously trying to put it into action, the ultimate responsibility for the sales forecast must rest with the chief marketing executive, who must ensure the forecasting is carried out, approve the forecasting method, ensure the forecast is monitored and constantly up-dated and who must also have made contingency plans if, despite the care taken, things go awry with the forecast.

Earlier in this work it was stated that the marketing philosophy had three distinguishing characteristics, one of which was its power to integrate the operations of the firm. The sales forecast is a mechanism for doing this for there can only be one forecast – there cannot be a variety of forecasts – one each for sales, production, finance, etc. The single sales forecast provides the basis for an effective, fully integrated planning system which is oriented to the market and while executives from many functions could and should contribute to it, the chief marketing executive bears responsibility for it to the board of directors (or board of governors in a non-profit organisation) who must approve it and receive regular reports on its up-dating.

The question of who does the forecasting must be related to the size of the firm. In a very small organisation, the chief marketing executive will probably make the forecasts. In a slightly larger firm it may be delegated to a marketing assistant. In medium and large firms the role may be allotted to an economist/market researcher. In a British Institute of Management survey, conducted some years ago, and reported by Wilson[4], 60 per cent of the responding firms stated that an economist/researcher figured in the forecasting process. This is not to say that the forecaster must invariably be a trained economist but what is important is that he or she should have a broad understanding of the economic environment and the working of the economy and be conversant with the many sources of published economic forecasts and other data. Where the organisation retains the services of economic or marketing consultants/advertising agencies it is important that the forecaster is able to work with them at an appropriate level of complexity and understanding.

It goes without saying that the forecaster must be competent in the standard forecasting techniques with an adequate appreciation of the more complex computer-based forecasting routines. What is salient is that the forecaster has a good knowledge of the organisation, its products or services, its objectives and policies, its consumer markets or user industries, channels of distribution, etc. Ideally, the forecaster will be closely involved with the development and operation of the marketing information system which informs and guides operations.

The level of accuracy of the forecast is obviously significant but must be related to the costs involved. The objective should be to develop a forecasting method that will be accurate enough for practical purposes within an affordable cost. Enthusiasm to 'get it right' can easily lead to over-elaboration and a situation where marginal increments of accuracy are clearly unaffordable or can only be obtained at highly disproportionate cost or take so long to produce results that marketing conditions have changed in the meantime. In this context, there is no shame in developing a method that will 'just do'. *Balance* is the criterion. Moreover, as Wilson[5] points out, while the forecasting tools available have reduced the margin of error, the human qualities of judgment and understanding are still pre-requisites. Willsmer[6] in a similar vein believes that human judgment and common sense applied to statistical projections and supported by market research and market tests, where both can be used and economically justified, 'will always produce the best results'. The chief marketing executive and his colleagues, including sales personnel and their supervisors, are responsible for contributing the vital ingredients of common sense, judgment and understanding to the forecasting process.

Forecasting methods

The author's initial intention was to title this Section 'The forecasting method', but this would be misleading, for the first point to be made is that no one method can be prescribed for all organisations. Once again, 'it all depends', and selection of the method best suited to an individual organisation will involve consideration of a number of factors. The following are prominent among them:

1 The type of business/field of activity involved;
2 The size of the organisation, the experience of the personnel at its disposal;
3 The type of 'historical' data available and its relevance to the forecasting problem;
4 The organisation's experience of forecasting;
5 The status of the forecast within the organisation i.e. its importance as an integrated planning tool;
6 The time period to be covered by the forecast and the time available to make the forecast;

7   The degree of accuracy required, i.e. the margin of error that would be acceptable for planning purposes.

To explain briefly the significance of each of these factors in turn:

1   In the consumer goods field, marketing activity is much more widely documented, with retail stock audits and numerous continuous research services and ad hoc surveys providing information on market trends, brand shares, etc. This is not the case in industrial marketing. Moreover, the action taken by the consumer goods company on such matters as price, discount policies, consumer and trade 'deals' usually has a much more direct influence on marketing results than in the industrial goods field where demand is derived.

2   The size of the organisation will determine the number of forecasting personnel at its disposal (the very small firm may have none), and the extent of their qualifications and training. The small firm will not, as a rule, be adept at the origination and use of complex, sophisticated techniques using econometric models. The experience of personnel is equally important. Most methods are a combination of objective (i.e. statistical) and subjective (i.e. judgmental) techniques. Executive judgement, based on up-to-date and valuable experience of the products, the market, competition, user and distributor attitudes, etc., is a vital element in realistic forecasting.

3   The amount and quality of internal data (sales by products, markets, calendar sales, sales expenses and expense ratios, promotional appropriations, unit costs of production, etc.) and the time period through which this has been accumulated will clearly be of great significance as will the availability of market data and its relevance to the forecasting problem.

4   The more experience of forecasting the organisation has, the more likely it is to 'get better at it', the more chance it has of determining which particular factors most influence its marketing results and the more prepared it should be to use the more sophisticated forecasting techniques.

5   The value put upon the forecast as an aid to planning will determine the resources made available for forecasting, hence the time and care devoted to it and the extent to which sales, production and finance personnel can be mobilised as part of the forecasting team.

6 Some factors may significantly influence short-term forecasts but have little significance for other time-periods. It may be that changes in customer/distributor stock levels markedly affect short-run demand, but this factor may safely be discounted for a five year forecast. The time available for forecasting may necessarily be short, e.g. prior to introducing a contingency or emergency plan, and an outline forecast may be quite adequate.

7 Accuracy must be approached on a cost: benefit basis – a point that has been made earlier in the Chapter. Moreover, the purpose of the forecast is relevant here. Greater accuracy is required for a forecast related to incremental improvement in net profit performance than one which relates to the decision to enter a new market, where perhaps only a 'broad brush' estimate of size may be all that is required for a 'go/no go' decision.

In addition to the above factors, the extent to which the organisation plans to do something different in the ensuing period (introduce new products; enter new markets; change marketing, promotional or distribution policies, etc.) may well affect the choice of forecasting methods.

With the knowledge and approval of the chief marketing executive, the forecaster or the forecasting team must make a choice from the welter of techniques, with their wide range of sophistication and their diverse standpoints. It is almost certain that a number of techniques will have to be used in combination. The single technique *may* suffice for the most simplistic decision where a high level of accuracy is unimportant. As part of the process, the forecast will be making certain assumptions about the economy and about the activities of competition. These need to be entered formally as part of the forecast. If the assumptions prove to be incorrect, they will need amendment and it is highly probable that the forecast will need amendment on that account. To discover the method of forecasting best suited to the organisation the forecaster will doubtless try a number of approaches. These will be compared and reconciled until one forecast emerges. The separate methods can be evaluated by comparing their forecasts for the period in question with the actual sales obtained. By this iterative process of evaluation the organisation will be constantly seeking to improve the method employed.

The process of forecasting will perhaps be better understood if we now examine in outline some of the main forecasting techniques.

Quantitative techniques

One of the most common statistical techniques used in sales fore-casting is that of *time series analysis*. Statistics relating to changes in the values of a variable over time (in this case, sales) are known as a time series. Examinations of such series of data commonly reveal four different effects of changes over time. The Figures below illustrate these.

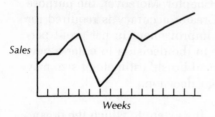

Fig. 10.3   Arnold Ceramics random fluctuation

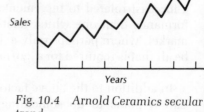

Fig. 10.4   Arnold Ceramics secular trend

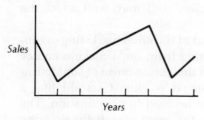

Fig. 10.5   Bennett Engineering cyclical variation

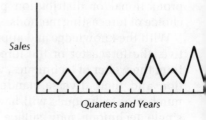

Fig. 10.6   Nonsuch Fashions seasonality

Figure 10.3 illustrates the sales of Arnold Ceramics during what normally would have been a busy quarter of the year. Unfortunately, a transport strike one third of the way through the period resulted in curtailment of deliveries of ceramics and a break in supplies of raw materials. Sales were adversely affected by the unforeseen event (*random fluctuation*) and only began to recover towards the end of the quarter.

Figure 10.4 depicts the long-term movement of Arnold Ceramics sales volume. It can be seen to have been increasing for several years. Such long-term movement is called the *secular trend*. It can be positive (upwards) or negative (downwards). Fortunately for Arnold Ceramics their secular trend is positive.

Bennett Engineering have plotted their sales over a long period of time (Fig. 10.5 is merely a section of a much more extended graph) and discover that in their section of the industry there is a cycle of growth and contraction over each six year period. This series of peaks and depressions, when occurring regularly over an extended period of time is a *cyclical variation*.

Nonsuch Fashions have chronologically classified their sales data (Fig. 10.6). The type of fashion goods they produce have peak sales in the stores in the summer season and in the months before Christmas. Their own sales to the trade have peaks in the Spring and September. The sales curve shows this *seasonality* and it is notable that despite the sales growth of recent years, the level of sales in the off-peak periods is quite static. Nonsuch intend to revise their product policy in order to improve this situation.

Recording these data graphically helps the firms in question to assess their future prospects to some extent (and, of course, it is perfectly possible for the sales curve of a single firm to exhibit all of these effects over time. And certainly in the case of secular trends, cyclical variations and seasonality, knowledge of the direction and magnitude of such changes will prove of some value in forecasting). In order to be more directly valuable, the trends in sales data require smoothing so that the overall trend lying behind the fluctuations becomes more apparent. One method of smoothing the trend is by the use of *moving averages*. An example may help to illustrate the process.

Potterstown Preserves

The company, relatively small but dynamic, manufactures jams and marmalades and markets these almost exclusively in the UK. Growth has been good but laboured at some stages due to the contraction in the number of independent retailers (their main outlet), keen price competition from larger manufacturers and the appearance on more and more tables of substitute 'spreads' (e.g. peanut butter, chocolate). Sales data since 1970 are shown on page 356.

In addition to the calendar sales, the forecaster has calculated the three year moving totals and the three year moving averages applicable to these sales figures (the supplementary note below the table outlines the method of calculation). The calendar sales are illustrated graphically in Fig. 10.7.

Also illustrated in Fig. 10.7 is the smoothed trend produced by plotting the values of each of the three year moving averages. Projecting the straight line (a process known as *trend extrapola-*

Table 10.1   Potterstown Preserves yearly sales (standard packs)

	Sales (calendar year)	Moving 3 year total	Moving 3 year average
1970	500	–	–
1971	622	1602	534
1972	480	2010	670
1973	908	2400	800
1974	1052	2775	925
1975	815	3270	1090
1976	1403	3630	1210
1977	1402	4080	1360
1978	1275	4500	1500
1979	1823	4848	1616
1980	1750	5364	1788
1981	1791	5706	1902
1982	2165	6210	2070
1983	2254	6588	2196
1984	2169	–	–

Note 3 year total: 1971 = *1970*(500) + *1971*(622) + *1972*(480) = 1602
   1972 = *1971*(622) + *1972*(480) + *1973*(908) = 2010 etc
   3 year average 1971 = $\frac{1602}{3}$ = 534 (recorded against mid year–1971–in each 3
   year cycle)

tion) it is possible to deduce that on a continuance of the trend Potterstown Preserves could sell 2460 standard packs in 1985, a figure which it would be difficult to project from the episodic twists and turns of the curve of calendar sales (and despite the fact that the secular trend it portrays is so markedly positive).

The reader will doubtless have realised that trend projection from a time series has the major drawback that it assumes that conditions in the past will be largely the same in the future. The technique clearly takes no account of changes in the economic environment, in competitive activity, or changes in the firm's own product, promotional or other policies. For this reason, its results must be cautiously interpreted and, in practice, it is seen as one input to the total forecasting process. A forecaster relying substantially on other techniques will invariably carry out a trend projection merely to serve as a starting point for subsequent ideas – to orient oneself to the task as it were.

For trend projection using moving averages it can be said that the technique is objective at least (i.e. not reliant on impressions and judgement) and simple to carry out. A refinement of the approach is provided by *exponential smoothing*.

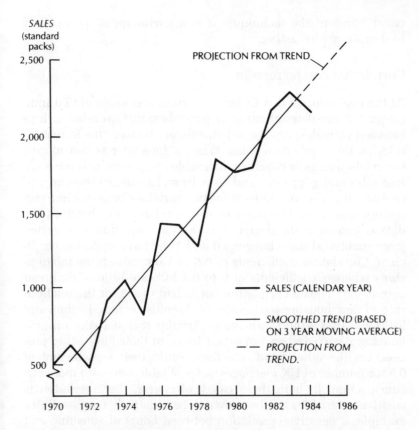

SALES
(standard
packs)

2,500

PROJECTION FROM TREND

2,000

1,500

1,000

——— SALES (CALENDAR YEAR)

——— SMOOTHED TREND (BASED
ON 3 YEAR MOVING AVERAGE)

–– – PROJECTION FROM
TREND.

500

1970   1972   1974   1976   1978   1980   1982   1984   1986

Fig. 10.7   Potterstown Preserves: calendar sales and smoothed trend
(using 3 year moving average)

In the example we have just examined, data from all parts of
the time series were given equal weighting in the process of calculation. Exponential smoothing is one of the techniques by which
because more recent data are judged to have greater typicality
for the future than older data, the more recent data are given
greater arithmetic weight. The weighting given to the data
increases exponentially as the calculation progresses from older
to the more recent data. Of great importance in the technique
is the determination of an appropriate value for the *smoothing
constant* or weighting factor which is applied. An approach would
be to compare past forecasts with actual sales and to adopt the
smoothing constant which would have produced the smallest
forecasting error. The computer can be used for the most sophisti-

cated forms of the technique. It is a useful input, particularly to short-term forecasting.

Correlation and regression

At the beginning of this Chapter mention was made of tied indicators and the determination of possible statistical relationships between variables, e.g. gross domestic product and the industry's sales or the firm's own sales. When a forecaster is considering the relationships between two variables (e.g. sales and advertising; sales and gdp; sales and rises in real incomes) then he will compare the relative values of the two variables by *regression/correlation analysis*. The strength of the relationship between the data is known as the *degree of correlation* and this is indicated (on a numerical scale between 0 and 1) by the *correlation coefficient*. Correlation coefficients of 0.8 to 1 indicate strong relationships whereas coefficients of 0 to 0.2 indicate little or no linear correlation. Thus a correlation coefficient of 0.8 for the relationship of new housing starts:sales of Arnolds ceramic kitchen and bathroom tiles would indicate to Arnolds that statistics on new housing starts were an important input to their forecasting process. On the other hand, the firm would treat a coefficient of 0.5 for number of UK marriages:sales of tableware with more circumspection. In both these cases, of course, the correlation is positive – variables can be shown to be negatively correlated (for example, a negative correlation between hours of sunshine and sales of heavy, durable clothing would hardly be surprising).

In order to study the relationship between the two variables, the forecaster will probably construct a *scattergraph* (Fig. 10.8). In the example below, the relationship between the sales of a basic raw material (e.g. china clay) and the output of some key 'customer' industries (ceramics, paper, paint and cosmetics industries) is being examined. The values of the dependent variable (sales) are plotted along the vertical (y) axis and the values of the independent variable (industries' output) along the horizontal (x) axis. The scattergraph is measuring *annual percentage changes in output* (in order to overcome the difficulty of plotting values of vastly differing orders of magnitude). Sales and industrial output could be measured on a quantities basis, if this was feasible, or on a money values basis in which case, in order to compare like with like, the values would be computed at constant and not current prices.

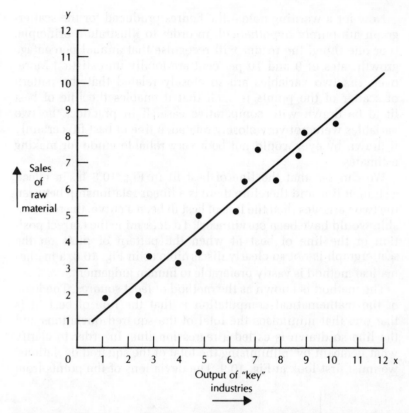

Fig. 10.8 The relationship between sales (raw material) and output of key industries

The reader will note that each single point on the graph is the plot of the pair of figures (industries' output; raw material sales), the values having been obtained from a time series (1970–84). It will also be seen that a line has been added which passes approximately through the centre of the graph of the points. This is the *line of best fit*. It has been drawn by eye and in such a way as to minimise the total divergence of the points from the line. The value of incorporating the line of best fit is that for any value of the independent variable (in this case, industries' output) an appropriate value for the dependent variable (sales) can be read off from the graph. Thus, if for the forthcoming year a 3 per cent growth in output is being forecast an estimate of 2.8 per cent growth in sales of the raw material seems reasonable.

Now for a warning note – the figures produced for the scatter-graph are *purely hypothetical*, in order to illustrate a principle. (For one thing, the reader will recognise that annual percentage growth rates of 9 and 10 per cent are totally unrealistic.) More-over, the two variables are so closely related that the pattern of scatter of the points is such that it enables the line of best fit to be drawn with comparative ease. If in practice, the two variables were not very closely related, a line of best fit, certainly if drawn by eye, would not be a very reliable guide for making estimates.

We can see that the line of best fit in Fig. 10.8 is, in effect, a straight line and therefore there is a *linear* relationship between the two variables (had the line of best fit been a curve, the relation-ship would have been *curvilinear*). To determine the correct posi-tion of the line of best fit when the pattern of plots on the scattergraph is not so clearly discernible as in Fig. 10.8, a mathe-matical method is vastly preferable to human judgement.

The method is known as the *method of least squares*. The logic of the mathematical computation is that the line of best fit is that one that minimises the total of the squared deviations and the line so drawn is called a *regression line*. In order to clarify what is meant by 'minimising the total of the squared deviations' we must first look at Fig. 10.9. The deviations of the points from

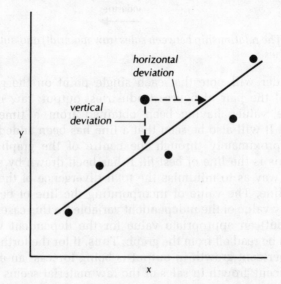

Fig. 10.9   *Horizontal and vertical deviations and the line of best fit*

the line are calculated by measuring either the *vertical* distance between a point and the line or the *horizontal* distance between a point and the line.

The general equation for a straight line on a graph is: $y = a + bx$ (where a and b are constants).

The two different methods of measuring the deviations, one minimising the total of the squared deviations measured vertically, the other minimising the total of the squared deviations measured horizontally would produce two different regression lines:

the regression of y on x (vertical deviations)
the regression of x on y (horizontal deviations)

The first of these (regression of y on x, to predict y from x), is the one most commonly employed. Determination of the line of best fit means finding the appropriate value of the constants a and b in the equation

$$y = a + bx$$

and for the regression of y on x, these can be discovered by the solution of the following two simultaneous equations:

$$\Sigma y = an + b\Sigma x$$
$$\Sigma xy = a\Sigma x + b\Sigma x^2$$

(where n = the number of *pairs* of figures)

(To the uninitiated, the above notes may be daunting. They are really very simple. For a straightforward practical example of these calculations in use, see the reference in Harper[7] in which he deals with the relationship between the two variables – advertising and sales.)

So this, in outline, is how *linear regression analysis* can be used as a *contributor* to the forecasting process. Again, the point is emphasised that an organisation would be foolhardy to rely on the projections from a single technique. Let us think, for example, of the warning notes we have to sound about the technique just described.

1 It assumes that the future will simply be a projection of the past, and given the dynamic nature of most markets not much reliance can be placed on this.

2 It assumes that the same relationship has existed between the two variables during the period from which the data is drawn – it is open to executive judgement as to whether this is true or not.

3 It assumes that one independent variable explains the variations in the dependent variable (e.g. sales) when we know that marketing outcomes are the result of the influence of several independent variables; some within the control of the firm, some which are features of the environment, the uncontrollable variables.

4 To be useful, the technique requires data extending over a lengthy period to be available. Stanton[8] suggests that 'to do a really good job, researchers need about 20 periods of sales records'. Whether or not this is true for each individual firm, the availability of an adequate 'bank' of data is a key factor.

These comments should not discourage the fledgling forecaster, but should serve to remind us that in attempting to forecast a highly unstable and dynamic situation we cannot allot too much importance to a single formula. Moreover, *multiple regression* techniques are available which do take into account the independent variables which are judged to be significant – e.g. employment, income, population, output, level of advertising support, level of competitors' advertising, level of own advertising, or whatever. Obviously the technique is complex, for separate forecasts must be made for each of the independent variables and an assessment made of the relative importance of each independent variable. The technique of *discriminant analysis* can be employed to provide estimates in this latter regard.

Qualitative techniques

Having taken a brief glimpse at the use of statistics in forecasting, we must now consider that side of the forecasting approach which depends upon the application of experience and judgement.

Surveys of buyer intentions

This method consists of asking a representative sample of users about their buying intentions (how much of a given product they will buy at a given price). The approach has been used in both the consumer and the industrial goods fields and is said, if anything, to be more reliable in the latter field (especially when the market consists of a limited number of firms) since industrial users are very much more clear about what materials and equipment they will purchase in the year ahead, than is the average housewife. The sample must be large enough for prediction purposes and some organisations (e.g. the BBC) maintain continuous *consumer panels* to assist their forward planning. The purchase of 'question units' in omnibus surveys as described in Chapter 3 would be another way of gaining this information and related to it are the techniques of *attitude measurement*, a subject mentioned in Chapter 5.

The limitations of the approach include the doubt which attaches to the relationship between *attitudes* and *behaviour* (and as explained in Chapter 5 various forms of multivariate and taxonomic analysis are being applied to attitudinal data in order to illumine this area).

Published information, such as the CBI forecasts, *The Financial Times* surveys, and the economic forecasts mentioned in the early parts of this Chapter, may well contain suitable contextual data for this method.

Surveys of expert opinion (internal and external)

Such surveys are usually a significant element in most approaches to forecasting. The chief marketing executive and his senior marketing colleagues are judged to be the internal experts and their knowledge of the firm's products, its markets, its competition, etc. constitute their expertise. In forming their judgements they will typically have access to any statistical projections derived from the objective techniques (described in the last section) and these will serve as a starting point for their own ideas.

The external experts usually comprise any marketing consultants or advisers retained by the firm, advertising agency executives, and senior personnel in customer organisations. In addition to their knowledge of the firm, these experts may be able to make comparative assessments based on their knowledge of the market performance of competitive products or of similar products in other markets.

The procedures employed might be either formal or informal. For example, the external and internal experts may be gathered together formally, having already prepared their own personal analysis of the situation and within the meeting may have to defend their viewpoints against alternative predictions. The objective of the 'jury' or 'conclave' of experts would be ultimately to arrive at some mutually agreed forecast. This is undoubtedly a valuable element in the forecasting process although the external experts are less likely to be able to make forecasts for individual products of the firm than to be able to provide some reasonable estimate of its *general* prospects.

Surveys of sales force opinion

The concept of building the forecast 'from the top down and the bottom up' has two aspects. There is firstly the idea of proceeding through stages of the forecast – from the macro to the micro, as illustrated in Fig. 10.2. There is also the idea of including *all* relevant personnel in the process, from whatever level in the hierarchy. Thus the contribution of the senior marketing executive and his team, and the opinions of external experts, may be thought of as the top down element, whilst including a survey of sales force opinion would be the bottom up part of the process. Involving the sales force has at least three points in its favour:

1 The sales force is closer to the market and user and distributor opinion; therefore it would be completely imprudent to overlook this source of opinion.
2 Since the targets and quotas of the sales force will be derived from the forecast it makes good sense to involve the sales force in the calculations for this increases their sense of responsibility in achieving targets.
3 When management canvasses the salesman's views, it increases his sense of importance to the organisation and acts as a motivator to his performance (shades of Herzberg).

The process is one in which the forecast of each salesman for his own territory becomes a *composite* forecast for the organisation when individual territory forecasts are aggregated. There is always the possibility that since the sales quota is derived from his forecast the salesman might be tempted to produce an artificially low forecast. Two points can be made here:

1 The process is one that can, and should, be approached in stages, each individual forecast being 'reconciled' with that of the salesman's immediate supervisor before being passed on to the next stage where 'reconciliation' again takes place. Thus territory→ area→ regional→ company stages each provide a device for filtering out artificially low forecasts.

2   Another check against the low forecast is by relating the level of approved sales expenses to the forecast.

The *sales force composite* is such an important aspect of the forecasting process that it would be an irresponsible management which excluded such opinion from the process. It could, of course, be argued that salesmen are not sufficiently au fait with general economic considerations to take sufficient account of them in their individual estimates. Management must make allowance, where this is deemed to be so, in its own assessment of the sales force composite forecast. Alternatively, as it develops experience with its forecasting and is able to isolate those environmental variables exercising the greatest influence on sales performance it can show the salesman how to adjust his own estimate accordingly. In one organisation where the salesmen were 'trained' in this way, the sales force composite came to within three per cent of its own top down forecast.

The Delphi technique

This is a technique which canvasses opinion from experienced executive members of the organisation by a structured research method making use of a questionnaire. The executives do not meet in committee and therefore the respondent is not inhibited by the group dynamics of the committee situation. The responses from the first round of questionnaire distribution are collated and fed back to each respondent, so that if one executive's views are challenged by what appears to be the majority opinion that executive may be asked whether he would wish to modify his views or submit extra supporting evidence for them. In this way it is hoped that some consensus view will emerge which can be used as a basis for forecasting. The approach can be varied in that personal interviews may be conducted with each respondent at the feed-back stage rather than the impersonal distribution of feedback notes and further questionnaires. Also, rather than deeper probing of a single issue, further questionnaires may proceed from the macro to the micro stages of forecasting (Fig. 10.2).

The method has been frequently used and while some observers feel that Delphi is better suited to estimates of general trends in markets and technologies rather than to detailed estimates of individual product sales, some success has been reported with forecasting of the latter type.

Forecasting and the computer

There are endless possibilities for the use of computers in marketing. There are the routine administrative tasks relating to sales, invoicing, order processing, stock control and so on. The volume of data thus assembled can be then aggregated and analysed so as to present information for decision making – qualitative judgements can be made on the performance of salesmen, products and market segments from the fine divisions of quantitative data which the computer can so speedily make available. At a higher level of abstraction, models of markets can be developed enabling the sensitivity of a market system to changes in inputs (e.g. price levels, advertising expenditure, etc.) to be reviewed. At the highest levels of complexity such models can encompass a large number of variables. In closing this Chapter we shall consider briefly the role of the computer in sales forecasting.

When we speak of a computer, the physical system used, the *hardware*, can range from a *microcomputer*, costing relatively little and providing relatively limited facilities to a *mainframe* based system, providing extensive print-outs, data security and a vast range of facilities. For the process of forecasting, the part of the computer system which stipulates how data are to be manipulated, the *software*, can range from simple *spreadsheets* to advanced statistical *packages*.

A spreadsheet is a form used for organising and calculating numeric information. The use of computer-based spreadsheets has eliminated errors in calculating relationships between data and has also made it possible to rapidly change data. An electronic spreadsheet 'remembers' the relationship between data and thus provides a 'what if?' facility. What if the cost of a basic raw material increases by 10 per cent? How would this affect the price of the finished product? What would be the consequent effect on sales and profits? The value to the forecasting process is clear and whereas manual techniques would take a considerable length of time to produce answers, the computer makes the information available in seconds.

At a more sophisticated level is the typical general-purpose statistical package MINITAB (trademark of Minitab Project, Pennsylvania State University). The package is designed especially for people with no previous knowledge of computers. It is especially useful for exploring data in the early phases of analysis, for plotting and for regression analysis. As well as normal arithmetic operations on data, it enables correlation coefficients, regression, binomial probability and other routines to be easily performed.

A software package at a higher level of sophistication is SPSS (trademark of SPSS Inc, Chicago). This is a comprehensive tool for managing, analysing and displaying data. Facilities available include scattergrams, factor analysis, cross tabulations, hypothesis testing, time series analysis, etc. If, for example, we are trying to explore the relationship between sales and advertising as we have seen earlier in the Chapter a scattergraph enables the two variables to be studied together. SPSS enables scatterplotting to be used in this context. Beyond this primary step in studying the relationship between two variables it is often useful to quantify the strength of the association by calculating a *summary index*. One commonly used measure is the Pearson correlation coefficient, r.

$$\text{It is defined as } r = \frac{\sum_{i=1}^{N}(X_i - \bar{X})(Y_i - \bar{Y})}{(N-1)S_xS_y}$$

where N is the number of cases and S_x and S_y are the standard deviations of the two variables.

The absolute value of r indicates the strength of the linear relationship. By this method it is possible to estimate the amount of sales generated from a certain level of advertising. Also within SPSS, the *Box-Jenkins* procedure can be used to fit and forecast time series data. This procedure is designed to provide for easy and flexible model identification, estimation and forecasting. Several models can be examined in a single invocation of the procedure. Parameter estimates, forecasts and plots of the auto correlation function, partial auto correlation function and forecasts at different levels can be included in the output.

Analyses that would literally take weeks of work can now be conducted economically and at great speed. The nature and impact of the computer enables better decisions to be made within the forecasting function, as it does in many other areas of marketing management.

Self-assessment questions

1 What is a sales forecast? Which comes first, the plan or the forecast?

2 Show how the operations of a business are governed by the sales forecast.

3 How are economic indicators used in the forecasting process?

4 Outline a logical sequence of the steps in forecasting sales for an organisation with which you are familiar.

5 Define: short-term; medium-term; long-term forecasting. Explain the value of each of these types of forecast to a business organisation.

6 What is meant by developing a forecasting method that will 'just do'?

7 What factors determine the selection of a forecasting method?

8 What is meant by: elasticity of demand; time-series analysis; secular trend; moving average; trend extrapolation; exponential smoothing; correlation coefficient; scattergraph; regression line; multiple regression; composite forecast?

9 Describe some of the qualitative techniques of forecasting.

10 How does the computer assist the forecasting process?

References

1 Willsmer, Ray L. *The basic arts of marketing*, London, Business Books, 1976, p. 166
2 Schwartz, David J. *Marketing today*, 3rd edn, New York, Harcourt Brace Jovanovich, 1981, p. 68
3 Wilson, Aubrey. *The assessment of industrial markets*, London, Cassell/Associated Business Programmes, 1973, p. 289
4 Ibid. p. 282
5 Ibid. p. 281
6 *The basic arts of marketing*, p. 192
7 Harper, W. M. *Statistics*, 4th edn, Plymouth, Macdonald & Evans, 1982, pp. 109/125
8 Stanton, William J. *Fundamentals of marketing*, 6th edn, New York, McGraw-Hill, 1981, p. 515

11 DEVISING, IMPLEMENTING AND CONTROLLING THE MARKETING PLAN

Objectives

The whole rationale of the marketing approach is that it is set within a planning process. Arguments in favour of planning are advanced in this Chapter; the planning process is reviewed and the component parts of a marketing plan are described. An explanation of how plans are evaluated is then provided, leading on to the important issue of productivity in marketing.

In this last respect, the reader is introduced to marketing cost analysis and the mechanism of the marketing audit. The objective the author has set for himself is that by the end of the Chapter, the reader will have grasped Eisenhower's axiom that: 'Plans are nothing; planning is everything.'

Introduction: planning and management

Henri Fayol (1841–1925) was trained as a mining engineer. He later became famous for his writings on the process of management. Though he is now considered to belong to the 'classical' school of thinkers on management, along with such historical figures as Max Weber and F W Taylor, much of what he said about management is still highly appropriate. Fayol[1] defined *management* as comprising five elements:

1 Forecasting and planning;
2 Organising;
3 Commanding;
4 Co-ordinating and
5 Controlling.

In effect, Fayol saw the central activity of business management as *forecasting and planning*. In his words, management is obliged to 'assess the future and make provision for it'.

In Chapter 2, we made a preliminary examination of the planning process and saw how the marketing plan is derived from the general objectives of the organisation in order to:

1   serve the attainment of these objectives; and
2   provide a basis from which plans for the other parts of the organisation (production, finance, personnel etc) can be developed.

Before going further in the present Chapter, the reader is invited to re-examine those parts of Chapter 2 which deal with organisational objectives and the role of marketing management. It will also be helpful to study the following:

Figure 2.3 The marketing plan and the manpower plan.

Figure 2.4 The creative alignment of the organisation with its environment.

Figure 2.6 The marketing management process within an organisation's operations.

Figure 2.7 A marketing strategy within an environmental system.

Echoing Fayol, Stanton[2] suggests that the process of management consists of planning a programme, putting it into operation and evaluating its results. He also distinguishes three planning concepts: total company planning; marketing planning and the annual marketing plan. Now it will be useful for us to dwell on this briefly because it disposes of the notion of planning as some over-enthusiastic process in which self-indulgent managers, after great expenditure of time and effort, produce an immensely detailed plan for next year which is then filed away and promptly forgotten until the time comes around again for the ritual planning rites. What Stanton has in mind is a process where the senior management of the organisation are involved in *long-range planning* (e.g. for periods of 5, 10 or even 15 years ahead) to serve broad corporate objectives and covering the acquisition of factories, major equipment, other companies and the development of products and markets. It is within this type of planning that organisations must address themselves to Levitt's question: 'What business are we in?' (see Chapter 1). Collateral to this long-range planning, managers lower in the hierarchy will be planning for marketing operations to serve this total company plan and the bricks from which longer range plans are constructed are the *annual marketing plans* which contain detailed marketing forecasts, targets, programmes and budgets which are controlled, continuously monitored and amended when necessary, but hopefully attained in order that the longer-range objectives of the organisation can be attained.

In this Chapter we are primarily concerned with the annual marketing plan (though we must recognise that it is only one element in a longer and larger-scale planning process). As with the sales forecast, so with the marketing plan – whether or not he is involved in the planning details, ultimately the plan is the responsibility of the chief marketing executive. Although it is true that the various sections and sub-sections of the marketing department will contribute to the plan, it is the chief marketing executive who will oversee the various contributions, appraise and ratify the overall plan as an entity and present it to senior management for examination and approval.

There are no fixed rules for the style and presentation of the plan, nor of the amount of detail it should contain. The ideal plan in this respect is the one that is closely fitted to the requirements of the organisation. 'Keep it simple' should be the overriding philosophy, with the statistical details contained in appendices where the supporting evidence for the recommendations contained in the plan itself can be scrutinised as necessary.

Precise achievement of the plan is not the first consideration. As Willsmer[3] points out, the odds against this are extremely high. The value of plans and planning lies more in their function of structuring organisational thinking; providing a basis for the allocation of resources; co-ordinating the activities of the separate departments and furnishing a bench-mark for monitoring progress towards company goals. So the plan should be as realistic as possible and the organisation should look towards minimising the degree of error but the touchstone is not whether the plan is accurate in the end. Such an aspiration is illusory for 'life is not like that'. Perhaps General Dwight D. Eisenhower had this in mind when he said: 'Plans are nothing; planning is everything.'

A single marketing plan is then an important but nonetheless individual feature within the organisation's larger planning landscape. And the larger plan will be grounded upon overall company goals, or policy or general objectives or what some call the 'company mission' (a label that does not particularly appeal to this writer).

General objectives will be couched in the broadest terms but will set the direction in which strategy will be applied. Thus an airline company which is nationalised may express these objectives as being to provide an aviation transport service acceptable in terms of speed and cost to its customers, effective in earning some target rate of return on its assets, in a manner which reflects credit on the nation for which it is the 'flag carrier', consistent with leadership in the field for safety.

The reader will note here that overall goals may be a mixture of economic and non-economic objectives (a target rate of return and 'safety'). Thus, in addition to effectiveness in economic terms, an organisation may pursue within its overall goals non-economic objectives, such as:

leadership in its field for innovation;

leadership in its field for quality;

leadership in its field for financial security (particularly important to a bank or a building society);

leadership in its field for environmental concern (perhaps of great significance for a chemical company).

It can be seen that the pursuit of economic and non-economic objectives may give rise to a *conflict of objectives*. An organisation aiming to provide 'value for money' may find this difficult to square with its goal of 'environmental concern'. Similarly a bank may see the prospect of increasing its return on investment but only in high-risk ventures which might militate against its goal of a market image of reliability and security. Arnold Ceramics may see lucrative opportunities in plastics but decide that this will damage their standing as producers of good quality, aesthetically pleasing tableware. These conflicts have to be resolved before overall goals can supply the context for strategy.

Moreover when senior management is asking itself 'what business are we in' it will need to be realistic. Lifting the 'planning horizon' is one thing, but declaring the field for action to be 'transportation' or 'communications' or 'domestic comfort' may leave management confronted with far too wide a range of alternatives. If broadening organisational outlook is well beyond its capital resources, the organisation may have to settle for a more restricted planning horizon (hence the point often made that marketing means giving customers what they want but within the constraints imposed by the organisation's current, or affordable, resources).

In favour of planning

The arguments in favour of planning can be summarised as follows:

1   Planning entails an examination of the marketing environment and the duty to forecast future events. This clarifies the options available to management and leads to *better decision making.*

2   Planning clarifies the threats and opportunities that are open to the organisation.

3   Planning provides the framework by way of which:

(a) organisational objectives can be pursued;

(b) standards for performance can be established and monitored;

(c) organisational, departmental and individual effort can be assessed and rewarded.

4   By clarifying alternative strategies and their costs and benefits, planning assists the efficient allocation and utilisation of resources.

5   Supported by appropriate procedures and organisation structures, planning helps in the development of effective horizontal and vertical channels of communication.

6   Relying as it does on a continuing input of reliable information, planning helps the organisation to monitor change and makes it better prepared for sudden developments.

7   Sound planning increases employee participation and commitment.

When planning (or so-called 'planning') fails it is because the planning is poor. Poor planning results from lack of realism in corporate/departmental objectives; inadequate communication; inept leadership; failure to implement the plan by not 'following the plan through' to individual tasks and responsibilities and monitoring their performance and finally, failure to adjust the plan where market information indicates this to be necessary.

To improve planning performance, the chief marketing executive needs to:

1   Recognise the necessity to improve the quality of management and acknowledge the assistance that information technology can provide in this regard.

2   Develop adequate and practical planning processes that are sensitive to market opportunities yet grounded in realism.

3   Ensure that senior management understands and effectively supports what the marketing plan is setting out to achieve.
4   Obtain effective participation and support of marketing personnel, rendering them effective technical and other assistance in their planning and operations.
5   Fix, define and publish decision making responsibility and authority and provide an adequate level of continuing information.

Markin[4] believes that successful marketing organisations do three things well:

1   quickly recognise the existence of a marketing opportunity;
2   develop an appropriate strategy for the given situation;
3   execute the strategy with a high degree of proficiency.

He believes that increasing uncertainty and a rigorous competitive environment will heighten the necessity for proficient strategic marketing planning. It is difficult, if not impossible, to quarrel with his judgment particularly since in addition to its other benefits, effective planning creates a benevolent climate within the organisation for the management of change.

Stanton[5] believes that formal planning is one of the most effective management tools for risk reduction. Mark Stern[6] suggests that the purpose of planning is not the elimination of risk but rather to increase the capacity of the organisation to take greater risk. Whatever their differences, which appears to be more of degree than of principle, they are both firmly in favour of planning.

The planning process

The essence of the planning process is depicted in Fig. 2.6 which outlines the nature of the marketing management process. The aim of this Section is to take a more detailed look at that process. (Re-examine Fig. 2.6 and also take another look at the four questions listed under 'Organisational objectives' in Chapter 2.)

In fact, in order to complete our picture of the planning process we need to add three more questions, as shown in Fig. 11.1.

It can be seen that we have now posed ourselves three questions in addition to the four set out in Chapter 2:

1   Where are we now?
6   How much will it cost us?
7   Who will be responsible for getting us there?

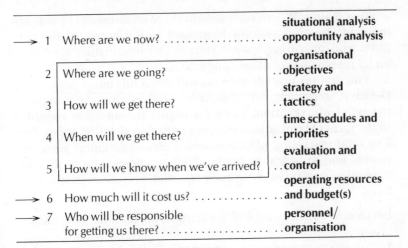

→ 1	Where are we now?	situational analysis .. opportunity analysis
2	Where are we going?	organisational .. objectives
3	How will we get there?	strategy and .. tactics
4	When will we get there?	time schedules and .. priorities
5	How will we know when we've arrived?	evaluation and .. control
→ 6	How much will it cost us?	operating resources .. and budget(s)
→ 7	Who will be responsible for getting us there?	personnel/ .. organisation

Fig. 11.1   *A framework for planning*

To the right of Fig. 11.1 the procedures which relate to these questions are set out in more formal language and we must now consider what these formal procedures entail. Before doing so, it might be helpful to make a few more general points:

1   No planning process is likely to succeed unless the personnel involved are *adequately motivated* – this is the responsibility of senior management who must ensure that everyone recognises the value of planning.

2   The planning process, like forecasting, is a top down and bottom up process – the bottom up process meaning that each department or section involved will review its performance in the immediate past period, examine the factors underlying its successes and failures and make plans to capitalise on success and to minimise failure – its projection will take account of any new products and services to be available in the next period and the scope of allocated resources. This procedure can be wasteful unless the organisational objectives are adequately communicated to individual personnel – for the parts must be made to fit the objectives of the whole. Effective communications networks, horizontal and vertical, are also the responsibility of senior management. There is no problem for the owner of a small business to communicate his general objectives. Communications networks extending over an organisation with a number of product managers, within each of several operating divisions, are

another matter. Where such networks are cross-braced by management information systems harnessed to the power of the computer and providing instant retrieval of information they stand an increased chance of being effective.

3 The aim on presentation should be to minimise paper-work. Detail is important, but should be kept as close as possible to the point of execution. Plans for higher management should be in the form of brief summaries, supported by detailed appendices. The total marketing plan becomes a consolidation of such summaries and appendices prefaced by a statement from the chief marketing executive as to how the plan serves corporate objectives.

Let us now consider each of the steps in the planning sequence.

1 *Situation/opportunity analyses.* The situational analysis ('where are we now') comprises an objective examination of current activities – marketing programmes, product performance, sales and profit trends, environmental influences (economic, governmental etc) and the performance of competitors. Within the situational analysis, the company will pay special attention to its operational strengths. Arnold Ceramics, for instance, may feel that its production equipment; the skills of its labour force; its knowledge of raw materials, technological processes, and quality control; its market standing or its marketing skills are all factors that at present are being under-utilised and in its planning may decide to capitalise on one or more of these.

The opportunity analysis will provide a screening survey of trends in population, gross domestic product, sales of customer industries, consumer attitudes, i.e. of whatever appear to be the relevant variables – the 'tied indicators', perhaps.

Market opportunities may consist of:

(a) *market penetration:* selling more of existing products to existing markets by increased promotion or sales force activity

(b) *market development:* increasing sales volume and profits by finding new markets overseas, perhaps

(c) *product development:* introducing new or improved products to its present markets

(d) *forward integration:* by diversing its activities – Arnolds, for example, may diversify from tableware into wall and floor tiles, into industrial ceramics, laboratory ceramics, refractories etc. Diversification may take place through mergers with other companies, the acquisition of other companies and may be *horizontal* (e.g. the acquisition of competitors), or *vertical*, and if the latter, may consist of acquiring raw materials producers.

Again, the organisation may see opportunity for growth by acquiring its own retail outlets.

2 *Organisational objectives.* Quite a lot has already been said about objectives but it is worth emphasising that planning can hardly be successful unless it is based upon clear, realistic and internally consistent objectives (n.b. see 'conflict of objectives', page 372). Moreover, whilst objectives can be couched in both qualitative and quantitative terms, as we have seen, it is important that marketing objectives are translated into some quantitative form so that the actions necessary are clearly apparent and performance can be measured.

In this way, objectives provide direction for the various managerial levels, serve as motivators to achievement, provide a basis for monitoring and control, make corporate philosophy abundantly clear and help to create a unity of purpose throughout the organisation.

What is termed the 'organisational mission' will derive from some formally written response to the question 'what business are we in?'. Unless the basic ground rules are put into writing it is conceivable that plans could be produced which lead in the wrong direction.

'Company mission' helps to clarify 'company goals' and these goals, which may set an acceptable rate of return on investment, or an increased share of market(s) or projected growth rates of revenue and profits, enable each department – production, finance, marketing, personnel – to clarify its objectives and thus to consider its *strategies* and *tactics*.

3 *Strategies and tactics.* The company mission entails making broad policy statements which are long-term (valid perhaps for ten years or more). Statements on strategy are similarly broad in scope, indicating the directions in which the organisation will move to achieve its objectives and are, as often as not, quite long in term, e.g. two to three years. Tactics are the actions deemed necessary if particular strategies are to be adopted and are usually short-term (usually reviewed yearly).

An example may help here. The company goals may hinge on a particular growth rate of sales and profits. The strategies being evaluated may consist of:

retention of existing markets;
entry into new, but similar markets, with existing products;
entry into new, but similar markets, with new products;
diversification into radically different markets;

The strategies are not mutually exclusive and some combination of them may be adopted.

A sequence of questions of the following types will be used to determine the tactics:

(a) *retention of existing markets:* what tactics best serve this strategy?... product modifications? increased advertising? extension of the distributive network?

(b) *entry into new markets with existing products:* how best do we enter overseas markets?... through export houses? agents and distributors abroad? UK based representatives?

(c) *entry into new markets with new products:* how should these be priced, promoted, distributed? shall we adopt the tactics prevailing for the marketing of similar products or devise new tactics?

(d) *diversification into radically different markets:* the manufacturer of ceramics may decide to enter the market for high-performance ceramics in the space programme; the manufacture of engineering products may decide to seek contract work for suppliers to defence programmes; but a warning note here; where such diversification can be undertaken with minimal modification to production techniques, manpower planning and organisational structures it is essentially tactical, otherwise strategic decisions are entailed.

The reader will be aware, of course, that like the other steps in the planning process, tactical decisions call for an accurate appreciation of competition and realistic assessment of the resources which will be available. Thus, although we shall be considering resources below ('how much will it cost us?'), these steps do not follow each other. In practice, resource considerations are weighed in the balance when alternative strategies and tactics are being studied for their feasibility.

4   *Time schedules and priorities.* Planning takes place within a time framework – 'a planned growth of profits over a five year

period'; 'the annual marketing plan'; 'the *time* required to develop and launch the modified product', etc. Time scheduling specifies what must be done and when it must be done, which actions must precede others and where necessary what aspects of the plan are the priorities for action.

Moreover, setting the marketing plan within a time frame provides a time frame for the other departments of the organisation. For example:

A marketing objective of £3 000 000 revenue in the ensuing financial year *means*

$$\downarrow$$

A production objective, having adjusted for opening and closing stocks and work in progress, of 1 000 000 units at an ex factory price of £3 per unit *means*

$$\downarrow$$

A financial objective based on time scheduled raw materials purchases, labour costs, direct and indirect, overhead costs, marketing and administrative costs, packing and transport costs, projected borrowing for peak periods in business activity and projected cash flow *means*

$$\downarrow$$

A personnel objective based on a time scheduled plan of, the labour to be employed, the labour to be trained, the provision for recruitment and redeployment, etc.

Figure 11.2 (p. 380) depicts the *means-end chain* by way of which the attainment of the time scheduled objective set for each departmental function constitutes the means by which the ensuing department attains its objective which in turn enables the organisation to attain its objective.

(Note: The operation of the financial and personnel functions cannot be set out in sequence to the other functions – they serve each of the functions directly and concurrently. The diagram attempts to show this. In effect, 'personnel' and 'finance' may be thought of as 'cross-bracing' the chain or staircase, thus adding to its strength and durability!)

The plan of schedules and priorities can be as simple or as complex as circumstances dictate. The small firm with a limited range of products or services may find a simple typewritten sheet completely adequate. A complex organisation with several operating divisions may plan its sequential, interrelated activities utilising such techniques as *network analysis* (e.g. either the criti-

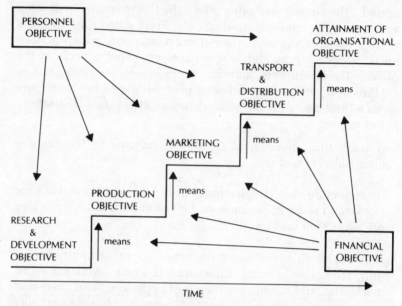

Fig. 11.2   *A means-end chain of objectives within a time schedule*

cal path method or the program evaluation review technique). Planning the development of a new, complex product which will affect production methods, manpower planning and marketing programmes over an extended period of time and require successive increments of capital investment will require quite sophisticated scheduling. A modification to an existing product entailing minimal 'adjustment' to the way in which departments operate will require clear but relatively simple scheduling methods.

5   *Operating resources and budgets.* This is the 'how much will it cost us?' question and, as one writer[7] has put it, it enables the organisation to develop 'a programme of action with price tags'. Here the organisation is evaluating alternative courses of action and assessing their costs and benefits so that ultimately a plan is agreed with an accompanying logistical appreciation which will enable the managers concerned to obtain the right resources, of the right quality and quantity, in the right place, at the right time and at the right (i.e. acceptable) level of cost.

The process entails making forecasts of sales revenue, capital, manufacturing and marketing expenses, labour costs, plant capacity and projected return on investment, among the many other factors involved. The plan for the immediate period ahead (usually one year) will have detailed forecasts and budgets; the plans for succeeding periods (so as to complete a three or five year period, for example) will be less detailed. Planning procedures at this stage do not call for strict mathematical accuracy so much as sound indications of the 'gap', if any, remaining in the desired quantum of sales volume, revenue, profits or whatever.

One other important point: the 'how much will it cost us?' question is only a convenient shorthand to describe this stage in the planning process. Financial considerations are important here, but a review of resources means screening *all* the wealth producing assets that are available to the firm – its plant capacity, its equipment, the skills of its labour force, its technical know-how, its 'institutional image' in the market, the opportunities for selling its by-products, etc. In short, 'positive thinking' is important here and the review of resources must be undertaken not in the spirit of what constraints it will impose but with an eye to the opportunities it will offer.

6 *Evaluation and control.* We shall be looking at the evaluation process in some detail later in this Chapter. At this point let us establish that in order to know whether we have arrived entails:

(a) continually monitoring the results actually achieved against forecasts and budgets, so as to affirm progress to objectives or determine any differences between projections and performance;

(b) where differences do exist, probing into the causes for those differences;

(c) taking corrective action, either within the current programme or by making necessary adjustments to the programme for the immediate next-period(s).

Statistical analyses of sales volume and marketing costs are the typical instruments of the evaluation process.

7 *Personnel/organisation.* Responsibility for obtaining the results must be defined, fixed and published. The organisation will need to be clear on the numbers of personnel involved, their grades and level of training and how their activities are to be organised and co-ordinated. Within the marketing department,

such issues as the size of the sales force, the availability of personnel for merchandising/demonstration, etc, are typical at the tactical level while at the strategic level planning consists of applying the existing organisation structure to projected operations and measuring it for its 'fit'. Moreover the marketing plan may call for some radical alteration to the organisation structure, e.g. moving sales force organisation from a structure based on products, to one based on industries or markets (see Chapter 12).

Results are only obtained through people and they must be clear what they are expected to do, what authority they have to do it, how their performance is to be measured. *Performance appraisal* is a factor implicit in the planning process and this may be carried out at different levels of sophistication. Performance appraisal for a salesman in a small firm may simply mean continual scrutiny of his sales and his expenses. For a marketing executive in a large organisation, operating a system of management by objectives, it may mean an appraisal interview and the subsequent documentation of the objectives formally agreed with his superior, his performance being subsequently reviewed at fixed intervals.

The skills and the motivation of the people involved, their numbers, the methods of organisation and delegation employed and the way their activities are reviewed and rewarded will have a critical influence on the effectiveness of the plan.

The marketing plan

There are no universal formulae which will determine what the marketing plan actually looks like. The content, the period covered, the amount of detail it contains and the number of statistical appendices incorporated in it will all be determined by the needs of the individual organisation. There are important axioms viz 'keep it as simple as possible', 'be realistic'; 'senior executives require clear communication of the plan's objectives, preferably by short summaries which invite subsequent examination of the statistical tables', etc, but these exhortations do not tell us much about what should constitute an effective format for the plan.

Yet, from what has already been said about plans and planning it should be possible for the reader to deduce what an adequately constructed plan should contain. Let us think about it.

Plan summary

If the company's board of directors read no more than this introductory section they can grasp the essential philosophy of the
plan and its major recommendations. The section provides a
summary of products or product groups or operating divisions
covered by the plan, the period for which planning has been
undertaken, the sales and profit targets which are to be achieved
and the scale of the resources which are to be committed.

Usually targets and budgets will be described in relation to
some comparable preceding period, e.g. 'A target of sales has been
set at £15 000 000, an increase of three per cent on 1986/7 sales
in real terms. The projected net profit before interest and taxation
is £1 200 000, an increase of two per cent over the 1986/7 performance. It is anticipated that this will be achieved by the improved
economic position, resulting in increased demand on customer
industries, projected stability of our own price levels and a reduction of four per cent, in real terms, in our own marketing budgets.'
Some short statement on the assumptions made about competition, the launching of new products or the entry into new markets
may also feature in this section. Reference will be made to the
appropriate statistical or financial information contained in the
Appendices.

Current situation

This section will describe 'where we are now' in terms of present
market shares and market standing; current strengths and weaknesses; the opportunities and threats which emanate from current trading conditions, business outlook, technological change
and so on. The assumptions that have been used in making forecasts will be fully amplified. This section sets the scene on the
alternative routes to its objectives which the organisation might
take.

Objectives of the plan

This section of the marketing plan makes a proposal for where
the business should go. Senior management will have defined
what the overall objectives for the organisation should be. This
is one planning parameter. Another parameter will be the description of the alternatives available in the preceding section of the

plan (based on the opportunities and threats outlined there). This section now sets out the objectives and goals which the chief marketing executive and his colleagues believe will best support the company objectives.

Statement of strategy and tactics

Here is the proposed answer to the question 'How will we get there?' Possibly, before the recommended strategy is suggested, a number of alternative strategies may be reviewed in this section. The 'tactics' comprise a full description of the proposed marketing mix: details of product plans, including modifications to products and the product range and proposals for the introduction of new products; pricing strategy including plans for changes in trade margins, discounts, introductory offers, etc; proposals on physical distribution, channel policy stock levels, 'key account' policy, etc; and promotional plans including the type and level of sales force activity, the creative approach, the appropriation and the recommended media for advertising, details of sales promotion schemes (consumer and trade), public relations and publicity campaigns.

Action schedule

This section details the list of marketing activities scheduled through the time period (i.e. in 12-monthly or 52-weekly sections) and fixes which personnel will be responsible for seeing these marketing activities through to completion (typical activities here covering the monitoring of advertising campaigns, participation in exhibitions, the production of publicity material, price lists, press releases, etc).

Personnel must know what is expected of them and when, the dates for review and completion of their activities and must accept the commitment. Management, for its part, must have a clear appreciation of the interrelationships between activities and how best these may be co-ordinated throughout the time period.

Budget proposals

This section sets out the projected volume of sales for each product, the anticipated selling price and thus the revenue that will be generated during the period of the plan. Against this will be set the operating expenditure required to achieve this revenue – the manufacturing costs, the costs of packing and transport, the costs of marketing. In essence the budgetary proposals are a projected profit statement.

Once the budget, in its original or modified form, has been adopted formally by senior management it becomes the master plan from which all the other operating budgets are constructed. The projected *sales budget*, when adjusted for opening and closing stocks and work in progress, will become the *production budget* and will indicate desired levels of monthly output if the sales targets are to be achieved. The *financial budget* will be constructed from the predicted sales revenue, enabling the financial controller to calculate cash flows and the amount of borrowing (if any) required for critical points in the plan's activity (critical in the sense that heavy expenditures may have to be undertaken well in advance of revenues from sales). Similarly the organisation's manpower planning and its purchasing schedules will be constructed in line with the requirements of the approved marketing plan.

Control mechanisms

The plan has been devised and approved but it does *not* become a plan for action regardless of the consequences. When it is put into operation, the company's progress to the plan is carefully monitored, with particular regard to the sales being achieved compared with the stock levels being built up. This section of the plan will therefore make clear how and when (e.g. monthly, quarterly) the plan is to be reviewed by senior management. For these reviews, the chief marketing officer will survey the current scene and make recommendations for changes in strategy, if need be. These may entail reduction of projected expenditures if sales are not up to forecasts, or increased expenditures, or other activity to exploit a favourable situation if this should arise.

Also, if only in 'broad brush' terms, the marketing department is usually expected to have devised a *contingency plan*, so that if unforeseen challenges occur the organisation will have already thought about response strategies and a change of direction can be taken but the upheaval involved can be minimised (more of this later in the Chapter).

Additional information

Since the plan is but one element in a continuous planning process, it may well be that the plan will refer to *marketing research*
and *product development activity* that it is necessary to undertake before, during and after the tenor of the annual marketing
plan. This enables the planners to demonstrate how the annual
plan coheres with and serves the longer term objectives of the
organisation.

Evaluating the marketing plan

We now have an approved marketing plan and personnel have
been designated to direct and operate it in its various parts. As
soon as possible after the plan begins to operate management
must begin to evaluate its results by:

1   Comparing results with the standards established and set out
in the budgets;
2   Where there are differences between standards and results,
discovering the reasons for this;
3   Deciding what further action is necessary, either to remedy
unsatisfactory performance or to capitalise upon unexpected
opportunity – and implementing that decision before the next
review period.

In other words, planning and evaluation are inextricably bound
up together so that the whole monitoring and control process
is an iterative one leading to further actions. This process of
adjustment or 'fine tuning' of the plan will allow for the emergence of new factors (e.g. the appearance of a new competitive
product; a sudden increase in the price of a basic raw material)
and will lead to some appropriate action (e.g. the introduction
of extra incentives for distributors; a modification to the product). Fig. 11.3 attempts to depict the iterative process of evaluation and control.

To consider some of the practicalities of Fig. 11.3, the organisational objectives for business organisations will probably be set
in terms of profit, return-on-investment, annual rates of growth
or profit, sales revenue, or some similar standard of performance
with a monetary dimension. Each product or product group will
then have a calculated contribution to make to the overall profit

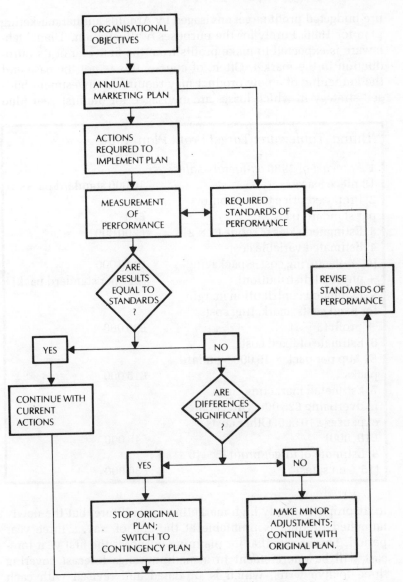

Fig. 11.3 *Evaluation and control as an iterative process*

objective. In Chapter 6 mention was made of the idea of Arnold Caramics introducing a range of 'Diana' tableware. The table overleaf gives a simple outline of how Arnolds might calculate a target profit plan for this tableware as its contribution to the overall pre-budgeted profit target envisaged by Arnolds annual marketing plan for 1986. Purely for the purposes of illustration, 'Diana' tableware is expected to make profits from the first year of its introduction to the market. Often, of course, this is not the case and the launching of a new product may require an 'investment budget' strategy in which losses are envisaged for the first year (due

---

'Diana' Tableware: Target Profit Plan, 1986

1 Forecast of 1986 ex-factory sales:	
18 piece teasets	10 000 standard packs
2 Proposed price to distributor per standard pack	£20
3 Estimated sales revenue (1 × 2)	£200 000
4 Estimated variable costs (manufacturing cost + packaging + physical distribution)	£110 000 (£11 per standard pack)
5 Estimated contribution margin for fixed costs, marketing costs + profit (3 − 4)	£90 000
6 Estimate of fixed costs: £1.50p per pack × 10 000 standard packs	£15 000
7 Estimated marketing costs (Advertising £25 000, Direct Sales expenses £10 000, Other costs £10 000)	£45 000
8 Estimate of target profit [5 − (6 + 7)] (15% on sales)	£30 000

---

to disproportionately high marketing expenditure) but the newly launched product is profitable at the end of, say, a three year period. This means that for planning purposes the first year forecast will be one element in a medium-range forecast covering three to five years, which is up-dated and revised with each annual marketing plan. Similarly, for evaluation and control purposes, the initial forecast for a new product may be part of a long-run forecast which covers its anticipated life-cycle (say five to seven years) with forecasts being made, albeit in outline only for each of the *introduction; growth; maturity* and *decline* periods of the life cycle, again with a yearly revision to the next-period forecast and the remainder of the long-run forecast as marketing experience is gained with the product. And so, with profit organisations, the marketing executive has two primary standards by which to measure performance:

1 *Sales volume* analysed by products, territories, customer groups, industries, etc, as well as by time periods (daily, weekly, monthly, quarterly and cumulative).

2 *Marketing costs* analysed under the headings in which they appear in the company accounts (e.g. salaries, commissions, travel expenses, advertising expenditure, etc) or better still by functions (e.g. advertising, sales force, distribution, etc), or even better still by market segments (e.g. by customers, territories, industries, etc) – the degree of refinement of the marketing information system being a function of the size of the firm and its affordable budgets for the administration of its controls systems. Certainly the higher the degree of refinement the better management can determine where the 'trouble spots' lie.

Non-profit organisations

However, as Markin[8] points out, non-profit organisations that use marketing techniques to serve their clientele need control procedures too. Thus, hospitals, higher education institutions, social service institutions and churches must define the criteria by which their own performance can be assessed (it is interesting that one or two countries in reducing their higher education expenditures, as part of their public sector spending curbs, are considering funding their universities on 'output' statistics, graduate and post-graduate, rather than on the numbers of student admissions).

It may be that standards of performance here are preponderantly qualitative rather than quantitative and are based upon the reputation being gained among clients and the extent and quality of the services being offered. Whatever the standards chosen, the fundamental question for every marketing-oriented organisation is 'are we delivering what we promised?'

Measuring performance

Comparison of results:standards usually begin with *sales volume analysis* in profit organisations. The internal measures are based on target sales compared with actual for individual salesmen, territories, industries, outlets, etc – whatever analytical breakdown is appropriate. Comparisons are made for a specific time period (daily, weekly, monthly) and cumulatively. Where the market is sophisticated in terms of *continuous research facilities*, valuable external measures are available with which to monitor progress (the services of AC Nielsen Co Ltd and MEAL provide data on comparative brand shares and advertising expenditure – see Chapter 8). Marketing management can then probe causes, taking remedial action where necessary, as has been said.

To illustrate the point, let us imagine that for the first quarter of 1986, the sales and profit targets for the new 'Diana' range of tableware were in line with forecasts. Then the sales/profit picture declined. Questions that Arnold's marketing director might ask could well include the following:

- Are the original standards of product quality being maintained?
- Are delivery promises being kept?
- Are sales in decline generally or only in certain territories and if the latter, which territories?
- Have there been any changes in the costs of labour, raw materials, distribution costs, which have adversely affected profitability or is the profits decline a function of the decline in sales?
- What are the reports of trade reaction and consumer reaction to this range of tableware?
- What is the pattern, if any, of repeat business from distributors?
- What is competition doing? ... is there news of new products or changes in trading terms, profit margins, discounts or increased advertising?
- How is our own advertising and sales promotion being received? – what evidence is there of its effectiveness?
- Has the target of in-store displays been achieved?
- Have deliveries of the standard packs been received in retail outlets undamaged and in good condition to display?
- Is consumer and trade reaction/acceptance of the retail selling price in line with our preliminary research predictions?

It can be seen that the list of questions ranges over all the elements of the marketing mix and also concerns itself with profit, for if marketing means what it says and is concerned with return on investment then the marketing executive must be dealing with it during the life of each marketing plan and not receiving it in some post mortem fashion when the year's accounts are finalised.

Marketing cost analysis

Since marketing, for business organisations, implies attention to profit performance, this in turn means that the marketing executive must not only be concerned with the revenue being generated, but what it is costing to generate it. As has been said on page 389, the higher the degree of refinement in classifying costs, the better management is able to discern the 'trouble spots'. Does management have an information system that enables the organisation to classify the costs and profitability of individual customers, for instance? Is management able to take sufficiently competent decisions on the minimum turnover necessary to justify direct dealing with customers? Consider the table below.

In this example, the organisation's customers, its sales, costs and profit have been expressed as profiles adding to 100. On the basis of its marketing cost analysis it discovers that 51.8 per cent of its customers are responsible for 87.5 per cent of its sales. 48.2 per cent of its customers add a mere 12.5 per cent to its

Table 11.1   Marketing cost analysis (profitable/unprofitable customers)

	All customers	Profitable customers	Unprofitable customers
Number of customers	100	51.8	48.2
Sales volume (£)	100	87.5	12.5
Gross profit (£)	100	88.1	11.9
Marketing costs(£)	100	55.3	44.7
Profit/loss (£)	100	143.5	−43.5

sales volume. However, they are responsible for no less than 44.7 per cent of its costs. On the other hand, the 87.5 per cent of turnover is being obtained more cost effectively (55.3 per cent of total costs). In fact if the profit is expressed as 100, 51.8 per cent of the customers must be responsible for 143.5 per cent of it, because there is a loss of 43.5 per cent as a result of dealing with 48.2 per cent of the firm's existing customers. This may well be a function of the changing pattern of distribution and there may be a number of ways of dealing with the problem – one of which would be to divert the requirements of some of these customers, all of whom have hitherto been supplied direct, to wholesale distributors. Mention of the changing pattern of distribution brings to mind the 80/20 tendency, and how as a result of the concentration of buying power, it is the case in both consumer and industrial markets that frequently 20 per cent of the buying points are responsible for 80 per cent of the demand.

The reader will recall that in Chapter 6 (page 210) we saw that the 80/20 rule can also apply to the product range, where a large proportion of the firm's product range is responsible for only a small proportion of sales, or profits or both, whilst a relatively small proportion of the output is responsible for most of the sales/profits. This may require rationalisation decisions – and a strategy which dispenses with the unprofitable products and the marketing of a 'leaner' but more effective range.

A product range that effectively results in too wide and deep an assortment being offered frequently results in production bottle-necks, uneconomically short production 'runs', split deliveries to customers – all tendencies which have a detrimental effect on profits. Marketing cost analysis can provide information on the average costs of individual consignments and the correct, economic, level for order sizes. Similarly it can be applied to determine the profitability of individual salesmen, sales territories and sales regions perhaps leading to decisions on how these may be economically adjusted. It is hoped that these comments will clarify for the reader the importance of:

1   the annual marketing plan: which supplies a blueprint for action in pursuit of marketing objectives;
2   a marketing information system: which enables management to monitor progress and to probe deeper into causes if results do not compare with standards (particularly with respect to sales volume and costs).

The marketing audit

Field Marshal Lord Montgomery once remarked that every organisation, no matter how effective, would benefit from 'spring-cleaning'. In the control processes we have examined in this Chapter, we have been considering the evaluation of *particulars* – products, territories, costs, etc – within the annual marketing plan. However there is a broader, total approach which an increasing number of organisations employ to complement the evaluation of particulars which have been described. This total approach is the marketing audit and it is akin to the 'spring-cleaning' process which Lord Montgomery favoured. A marketing audit is the planned, systematic, periodic evaluation of the total marketing function and it encompasses an assessment of:

1   the formulation of marketing objectives;
2   the process of devising strategies and tactics to meet those objectives;
3   organisational performance – i.e. the extent to which the strategies and tactics achieve the stated objectives;
4   the manner in which the activities necessary to achieve the goals are organised;
5   the selection, recruitment, training and performance of the personnel carrying out the marketing activities;
6   the procedures involved in the total marketing function including forecasting, planning, administration, and control.

The audit approach can be applied to any marketing organisation – profit or non-profit; large or small; private or public sector – and can be as simple or as complex as the needs of the organisation dictate. The general requirements are that:

1   Everyone concerned – auditor(s) and 'audited' – must be in agreement as to what the audit is intended to achieve and how it is to be carried out.
2   There must be an agreed framework for the way in which the audit is developed (a series of suggested headings is given below).
3   An audit report must be prepared, with conclusions and recommendations for action, and presented to senior management so that the necessary authoritative actions can be undertaken.

As to who carries out the audit – this will depend upon the size and resources of the organisation. A large organisation may appoint an independent consultant, or set up an audit group or department within its own structure. The smaller organisation may designate one of its executives as auditor or the chief marketing executive may simply be asked to arrange for the auditing to be done from within his own resources. In the last case, pressure on already busy marketing personnel may impair the necessary time, care and attention being given to the audit. Where a separate audit group or department is set up, the staff concerned should, theoretically at least, be able to provide that nicety of balance between the detached viewpoint and close working knowledge of internal policies and procedures. The external consultant(s), for their part, should certainly ensure independence of judgement and, if chosen well, the level of professional skill which derives from up-to-date and comprehensive knowledge of evaluation techniques. The internal or external argument should ideally be grounded in the maxim that 'no man can be a judge in his own case', but as with so many other decisions 'it all depends upon the budget'.

The word 'period' is important – ideally, the exercise should be done annually and where much of the work involved has become routinised, this should not be the burden it may appear to be. If the annual pattern cannot be achieved, regular audits should be the aim – the more dynamic the markets in which the organisation operates, the more regular the audits.

A framework for the marketing audit

As has been said, the length and complexity of the audit report and the ground covered in the audit process depend on the needs of the organisation and the resources available. What follows are some suggestions for an *audit framework*.

1 *The general marketing environment* (see Chapter 2). This would cover an evaluation of the likely *economic, political, social, technological* and *legal* influences affecting its future operations.

A lawn mower manufacturer, for example, might be concerned with:

(a) stability of price levels and levels of unemployment, affecting home ownership (*economic influences*)

(b) government policy on imports and investment (*political influences*)

(c) changes in life styles and values as they affect gardening as a leisure-time activity (*social influences*)

(d) developments in polymer engineering which indicate the replacement of sheet-steel by heavy duty plastic in garden machinery (*technological influences*).

(e) legislative trends as these affect safety standards and manufacturers' warranties (*legal influences*)

2 *The particular marketing environment.* Here the department will be concerned with: market size (total and by segments); market growth and market share(s); the company image with users and distributors, its rating against competitors; trends in competitors' performance, news of competitors' new products; relationships and market standing with suppliers and facilitators (e.g. transport, finance and insurance companies, advertising agencies, trade associations etc); trends in buyer behaviour and expectations (user and trade).

3 *Marketing objectives and marketing strategy.* Here the factors concerned will hinge on examination of how corporate objectives are devised and stated and their implications for clear marketing objectives, in turn; how well marketing strategies seem to be serving corporate objectives and how effectively resources are allocated to the elements of the marketing mix in order to achieve objectives.

4 *The marketing mix.* Current performance against objectives will be evaluated to determine the effectiveness of products, pricing strategy, distribution, the salesforce, and the organisation's advertising, sales promotion and publicity activities. Questions that may emerge are these, among others:

what products should be phased out?
what existing products should be modified?
what entirely new products should be introduced?
should the product range be rationalised?
is there an 80/20 tendency?
are our pricing policies based on continuing sound criteria?
what is the current price/value dimension of our products?
are changes required in our trade mark-up and payment discount policies?
is the level of availability/service adequate through existing distribution policies?
are we taking sufficient account of changes in transport techniques and warehousing systems?
are there any significant changes in the pattern of distribution: do they alter the balance between market coverage by distributors; the sales force, etc?

is the sales force effectively deployed (e.g. by market segment, geographical territory, industry, outlet) so as to achieve its objectives?

is the sales force of adequate size?

does it possess the necessary technical/sales skills?

is it adequately motivated and trained?

how does its performance compare to internally established standards (targets, quotas)? external standards (e.g. competitors sales forces)?

how are the objectives/incentives devised for the sales force? are there adequate incentives?

are the procedures adequate for establishing standards and monitoring performance?

are the aims and policies of promotional campaigns soundly devised?

is the correct creative approach being employed?

are appropriate media being chosen?

how do our advertising campaigns compare with those of competitors? what is the reaction of (i) users, (ii) distributors?

is the funding for promotion being effectively determined? does it appear to be adequate?

how do results compare with effort?

5 *Marketing productivity.* What is the respective performance of the organisation's products, markets, market segments, territories and channels of distribution with regard to:

revenue,
costs and
profitability?

Are there any markets or market segments which we should enter or from which we should withdraw? and what would be the short and medium-term effect on profits? are there any ways in which we might reduce costs?

6 *Marketing organisation.* The type of issues appraised under this heading would include the following:

the lines of responsibility and authority established for the marketing function and their appropriateness and adequacy for user and distributor satisfaction; the efficiency and productivity of individuals and groups within the marketing function (market research, sales, advertising, etc) and the way in which their efforts are co-ordinated; the quality and effectiveness of the working relationships between the marketing function and the other functions of the organisation (production, finance, personnel, purchasing, etc).

(*Note* these and other organisational issues are developed more fully in Chapter 12, which follows).

7   *Marketing systems.* The audit would range over the separate systems employed within the marketing function in order to evaluate their effectiveness in relation to objectives. The following are the major systems:

    (a) the marketing information system;
    (b) the system for developing new products/services;
    (c) the system for forecasting, planning and setting performance standards;
    (d) the system(s) for the monitoring and control of marketing operations;
    (e) the general administrative system(s) supporting marketing, including procedures for dealing with complaints from users and distributors.

From this brief survey it can be seen that a well conceived and conducted marketing audit can do a great deal to improve performance. Its objective, as the old chestnut goes is 'to examine the past, here in the present, in order to provide for the future'. Shuchman[9] expresses it more imaginatively when he says that the audit is intended for: 'prognosis as well as diagnosis... It is the practice of preventive as well as curative marketing medicine'. Also, if the audit procedure is conscientiously followed the company should have a clear picture as to how objectives relate to resources. It is good to remember again Foster's observation[10] that marketing is not an open-ended process with regard to expenditure but is 'the art of doing what is possible' in order to attain profit or other objectives.

Other thoughts

In concluding this Chapter, it might be helpful to make some new points and re-state some old ones. Firstly, plans can only be achieved through *people* (the subject of the next Chapter). Information technology has not yet dispensed with the need for people, nor is it likely to, nor should it ever do so. People need to be motivated and they need to be *informed* – a plan is no better and no worse than the way it is communicated and accepted by the people chosen to carry it through. Next, a plan is no better and no worse than the forecast on which it is based. Realism should pervade the whole of the planning process. Planning which becomes an end in itself might well induce a state of euphoria among the planners, leading to the development of objectives which are well beyond the prospect of achieving them. Objectives that cannot be attained, either with current resources or by affordable investment, have no place in marketing planning and can, in fact, threaten the organisation's existence if the worst happens.

The plan should contain no more detail than is necessary. Plans that are long on statistics and short on clear lines for action are likely to bore rather than inspire and increase their chances of rejection.

Then as Cannon[11] indicates, suggested frameworks for planning only reflect the approaches employed by organisations and, in practice, the range of approaches is wide. So the planning format should be the one that best suits the organisation devising it. The touchstones are – is it clear? does it suggest action? can it be carried out? is is based on sound data?

Finally, as Boone and Kurtz[12] have pointed out, most markets are so dynamic that forecasting the future is nothing if not risky. This therefore calls for a strategy in which: monitoring of progress to plan is a diligent and continuous process; forecasting approaches are being continually refined in the light of 'feed-back' from the changing scene; and the organisation is managed in such a way that it is nothing if not adaptable.

Self-assessment questions

1   Why is it that 'plans are nothing; planning is everything'?
2   What are non-economic objectives? Why are they important to a business organisation?
3   What are the arguments in favour of planning?
4   Suggest some things the chief marketing executive might do to improve planning performance.
5   Outline a framework for planning.

6 Explain, with examples, the difference between strategy and tactics.

7 What do you think a well-constructed marketing plan should contain?

8 How would you evaluate a marketing plan?

9 Explain the scope and purpose of marketing cost analysis.

10 What is a marketing audit?

11 Why should planning be a continuous process?

References

1 Fayol, H. *General and industrial management*, 1949 Pitman, reported in *Writers on organisations*, (eds D. S. Pugh, D. J. Hickson, and C. R. Hinings), 2nd edn, Hardmondsworth, Middx, Penguin, 1971, pp. 61–62

2 Stanton, William J. *Fundamentals of marketing*, 6th edn, New York, McGraw-Hill, 1981, pp. 509–511

3 Willsmer, Ray L. *The basic arts of marketing*, London, Business Books, 1976, p. 134

4 Markin, Rom. *Marketing – strategy and management*, 2nd edn, New York, John Wiley, 1982, p. 66

5 *Fundamentals of marketing*, p. 510

6 Stern, Mark E. Thinking through policies, objectives and strategies, *Handbook of modern marketing*, (ed Victor P. Buell), New York, McGraw-Hill, 1970, p. 7–15

7 Green, Edward J. The concept of marketing planning, *Handbook of Modern Marketing*, p. 7–13

8 *Marketing – strategy and management*, p. 84

9 Shuchman, A. The marketing audit: its nature, purpose and problems, *Management report No. 32*, New York, American Management Association, 1959, pp. 11–19

10 Foster, Douglas. *Mastering marketing*, London, The Macmillan Press, 1982, p. 5

11 Cannon, Tom. *Basic marketing – principles and practice*, London; Holt, Rinehart and Winston, 1980, p. 252

12 Boone, Louis E. and Kurtz, David L. *Contemporary marketing*, 3rd edn, Hinsdale, Ill., The Dryden Press, 1980, p. 455

12 MARKETING ORGANISATION

Objectives

For 'organisations' read 'people'. Whatever an organisation achieves is achieved by people.

The Chapter describes ways in which groups of people may best be organised in order to achieve objectives. Various forms of organisation structure – including product or brand management are discussed.

The element of the marketing concept known as 'organisational integration', and its root-and-branch significance, are also examined.

Introduction – organisational principles

We have seen that strategic planning consists of scanning the environment, developing objectives, forecasting and planning to achieve those objectives, developing strategies, developing tactical plans to implement the strategies and periodically reviewing progress towards objectives, with a revision of the plans if necessary.

The effective plan suggests *actions* and these are performed by *people*. This Chapter offers some ideas on how people might best be organised so as to achieve objectives. The way in which the marketing function is organised will not only exercise great influence on the organisation's focus and success, it will also leave the chief marketing executive more time to think strategically rather than tactically and free to consider the medium and the long-term rather than the short-term.

Organising the marketing function is similar to organising any other function so far as the general principles are concerned. Let us think about those principles.

The organiser must examine the activities entailed in the marketing plan, group these into units or departments according to their homogeneity and then establish structural relationships between the units in a manner best fitted to achieve the ultimate goals. Marketing departments that are well organised to achieve goals have a number of distinguishing characteristics. Listed below are some of these.

1   Every individual has a clearly defined role and an adequate understanding of how that role relates to other roles in the organisation structure. Conflict and duplication of effort are thus minimised.

2   Each individual knows the exact extent of his responsibility and authority; knows his/her functional relationship to subordinates and superiors. Each individual is responsible to one immediate superior (the principle of 'unity of command').

3   The organisation has well established and effective lines of communication, both 'vertically' (i.e. through the levels of responsibility and authority) and 'horizontally' (i.e. across the functional areas or departments of the organisation). These lines of communication permit information to ascend or descend rapidly through the organisation structure and to move laterally through departments. Above all, the communications network permits rapid dissemination of organisational objectives to every member and a clear indication of each member's expected contribution towards their achievement.

4   The organisation has a system of appraisal whereby the contribution of each member is evaluated. Upgradings, changes in role and training programmes are systematically linked to this system of performance appraisal.

5   Following careful analysis, administrative and other systems are established that make for integrated, trouble-free work flows. These systems are set out in manuals of procedure enabling the induction of new employees, and members on job-transfer to acquire the necessary operational skills in the smoothest and speediest manner.

6   A system is established for the satisfactory deployment of financial and other resources to achieve objectives and provision is made for adequate monitoring and control of these resources.

7   Operations are undertaken against planning based on sound data and the plan is used as a powerful integrating force so that all departments make their due contribution to the attainment of organisational goals.

8   Above all, the organisation is customer oriented in all phases of its operations and management and no decisions, either strategic or tactical, are taken without due consideration of the impact of those decisions upon customer satisfaction.

The Section which follows will describe how individual tasks and work-roles are fitted into structures.

Forms of organisation structure

As a general rule, and taking a manufacturing organisation, Arnold Ceramics, as our example, the overall structure is based upon *functions*, as shown in Fig. 12.1.

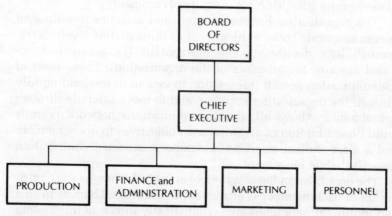

Fig. 12.1   *The functional structure of Arnold Ceramics*

In the simple diagram we see how each of the main functions of the business (under senior managers reporting to the chief executive, or managing director), are shaped into a structure controlled ultimately by a board of directors.

We are primarily interested in the marketing department of the firm and if this is organised on functional lines, we have a structure as shown in Fig. 12.2.

Again, this is a relatively simple structure in which managers of medium seniority in charge of the marketing research, marketing communications, marketing administration, physical distribution and the sales function are responsible to the chief marketing executive.

Fig. 12.2   *Arnold Ceramics: marketing department – functional organisation*

The other main functional areas of the business – finance, personnel, production would probably be organised into appropriate sub-functions, in the spirit of Fig. 12.2. Because of its simplicity, the functional approach is found to suit Arnolds at that stage of its growth where products and markets are relatively few in number. As the business grows, however, so does the scale and complexity of its organisational problems. Unless the sub-functions are working to a carefully co-ordinated planning system, the chief marketing executive may discover that insufficient attention is being given to certain products and markets; that he is becoming occupied with operations at too low a level of detail; that the marketing function as a whole is becoming more difficult to co-ordinate and that each of the sections within the marketing department (marketing research, advertising, sales, etc.) is developing a sectional outlook and sectional goals instead of co-operating to achieve overall marketing goals. In such a situation, the head of marketing finds himself too often cast in the role of 'referee' as sections compete with each other for resources.

Because of this, Arnolds might, at the next stage of their organisational development, group sections that cohere in some sense and add another tier of management. Fig. 12.3 depicts such a development based on a division into the two principal areas of 'planning and services' and 'operations'. This reduces the chief executive's *span of control* from five (Fig. 12.2) to two (Fig. 12.3) freeing him from a large measure of tactical detail and increasing the time available for strategic thinking.

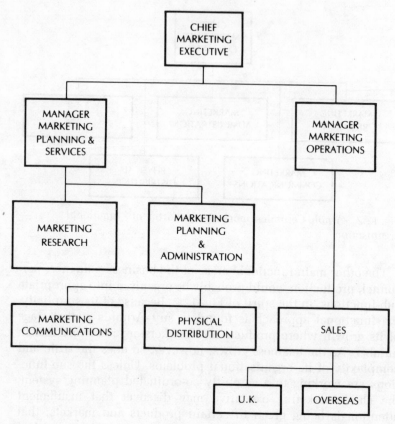

Fig. 12.3   Arnold Ceramics: marketing department – functional
organisation (stage II)

Product management

Happily, Arnolds continue to grow, but growth brings with it
organisational pressures. Even the developed functional organisation depicted in Fig. 12.3 becomes a creaking door when faced
with the growing number of products being added to the range.
Planning becomes more complex and the problems attaching to
the marketing of each individual product increase. It becomes
apparent that insufficient planning and operational attention is
probable at the level of the individual product given the current
organisation structure (Fig. 12.3).

Arnolds survey the total range of products and decide that these can be divided into four relatively homogeneous clusters:

Tableware (domestic)
Hotel and institutional ware;
Tiles and Building supplies
Industrial ceramics.

The company decides to adopt a *matrix organisation* for its marketing which it aligns with its functional organisation in a general sense (i.e. covering production, finance/administration, marketing and personnel) to produce the structure shown in Fig. 12.4. Each of the four divisions identified have now been placed under the supervision of a product manager. (*Note* Generally the role is described as one of *product* management in industrial marketing and *brand* management in consumer goods marketing.)

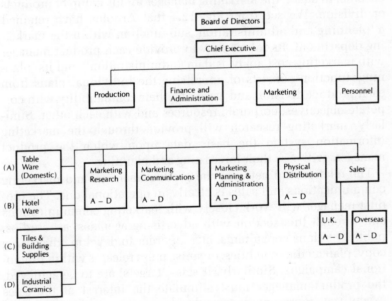

Fig. 12.4 *The introduction of product management at Arnold Ceramics*

Each product manager is charged with the following responsibilities for his division:

1 the development of short and long-term marketing plans which serve overall goals of growth and profitability – the plans

being based on skilled assessment of the market, competition, business/economic trends, etc.;

2 the development of strategic and tactical programmes to achieve those plans;

3 effective co-operation with the various sections within marketing (sales, marketing communications, marketing research, etc.) and with other management functions (e.g. production) so as to obtain full support for the achievement of the divisional plan;

4 the development of evaluation and control procedures which ensure that progress to objectives (e.g. sales growth, profit targets) is constantly monitored and contingency plans are brought into action if necessary.

From these duties we can see that the product manager has become, in effect, the marketing manager for his group of products or division. We see from Fig. 12.4 that Arnolds have retained a 'planning and administration' sub-function within the marketing department. Its role is now to provide each product manager with marketing cost analysis data ('administration') and its 'planning' function consists of appraising the individual plans from each product division and assessing their compatibility with corporate objectives, corporate resources and with each other. Similarly, marketing research will provide through the marketing information system the basic data upon which the product managers will base their forecasting and planning.

The relationship between the product manager and marketing communications and sales is clearly an operational one. The product manager will work closely with marketing communications and through this section with advertising agencies, art studios, public relations consultants, etc., in order to develop advertising copy, plan media schedules, organise press releases within promotional campaigns. Similarly, if sales 'targets' are to be achieved, the product manager must stimulate the interest of the sales executives, representatives and sales agents so that they give their fullest support to his plans and programmes.

Where the product managers are given responsibility for profit performance as well as sales targets, then in effect they will 'buy' the time of the sales force and the marketing research section within their budgets. Similarly the costs of advertising campaigns, sales promotion schemes, etc. will be debited to their trading account and so they will be keenly interested in the productivity of every pound spent on marketing communications. A word on the physical distribution section might be useful here. Arnolds have for some time now incorporated physical distribution within the marketing function since they recognised the implications of the newer transport techniques (containerisation, air freight, 'roll-on/roll-off') not only for marketing costs, but also for product design and development. Under the product management reorganisation, individual product managers will be similarly concerned with physical distribution on both of these counts.

The product or brand management concept, both in the UK and the USA, is synonymous with the Procter and Gamble organisation, and since the Second World War it has proved an excellent nursery for the development of marketing talent in the UK (the system was introduced in the USA by the company as long ago as 1927).

It can be seen that the system improves upon the simple functional structure in its ability to cope with organisational growth and organisational complexity. Even the smallest product will have the close attention of a marketing executive; this close attention assists speedy reaction to problems whether these arise in the organisation or in the market place; the system allows the various resource and managerial 'inputs' to be balanced and co-ordinated and this at the level of the individual product. Lastly, as has been mentioned above, the system provides a good mechanism for the development of marketing managers.

Nonetheless, the approach can have drawbacks in practice. Where the system has been tried and has failed it has been due to the product manager being given responsibility without commensurate authority. Frustration and disappointment have been experienced, not least by the product manager himself, when conflict has arisen between this 'junior' marketing manager and more senior colleagues in charge of other functions and sections-within-functions. The problem is neatly summarised by the comment that product managers are expected to: 'cross organisational lines without making the organisation cross'.

If the product manager system is to be made to work, Winston Churchill's dictum of 'no responsibility without authority' has to be borne in mind: it is simply not good enough to saddle the product manager with profit responsibility and not allow him sufficient influence upon the variables that affect profitability. Obviously clear delineation of roles, with appropriate job specifications, will reduce the chance of conflict between the product manager and other managers, inside and outside the marketing department. Kotler[1] suggests that product managers and the functional line managers should be formally required to report in writing to general management on all conflict-of-interest situations, with final decisions being made at that level.

Initially, as has been mentioned, the product manager system emerged in the consumer goods field. Oliver[2] reports on its successful employment in industrial markets adding, with one example, that where technical expertise and consultancy are very much a part of the service, the product manager is technical expert and able to operate as consultant. This is all to the good so long as we remember, in the consumer goods field, that as Thomas[3] warns, excessive preoccupation with the product can develop a product-oriented outlook in the product manager, to the detriment of sensitivity to market needs and the probable necessity to develop new products. The key is not to impair his strategic thinking by making the product manager too much a manager of operations only.

The foregoing outline covers many of the main features of the product management concept, except to add that in very large organisations with an extensive range of products and brands, a 'senior' or 'group' product manager is introduced into the organisation structure. With three or four product managers reporting to each group product manager, the span of control of the chief marketing executive is kept reasonably short. His time for strategic thinking is also that much more protected although the 'trade-off' here is that the insertion of another level of management into the structure takes him further away from the scene of actual marketing operations.

The pitfalls of the product management system can be foreseen and circumvented by planning and therefore it is really for the individual organisation to decide whether it is at that stage of development where a closer and more comprehensive marketing/profit orientation can be brought to each of its products by the adoption of the product management concept. A good example of its applicability to non-profit organisation is provided by the field of education. Many junior and middle managers in this field are not sure where their responsibility for academic leadership ends and their duty of resources allocation and control begins, and vice versa.

Some establishments have introduced the idea of the matrix

organisation with the objective of maintaining the required standards of quality and cost-effectiveness.

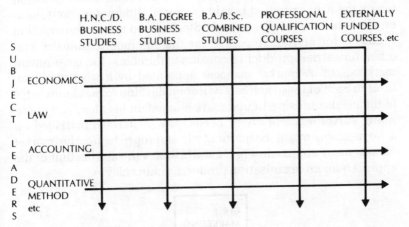

Fig. 12.5   *The matrix organisation within a Faculty of Business Studies*

Fig. 12.5 demonstrates how, within a Faculty of Business Studies *course leaders*, who in this sense we may call the product managers, commission the services of *subject leaders* to provide for the needs of their courses. Here we could say that the 'product' is the course and its leader is responsible for its quality, cost effectiveness and marketing performance (judged, on one dimension, by the number of students recruited). The subject-leaders are somewhat similar to the Section Heads in Fig. 12.4 (research, planning, distribution, etc.). We must not push the comparison too far since there are some important differences. Fig. 12.5 is offered, however, as an illustration of how pressure for effective marketing performance on a public sector service (i.e. education) has generated revised thinking on organisation structure.

Market management

An alternative approach to the problems of organisational growth and complexity is that of *market management* in which a number of managers are each made individually responsible for the servicing of a single market through the entire range of the firm's product possibilities. In a sense, the product manager and the market manager approaches are the same thing writ differently in that they both focus the efforts of a junior or middle manager onto sub-divisions of the firm's products or markets. The *market management* approach is best suited to the situation where the firm's product is sold in several different markets, each of which have specialised needs. Steel is used for the construction industry, for civil engineering; for the automobile industry and other industries producing consumer durables; for government markets, etc. A market manager appointed by a steel manufacturer to each of these markets will soon develop expert knowledge of the needs of his particular market based on his close and continuing surveillance of client needs. Raw materials, marketed on a large scale, might be particularly appropriate for the market management approach. Fig. 12.6 illustrates the application of the approach for an organisation producing china clay.

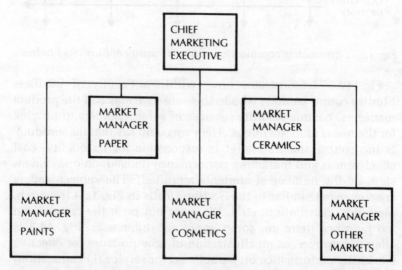

Fig. 12.6 *Wessex China Clays: a market management organisation*

The market management approach is best suited to a pattern of marketing activity in which total demand comprises the sum of the demands from a number of types of user, each with clearly differentiated needs. Serving each of these market segments requires close and often expert attention to those needs and a continuing, skilled servicing activity in the post-sale situation.

If, on the other hand, a standardised product is sold to a large number of user industries, each of which comprises a considerable number of member organisations which are geographically spread, then the *geographical approach* to organisation structure might be the most effective. According to the work-load that each geographical cluster of user organisations entails (see Chapter 9), an appropriate number of organisations determines each salesman's *territory*. In turn, a number of territories will form a *sales area*, with an appropriate number of areas comprising a region – if the total number of actual and potential users justifies this number of tiers in the organisation structure. If we look back to Fig. 12.3, the sales manager reporting to the manager of marketing operations would in turn probably have five or six UK regional managers reporting to him, this number comprising an effective span of control for the extent and complexity of such selling operations. It can also be seen from Fig. 12.3 that there is an overseas department within the total sales operation. Needless to say, where marketing organisations are well-developed internationally, the geographical approach to structure is very suitable. Standardised products sold to industrial users for which a geographical organisation might be the most effective approach include office equipment and stationery, laboratory equipment, engineering tools and maintenance equipment and supplies. Intermediary suppliers (e.g. distributors, agents) might be used, in addition to direct representation, particularly in geographical areas where users are not so numerous. In the consumer goods field, such standardised products as foodstuffs, confectionery and household products might be marketed within a geographical framework although the structure will again allow for 'key accounts' and 'super-distributors' to be serviced from head office, according to the concentration of buying power (see Chapter 7).

Services lend themselves to geographical organisation. Banks, building societies, insurance and travel organisations as well as the public utilities (gas, electricity) are so structured. The branch/head office structure gives rise to issues of *centralisation/decentralisation*, which are discussed in a later Section of this Chapter.

Finally, and reverting to product management and market management, it should not be thought that these are mutually exclusive. The product manager specialises in a narrow range of products and must develop knowledge of the needs of several, perhaps highly divergent markets. The market manager specialises in one or a few markets and must commission knowledge of the many, perhaps highly divergent products bought by the market. Where a single organisation is producing multiple products for multiple markets it may well be that it can combine the two concepts into a product management/market management organisation.

For example, imagine an organisation specialising in polymer engineering. Let us say it produces four grades of plastics and that these can be used in a number of different markets – *industrial* (e.g. capital equipment; commercial motor vehicles) *consumer durables* (e.g. refrigerators, private motor vehicles, household equipment) *leisure and amenities* (e.g. sailing craft, toys and games) and *construction* (e.g. pipes, sanitary fittings, windows, downspouts, etc.). The organisation structure – a product management/market management structure may be as depicted in Fig. 12.7.

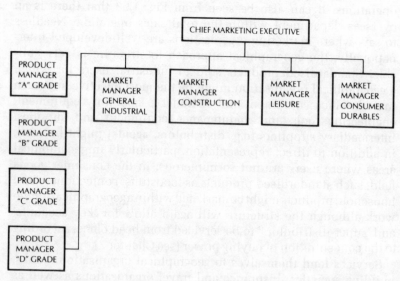

Fig. 12.7 *Peerless Petrochemicals: a product management/market management structure*

The four product managers have sales and profit responsibility for their respective grades of material. They will plan for the use of their material in each of the four existing markets plus any others that may be developed by the Peerless organisation. Their points of reference for planning purposes will be the individual market managers and the total sales forecast for each grade of plastic will comprise the estimate of sales made in consultation with each market manager.

The market managers are primarily concerned with the changing composition of user needs in their respective markets and the development of products appropriate to user needs and the profitability of the market for which they are responsible. The development of sales for specific grades of plastic is not their first consideration, therefore, but they will liaise closely with each product manager on the matters of prices and output capabilities. The total forecasts of the market managers should equal those of the product managers, given that Peerless is entirely self-supporting in the matter of materials supply. The planning horizon of the market managers will be necessarily more extended than that of the product managers, for the monitoring and evaluation of medium and long-term trends affecting the use of plastics and the importance of these for product development will be a significant part of their role.

Large-scale organisations: corporate marketing

As organisations become larger and more complex with perhaps a number of operating divisions which are geographically spread, as is the case with many multinational organisations and conglomerates, a decision may be made to establish, usually at the head office location, a *corporate marketing department*. The individual divisions, or member companies, typically concentrate on production and selling, leaving the strategic marketing role and the planning that accompanies it to the headquarters organisation.

The advantages of centralising the marketing function in this way include the employment and utilisation of specialists (forecasters, planners, media buyers, designers, researchers, etc.); the economies of purchasing co-ordination, particularly for promotional expenditures and the development of a unifying corporate image with which to support the many and diverse marketing operations of the organisation as a whole.

The disadvantages are that decision making is somewhat removed from the scene of operations; that cumbersome bureaucracies can develop which increase costs and decrease motivation and that the flexibility of individual divisions may be impaired by having to 'go through channels' so that many a marketing opportunity will be lost.

The arguments for and against centralisation will continue and for every organisation that has set up a corporate marketing department to its advantage, there is another which has tried it and failed. For every opinion in favour of a group of highly trained corporate planners there is another to support the view that marketing plans are best developed and operated by experienced practitioners. There are no 'absolutes' here. The best marketing structure is the one that best suits the objectives of the organisation at that particular stage of its development at that particular point in time. The ideal solution may, or may not, justify the establishment of a corporate marketing department.

Organisational integration

Mention has been made earlier in this work of the view of Giles[4] that a vital part of the marketing concept is the proposition of organisational integration. This view is easily understood, for no organisation can be adequately user-oriented or obtain an adequate return on investment if it believes that its marketing responsibilities can be left entirely to marketing personnel.

Indeed, the purpose of the marketing concept can easily be misunderstood unless its introduction to the organisation is handled effectively. Some departments may construe it as a thinly-veiled take-over bid for their own power and influence and may feel that decisions which are properly their own province are being absorbed into marketing planning. Badly handled interpretations of marketing often stem from explanations that fail to emphasise that it is the *customer* who is the focus of activity and not marketing as such. Once service and satisfaction for customers become established as the ethic then all departments can properly be regarded as having an important role in marketing.

Of course in any organisation there will be in-built tensions between the marketing department and other departments. Production may wish to enjoy the cost benefits and the manufacturing efficiency of lengthy production runs on standardised products – marketing may be seeking flexibility from production and the introduction of non-standard models. Purchasing may wish to confine expenditures to bulk purchases of standard materials and components so as to secure the fullest discounts from suppliers – marketing may insist that this imposes a deadening uniformity on the product range and impedes sales growth. Credit control insist that new customers must only be extended the most cautious terms until experience has been gained of trading with them – marketing emphasises that certain risks must be taken if some edge over competitors is to be attained. Finance wish to see a closely reasoned analysis underlying all budgeted expenditures – marketing state that the organisation can suffer from the 'accountancy mind' – that dynamic markets require a dynamic approach, which entails action even in the face of some imponderables.

The opportunities for suspicion and mistrust are greater when marketing is seen as a threat to status and power. Thus, the relationship between the marketing department and the other departments of the organisation has a great deal to do with the ultimate success or failure of the organisation as a whole. Because the marketing concept implies that all personnel possess a positive, supportive attitude to creating and keeping customers a number of strategies have been adopted to achieve integration. Some of these are now listed.

1   It is a truism that 'the standards in any organisation are set at the top'. This also applies to the marketing philosophy as an operating concept without doubt. Unless the board of directors and its chief executive are 'marketing minded', the concept has little chance of permeating the rest of the organisation. The leadership must therefore demonstrate its belief that marketing is the key to organisational prosperity and ensure that the outlook is shared and acted upon by all personnel.

2   The installation of a marketing planning system which impinges upon the activities of all departments can be a powerful integrating force and should help to ensure that all in the organisation recognise the salience of customer satisfaction.

3   Some companies achieve marketing orientation by ensuring that personnel from other departments spend some of their time in the marketing department. In the UK, Beecham Toiletries have utilised this approach. Firms in the industrial goods field have formed teams of personnel, drawn from marketing, design, finance, production, etc., to introduce new products to the market. Reciprocal attendance at departmental meetings: marketing personnel at the production committee, production personnel at the marketing planning group, is another useful strategy.

4   It is often of great advantage to the organisation for each departmental head to spend some time 'in the field' or to attend exhibitions. This provides an opportunity to meet customers and supports the efforts of marketing and sales personnel to bring the 'atmosphere' of the market into the firm.

5   The marketing approach is democratic in nature and democracy can become a cumbersome beast not least because of its power in generating committees. Some firms have avoided becoming 'committee-ridden' by forming working parties – carefully briefed, working to strict time-schedules and drawn from all parts of the organisation, in order to solve marketing problems. Again, this idea has gained favour in industrial marketing.

6   A popular means of bringing the market to the organisation is by arranging factory visits and tours by users, distributors and overseas agents. Jaguar Cars have also done a great deal to purposefully integrate the efforts of their personnel by the use of video presentations. This enables executives and other key figures to talk to shop-floor workers without interruption to the work-flow.

7   Marketing seminars, films and presentations are also useful and some organisations hire the services of lecturers and consultants in order to explain and interpret what the introduction of marketing to the organisation entails. The author has conducted courses of this kind for foremen and office supervisors in a number of companies, over a range of products as diverse as motor gears, electronic equipment, surgeons' gloves, fine chemicals, carpets and confectionery.

An organisation is a group of people driving towards objectives that can better be reached by a group than by individuals. Primitive man recognised this – the tribe came into being with the realisation that perils could be better confronted, and more could be achieved, if man began to co-operate with other men. The old truths still stand, but the whole will only be greater than the sum of the parts if everyone is pulling together and, as marketing implies, in the direction of the customer.

Human resource accounting

Some years ago, authors Brummett, Pyle and Flamholtz[5] made the point that the amount of money required by an average business organisation to recruit, train and replace staff must form a highly significant proportion of the value of the business as a whole. They proposed the development of a conceptual framework for the recording and analysis of the costs and values of the human resources employed by the business, reasoning that the technical and managerial skills of the staff of a business are more critical for the success of the business than any other factor yet the recording of their 'cost', 'depreciation' and 'profit and loss' receive scant attention compared with, for example, the accounting processes surrounding the acquisition, use and disposal of a relatively insignificant asset such as a minor piece of capital equipment. They proposed a system of *human resource accounting* – a 'process of identifying, measuring and communicating information about human resources to facilitate effective management within the organisation'.

The extent to which their proposals have been accepted or not is beside the point, for this author at least. What the paper did, if nothing else, was to identify the importance of the human assets which a company acquires and trains in the expectation of realising an adequate return on its investment. The 'fitting the man to the job' and the 'fitting the job to the man' model outlined in Chapter 9, is one aspect of good husbandry of human resources. An equally important aspect is how best those resources can be moulded into effective organisational shape – a decision to be based on careful study of the structure, functioning and performance of organisations and the motives and behaviour of groups and individuals within them, as Pugh[6] has indicated. This Chapter has offered some examples of current thinking in this regard.

Finally, and in the context of current thinking, mention should be made of the emergence of the post of *marketing controller*. In Chapter 11, the scope and function of the marketing audit was explained. McDaniel[7] suggests that where the audit is conducted from within the organisation's own resources, responsibility for the audit should be given to a marketing controller whose role would encompass the administration of the financial/marketing planning function, liaison with all operating departments and provision of help and advice to marketing executives particularly for plans, budgets and analyses. The marketing controller should be particularly competent at monitoring progress to profit objectives, the preparation of budgets and the control of media expenditure, as well as the measurement of marketing costs and profitability in relation to customers, territories, promotional schemes, etc.

It is easy to discern the adherence to the return on investment aspect of marketing through the effective discharge of the role of the marketing controller as described by McDaniel. Reporting on the American experience he adds that while the role is not yet widely established and is restricted to a few very large compa-

418 **Principles and Practice of Marketing**

nies, one study[8] shows that 'many companies had either just embarked, or were about to embark, on the creation of the position...' McDaniel concludes:

The skills required for the job are a unique blend of marketing, finance, and quantitative training. Perhaps this will be a significant career field for MBAs during the late 1980s.

Self-assessment questions

1 What are the distinguishing characteristics of departments that are well organised to achieve goals?
2 Explain the rationale of product management. What are its drawbacks?
3 In what circumstances might it be desirable for the organisation to adopt a market-management approach?
4 What is the justification for a corporate marketing department?
5 List some of the strategies by which all departments of the organisation can be integrated, with the objective of customer satisfaction.
6 Design a job description for a marketing controller.

References

1 Kotler, Philip. Marketing management – analysis, planning and control, 4th edn, Englewood Cliffs, NJ, Prentice-Hall, 1980, p. 587
2 Oliver, Gordon. Marketing today, London, Prentice-Hall, 1980, p. 300
3 Thomas, Michael J. The organisation of the marketing function, Marketing handbook (ed. Michael Rines), 2nd edn, Aldershot, Gower Publishing, 1981, pp. 167–168
4 Giles, G. B. Marketing, 3rd edn, Plymouth, Macdonald and Evans, 1978, p. 4
5 Brummett, R. L., Pyle, W. C., and Flamholtz, E. G. Human resource accounting, Michigan Business Review (March 1968), reprinted in the Canadian Chartered Accountant (June 1968)
6 Pugh, D. S. Organisation theory, Harmondsworth, Middx., Penguin, 1983, p. 9
7 McDaniel, Carl, Jr. Marketing, 2nd edn, New York, Harper and Row, 1982, p. 660
8 Goodman, Sam R. The marketing controller concept: an inquiry into financial/marketing relationships in selected consumer companies, Cambridge, Mass., The Marketing Science Institute, 1970, p. 48

13 INTERNATIONAL MARKETING

Objectives
We are now about to look at why a firm might seek markets abroad and ways in which this might be done. We shall also see why international marketing is not just marketing 'writ differently', for in this Chapter quite a deal of attention is paid to export procedures and the export marketing mix.

Some particulars of HM Government services for exporters are provided, including the important issue of covering the credit risk.

Finally we shall see that the market abroad might well consist of trading opportunities for technical and managerial skills as well as for products.

Introduction

International trade is of great importance to Britain. By the end of the 1970s exports of goods and services accounted for 34 per cent of gross domestic product. In 1979, she was fifth in the 'league table' of world trade (preceded by the USA, the Federal Republic of Germany, Japan and France) and attained a six per cent share of total world trade. She is a significant customer for primary products (taking over 7 per cent of the world's exports) and contributes very nearly one tenth of the main manufacturing countries' exports of manufactured goods. She is one of the world's most important exporters of aerospace products. Motor vehicles, electrical equipment, textiles and machinery of most types also figure prominently in her exported output. On the import side, Britain is one of the world's most important markets for agricultural products, raw materials and semi-manufactures.

Now we know from the economics textbooks that international

trade is based on the *theory of comparative advantage.* The theory states that nations usually produce and export those goods in which they have the greatest comparative advantage and import the goods in which they have the least comparative advantage – the nation having comparative advantage in a product if it can produce it more efficiently (i.e. at a lower cost) than it can produce alternative products. Hence, the pattern of Britain's exports and imports described above. But, while this theory has its place at the macro level of economic activity, as Chisnall[1] points out:

At the micro level, however, a businessman is not directly affected by the theory of comparative advantage; other motivations spur him to seek overseas trade. Self-interest is the prime motivation of individuals and trading organisations . . .

And what could be classified as 'self-interest' in this context? Such motives as:

1   the desire to obtain economies of scale;
2   the opportunity to increase profitability in the face of a depressed home market or one in which prices are rigidly controlled by government intervention;
3   as a counter to increased competition in the home market from foreign firms.

These are typical reasons why business organisations seek to enter overseas markets.

Ways in which the organisation might enter foreign markets include the following:

indirect exporting;
direct exporting;
licensing and royalty agreements;
contract manufacturing;
management contracting;
joint ventures;
wholly owned subsidiaries *leading perhaps to*
multinational companies.

All of these terms will be explained in this Chapter. At this point let us be clear what we mean by international marketing for the term is often used interchangeably with exporting, and this is not correct. To quote Tom Cannon,[2] a British Professor of Business Studies:

Export marketing is the marketing of goods, produced in one or more countries, in other countries. International marketing, on the other hand, gives weight to the development of business in a number of countries or regions, with a framework capable of incorporating the establishment of local manufacturing, distribution and marketing systems.

Or, as Foster[3] puts it:

It is now generally accepted that 'international marketing' covers all activities from direct exporting of finished products to overseas markets, to wholly or partly owned subsidiaries of all kinds, joint ventures with foreign organisations and the big multinational corporations.

In short, the greater (international marketing) includes the less (exporting; export marketing).

The meaning of international marketing

If we were to ask a successful businessman what was required to succeed in international markets – user orientation? sensitivity to an adequate return on investment? organisational integration? ... he would doubtless answer 'Yes' three times over. In fact, he would probably emphasise the increased importance of all three tenets of the marketing philosophy, pointing out perhaps:

1 the increased risk inherent in developing products or services for people of different races, cultures and religions (hence the need for adequate user orientation);
2 the increased difficulties of competing with another nation's domestic producers in their home market, of abiding by the nation's laws and observing its regulations (hence the need for a proper appreciation of return on investment requirements);
3 the fact that no firm can hope to be successful in foreign markets unless all functions of the organisation – research and development, production, finance, marketing and personnel are inured to the idea of customer service (organisational integration).

What then is international marketing? If the same operating philosophy will do – is even more relevant, in fact – isn't it all simply 'marketing'? There are some who reason in this way. The author prefers not to do so because he feels that greater service is done to students and practitioners to emphasise the differences rather than to dwell on the similarities of domestic and foreign marketing. Stanton's maxim[4] is appropriate here:

Marketing fundamentals are universally applicable. Whether a firm sells in Toledo or Timbuktu, its marketing program should be built around a good product or service properly priced, promoted and distributed to a market that has been carefully analysed... however, ... there are considerable differences in the *implementation* of marketing programs in foreign markets. Modifications are necessary because of the environmental differences that exist among and within the many nations... Consequently, executives should try to understand each environment and anticipate its effect on their marketing programs. What complicates this task in international marketing is the fact that the environment – particularly the cultural environment – often consists of elements very unfamiliar to marketing executives. A further complication is the tendency for people to use their own cultural values as a frame of reference when in a foreign environment.

In this Chapter then an attempt will be made to explain in some depth the special features of international marketing. One other thing should be said. Again, this is linked to the author's perception of the service values of this Chapter to the reader. The various aspects of international marketing – licensing, joint ventures, multinational operations etc – will all be described. But the greatest attention will be paid to *exporting*, for this is the starting point for nearly all organisations in the international field and many, though successful, do not move on beyond it to the other forms of international activity. The author's perception is also based on data, for he recalls the public acknowledgement[5] of a number of ministers from EEC countries that small and medium-sized companies account for 90 per cent of businesses in the Community. For them, and for the students and practitioners associated with them, international marketing *is* exporting.

Indirect exporting

For many successful organisations in the international field, their first introduction to overseas business came via an *export house*. The British Export Houses Association[6] defines an export house as:

any company or firm not being a manufacturer, whose main activity is the handling or financing of British export trade and/or international trade not connected with the United Kingdom

In the Directory of the Association, the specialist functions which an export house may fulfil are listed as follows:

(a) *the merchant* serving neither manufacturer nor buyer but acting as principal on the contract of sale, buying in the best market and re-selling in the best market, and accepting the risk of loss as well as the hope of profit;

(b) *the manufacturer's agent* holding sole rights from a manufacturer for the promotion of the sale of some or all of his products in one or more markets on an agency basis;

(c) *the export manager* acting as the export department of one or more manufacturers and selling in the name of the export house or of the manufacturer and sometimes also bearing the credit risk;

(d) *the buying/indent agent* acting on behalf of, or as agent for the overseas buyer, either buying with wide discretion on orders received, or placing indents with specified manufacturers. The export house may act as principal on the contract with the manufacturer, thereby accepting responsibility for payment;

(e) *the confirming house* serving the overseas buyer by confirming 'closed' indents, assuming responsibility to the manufacturer for payment of consequent trade debts, and normally arranging the shipping and insurance and extending credit to the importer where required;

(f) *the factor* providing a series of services on behalf of the manufacturer including principally, finance, but not normally taking any active part in selling overseas;

(g) *the export finance house* mainly providing medium or long-term export credit, principally for capital goods. Serving the buyer, in the main, and receiving from him payment of charges and interest, sometimes separately from payment for the goods.

Note
   (i) in the above list of functions, 'manufacturer' should also be taken to include 'supplier', for example, a wholesaler.
   (ii) a 'closed' indent is one in which the manufacturer/supplier is specified by the overseas buyer, in contrast to the 'open' indent in which the export house uses its own expertise to determine the best source of supply; occasionally too, the 'open' indent may leave the specification of the product in broad terms, the buyer again relying on the expertise of the confirming house.

The importance of Britain's merchants and confirming houses to the pattern of her international trade has its roots in her imperial history. Yet while the export houses are still well represented in the former Empire and Commonwealth countries (despite the economic nationalism of the post-1945 period), their connections extend to Europe and the Americas, as well as Britain's traditional markets in Africa, the Middle East, Asia, Australia and Oceania. The following is a representative list of the products in which they trade;

> Abrasives, building materials, cables, clothing, construction equipment, cutlery, educational equipment, electrical goods, fancy goods, furniture, jewellery, medical equipment, petroleum products, toys, travel goods, wire and wood.

It is beyond the scope of this work to describe the work of the Export Houses in detail although they have been described at some length in a previous work by the author.[7]

Suffice it to say that most of the export houses in the UK are members of the British Export Houses Association, whose headquarters are at 69, Cannon Street, London EC4N 5AB and that they are involved in a substantial amount of Britain's annual export turnover. From the author's own experience, he can concur with the statement in the BEHA Directory that export houses play a most important part in promoting exports and their knowledge and experience are of great value to manufacturers and other types of suppliers who are new to exporting or who wish to expand their overseas business.

In essence the export houses enable the firm new to overseas business to enter overseas markets without first accumulating the specialist administrative and financial knowledge required to service customers abroad.

When the export house is operating as a *merchant*, it is buying and selling on its own account, relying on its own experience and knowledge of international markets and of the developing needs and tastes of foreign users. From the supplier's point of view when he trades with an export merchant he is virtually dealing with another UK 'domestic' customer.

Similarly, when the export house is operating as a *confirming house*, it takes full responsibility for payment, operating as principal on the export contract of sale even when the order is placed direct from overseas (in which case it will be franked 'Await confirmation by XYZ' – the confirming house). The function of the export house as confirmer, provides the supplier with:

1   a contract of sale enforceable in the UK;

2 prompt payment in sterling against presentation of 'clean' documents;
3 full provision of despatch instructions and documentary requirements (see page 440)
4 full coverage of the credit risk.

With regard to the last point, the supplier will find the granting of credit by the export house is a useful way of building business with those markets where credit is vital to the development of turnover without extending the supplier himself financially.

Where the export house operates as export manager, it becomes, in effect, the export department of the supplier. The supplier is thus relieved of the overhead expenses of establishing an export department, for the export house corresponds and sells on the supplier's behalf, arranges shipping space, insurance, all related documentation and, where agreed, bears the credit risk.

Before leaving this Section, it is important to add that through their network of branch offices, subsidiaries and affiliates export houses can also undertake certain specialist functions in markets abroad. These include:

(i) acting as stockist/distributors – usually by means of a territorial franchise or other type of exclusivity;

(ii) acting as wholesalers/retailers – usually through their own outlets and thereby providing a well integrated link between the UK supplier and the foreign user;

(iii) acting as 'manufacturer' – this is an increasingly significant role in those developing countries which are now becoming industrialised and especially suits suppliers who would wish to establish manufacturing facilities abroad but are prevented from doing so by financial or legal impediments.

Finally, it is worth noting that another form of 'exporting by proxy', as Day[8] puts it, consists of the use of UK buying offices of foreign organisations, such as the US department stores. These buying offices are usually situated in London and offer fledgling exporters the opportunity to launch their products in foreign markets – the USA, Japan, etc without the initial expense of organising sales trips to the markets. At the entry stage, the retail organisations typically involved in this method of trading offer the supplier a 'shop window' in the market (often linked to a name of considerable prestige) and a source of market research data on product acceptance and the need for modifications where this is necessary.

Direct exporting

Frequently the route into direct exporting happens by chance. A foreign buyer visits the firm's showrooms, expresses interest and orders a sample consignment to 'test the market'. Or an intending agent may visit the firm's stand at a UK exhibition and ask for samples with which he can canvass business in his home market, subject to his 'usual commission'. From these casual beginnings, sales volume may build to the extent that the organisation begins to wonder what would happen if it made a serious and sustained effort, on its own account, to obtain business from abroad. Thus it is led into direct exporting and whilst the 'casual trade' just described has a positive value of its own and should never be disregarded, most firms would recognise that if worthwhile and continuing sales volume is to be achieved, direct exporting calls for investment on three counts:

    an investment of time
    an investment of finance
    an investment of personnel

Before the explanation of this statement, the reader is invited to examine Table 13.1, which shows the changing pattern of Britain's 'top ten' export markets (based on percentages of UK exports) in the period 1948–1982.

Table 13.1   The changing pattern of Britain's top ten overseas markets (percentage of UK exports)

1948	1958	1968	1982
1 Australia	USA	USA	USA
2 S. Africa	Australia	Australia	Fed. Rep. Germany
3 India	Canada	Fed. Rep. Germany	France
4 Ireland	S. Africa	S. Africa	Netherlands
5 Canada	India	Canada	Ireland
6 USA	New Zealand	Sweden	Belgium/Luxembourg
7 Sweden	Fed. Rep. Germany	Ireland	Italy
8 New Zealand	Sweden	Netherlands	Sweden
9 Argentina	Ireland	Belgium/Luxembourg	Saudi Arabia
10 Netherlands	Netherlands	France	Nigeria

Source: *Export* Journal of the Institute of Export and *Overseas Trade Statistics of the UK* HMSO

What this Table demonstrates is a move away from a pattern of trade with the Empire and Commonwealth (which was based on Imperial preference, generally conducted in sterling and comprised the exchange of manufactures for food and raw materials)

to a pattern of trade conducted principally with other industrialised countries, particularly the United States and Western Europe (based on the exchange of manufactures for manufactures
and conducted in US dollars and Euro-currencies). The predomi-
nance of Europe in Britain's external trade is illustrated by the
fact that in the 12 months ended December 1982, the value of
Britain's exports to the European Community totalled a little
over £23 billion.*

Today, the pattern of Britain's export trade is one conducted
with markets in which there is extensive competition from both
resident and foreign suppliers. To be successful, new suppliers
to the market must 'go one better' in one or more elements of
the marketing mix. Also, patience and a serious and sustained
effort may be necessary before the correct combination of product
and marketing strategy is found – and this is especially so in
lucrative markets, where the most effective agents and distributors have long since been taken up by competitors. This is but
one aspect of the *investment in time* that is required.

Breaking into highly competitive markets may require some
type of *investment budget* procedure – with a subsequent 'pay-
back' period of two, three or more years . . . an aspect of the necessary *investment in finance*.

Exporting, even on a limited scale, poses particular problems
and calls for specialised administration. 'Making it easy for the
buyer to buy', intrinsic to the marketing approach, means, ideally,
quoting a delivered price. In turn, this calls for a knowledge of:

   shipping procedures;
   appropriate routes and modes of transport;
   the related freight and insurance rates;
   other expenses entering into the contract of sale.

The organisation quickly becomes involved in a study of tariffs,
quotas, import licensing restrictions, exchange control procedures, packing and marking regulations, the credit and 'political' risks involved (see page 461) and so on. Now it is true, of
course, that expert advice is readily available, from the exporter's
bank, from shipping and forwarding agents, from ECGD (page 462).
But someone has to co-ordinate all this advice and information.
Lumping the responsibility on to a marketing executive already
pressed with problems of the UK domestic market dooms the
project to failure. Hence the need for an *investment in personnel*.

* Her exports worldwide amounted to £55.5 billion approximately.

If these facts point to anything it is that enthusiasm and the positive attitude, though important, are not enough. Vital to success is the marketing research function. The decision to export often means 'the world is our market'. Yet we can see that all markets are becoming increasingly difficult to penetrate. Often, when firms try to export and fail, it is because they have spread themselves too thinly over too many markets, have been represented by agents already carrying too many products, and in consequence, have failed to build substantial sales volume in any market. If they have established a foothold, it is possible that competitors have found them easy to dislodge because of their lack of a thought-out plan or because of the limitations of their marketing budget. Therefore, researching the potential markets(s), efficiently arranging the documentation, the transport, the channels of distribution etc, are the very stuff of the marketing philosophy, but so also is the return on investment consideration and this necessitates that the firm assesses:

1   the scale of investment involved;
2   the funds it can make available;
3   any limitations that 2 might impose.

The Sections which immediately follow offer some thoughts on *export marketing strategy*.

An approach to export markets

A strategy for the approach to overseas market(s) should be based on an accurate assessment of at least these factors:

1   the present and potential size of the market(s);
2   the degree and type of competitive activity;
3   prevailing price level(s), including trade margins and discounts;
4   the degree of advertising, promotional and servicing support that is required;
5   quality and performance comparisons with competition, together with suggestions for product modifications;
6   assessment of tariff and non-tariff barriers to trade;
7   assessment of the relative effectiveness and cost of various methods of transportation and distribution;
8   the establishment of short and long-term targets for return on investment;

9   the related financial implications of headings 1–8, including an assessment of the credit and political risks attendant on market entry.

Such a strategy is important because it is essential to:

1   carry out basic research to determine which market(s) offer the best opportunities;
2   assess the scale of investment required to exploit market opportunities;
3   match the investment required with the resources available, and *construct a priority list of markets if necessary*.

The last point is worth emphasising, for by following these steps the firm will not get out of its depth on costs and the most favourable markets can then be approached without sacrifice to general corporate objectives and without making inroads into the projected return on investment. In essence, the approach is to determine those markets which offer the best prospects and then to penetrate these in depth. In turn, this means that if the supplier has to work on a limited budget then, to use a military analogy, he must 'move in on a limited front'.

It is also worth repeating that the 'casual trade' which emanates from overseas without direct effort by the exporter, is undoubtedly valuable and must never be ignored. The structured approach outlined above and the list of priority markets is not intended to convey that it be ignored. The approach outlined does recognise, however, that in today's competitive picture of world trade, such casual business is becoming rarer and an organised approach is necessary if connections of solidity and permanence are to be built up.

Earlier in this Chapter brief reference was made to the marketing mix and the requirement that, in highly competitive markets, it must 'go one better'. Some thoughts on this are now explained.

The export marketing mix

We saw in Chapter 2 how the marketing management process attempts to co-ordinate a set of controllable variables (the marketing mix) within a framework of uncontrollable variables (the environment). Stanton[9] also reminds us that while marketing fundamentals are universally applicable, modifications are often necessary because of the environmental differences existing among and within foreign nations. The implications for the four key variables in the mix – product, price, place and promotion – are worth considering carefully.

Product

Clearly, it must possess such characteristics (e.g. size, colour, shape, nutritional value, warmth, taste, speed, output, etc) as make it totally acceptable to the market. Differences arising from climatic and geographical factors, language, tribal customs, cultural factors, health and safety legislation, types of power supply, etc, often mean that developments or adjustments are necessary to products and services if they are to be successfully marketed overseas. The journals and text books contain countless examples of how such diverse products as shock absorbers, gas turbines, printing materials, air compressors, lawn mowers, furniture and many other types of production have been successful in foreign markets through product strategies derived from a rigorous assessment of market needs. We might begin our considerations by reflecting on the total product concept described in Chapter 6. As we saw there, the total product means more than the product itself for it may incorporate accessories, an installation service, a user guarantee, after-sales service, an operating manual, a package and a brand name. These additional factors count for a great deal at any time but they have an added significance in export marketing, for the user is entitled to trouble-free, continuous use of the product despite being a considerable distance away from the exporter's premises. There is no question that adequate after-sales service, for instance, is often a 'make-or-break' aspect of marketing abroad. No matter how difficult or costly it is to arrange, it simply cannot be neglected. Unfortunately, all too often Britain's competitors, and particularly the Japanese and the Germans, have been seen as pre-eminent in this regard. Of course, we must also bear in mind for a satisfactory total product the supplier is entitled to ask a reasonable price – a point to which we shall return.

Also, product policy for exporting must be based upon those tenets of product policy set out in Chapter 6, i.e.:

1 new products and product modifications must be related to a planned return on investment;

2 anticipated revenues from existing products and markets must be related to projected growth of sales/profits;

3   the firm must then find sufficient new or modified products
to correct any shortfall in profit objectives;
4   product policy must be related to the resources available, bearing in mind that investment budgets may be necessary, perhaps
with lengthy pay-back periods;
5   new product development must therefore be operated upon
a stable base of existing products.

It follows that new and modified products for overseas markets
must be subjected to this same planning framework.

In practice, product decisions for international operations
usually entail modifications to existing products rather than the
development of completely new products. And therefore, some
or all of the following strategies are open to the organisation:

1   *Reformulation of the product itself.* This is usually related to
such factors as: differences in the voltage rates of electricity supply; the need for different design features, colours, materials, etc;
differences arising from geographical or climatic conditions; differences in the levels of technical skill of operatives; differing
legal requirements re health, safety, labelling, etc; taxation and
political requirements necessitating the use of locally made components; economic considerations (e.g. 'a cheaper version for
developing countries'); cultural considerations affecting the use
of foodstuffs, additives, ingredients, brand names, symbols, etc.

2   *Changes in pricing strategy.* These are discussed on page 434.

3   *Changes in packing and presentation.* Climatic, geographical,
economic or cultural considerations may give rise to the need
for these. The question is one of balance – between suitability
to the market, and the preservation of identity and reputation
of the company or brand where this is significant.

4   *Changes in promotional expenditure and content.* In some
cases, extensive consumer 'education' is necessary in order to
launch a product in a foreign market. Heavy initial expenditure
may be required on an 'investment budget' basis.

Or again, the advertising message may have to be modified so
as to take account of the market's level of literacy or its cultural
factors.

These points apply equally to completely new products or to
products which have already been successful in the UK. In the

latter case, changes in promotional expenditure and content may be necessary in order to more clearly align them to the wants and needs of the market. In the strict sense, therefore, the established product may be said to have become a 'new' product.

Harking back to product policy, important general considerations usually arise. For example,

1   whether and to what extent a completely standardised product can be sold worldwide;
2   whether and to what extent the marketing communications strategy can also be standardised.

A number of multinational organisations have been able to operate successfully with a completely standardised product. Perhaps the best examples are the American manufacturers of soft drinks (Coca-Cola; Pepsi-Cola). Within this policy, an internationally known brand name is used to identify a standardised product and local manufacturers are licensed to supply the product under the multinational's brand name, subject to satisfactory performance by the local supplier on quality and output.

It is sometimes the case with a standardised product that the product itself requires no variation, no matter where it is sold. Perhaps the best example here is that of photographic film.

The worldwide growth of advertising, and the way in which it influences wants is another factor assisting product standardisation as is the growth, internationally, of voluntary groups and other forms of distributor cooperation. In such cases, it is often possible for the supplier to launch his product as an *international brand* – by supplying a major distributor with his 'own brand' (as in the past, for example, under the 'Spar-Europ' and 'Euro-Végé' labels).

Packing and packaging are an integral part of the product offering and the design of these for overseas markets should obviously be based not only on a study of market needs but also on the nature of the journey to the market. 'Armchair research' (about which more later) will have clarified:

the nature of the overseas journey;
the nature of transportation and distribution facilities for the overseas journey and within the market;
the climate and geographical features of the journey and the destination market.

Such details will serve to establish:

1   whether it is necessary to devise special outer packs (e.g. to withstand rough handling);
2   whether, because of tropical conditions, particular printing processes should be avoided for packaging/merchandising material;
3   whether any special precautions should be taken for the transit journey (e.g. for products which have a low flash point or are inflammable in solution);
4   whether, because of cultural and religious factors in the market, certain colours and symbols should be avoided.

The size(s) of packages will be influenced by information on:

per capita income; average size of family; storage facilities in the home; level of car ownership; incidence of the newer forms of retailing – e.g. hypermarkets, discount houses; frequency of shopping trips; 'cultural' aspects of the market (e.g. the largest size British package may be among the smallest in the USA; German and Italian users usually prefer larger packages than do French users)

Legal requirements often influence the design of packaging and packing, particularly with regard to the *description* of the product(s) and the declaration of ingredients. Allied to the question of legal requirements is the important issue of *protection of the supplier's trade-mark(s)*. Walsh's book[10] contains some useful notes on these matters.

Beyond these factors, marketing research can usefully demonstrate how best to maximise the promotional value of packaging. Basic data may also indicate whether packaging economies are possible. For example, in countries with a low per capita income, the corrugated 'tube and slide' type of package, with a simple label, might adequately replace the 'presentation' package used in richer markets.

Recent *developments in transport methods* offer some opportunity for manoeuvre on how best the product might be offered to a market. Here are just two examples:

1   because the consequent savings in packing more than compensates for the increased freight rate, a manufacturer of machinery might decide to airfreight his product to the market (an illustration in a previous work by the author[11] shows bottling machinery, devoid of any outer packing, being placed by scissor-lift into a nose-loading aircraft, en-route to Western Europe).

2   Arnold Ceramics might decide to reduce the height of their teacups, enabling them to add an increased number of standard packs of these within the 8 × 8 foot container module – they might then use the resultant savings in distribution costs in order to reduce prices.

The second example presumes that market research has shown that such a change in size would make no difference to user appeal. It is an example which does demonstrate the integrating effect of the newer transport techniques on the various elements of marketing activity. Since these techniques, as described in Chapter 7, offer clear opportunities to reduce distribution costs and also influence design policy and sales policy, they can be seen to bring important considerations for product policy.

Having examined some ideas on product policy for overseas marketing, let us now turn to the closely related variable in the marketing mix – that of price.

Price

In Chapter 6 we saw why pricing is such a fundamentally important process and how pricing policies can be made to serve particular marketing objectives. Such concepts as the price/value dimension; the price/sales volume relationship and its implications for return on investment; price elasticity of demand; external constraints on pricing; price and the product life cycle; price confidence level and pricing techniques (e.g. skimming; penetration) have equal validity whether the market in question is at home or abroad. Certainly no marketing executive should undertake pricing responsibilities in the international field without a sound grasp of general pricing principles. This Section will take such knowledge as 'given', and concentrate on the special, additional requirements of the approach to pricing for foreign markets. In order to introduce the topic, what follows is an outline of a single approach to pricing an individual product for a market abroad (any unfamiliar terms will be explained before the end of the Chapter).

An approach to pricing strategy for an overseas market:

1   Define the product's tariff classification in the importing country (through initial research in the UK).
2   With the assistance of forwarding agents, calculate freight

and insurance costs, handling and storage costs, customs duties, etc, either on the individual product or on a 'standard consignment'.

3   Through contacts in the overseas market (e.g. intending agents and distributors, UK Government commercial representatives) obtain information on: agents' sales commission rates; trade margins and discounts at all stages of distribution; local taxes, including any taxes specific to the exporter's product.

(*Note.* 1–3 above should all be re-checked during subsequent market visits.)

4   The foregoing information will provide a reasonable idea of the product's ultimate selling price in the market. The assessment is usually based on the 'prevailing method' of distribution, is calculated upon some base price determined by marketing policy (e.g. 'cost plus'; marginal costing) and is usually calculated upon the ex works or f.o.b. price for a standard product in standard packaging and packing. The 'final' price so determined can then be compared with prices of competing products.

5   If the final price is higher than the confidence level established by competing products some options may be open to the exporter. These are set out below.

(*a*) Does an analysis of competing products show that the exporter's product has:

a better specification,

or better performance,

or better design

or greater durability

or better accessories

or better after-sales service

than competing products? i.e. is the higher price offset by compensating advantages? If so, can this superior value for money be effectively communicated to the market? Is the price confidence level well established, or might it be possible to 'trade up' the price? Might it be better to direct the sales campaign to a richer segment of the market?

(*b*) Could designers/production engineers conduct a *value analysis* study, comparing costs with functions, to clarify whether the same performance could be obtained at lower cost (e.g. by using a brazed instead of a soldered assembly)?

(*c*) If it was intended to provide accessories within the final selling price, are these necessary or are they merely marginal to the use of the product overseas?

(d) Can economies be made in packaging/presentation?... e.g. by replacing presentation packaging with a plain package + label?

(e) Could costs be reduced by using a different type of outer packing?... or by increasing the size of the standard pack for distributors?... or by using different transport methods (e.g. containerised or other 'unit load' methods)?

(f) How does the proposed marketing communications budget compare with those of competitors?... can economies be made here?... e.g. can market entry be switched to the production of 'own brand' merchandise for leading distributors?

(g) What are the credit terms and levels of after-sales service being offered by competitors? If the exporter's proposed level of after-sales service is clearly superior, can this be exploited by promotion (as in (a) above), or could sales be maintained although economies were made in the service level (Note the exporter would have to consider such a strategy very carefully, particularly in an overseas market, and (a) would appear to be the sounder idea).

(h) Would it be useful to conduct some form of 'price/volume' study? (see Chapter 6). The price would be chosen which best serves the overall marketing strategy and planned growth of profits.

(i) The implications of the marginal costing approach are that when total fixed costs have been recovered, any price beyond the variable cost per unit of production will yield some return. Related to this is the desirability of considering fully any manufacturing or other economies (e.g. in the purchase of components, raw materials, etc) which would result from the extra sales volume. Possibly these may support a price reduction.

(j) Thus far, the assumption may have been that the product would be marketed by using the prevailing method of distribution. This raises the question whether, with a consumer product for example, the competitive position might be improved if the importer/wholesaler position was skirted, by 'going direct' to central buying organisations and large retailers. Similarly, there might be a possibility of obtaining standard shipping quantities from retailers by granting them exclusive selling rights within defined areas.

(k) Further to (j), where products are subject to a turnover tax, levied each time the goods change hands, then the longer the chain of distribution, the greater the effect of the tax on the

final selling price. The problem is intensified if the tax is cumulative in its effect (i.e. the 'cascade' effect) rather than a tax
on value added (which allows the trader to deduct from his
liability for tax the amount of tax levied on the product at
earlier stages).

The aim of the approach outlined above is to demonstrate some
of the typical issues that relate to pricing decisions for foreign
markets. There are one or two other points which should be made
clear. The first concerns *price quotations*. There are many variants
in overseas trade, ranging from *ex works* at a named town of departure to *delivered, duty paid* at a named destination point in the
country of importation and, of course, they mean that a greater
or lesser degree of cost and responsibility within the export contract of sale fall upon the supplier. For example, the main types
of quotation between the 'ex works' or 'delivered, duty paid'
quotations are:

F.a.s. (free alongside ship). These initials would accompany the
name of an appropriate port ('f.a.s. Liverpool, Garston Dock').
Under this contract, transit charges in the UK and insurance cover
as may be appropriate, up to the point where the goods are placed
alongside the designated vessel, are the responsibility of the
seller. The buyer must secure the shipping opportunity, pay the
loading charges from the dockside to the vessel and bear all
expenses thereafter, including freight and insurance costs from
that point onwards and any duties payable before delivery to
final destination.

F.o.b. (free on board). Again the letters do not stand alone but
are used as a prefix to a named port, e.g. 'f.o.b. Felixstowe' or
perhaps 'f.o.b. UK Port'. When the buyer agrees an f.o.b. price,
the exporter will meet all costs up to the point where he has
placed the goods on board a designated vessel and the buyer meets
all the costs from that point onwards.

C.i.f. (cost, insurance and freight). This quotation tells the buyer
the cost of goods at a port or airport in his own country (e.g.
'c.i.f. Schiphol'). Under the c.i.f. contract, the exporter's costs
include all those entering into the f.o.b. price with the addition
of sea or air freight charges plus insurance. The quotation makes
it 'easier for the buyer to buy' for it tells him the complete cost
of the goods at some destination convenient for his own premises.

He is also relieved of the tasks of arranging shipping space and insurance.

Of course, when it is stated that the 'exporter bears the costs' of particular operations these are not a charge against his own profits and are fully recoverable in the export quotation. The point being made is rather that certain quotations place greater duties and responsibilities on the seller but make it easier for the buyer to buy and vice versa. Obviously, a quotation delivered, duty paid to the buyer's warehouse, and expressed in the buyer's currency, or a main trading currency such as the US dollar, leave the buyer free to compute trade margins and local taxes in order to arrive at his final selling price. Taking these extra pains can be profitable, since it might project the exporter in a more favourable light than less caring suppliers. Making it easy for the buyer to buy is at the core of the marketing philosophy but the prudent exporter always has to bear in mind that against the increased chances of doing business must be measured the degree of risk which might emanate from adverse movements in transport costs and exchange rates (although these can always be guarded against – for instance, by entering into a forward contract with the exporter's own bank for the sale of the foreign currency).

A final point concerning export quotations: it is very important that the exporter sets out the precise nature of his meanings and intentions so that the responsibility and expenses of both parties are definitely and unmistakably fixed. The International Chamber of Commerce has done significant work in eradicating the dangers of misunderstandings. In its *Incoterms* it has published standard interpretations of the most commonly used quotations (f.o.b.; c.i.f. etc), setting out clearly the obligations of both buyer and seller and this has been widely adopted for application to international sale contracts. The exporter can therefore make the proposed extent of his own responsibility transparently clear merely by adding the expression 'Incoterms' as a suffix to his quotation. If the buyer agrees to be bound by these terms, there will be no problems and the seller should refer the buyer to the latest edition of the International Chamber's Incoterms publication for this purpose (1980 edition, at the time of writing).

Note The author was associated with the Export Committee of the Northamptonshire Chamber of Commerce and Industry. To assist members, a wall chart has been produced depicting Incoterms. A number of members have reduced the chart to A4 size – as depicted in Fig. 13.1,

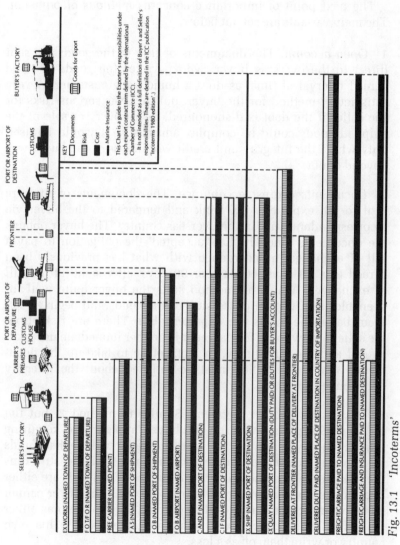

Fig. 13.1 'Incoterms'

KEY
☐ Documents
▥ Risk
■ Cost
▬ Marine Insurance

This Chart is a guide to the Exporter's responsibilities under each export contract term defined by the international Chamber of Commerce (ICC).
It is not intended as a full definition of Buyer's and Seller's responsibilities. These are detailed in the ICC publication 'Incoterms 1980 edition '.

▥ Goods for Export

SELLER'S FACTORY   CARRIER'S PREMISES   PORT OR AIRPORT OF DEPARTURE CUSTOMS HOUSE   FRONTIER   PORT OR AIRPORT OF DESTINATION CUSTOMS   BUYER'S FACTORY

EX WORKS (NAMED TOWN OF DEPARTURE)
F O T (F O R (NAMED TOWN OF DEPARTURE)
FREE CARRIER (NAMED POINT)
F A S (NAMED PORT OF SHIPMENT)
F O B (NAMED PORT OF SHIPMENT)
F O B AIRPORT (NAMED AIRPORT)
C AND F (NAMED PORT OF DESTINATION)
C I F (NAMED PORT OF DESTINATION)
EX SHIP (NAMED PORT OF DESTINATION)
EX QUAY NAMED PORT OF DESTINATION (DUTY PAID) OR (DUTIES FOR BUYER'S ACCOUNT)
DELIVERED AT FRONTIER (NAMED PLACE OF DELIVERY AT FRONTIER)
DELIVERED DUTY PAID (NAMED PLACE OF DESTINATION IN COUNTRY OF IMPORTATION)
FREIGHT/CARRIAGE PAID TO (NAMED DESTINATION)
FREIGHT/CARRIAGE AND INSURANCE PAID TO (NAMED DESTINATION)

and include a copy with their quotations to foreign buyers. In this way, what is being proposed by the seller in the export quotation can be made absolutely clear.

The next point of importance concerns *methods of payment*. The main variants are set out below.

1 *Open account*. The documents of title to the goods are sent direct to the overseas buyer, who pays for the goods at some agreed interval of time, as does a home trade customer. A very satisfactory method for the buyer, but involves serious risks for the seller if the debt is dishonoured, for recovery or sale of the shipped goods could be complex and costly. It would be used only where the integrity and credit worthiness of the buyer was beyond doubt.

2 *Documents against acceptance*. The documents of title are sent to the exporter's UK bank and tendered to the buyer via a correspondent bank in the overseas country. The buyer obtains the documents when he has 'accepted' the obligation to pay a bill of exchange in accordance with what has previously been agreed (e.g. 30 days, 60 days or 90 days 'after sight' of the bill of exchange). Again the method suits the buyer quite well for it enables him to take possession of the goods and begin to sell them before he meets the exporter's bill. There are risks from the seller's viewpoint, for payment is neither immediate nor guaranteed and the buyer may, in fact, refuse to take up the documents. Again, the seller must be satisfied about the integrity of the buyer.

3 *Documents against payment*. Similar to method 2, but the bill of exchange is drawn on the buyer 'at sight' (i.e. requiring immediate payment). In this case the seller will realise funds for the transaction without extending credit but he still runs the risk that the payment is not guaranteed. The goods are either at a foreign port or airport or in transit to it. If the buyer cannot make payment or repudiates the contract, the exporter has either to find an alternative buyer, ship the goods back to his own country or write them off as a loss.

4 *Documentary letter of credit*. This is a sure and prompt method of obtaining payment. The buyer is required to arrange through his own bank for a letter of credit to be established and he agrees

that his bank instructs a bank in the exporter's country to pay the exporter provided documents are presented which *exactly conform* to the buyer's instructions and descriptions as specified in the documentary credit.

Where the letter of credit is *irrevocable*, the exporter has the irrevocable undertaking of the issuing bank that if he complies with the terms of the credit, drafts on the bank appropriate to the credit will be honoured. If the credit is *revocable*, on the other hand, it can be altered or cancelled by the buyer without the seller's consent and without notice to him. With the irrevocable credit the exporter's position is improved and further improved if the issuing bank will authorise a UK bank to add its own *confirmation* to the credit. Although this confirmed, irrevocable credit completely secures the seller, provided he fully complies with its conditions, it involves the buyer in greater trouble and expense. He may be required to pay over immediately an appropriate sum in his own currency in order for the issuing bank to establish the credit including an appropriate fee for his bank's guarantee, plus the confirmation fee of the UK bank.

5 *Cash with order.* It is difficult to imagine an exporter developing worthwhile sales turnover if he insisted upon payment from his foreign customers before despatching the consignment, or even perhaps producing the goods. Nevertheless it is a method of payment and might well be used if the manufacture of a costly, purpose-built product of exclusive design was being undertaken. Where considerable expense is involved, provision may be made for progress payments at succeeding stages of manufacture.

The methods of payment to be adopted will depend upon the financial resources of the exporter, the type of products involved, the creditworthiness of customer(s), etc, but it would be true to say that the easier it is for the buyer to buy, the greater the risk to the exporter and a skilled marketing approach will achieve a nicety of balance here. Fig. 13.2 (p. 442) depicts diagrammatically the risk/opportunity aspects of financing exports.

It should also be noted that the credit risk can be covered by insuring against such loss, particularly through the services of the Export Credits Guarantee Department of HM Government (ECGD). The work of ECGD is outlined in a later Section of this Chapter.

Before leaving this necessarily brief glimpse of price as an element of the export marketing mix there is a third point to make.

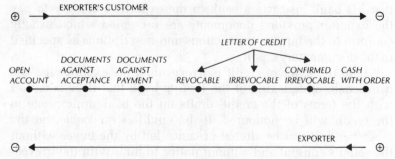

Fig. 13.2 Export methods of payment: risk and opportunity

In some sense, it has been made before but it is worth repeating. 'Being competitive' does not necessarily mean quoting the lowest price. Research demonstrates that in many overseas markets the reliability of the supplier, the level of after-sales service and the consistency of quality of his products often count for more than price. The axiom 'to be clear what we mean by price' is an important one. Marketing organisations must clearly convey what is being offered for what is being asked. This is important for all products and has added significance for industrial products, when the price being asked is for a *total product* which often comprises not only the product itself but an equally vital installation service, user guarantee, after-sales service and may even extend to the training of operatives.

Place

We now come to the third element in our export marketing mix. As we recognise from previous reading (Chapter 7) distribution policy is based upon considerations of methods of physical distribution and of marketing channels.

Balancing the costs and benefits of various methods of physical distribution includes a consideration of such factors as:

any special requests of the customer;

the required speed of transit;

the climatic and geographical conditions of the journey;

the volume/weight/value of the consignment(s);

the physical nature and chemical composition of the product(s);

the freight, packing and insurance charges incurred by the various methods of physical distribution.

Reviewing these factors will mean, in many instances, the review of:

the whole broad field of containerisation;

the economics of palletisation and the 'unit load';

the pros and cons of 'roll-on/roll-off' road vehicle services, air freight services, train ferry services;

other considerations, including the use of company transport or contract haulage and the availability of forwarding agents, 'groupage' services.

For many companies, particularly exporting companies, the best prospects to out-distance competitors may lie in the field of distribution rather than production. Imagine that an organisation new to exporting employs the latest production techniques and has a highly trained labour force so as to fully match its competitors. Might it not have its priorities wrong if it is pushing its labour force to the limit in order to make marginal improvements on product quality and product costs when at the same time it has little or no idea of its total distribution costs? It is an issue worthy of close thought when one recalls that, with many of the newer transport techniques, the cost savings are *indirect* rather than direct (that is, in cost elements such as packing and insurance rather than freight rates). It is also worth remembering that, according to research sponsored by the Centre for Physical Distribution Management[12] freight transport as an element of the distribution cost is likely to increase from an average of 5.5 per cent of retail sales price in 1978 to an average of 7.4 per cent in 1990.

There are countless examples available from transport organisations of how preoccupation with freight rates can lead to incorrect assessments of the least-cost method for a particular export consignment. The point being made seems commonplace – items additional to the freight rate clearly have to be taken into account. Yet when we consider *total* distribution costs, we are only at the beginning of the calculation, for we have also to consider factors such as warehousing costs and interest on capital. It is interesting to note here that the cost of carrying stock to service a customer or a market can amount to as much as 25 per cent of production cost. Even at that point, we are merely considering which transport technique offers the least cost method for moving a specific consignment to a particular market. If we consider the *total predicted sales volume* for that market, total distribution cost analysis can be employed to inform us of the least-cost method at that volume and at significant 'break-points' above and below that volume.

The transport developments since the mid 1960s have been significant for Britain's exporters. Being separated from her markets by a stretch of water was more than a psychological barrier to her performance for it gave rise to real problems connected with delivery times and delivery costs. The newer techniques have done a great deal to close the gap between Britain and her more favourably placed competitors but to secure full value from them it is important that management takes an adequately sophisticated view of their costs and benefits. Raising as they do important questions of financial policy and product policy as well as distribution policy, the time is gone when the export manager can say 'I leave such things to the transport manager, he has a good head on his shoulders'.

Of course, the new exporter will have little use for more complex applications of total distribution cost analysis but in his case there is still significant work for the lower reaches of the technique to do, if it only ensures that he does not stay preoccupied with freight rates. And again, as hopefully, sales turnover develops total distribution, cost analysis can be extended to solve more complex problems. Consider, for example, a manufacturer of engineering components pondering whether to establish a warehouse on the European mainland in order to give an intensively good service to its mass assembly plants. He may do one of two things:

1   he may make a purely subjective judgement and say: 'the business is building up, it's about time we put a warehouse there', or

2   he may make a thorough cost analysis of the whole project and compare the alternatives, e.g. by sea ex UK/European warehouse thence by road to customers or by air transport ex UK thence by local delivery to customers,

in order to establish the volume break-points at which each of the alternatives becomes the least-cost method. Since the matter is too complex and expensive for subjective judgement, the exporter will be better served with the second approach. The earnest student of marketing will remember that it is to do with measurement and return on investment and he will therefore find a fruitful field of enquiry in the field of physical distribution for exports.

Marketing channel policy usually entails, at the first stage, an examination of the prevailing method of distribution. On the one hand, it may be completely unrealistic for a new exporter to attempt to divert business from the customary channels. On the other hand, the exporter may see competition so strongly entrenched that market entry can perhaps best be obtained by adopting a different policy, perhaps through concentrating upon a specialised segment of the market. There are no absolutes except perhaps to note that the prevailing method of distribution can, and frequently does, vary from the UK prevailing method. What is more, within what may seem a fairly integrated marketing region of the world, such as Western Europe, there is usually a variety of prevailing methods to be found.

Indeed, we need look no further than Western Europe in order to underline the importance of studying each market closely and individually before deciding upon distribution policy. If we look at the Table on page 426 we see that Federal Germany and France are both in the top tier of Britain's markets. They are neighbouring countries and have been partners in the European Community since its inception. They are both industrialised countries with high purchasing power. Yet in the distribution of consumer goods they exhibit decidedly different structural patterns. In the Federal Republic, for example, central and co-operative purchasing is even more highly developed than it is in the UK. In fact, concentration in the following main groups:

1 Central purchasing (purchasing co-operatives)
2 Department stores
3 Hypermarkets
4 Cash and carry outlets

has been regarded by some observers as one of the major obstacles to selling in Western Germany. Throughout the 1970s the growth of large retail groups (with five or more branches) has continued to make inroads into the market share of the independent retailers, as the table on p. 446 shows.

The German Institute for Economics (IFO) has studied the share of the total retail market obtained by the major outlets and it estimates that against a 31.2 per cent share in 1970 and a 36 per cent share in 1977, they would have reached a 50 per cent share by 1985.

In France, by contrast, the small independent shopkeepers account for 70 per cent of all retail sales and shopping areas

Table 13.2 The Federal Republic of Germany: retail turnover in major outlets (percentage of total retail trade)

	Specialist retail stores				
Year	1–4 branches	5+ branches	Department stores	Mail order	Co-operatives
1965	72.4	11.1	9.3	4.2	3.0
1974	65.3	16.5	10.4	4.7	3.1
1975	64.4	17.5	10.4	4.6	3.1
1976	64.4	17.9	9.9	4.7	3.1
1977	64.0	18.6	9.5	4.8	3.1

Source: *Marketing consumer goods in West Germany* British Overseas Trade Board 1979

throughout the country are characterised by the absence of the multiples. The only national store networks are owned by the department stores (Printemps; Nouvelles Galeries), the variety stores (Prisunic; Monoprix) and certain chainstore organisations in the footwear and maternity wear fields. It is also significant that in the food sector the largest retail groups (Casino; Docks Remois) are still regional. With over 569 000 retailers and more than 85 000 wholesalers France has traditionally been regarded as a formidable market for British exporters because of its lack of concentrated buying power. A far cry from the distribution system in neighbouring West Germany where concentration has developed beyond the production capacity of some manufacturers to supply it effectively! A closer look at the prevailing method of distribution invariably raises intriguing questions. Why, for example, is the mail order trade in West Germany, with an approximate five per cent share, so dynamic, when in France, where it began, it has attained less than half that figure? There are, of course, significant geographical, social, economic and cultural reasons underlying all distribution statistics and until the marketing executive has scrutinised them he cannot begin to probe deeper into causes, which is his raison d'être. The moral, therefore, is to 'look at the figures' and to take nothing for granted bearing in mind too that the prevailing method may be a 'must' or may be the signal to do something different.

Comparing the effectiveness of various marketing channels means comparing the costs and efficiency of each method, 'efficiency' being taken to mean an adequate level of availability for the user (given the rate of stock-turn of the product(s) in question), an adequate level of after-sales service and an adequate level of dealer goodwill.

As indicated above, examining the 'structure' of the market

means discovering the relative importance of 'independent' retailers, multiples, department stores, consumer co-operatives and mail order organisations. The significance of the wholesale trade, franchising and direct distribution methods must also be weighed carefully.

Distributors' profit margins and discounts, quantity discounts, 'internal' sales taxes, the creditworthiness of the distributors, the necessity of stock-holding in the market and the possibility of negotiating contracts for the supply of 'own brand' merchandise must all be weighed carefully. For industrial products, complex plant and equipment, requiring a skilled installation and maintenance service would usually be marketed on a 'direct to user' basis. For other industrial supplies (e.g. small tools, industrial adhesives etc) the 'prevailing method' may disclose an importer/wholesaler stage is so well entrenched that to attempt to divert business from it might prove both costly and abortive. Some exporters have found, however, that concluding arrangements for the introduction of products through local manufacturers of allied or even similar lines has proved very effective. Mention of this underlines the fact that distribution policy is closely linked with a consideration of the costs and benefits of the various types of sales organisation which could be adopted within the foreign market. This aspect is discussed in the latter part of the Section on promotion which follows.

Finally, continuing attention must be paid to the structure of distribution in the market for if a changing pattern is becoming apparent, policy decisions must take account of it. For example, mention has been made of the fragmented nature of French retailing. Yet, as a BOTB survey[13] has remarked, important changes have been taking place. For example:

1 because of the decline of town centres, hundreds of new stores have opened on the fringe of urban areas – these include hypermarkets and also new specialist stores for furniture, household goods and garden requisites;

2 there has been rapid growth of suburban centres, such as Parly 2 and Rosny 2, near Paris – often these centres have a hypermarket at the core and are surrounded by a large number of shops and specialist boutiques;

3 these developments have had a marked effect on the traditional town centre retailers who have taken steps, including self-defensive convergences, in order to survive;

4   these and other protective groupings of independent retailers are now beginning to offer to British exporters the central purchasing organisations that make the task of distribution easier;
5   many foreign retail chains have now moved into France, including Burton, Habitat, Marks and Spencer, Jaeger and WH Smith (Britain); Quelle, Neckermann (West Germany); C & A (Holland) and Jelmoli (Switzerland).

The influence of such changes will clearly emerge in this decade and the enterprising exporter will obviously take them fully into account.

Promotion

Many of the general principles of planning marketing communications, as set out in Chapter 8, are equally applicable to both domestic and foreign markets. This Section will concentrate on points of particular relevance to overseas operations.

Typical objectives for promotional campaigns in foreign markets are these:

1   to enter the market by promoting products or services where, in this sense, both supplier and product are 'new' to the market;
2   to promote the sale of a new product or service in a market abroad where the exporter is already established;
3   to support the sale of established products or services in an 'established' foreign market; and/or
4   to inform and educate users and dealers about the exporting organisation and its objectives and to influence attitudes towards the organisation.

It is worth repeating that wherever the campaign is staged its ultimate objective must be to serve the company goal of an adequate return on investment (i.e. through 'buying' sales revenue at an acceptable cost). It follows from this that the strategic ideas of checks on expenditure and monitoring the campaign in relation to its objectives (strategic and tactical) as set out in Chapter 8 are just as valid when planning campaigns for overseas and therefore must not be neglected.

At the planning stage, some decision will have to be taken on how the campaign will be organised and controlled. The main options open are these:

1   through the overseas associates or subsidiaries of the firm's UK advertising agency;

2   via the firm's UK advertising agency, either working direct with overseas media or through the UK representatives of those media;

3   by the firm working direct with foreign advertising agencies or possibly foreign media;

4   in small, or undeveloped, markets (and perhaps at the first stage only), through the firm's foreign sales agent or main distributor.

The criteria for selection of one or other of these methods will include:

(a) the number and geographical spread of markets in which the organisation is seeking to operate;

(b) the size of funding available;

(c) the degree of sophistication required in media choice and creativity;

(d) the presence or absence of the firm's own manufacturing/sales organisation(s) in the market(s) abroad.

(*Note.* As a rule method 3 above is more appropriate to the large organisation with its own advertising department. Method 4 is not to be recommended unless the market is small and lacks promotional facilities and sophistication.)

Most campaigns will utilise some or all of the following three elements:

advertising,

sales promotion,

publicity,

(these elements having been defined in Chapter 8). The fourth element of marketing communications, personal selling, is of particular importance and will be discussed later in this Section.

The balance of the first three elements will be governed by the media sophistication and facilities in the market and the activities of resident and foreign competitors, but two general points should be noted:

1   the use of exhibitions abroad is often of decided value, particular to new exporters.

2   similarly the use of publicity techniques to create a favourable 'atmosphere' for the firm and its products is also very valuable.

Publicity is usually achieved by means of editorial articles in newspapers and magazines and programmes on radio and television in which the organisation, its products, processes or discoveries receive favourable attention. HM Government provides a great deal of help in this regard, as we shall see later in this Chapter. Public relations officers and consultants at home and abroad can also assist the exporter to prepare and utilise interesting, idiomatically translated, press releases, publicity films and tape and slide presentations – the very 'stuff' of export publicity.

We remember that *campaign planning* hinges on the questions of:

WHAT should be said,

WHERE it should be said, and

HOW it should be said.

The WHAT question has broad implications for overseas campaigns. Should it be a *standardised message*, for example? Taking the instance of Western Europe, such a strategy would entail a common brand identity, market segmentation policy, and creative theme for each country but it would permit of local variations to ensure that any particular linguistic, legal or social constraints were taken into account. Such an approach would be particularly appropriate where:

1   the user population is inured to sophisticated techniques of marketing communication (as in the USA, UK, Sweden, Switzerland and Federal Germany, for example);

2   the buyer motives and informational needs are the same for most, if not all markets (as would be the case for a complex, technical product bought by industrial users on specific details of price, rate and quality of output, durability, after-sales service, etc).

Standardisation of the promotional approach would also bring with it cost reductions in such ancillaries as blocks, artwork and film production but it might be self-defeating if the results were so bland that the campaign failed to achieve impact. In such a case, the sales message, from country to country, would need to be more particularised. For example, the message for a pharmaceutical product might range from a fairly detailed description of its beneficial action on the nervous system (for countries with a high level of literacy) to a simple 'before and after illustration' of its effects (for countries with a low level of literacy).

The *where* question in campaign planning relates to *the use of media* and, as explained in Chapter 8, this involves a consideration of the:

characteristics,

'atmosphere',
quantitative coverage, and
cost

of the media available in the market(s) under examination. One cannot usefully add much to what has been said in Chapter 8 on media characteristics, 'atmosphere' and cost but the factor of *quantitative coverage* deserves an extra word.

As we know, campaign planning is based on the matching of media characteristics to the user characteristics determined by market research. In the developed economies of the West, details of press circulation and readership and of the composition of television audiences are available from independent research sources. For example, in the United Kingdom, the Audit Bureau of Circulations, the National Readership Surveys and Audits of Great Britain (AGB) have a significant role in marketing communications. Such syndicated research services as the Target Group Index (TGI) relate media usage to actual purchasing behaviour. But the advertiser operating in foreign markets must satisfy himself that, insofar as local conditions permit, the quantitative data upon which media selection is to be based is as accurate and objective as possible (another point in favour of using the UK advertising agency in a co-ordinating role). Some foreign research data has necessarily to be approached with caution. An extremely useful publication in this regard is the latest edition of *The International Research Directory* of market research organisations published jointly by The Market Research Society and the British Overseas Trade Board.

Although cost and budget calculations are identical, in principle, to those for UK marketing, it is useful to note that entering markets abroad may have to adopt the *investment budget* technique, undertaking a disproportionately heavy expenditure in the introductory stages. The period before 'pay back' may be quite lengthy, particularly in highly competitive markets. Again, this points up the importance of accurate preliminary marketing research and the construction of a priority list for market entry if financial factors so dictate.

So much for the *what* and the *where* of campaign planning. The question of *how* relates to the *method* of transmitting the message. We have seen earlier (Chapter 8, pages 301–4) that this is usually taken up with considerations of:

1   the creative approach;

2   the relationship between the creative approach and the budget available
3   the market segment to which the message will be directed.

Some additional factors for campaigns abroad should be stressed, including:

1   the market's legal regulations affecting the *content* of advertising messages (especially concerning claims made for the product);
2   the social and religious conventions of the market (related to the role of women, for example);
3   the subjective attributes of colour in certain markets and cultures;
4   by no means least, the absolute necessity of obtaining correct, idiomatic translations of advertising 'copy'.

Readers seeking some practical reward from this book need look no further than point 4 above. If they are prevented from making some of the mistakes made in the past by aspiring exporters, the book will more than justify its price. Textbooks and business magazines are replete with grave warnings. Because the importance of correct translations seems such a truism, acknowledgment of its real significance is often ignored. Yet it would be an easy task to produce a compendium of international howlers from the mistakes we read and hear about. In order to demonstrate the substance of the issue, a short list of examples follows, together with the name of the writer to whom the author owes each particular point.

Marketing communications: some unintended outcomes

1   Stanton[14] points out that in some languages Pepsi-Cola's 'come alive' slogan translates as 'come out of the grave'.
2   McCarthy[15] indicates that some manufacturers have found that placing an illustration of a baby on food packages is unwise, for in markets with a low level of literacy the contents are taken to be a ground-up baby.
3   According to Walsh[16] a Thai national once recalled a translation of advertising copy in which 'out of sight out of mind' had become 'invisible things are insane'.
4   Kitler[17] writes: 'in Spain, Chevrolet's "Nova" translates as "no va", which means "it doesn't go"!'
5   Boone and Kurtz[18] make this observation: 'Consider the problems associated with using the "Body by Fisher" slogan for

General Motors cars. In some translations it comes out "Corpse by Fisher".'

The foregoing examples are humorous but they make a serious point. It is a point which came home to the author very early in his own career. He had cabled an Australian agent with enthusiasm to explain that samples of a product were on the way to him, adding that in Britain it had 'gone like a bomb'. The agent replied that he was sorry to hear this. In subsequent contacts, it emerged that in the agent's country a 'bomb' is the colloquial expression for a broken down motor vehicle.

In concluding this Section, further reference should be made to the question of the financial allocations to various media. UK campaigns typically employ certain media (e.g. the press, television) as *primary* media, with other media (e.g. radio, exhibitions, outdoor advertising) as *secondary*, or support, media. Now it is often the case that problems associated with literacy or the non-availability of certain media abroad demand a different approach. The importance of exhibitions and publicity as primary media abroad has already been touched upon – beyond this, radio, posters and other outdoor advertising often have a *primary* role, especially in developing countries, for the reasons just indicated.

Export marketing research

Having considered how the four key variables in the marketing mix might be co-ordinated into an export marketing plan, let us step back a stage further in the process and consider the marketing research process for export planning. This Section will provide supplementary information (in an international context, that is) to the general description of marketing research set out in Chapter 3.

The research process typically comprises:

1   desk or 'armchair' research (usually UK based)
2   field research (in the market abroad).

'Armchair' research involves the gathering and analysis of *secondary data*, as defined in Chapter 3, and sources of such data include the following:

• The British Overseas Trade Board and its Statistics and Market Intelligence Library

- The exporter's bank and its 'correspondent' banks overseas
- The local Chamber of Commerce
- The exporter's Trade Association
- UK forwarding agents and transport companies
- UK marketing research organisations specialising in international trade (e.g. the Economist Intelligence Unit, which conducts surveys on behalf of client companies and whose general publications include the monthly *Marketing in Europe* and quarterly *Economic Reviews* covering a total of 160 countries)
- The Export Credits Guarantee Department of HM Government (ECGD)
- The Confederation of British Industry (CBI)
- The Institute of Export
- The Institute of Marketing
- Foreign embassies in UK and UK embassies abroad
- Foreign trade organisations collaborating with UK (e.g. The British-German Trade Council, British Hellenic Chamber of Commerce, The Netherlands-British Chamber of Commerce – whose services are set out in Fig. 13.3)
- The Statistics Office of the European Community (Eurostat)
- Appropriate newspapers and journals (e.g. *Export* journal of the Institute of Export, *Marketing* journal of the Institute of Marketing and *The Financial Times* which publishes a great deal of relevant information, including detailed economic surveys of overseas countries).

The purpose of armchair research is to indicate those markets which appear to offer the greatest potential and which could be examined in greater depth by personal visits and discussions with potential users, agents and distributors. A check list for this type of research can be constructed from the strategy factors listed on page 428. The use of a check list for each market will then facilitate market comparisons.

Where desk research provides sufficient encouragement field research can be subsequently undertaken but it may well be that an intelligent analysis of secondary data will, of itself, point the way clearly to market opportunities. Let us consider an example. Jenner,[19] for instance, points out that in Western Europe:

The big importing countries, relative to population size, are Belgium, Norway, Netherlands, Switzerland and Denmark, small countries with a narrow industrial base.

Now the exporter may discover that data on the volume, value

Services of The Netherlands-British Chamber of Commerce

NB

General	Marketing	Management	Publicity	Regional
Group Telex	Marketing Research	Language Training	Publicity for members	Scottish Advisory Committee
Continuous Contracts	Market Reports	Critique Panels	Publicity for Chamber	North West Advisory Committee
Anglo-Dutch Trade Bulletin	Agents Search	Clearing House Scheme	Magazine "In Touch"	East Anglia Advisory Committee
Trade information	Names and addresses	Mergers/Joint Ventures	P. R. Service	British Business Association
Directories	Buyers Panels	Licensing Research		South West Advisory Committee
Exhibition information	Periodicals	Trade Regulations		Netherlands Regional Advisory Committee
Mailing services	Mini-surveys	Tariff and Customs		
Translations	Trade Announcements	Financial Reports		
Membership		Debt Recovery		
Computer		Taxation		
		Investment		

Information

A desk information service is available for quick replies for a wide variety of questions and problems relating to Anglo-Dutch commercial matters

Marketing Services

The Chamber's most important function. Staffed with qualified, fully bilingual personnel, the Marketing Service department offers a broad range of practical marketing facilities, involving all aspects of Anglo-Dutch trade.

Market Research

Brief or exhaustive, this service can be adapted to suit individual needs. Information can be supplied on:
* Market size
* Market structure
* Competition
* Distribution patterns
* Market preferences and trends
* Advertising media

General

Responsible for services other than marketing and information with special reference to investment, joint ventures and establishment of business in both countries

Agency/Distributor Search

The Chamber's research staff in Britain and the Netherlands obtain full details of your product or service in order to search for and select suitable trading partners, willing and able to handle the commodity you offer. This is accompanied by an announcement in the Chamber's widely read Anglo-Dutch Trade opportunities Bulletin.

Clearing House Scheme

This scheme is a service for members who are involved in the purchase of British, Dutch or overseas companies and in some cases the development of joint ventures.

Critique Panel

The aim of The Netherlands-British Chamber of Commerce Critique Panel is to provide a service whereby you as British and Dutch businessmen can be subjected to and learn about the differences in cultural and behavioural attitudes.

Public Relations

Our public relations officer has many long standing connections with the media in both Great Britain and The Netherlands. His most important task is helping Chamber members and others with their own publicity requirements and problems. You should always consider him as your first call when thinking about your own publicity.

The aim of the Chamber is to get the right Dutch and British businessmen to meet and discuss profit.

Regional Advisory Committees

meet monthly to encourage Anglo-Dutch trade.

Among the members are those already active in this two-way trade who are willing to help others in their regions.

In Touch

The magazine is published at the beginning of each month and is sent to all our members as well as to libraries and other reference sources in both countries.

Readership is at least 10,000 per issue. Incorporated in the centre of the magazine is our Anglo-Dutch Trade Bulletin which is printed on distinctive blue pages and gives you and others the opportunity to place announcements and advertisements.

PLEASE NOTE

A wide range of our services are free to members. Appropriate charges are made to members for special work or where exceptional expenditure is incurred. Work for non-members carries a 50% non-members surcharge.

Fig. 13.3   The services of The Netherlands – British Chamber of Commerce

and type of his particular products being imported into one or more of these countries when compared to statistics of the potential market and the volume of local production (if any) discloses that a significant supply-gap exists for an efficient exporter. Generally, however, desk research precedes a field survey in the market which sets out to obtain primary data on how best the 4Ps of the marketing mix can best be offered for maximum acceptability.

A warning note at this point. Desk research is a fundamental part of the research process and should never be neglected. However, it is important to ensure that the data so obtained:

1   is *relevant* to the marketing problem (bearing in mind that the original acquisition of secondary data is usually quite unconnected with the problem under review);
2   is *up-to-date*;
3   is sufficiently *accurate* for its intended purpose.

The reader must bear in mind that many foreign sources of data, particularly those of developing countries, fall markedly short of the UK Government's statistical service. There is no point in attempting to make assessments between markets unless a sound basis for statistical comparability is present.

Field research abroad requires careful planning and oversight. Problems arise because of the environmental factors – linguistic, cultural, geographical and economic, which differentiate international from domestic marketing. Some countries offer facilities for field research of equivalent standard to those of the UK. Other countries do not.

In the Federal Republic of Germany, for example, facilities exist for ad hoc and continuous consumer research, advertising research, industrial marketing research, packaging research, product testing, attitude and behavioural research, etc. By constrast, if facilities exist at all in many of the developing countries, they exist in the most rudimentary form. In such markets, the geographical spread of the population frequently makes representative sampling difficult, if not impossible. Linguistic difficulties hinder the gathering of objective information and cultural taboos may make interviews difficult to obtain. In his very good summary of the problems associated with personal interviewing in markets abroad, Walsh[20] makes the important additional points that in developing countries, particularly,

suspicions may arise of a political motivation on the part of the interviewers... in industrial research, businessmen are often accustomed to
keeping to an absolute minimum any disclosure of information to government, employees and shareholders, let alone market researchers.

In case readers are daunted by the mention of these difficulties,
Walsh does propose[21] some extremely useful guidelines to overcome them.

The various stages in the research process, the methods of sampling and the methods of data collection, are exactly as described
in Chapter 3 and, in practice, particular research methods (such
as telephone interviewing in the USA and group interviewing
in developing countries) have been found to be especially appropriate to particular countries.

Methods of collective research (e.g. 'omnibus' surveys) and syndicated research services (e.g. those of the AC Nielsen organisation) are often available abroad, particularly in industrialised
countries and of great significance, particularly to new exporters,
are the Government schemes to assist market entry, including
support for marketing research. These are co-ordinated, on behalf
of Government, by the British Overseas Trade Board and are described in the next Section.

International marketing research can be organised:

(a) by the exporting organisation itself;

(b) by the exporting organisation working via
a foreign agency;

(c) by a UK agency working directly on   } on
research projects abroad;   the
(d) by a UK agency supervising the work of a exporter's
foreign agency;   } behalf

(e) by the foreign subsidiary of a UK or multinational research agency

It would be for the exporting company to assess the pros and
cons of each method bearing in mind the nature of the research
problem and the amount of funding available. Many companies
new to exporting are small and medium sized companies and
for them the research function of the UK based travelling sales
representative is a valuable one. A great deal can be gleaned from
the work of the representative abroad on such matters as: distributors' reactions to products, prices, payment methods and credit
terms; the level of promotional support for market entry; basic
intelligence on patent and trade mark protection; the nature and

extent of after-sales service required and, of course, the suitability or otherwise of proposed sales agents and distributors.

Perhaps the last words in this Section can be left to Stanton.[22] Making the point that a key to satisfactory performance overseas lies in gauging which aspects of one's own domestic marketing techniques should be retained, modified or abandoned, he adds:

A marketing information system would seem to be even more essential in foreign markets than in the domestic market because the risks are so much greater.

HM Government services for exporters

Britain is a small country containing no more than 1.4 per cent of the world's population. Yet she is the fifth largest trading nation. This fact, coupled with the salience of her international trading performance for her balance of payments, has meant that HM Government has always had a significant supporting role in the post-1945 drive for exports. Much of Government's work in this field is co-ordinated by the British Overseas Trade Board which was set up in January 1972 to assist British exporters. Its members are drawn from Government and industry. Its President is the Secretary of State for Trade and the Chairman is a leading industrialist. Its responsibilities are:

1   to advise the Government on strategy for overseas trade;
2   to direct and develop the Government on export promotion services on behalf of the Secretary of State for Trade;
3   to encourage and support industry and commerce in overseas trade with the aid of appropriate governmental and non-governmental organisations at home and overseas;
4   to contribute to the exchange of views between Government and industry and commerce in the field of overseas trade and to search for solutions to problems.
(Source: *BOTB's Services*, British Overseas Trade Board, September 1982)

A copy of the handbook mentioned above provides a comprehensive guide to BOTB's services. Among the services are the following:

1   16 Area Advisory Groups responsible, on a geographical basis, for providing advice on the world's main trading areas, e.g. Western Europe, the Middle East, North America, South East Asia.

2   A London headquarters and 10 Regional Offices staffed to give advice on BOTB services, with the regional offices providing a counselling service tailored to meet the needs and capabilities of individual companies.

3   8 Market Branches, the Statistics and Market Intelligence Library and the Product Data Store, all situated at the Department of Trade headquarters (1, Victoria Street, SW1) designed to provide market information of the most detailed nature and utilising the network of commercial staff in the 200 or so UK Embassies, High Commissions and Consulates abroad.

4   A *Market Advisory Service* and an *Overseas Status Report Service* which provides, at a nominal cost, detailed information on market potential and particular organisations in foreign countries. This information is based on the specific enquiries of the individual exporter and also includes assistance with the costs of an initial visit to the market.

5   A *Technical Help to Exporters Scheme*, operating through the British Standards Institution and designed to assist with the technical requirements of would-be exporters. This includes the provision of information on:
   (i)   the laws of the land (safety, environmental, etc);
   (ii)   national standards;
   (iii) certification practices;
   (iv)   customer requirements.

6   An *Export Marketing Research Scheme* where, in approved cases, BOTB will make grants towards the costs of marketing research studies in overseas countries conducted on behalf of individual companies (up to 33.3 per cent of total cost) groups of firms (up to 50 per cent of total costs) or trade associations (up to 66.6 per cent of total cost).

7   Through its Fairs and Promotions Branch, financial assistance to groups of exporters travelling as an *Outward Mission*, sponsored by an approved trade association, chamber of commerce, etc.

8   Financial assistance to groups of companies wishing to bring to the UK overseas businessmen, journalists, etc as an *Inward Mission*.

9   *Assistance at Trade Fairs Overseas*, through the provision of space, shell stand or other appropriate display facilities at attractive rates and assistance towards travel costs, for firms taking part in group displays of UK products.

10   Financial assistance for the support of Seminars outside the

UK organised and sponsored by a trade association or other non-profit making body. The objective of such seminars must be to bring specific UK products, processes or services to the attention of specific buyers, users and technological experts. To qualify for support, the seminars must be organised in association with BOTB's Fairs and Promotion Branch.

The above 10 headings provide a very good indication of the valuable support services provided by HM Government through the Board. The reader should also refer to the many publications issued by the Board, taking care to obtain the most recent copies of these. In addition to the services listed above, other noteworthy BOTB initiatives have included:

1   EIS (*Export Intelligence Service*) a daily, computerised information service which distributes details of overseas enquiries for products or services, calls for tender, agents seeking UK principals, etc;
2   MEGS (*the Market Entry Guarantee Scheme*) which is designed to help smaller and medium-sized firms to enter new overseas markets and provides 50 per cent of certain overhead costs linked with such new ventures, and, not least
3   *Publicity Support for Exports* through the offices of the BOTB Publicity Unit, the Central Office of Information (COI) and the BBC External Services, resulting in the dissemination of news stories, films, colour slides, photographs and TV and radio programmes to a vast number of overseas markets.

One of the deterrents to export activity, particularly with smaller firms, is the fact that specialised administrative procedures are called for. In addition to the commercial invoice found in UK trade, exporting, even on a limited scale, typically involves the origination and distribution of additional documents frequently of some complexity. These include bills of exchange, bills of lading, air waybills, cargo insurance policies and certificates, certificates of origin, dock receipts, health certificates, etc. An already complex situation has been underlined by the striking improvements in transport techniques during the last two decades, with the result that the speed and efficiency of trade procedures and related documentation has fallen markedly behind the enhanced capability of rapid delivery that the newer transport techniques have made possible.

To counter this problem, a Board for the Simplification of International Trade Procedures (*SITPRO*) was established in the UK in 1970. Since that time it has been extremely active in working towards the simplification and reduction of the documentation required in invoicing, transport, customs and shipping procedures. SITPRO operates on an annual grant from the British Overseas Trade Board and has developed aligned export documentation systems as a move to simpler, speedier procedures. Its publications include:

(a) *Systematic Export Documentation*
(b) *Costing Guidelines for Export Administration*
(c) *Computers in International Trade and Transport* – *data standards*
(d) *Computers and International Trade Documents* (1981)

(Note. The intending exporter will obviously find these publications of great value. Significant advice is also available through Croner Publications Ltd – e.g. the *Reference Book for Exporters*.)

BOTB also publishes a series of booklets entitled *Hints to Exporters*. Currently over 100 overseas markets are included in the series and up-to-date information on currency and exchange regulations, passport and visa formalities, methods of business, social and economic factors, etc is provided for each market. The booklets are readily available to businessmen planning to travel abroad.

Covering the credit risk

Cash flow and credit control are important aspects of all commercial operations. In dealing with overseas markets, however, the risk that the seller will part with his goods and not subsequently be paid for them is exacerbated by distance, differing trading practices, differing legal systems, less comprehensive knowledge of buyers and differing standards of business ethics. Taken together, these factors constitute the *credit risk*. In addition, there is a *political risk* that the proceeds from sales to a particular country cannot be repatriated due to such unforeseen factors as war, expropriation or restrictions on remittances.

The reader will have deduced that a degree of protection is afforded by particular *methods of payment* (see pages 440–1) but as Day[23] has observed: 'Credit control is an aspect of international trading to be taken very seriously'. Certainly no organisation intent on building worthwhile turnover with overseas markets can realistically neglect insuring against the particular risks of international trading. In this milieu, any description of HM Government Services would be inadequate without mention of the Export Credits Guarantee Department (ECGD). This is a Government department responsible to the Secretary of State for Trade and has over 60 years experience in export credit insurance. It has a head office in the City of London, 10 regional offices (in the main industrial and commercial centres) and its primary function is to provide guarantees so as to encourage British exports of goods and services.

Assistance is provided in two main ways:

1 by insuring exporters against the risks of not being paid by their customers – deriving from such factors as default or insolvency of the buyer (buyer risk) or exchange difficulties or import restrictions (country risk) – both types of risk being covered in the same policy;
2 by giving medium/long-term specific guarantees to banks which enable organisations to obtain funding, for their export credit transactions, often at favourable rates of interest.

ECGD can also provide insurance against the main political risks (war, expropriation, restrictions on remittances) which might jeopardise new investment overseas. The significance of ECGD services is confirmed by the Department's booklet *ECGD – your questions answered*. The 1980 edition reported:

In the last financial year over 12 000 exporters insured their overseas business with ECGD to a total value of some £14 515 million. This represented about 33 per cent of all UK exports. During the same period the Department earned over £107 million in premium and paid out a record £134 million in claims.

With regard to the figure of expenditure on claims, it should be noted that ECGD, although a Government department, enjoys no subsidy from the taxpayer. The Department has to operate on a normal commercial basis and is expected to fund its own reserve against future liabilities.

Space does not permit dealing with ECGD services in detail here and intending exporters should consult the Department's publications as a preliminary to discussions with ECGD officials.

In concluding this Section we should make mention of the important functions of *Sales organisation* and *distribution* which

were covered in Chapters 7 and 9. Readers who are candidates
for export examinations are advised that, for revision purposes,
it would be sensible to return to the appropriate sections of those
Chapters before proceeding.

On page 420 the various ways in which organisations might
enter foreign markets were enumerated. The remaining methods
are now described.

Licensing and royalty agreements

Although basic marketing research is conducted to discover
whether an organisation's *finished products* can be sold to a foreign market, it is often revealed that the best method of entry
(or of retaining a market, or of increasing market share) is to conclude a licensing arrangement with a local manufacturer.

What factors would point towards such a decision? It could
be that import controls, or freight and distribution costs might
otherwise 'shut out' the products. Or possibly, the design and
specification required might be impractical for economic modification and development in the UK factory. Again, the organisation, though technically expert and naturally inventive, may well
lack the plant capacity or the capital funding to make a wider
return on its expertise. It might naturally wish to profit from
its possession of certain techniques of production which are
clearly ahead of established techniques. These are typical reasons
why a firm might pursue the possibility of a return by way of
royalty payments from overseas rather than by the invoicing of
finished products.

What deserves emphasis here is that *licensing as a method of
operation must be a fundamental aspect of the marketing
approach*. Perhaps it has been regarded as a last resort too often
in the past. Yet accurate assessments and costings may prove
it to be the best way – the way to trade for the best return on
investment.

In addition to any granted patents a firm may possess (and
protection in foreign markets is a matter on which it must obtain
specialist advice), it may also be possible to license the following
'know-how'.

(a) the results of technical research, e.g. the development of
a heat treatment to increase the mechanical strength of the
finished product;

(b) a novel, important feature of design, e.g. one which reduces loss or 'scrap' rates in manufacture;

(c) the use of the firm's name or trade mark where this has commercial value or prestige;

(d) specially developed features in capital equipment which increase output, enhance safety, etc.

It is true to say that as more and more countries become industrialised, international marketing becomes more a matter of marketing skills rather than products. Certainly when the marketing strategy is being considered, blueprints, drawings, prototypes and technical knowledge are as important to consider as finished manufactures.

Some of the usual forms of agreement are these:

(a) a licence to manufacture, for the payment of royalties, with or without an initial disclosure fee;

(b) the outright sale of manufacturing or process 'know-how';

(c) a comprehensive, continuing agreement for technical assistance.

With this last, for example, the UK organisation might undertake a feasibility study on behalf of the foreign 'partner', which would be followed by advice on setting up a manufacturing plant and perhaps include the training of operatives and the provision of production 'know-how' and guidance on quality control.

A properly constructed agreement, in consultation with legal advisers is obviously essential. Although Walsh[24] states that his listed headings of agreement are 'necessarily oversimplified' they do nevertheless provide a very good guide to the scope of such agreements.

Allied to the licensing strategy is *franchising*. This is a method of market entry whereby the franchiser provides a basic raw material, ingredient, or package of components together with management expertise, including advice on marketing strategy and sales promotion. The franchisee, an indigenous organisation or individual subscribes the capital, labour and knowledge of local conditions. Manufacturers in the soft drinks field rely heavily on this method. The agreement might provide for the remittance of payment to the franchiser for the supplies plus service fees for advice or might be based on a proportionate distribution of profits. The agreement might typically provide for the establishment of quality checks by the franchiser. The method has the advantage of providing an opportunity for market entry which provides protection to the licenser's brand name or trade mark since he has some control of the standards of final product or service, which, as a rule, are non-patentable. As with all such types of agreement, the prospective franchiser will have satisfied himself through basic marketing research that royalty payments, service fees, etc may be freely remitted to him by the franchisee and that if any payments to non-resident corporate bodies or persons are subject to local taxation, a convention exists between the UK and the country concerned for the avoidance of double taxation.

Contract manufacturing

Here, the organisation will seek a suitable manufacturer in the overseas country and conclude an agreement for the production of his products there. Although the method obviously permits variations, in most instances the agreement extends only to manufacture or assembly, with the UK firm retaining control over marketing and distribution.

As Kotler[25] points out, whilst contract manufacturing offers less control over the process of production, it does enable the 'outside' organisation to begin operations faster than would be the case if it was setting up its own manufacturing plant, yet it could constitute an important first step in that direction. So here again, we have a method of entry into markets which might otherwise be 'protected' through tariff and/or non-tariff barriers, in which local investment is on a limited scale and yet since operations are being conducted through an indigenous organisation, there is no danger of nationalisation or expropriation should the country become politically 'tricky'.

Management contracting

In essence, this is really the export of management and consultancy services. A local organisation seeking investment opportunities may decide to provide the capital for the construction of a tourism complex, including accommodation, entertainment and shopping facilities. Realising that it lacks the management expertise to control and operate such facilities it may arrange to 'import' the necessary know-how from some well-known international organisation with considerable experience in the field.

As Kotler points out, the Hilton chain of the USA has undertaken to manage hotels throughout the world in this way.

The contractual arrangements usually provide for the payment of service fees from the outset and thus the method provides low-risk market entry with the prospect of quick returns. Also there may be provision for the purchase of shares in the managed venture at a subsequent stage.

Once again, the initial screening survey must assure the provider of know-how that so far as return on time and effort is concerned there are no better openings for the deployment of expertise and that this method is more lucrative than setting up his own local provision, for example.

Joint ventures

Strictly speaking, the methods of market entry most recently described in this Chapter – licensing, franchising, contract manufacturing, and management contracting can be accurately described as *joint ventures*. An organisation abroad is identified as an appropriate partner for the development of market opportunity by a method agreed under the terms of a contract. In addition, there is the partnership venture which is based on *joint ownership*. It may be that the UK organisation will purchase an interest in an existing foreign company. Or a foreign organisation may similarly acquire a share of a company that a UK parent organisation has already established in an overseas market. Or again, a UK company and a foreign partner may jointly set up and operate a completely new business enterprise.

The UK firm may opt for one or other of these ideas for its own internal reasons (it may lack the capital to set up its own wholly-owned company) or because the economic and political environment in the foreign country dictates it should be so (joint ownership with a local company may be a stipulation for entry).

These methods can be successful but it is important that a great deal of thought is given at the outset to the type of potential partner required. Success will depend on unity of outlook on such matters as *dividend distribution* (should profits be distributed or re-invested for growth?), *commercial policy* (does the foreign organisation understand and support a marketing approach?) *business ethics* and important aspects of product policy (e.g. quality standards, health and safety factors, etc).

Unless there is clear and unequivocal understanding and *written agreement* on these and similar aspects, then the seeds of dissension, and possibly dissolution, could be implemented from the start. It is also important for the UK organisation to bear in mind that where local company law prevents majority shareholding by foreign nationals, it may not have the power to alter things which are not to its liking.

Wholly owned subsidiaries

A danger of producing for the reader, even in outline form, a summary of the various methods of market entry is that it may be assumed that the various methods so described are mutually exclusive. This is not so. A company marketing internationally, and doing so successfully may employ a variety of different methods: indirect exporting, direct exporting, licensing, contract manufacturing, etc, according to (*i*) their suitability for that company's own size and capital structure and (*ii*) the needs of the foreign countries and trading blocs in which the company is active.

Moreover, such a list of methods is often *developmental* or *transitional*, for having gained some experience of trading through a method with a given level of involvement with a market (e.g. direct exporting), if the signs are encouraging, the company may move to a method with a deeper level of involvement (e.g. a joint venture of some kind). So it is that after a period of successful trading with a market, a company may conclude that further expansion of sales will only take place there by setting up its own wholly owned company. These foreign subsidiaries of the UK parent may take the form of a marketing subsidiary (including showrooms and service depots) or may be a manufacturing organisation. Retail outlets, consultancy organisations or advertising agencies owned by UK companies and operating successfully abroad, particularly in Western Europe, show that the possibilities do not end with the manufacture and distribution of products.

But to stay with products, by way of example, UK organisations manufacturing or assembling in local markets are drawn from product groups as diverse as:

motor vehicles, electrical appliances, agricultural machinery, machine tools, confectionery, plastics, floor tiles and ready mixed concrete.

So the method itself does not pre-select any particular group – the options are quite wide.

When expert technical selling and detailed after-sales service are required, but no other factors point towards the need for local manufacture, a *sales/marketing subsidiary* will probably be established. And in Europe, for example, such subsidiaries have been set up by UK organisations drawn from diverse fields – contractors' plant, heating and air conditioning equipment, food machinery, motor vehicles, perambulators, accounting machines and product components of many types.

Whatever the class of subsidiary, owning and operating one abroad is not for the beginner and the list below indicates just some of the factors to be considered:

1   Size of the market; regulations on foreign investment; facilities for bank borrowing.
2   Trade policies, including duties and uplifts for duty on necessary imports (e.g. raw materials); company laws – including protection for foreign investors, transfer of dividends, eventual repatriation of capital.
3   The location of the market as a base for distribution to other markets, including membership of customs unions, free-trade areas.
4   The incidence and amount of taxation, including details of taxes on income/property (income tax, corporation tax, trade tax, etc) and taxes on transactions (import turnover tax, tax on value added, capital transactions tax, etc); existence or otherwise of a double taxation agreement (between UK and the country concerned).
5   Labour costs, labour productivity, incidence of restrictive practices; levels of salaries and wages; skills and adaptability of the work force; regulations in force concerning recruitment.
6   Potential locations for the subsidiary organisation; costs and ease/difficulty of securing premises; aspects of access to markets, labour, inducements offered in 'development' areas; transport facilities, etc.

Local manufacture or assembly may so reduce costs and distribution lead time that the firm's competiveness is signally improved. Full control of the manufacturing and marketing operations is retained and presence in the market should provide heightened awareness of changes in user needs. Of course, such a high level of involvement means a high level of risk, particularly if a changed political situation leads to expropriation of foreign assets. However, Britain's recent history demonstrates the steadily growing trend for direct investment by many of its companies. Such companies had, of course, previously recognised the importance of extensive marketing research, expert legal advice on company formation and taxation matters and accurate assessment of the capital and recurrent costs involved.

Multinational corporations

At the highest level of sophistication, so far as overseas involvement is concerned, stand the multinational corporations. Seddon and Appleton, reporting Tindall[26] define these as combinations of 'companies of different nationality connected by means of shareholdings, managerial control or contract and constituting a single economic entity'. Reporting Pickering[27] they add that a multinational will have annual sales of at least £100 million, 25 per cent of which will be earned by overseas plants. The multinational will have production facilities in six or more countries. Distinguishing features also include a head office in a 'parent country', with production and distribution plants in 'host countries'.

Clearly, relatively few firms enter the lists as multinationals on these definitions but British multinationals include British Petroleum, ICI and Dunlop whilst foreign multinationals operating in the UK number Esso, Gillette, ITT, IBM, Ford Motor Company, Phillips Electrical and Siemens in their ranks. However, their overweening importance and their significance for Governments lie not so much in their numbers as organisations but in the size of operations. For example, by the early 1970s it was calculated that almost one eighth of Britain's output and one fifth of her exports were produced by multinationals. In 1978, Seddon and Appleton[28] stated that 'in terms of gross national product if General Motors were a state it would rank fourteenth in the world'.

Thus it is that outside of Eastern bloc countries, the ownership and control of the means of production and distribution by these giant international corporations operating across national boundaries, often globally, has assumed remarkable proportions. Governments pay great heed to them for on the credit side they provide for host countries extended employment opportunities and an infusion of capital, technology and, not least, marketing skills, so that their presence brings many direct and indirect economic benefits. On the other hand, their very size and the fact that their strategies are planned internationally means that their pricing strategies, movements of capital and rationalisation of production may have profound effects on the individual nation and its balance of payments. Past thinking by Governments on controls have included equity participation by host countries, measures to ensure the appointment of locals to management structures and anti-trust legislation.

In concluding this Chapter, it is hoped that the reader has gained an appreciation of what constitutes international marketing, in the broader context, whilst at the same time paying due regard to those special aspects of exporting which are often overlooked in general summaries of this type. Where it is required, more detailed information on exporting can be found in the textbooks mentioned in the bibliography.

Self-assessment questions

1 List the various functions which might be carried out by an export house.

2 Write a short essay on the changing pattern of Britain's main overseas markets, indicating the implications for marketing strategy.

3 What are the factors upon which an export marketing strategy is based?

4 What alternative strategies are there for the development of new or modified products for overseas markets?

5 Draw up a planning approach for pricing a product you wish to introduce to a foreign market.

6 Define: f.a.s.; f.o.b.; c.i.f.; Incoterms; open account; documents against acceptance; documents against payment; documentary letter of credit; SITPRO; franchising; contract manufacturing; management contracting.

7 What factors need to be taken into account in establishing a distribution policy for an overseas market?

8 In what ways might an overseas promotional campaign be organised and controlled on behalf of a UK exporter?

9 List the sources of 'armchair research' data.

10 Outline the major sources of (HM) Government help for exporters.

11 List some types of 'know-how' which might form the basis of a licensing agreement.
12 What factors have to be considered before establishing subsidiary organisations abroad?

References

1 Chisnall, Peter M. *Effective industrial marketing*, London, Longman, 1977, p. 128
2 Cannon, Tom. *Basic marketing – principles and practice*, London, Holt, Rinehart and Winston, 1980, p. 132
3 Foster, Douglas. *Mastering marketing*, London, The Macmillan Press, 1982, p. 292
4 Stanton, William J. *Fundamentals of marketing*, 6th edn, New York, McGraw-Hill, 1981, p. 472
5 Woodcock, Clive (ed.) Small Business (Pressure for change in the EEC), London, *The Guardian*, 28 January, 1983, p. 19
6 British Export Houses Association (BEHA). *Directory of British export houses*, London, BEHA, 1978–9, p. 4
7 Frain, John. *Transportation and distribution for European markets*, London, Butterworth, 1970, pp. 97–101
8 Day, Arthur J. *Exporting for profit*, London, Graham & Trotman, 1976, p. 334
9 *Fundamentals of marketing*, p. 472
10 Walsh, L. S. *International marketing*, 2nd edn, Plymouth, Macdonald & Evans, 1983, pp. 44–45
11 *Transportation and distribution for European markets*, plate 8
12 Centre for Physical Distribution Management. Research reported in *The Director's Guide to storage, handling, freight and distribution*, London, Institute of Directors, 1980, p. 11
13 British Overseas Trade Board. *Marketing consumer goods in France*, London, BOTB, 1977, p. 15
14 *Fundamentals of marketing*. p. 480
15 McCarthy, E. Jerome. *Basic marketing*, 6th edn, Homewood, Ill, Richard D. Irwin, 1978, p. 606
16 *International marketing*, p. 124
17 Kotler, Philip. *Principles of marketing*, 2nd edn, Englewood Cliffs, NJ, Prentice-Hall, 1980, p. 584
18 Boone, Louis E. and Kurtz, David L. *Contemporary marketing*, 3rd edn, Hinsdale, Ill, The Dryden Press, 1980, p. 401
19 Jenner, Paul. *Europe: an exporter's handbook*, London, Euromonitor Publications, 1981, p. 10
20 *International marketing*, p. 25
21 Ibid. p. 26

22 *Fundamentals of marketing*, p. 480
23 *Exporting for profit*, p. 115
24 *International marketing*, p. 72
25 *Principles of marketing*, p. 581
26 Seddon, E. and Appleton, J. D. S. *Applied economics*, 2nd edn, Plymouth, Macdonald & Evans, 1978, p. 262
27 Ibid, p. 262
28 Ibid, p. 263

14 MARKETING AND SOCIETY; MARKETING AND THE LAW; MARKETING AND TOMORROW

Objectives

Finally, we are going to consider the organisation's social and ethical responsibilities. The proposition will not be that marketing should be defensive, but that in its fullest and best sense, the marketing concept will facilitate a proper response to such important forces as consumerism and environmentalism.

The UK's legal framework, as it impinges on marketing, is briefly and generally explained, as are the ways in which, through voluntary codes and controls, marketing disciplines itself.

The last pages look at marketing and tomorrow bearing in mind that, at the current rate of change, it is already tomorrow today.

Marketing and society

The rats were nuisances, and the packers would put poisoned bread out for them and they would die, and then rats, bread and meat would go into the hoppers together ... Men, who worked in the tank rooms full of steam ... fell into the vats; and when they were fished out, there was never enough of them to be worth exhibiting – sometimes they would be overlooked for days, till all but the bones of them had gone out to the world as Durham's Pure Leaf Lard![1].

This extract, from Upton Sinclair's *The Jungle*, an horrific account of practices in the US meat packing industry, and published in 1906 is a striking illustration of the fact that society has long been concerned with some aspects of industrial behaviour, with some of the failings of the 'market mechanism'.

Sinclair's work had much to do with the passage of the US Pure Food and Drug Act of 1906. We also know that concern about the power of the seller vis-à-vis the buyer resulted, in the UK, in the Sale of Goods Act 1893, which did something to improve the balance. The years between the two World Wars saw more socially conscious writers taking up the cudgels on behalf of the consumer. High pressure salesmanship was denounced, as was false and misleading advertising. Calls were made for the scientific testing of products and for more and better technical information to enable consumers to make more informed purchase decisions. As the cliché runs: 'consumerism is not new.'

The consumer movement

It is in the period since the late 1950s however that legislation to protect the consumer has burgeoned and a social force called *consumerism* or the *consumer movement* has gained influence and power in many countries of the Western world. Thirty years ago the warnings of Vance Packard, in his *Hidden Persuaders*, that advertisers were using motivation research and subliminal advertising to manipulate consumers received considerable publicity and attention. Shortly afterwards, biologist Rachel Carson[2], with passion, skill and closely reasoned argument, explained why man cannot allow the natural environment of living things, from which he himself has so recently emerged, to be destroyed in pursuit of economic progress. And so, well before the 15 March 1962 there was a growing social consciousness of the need to afford the consumer and the environment a greater measure of protection. The twin forces of *consumerism* and *environmentalism* were gaining strength.

March 15 1962 is a significant date in the chronology of the consumer movement, for on that date, President John F. Kennedy delivered to the US Congress 'A special message on protecting the consumer interest'.
Here is an extract from that address:

The march of technology – affecting, for example, the foods we eat, the medicines we take, and the many appliances we use in our homes – has increased the difficulties of the consumer along with his opportunities; and it has outmoded many of the old laws and regulations and made new legislation necessary. The typical supermarket before World War II stocked about 1500 separate food items – an impressive figure by any standards. But today it carries over 6000. Ninety per cent of the prescriptions written today are for drugs that were unknown 20 years ago. Many of the new products used every day in the home are highly complex. The housewife is called upon to be an amateur electrician, mechanic, chemist, toxicologist, dietitian and mathematician – but she is rarely furnished the information she needs to perform these tasks proficiently.

Whilst not itself acquiring the force of law, what came to be known as Kennedy's 'Consumer Bill of Rights', greatly influenced both lay and legislative thinking and provided the framework for much of the consumer legislation which has been enacted in the United States since that date. The President himself identified the following consumer rights:

1   *The right to safety* to be protected against the marketing of goods which are hazardous to health or life.

2   *The right to be informed* to be protected against fraudulent, deceitful or grossly misleading information, advertising, labelling or other practices, and to be given the facts needed to make an informed choice.

3   *The right to choose* to be assured, whenever possible of access to a variety of products and services at competitive prices, and in those industries in which competition is not workable and government regulation is substituted, to be assured satisfactory quality and service at fair prices.

4   *The right to be heard* to be assured that consumer interests will receive full and sympathetic consideration in the formulation of government policy, and fair and expeditious treatment in its administrative tribunals.

What specific aspects of industrial and commercial activity have given rise to concern at best and clear disaffection and distrust at worst? In some senses they can be identified from President Kennedy's Bill of Rights. More comprehensively, the questions with which consumers have been increasingly concerned during the last 30 years can be summarised as shown below.

1   Do distribution, advertising and packaging cost too much?

2   Aren't some selling techniques deceptive? Doesn't high-pressure-selling persuade people into buying things they don't necessarily need?

3   Are there not too many shoddy and unsafe products available?

4   Doesn't the technique of planned obsolescence do a disservice to the consumer?

5   Aren't many advertising campaigns short on useful information and long on exaggeration? Should not the 'truth quotient' in advertising be increased? Isn't the type of advertising which exploits sex, offensive, degrading and a form of cultural pollution?

6   Aren't pricing tactics too frequently deceptive? Isn't the true cost of obtaining credit sometimes obscured, concealed even?

7   Isn't the impact of marketing activity excessive? Does it not result in excessive materialism and engender in people a feeling of competition rather than co-operation?

8   Hasn't 'business' grown too big, so that what is ostensibly a free market is, in Galbraith's phrase: 'the organised market of the corporations'? What are the implications of this for consumer interests and freedom of choice? To what extent does the market really cater for the poor and the disadvantaged?

9   In a situation of steadily diminishing natural resources, isn't a great deal of marketing activity wasteful – as typified by the excessive use of scarce materials in packaging and the development of 'throw-away,' non-returnable containers?

10   Isn't the provision of before-sales and after-sales service too often inadequate? Isn't the legal jargon surrounding too many warranties impenetrable to the average consumer and purposely so?

In response to these questions some quite legitimate points can be made, namely:

1   That the consumer has an imperfect understanding of the service – values encapsulated in the distributive mark-up.

2   Similarly, that the consumer has no conception of the high research and development costs involved in the introduction of products.

3   That in comparison with other methods of selling, advertising is often the most economic method of promoting goods in the market place; that advertising and branding go together and that branding is a guarantee of the manufacturer's confidence in the product.

4   That people are not economic ciphers, that they buy concepts

as well as products and that the psychological value engendered by packaging and advertising is often as important to the consumer as the functional value.

5   That the marketing activity of many firms both large and small has contributed in large measure to the standard of living so many of us now enjoy, that their contribution through taxation has resulted in increased social welfare, that the majority of business organisations operate responsibly and ethically, that the media sensationalise the shortcomings of the minority and that the many should not be castigated for the villainous few.

Even so, we are all only too aware of what any reasonable-minded person could properly regard as unethical, as sharp practice, and each of us can provide examples from our own experience. A short time ago I was attracted by the poster in the window of a television rental company about what seemed to be an extremely attractive offer on the rental of a new set. On enquiring in the showroom, I was given a verbal catalogue of all the shortcomings of the set in question and advised how much better it would be for me to rent an alternative model, at a much increased rental fee – an example of hoary old 'bait and switch' sales technique. Even my understanding of, and goodwill towards, the selling fraternity has been strained to the limit by the ill-mannered persistence of the door-to-door salesman of encyclo-paedias or double-glazing, though my annoyance was tempered by knowledge of the fact that the sellers themselves, on little or no salary, were spurred on by the 'vast earnings' to be had from the 'generous commissions' and 'substantial prizes' the employers were making available. I have seen advertisements of many types that were undoubtedly obscene and in which the female so depicted had absolutely no connection with the product being advertised. Doubtless the reader can readily supply his or her own list of such examples and hopefully, he or she would agree with Kotler[3] that the attitude that a few excesses, abuses and wastes are a small price to pay for the creation of a high standard of living is surely a dangerous one.

Environmentalism

Parallel to the growth of forces seeking to protect the consumer from the worst excesses of twentieth century industrial and commercial activity has been the development of a strong international lobby designed to protect the environment. Environmentalism is a clumsy word to describe an important concept but its advocates have made some impression on business organisations by reminding them that it is no longer enough to operate within economic and legal frameworks. Business decisions have far reaching social consequences not least with regard to the pollution of the environment and the accelerating rate of depletion of the earth's natural resources. In retailing a catalogue of ecological disasters, David Attenborough[4] reminds us that a tree which took two centuries to grow can be cut down in one hour, that every year an area the size of Switzerland is being cut down and that once the trees have gone nothing holds the soil together, it is lashed away by rain and the land becomes a soil-less waste. He goes on:

We have to recognise that the old vision of a world in which human beings played a relatively minor part is done and finished. The notion that an ever-bountiful nature, lying beyond man's habitations and influence, will always supply his wants, no matter how much he takes from it or how he maltreats it, is false. We can no longer rely on providence to maintain the delicate interconnected communities of animals and plants on which we depend.[5]

In the recent past we have had three graphic illustrations of the extent to which the continued existence of life on the planet is threatened by man's economic activity:

1   The incident at the nuclear power station on Three Mile Island in the United States, in which the temperature of the gases within a pressurised water reactor became too high. The staff were inadequately trained to deal with this. The incident resulted in a leakage of radioactive gases into the atmosphere and the declaration of a state of emergency.
2   The escape of toxic chemicals from an industrial process being operated in the Italian town of Seveso. This resulted in widespread damage to human, plant and animal life and provided the clearest illustration up to that time of the disaster which could be induced by the encroachment of industrialisation upon the quality of life.
3   The more recent and even more horrific happenings at Bhopal in India where leakage of methyl isocyanate from a chemical plant resulted in the deaths of 2000 people and countless animals. A considerable number of people were seriously injured. The effects of the disaster upon the unborn are not yet clear.

Concern for the dangers of physical pollution, for the slaughtering
of animals in order to make fur coats and other 'luxury' products,
for the thoughtlessness with which scarce minerals, fuels and
other natural resources are being depleted and for the destruction
of the environment through intensive and extensive farming,
opencast mining and motorway and airport construction has
generated a powerful environmentalist movement which is international in scope and contains within it several notable organisations, some of them political, such as the Green Party of the
Federal Republic of Germany and the Ecology Party of Great Britain, as well as Animal Rights Campaigners, Friends of the Earth
and the Greenpeace Movement. From recent beginnings, the success of the Green Party, which obtained one fifth of the seats
in the recent national elections shows that the environmentalists
are not a narrow coterie of idealists remote from the practicalities
of operating modern economies. Rather do they constitute a
mechanism through which widespread and sincere human concern is being mobilised.

Summary

In the last thirty years then, the Western world has generated
a consumer movement which is firstly concerned with many
aspects of the exchange relationships between business organisations and consumers which it considers to be unsatisfactory. Nor
is this concern restricted to profit organisations. The health service, education, the police, and local and central government have
also been subjected to its concerns and its strictures. As the consumer movement has developed it has also concerned itself with
environmental matters and the careful husbandry of natural
resources – in short, with the quality of life. It is attempting
to achieve an adequate balance of power between the consumer
and the organisations that affect his life and well-being. Although,
as we have seen at the beginning of this Chapter, consumerism
is not new, its latter-day influence is significantly different and
more powerful because it is set against a revolution of rising
expectations. As Stanton[6] explains, today's consumerism exists
within a setting of high incomes, high employment and largely
filled subsistence needs. In consequence, as people's drive for possessions has abated, as people have become less 'things oriented'
they have become more concerned with the quality of life. Person-

al possessions have become less important than personal well-being and personal growth. Kangun and others[7] report on research which indicates the belief not only that consumerism is extremely important today but that its importance would be greater in the future. Moreover, these researchers express the view, echoed by Stanton[8] that consumerism has the capacity to grow because it has generated an institutional structure of governmental and quasi-governmental agencies to represent and protect the consumer interest.

Despite the fraudulent practices, the excesses and indeed the horrors which have been described earlier in this Chapter there is now a rising social consciousness deriving from:

1   mounting public pressure as a result of society's changing expectations of business conduct;
2   increased government intervention in the shape of legislative and other regulatory pressures;
3   not least, evidence of increased sensitivity to consumer and environmental interests from individual organisations.

The implications of these environmental forces for management, particularly marketing management will now be considered.

Marketing, business ethics and social responsibility

Review of what has already been written about the consumer movement might raise the question: 'has marketing failed?' Now if we take marketing to mean the marketing concept as we understand it, our first reaction must be 'no', for certainly there is nothing in that concept which could be interpreted as detrimental to the consumer interest or which is intended to threaten his environment. On the other hand, we should recall Kotler's description of the societal marketing concept (in Chapter 1 of this book) in which he queried whether:

the pure marketing concept constitutes an adequate business philosophy in an age of environmental deterioration, resource shortages, explosive population growth, world wide inflation and neglected social services.[9]

Kotler believes that:

The societal marketing concept is a consumers' needs orientation backed by integrated marketing aimed at generating consumer satisfaction and long-run consumer welfare as the key to satisfying organisational goals.[10]

Now here we note that Philip Kotler emphasises *long-run consumer welfare* and this is an important addition to the definition for it seems that public opinion is now justifiably demanding that organisations recognise that the social framework in which they operate is at par with the economic and legal frameworks. For the business organisation this implies a clear recognition that decision making has a social as well as an economic cost – that consumer and environmental welfare is as decisive a criterion for success as sales turnover, costs and profits. A graphic illustration of the impact of marketing decisions is provided by Galbraith[11]:

An increase in the consumption of automobiles requires a facilitating supply of streets, highways, traffic control and parking space. The protective services of the police and the highway patrols must also be available, as must those of the hospitals. Although the need for balance here is extraordinarily clear, our use of privately produced vehicles has, on occasion, got far out of line with the supply of the related public services. The result has been hideous road congestion, an annual massacre of impressive proportions, and chronic colitis in the cities.

The plea is for the success of the marketing system to be judged not only by the volume of goods consumed, the breadth of consumer choice and the attainment of organisational objectives (profit or non-profit) but the quality of life within that system.

If we look back to Chapter 2, in describing the stakeholder theory, the author wrote:

the stakeholder theory ... suggests that the objectives of the organisation should not stem from the organisation exclusively but from the claims upon it of its various stakeholders – its employees, suppliers, shareholders, distributors, consumers, the general public, central and local government – all parties who have a stake in its well-being and are affected by its operations. The proposed objectives should constitute a reasonable balance of all their claims upon the organisation.

The words 'the general public' have been displayed in this instance for the author intends them to imply what Kotler means when he talks of 'long-run consumer welfare'. What this means for the individual organisation is that it must be adaptively rational to such significant social developments as consumerism, the trend towards simplification, the reaction known as anti-bigness, concern for the environment and the many other manifestations of public doubt and worry. Nor can the individual organisation spend a great deal of time pondering over these issues when public reaction exhibits the frustration-aggression syndrome resulting in the dumping of suspected radio-active waste outside the premises of government departments and the claimed adulteration of chocolate bars on supermarket shelves. While we may think these actions excessive they do illustrate the strength of feeling on social issues among certain groups in the community. On a less dramatic but equally important level, aggrieved consumers are more than ever willing to provide evidence to investigative journalists and to the presenters of TV programmes.

Today, therefore, it appears that what is called for is a broader intrepretation of marketing, after the manner of Kotler's *societal* marketing concept. Organisations must also develop and exhibit a keen sense of social responsibility. Stanton[12] sums this up neatly when he says:

Executives must realise (1) that business does not exist in isolation in our society and (2) that a healthy business system cannot exist within a sick society.

It also appears important for there to be a heightened sense of what is *ethical* in business. Ethics, in this sense, goes beyond legal minima. Fraud and deceit are punishable by law. The use of an additive whose long-term effects are uncertain, the production and distribution of a film that glorifies violence, the television advertisement that extols the speed capability of a car or the power in petrol, are not. Yet an organisation with an adequate ethical sensitivity might ask itself whether following one or other of these approaches might not be doing society greater damage than could be justified by mere return on investment calculations.

The story of the consumer movement would be incomplete without some description of the legislation which has resulted from its development. In the Section which follows, recent consumer legislation in the UK, set within the framework of other law which governs marketing activity, is briefly specified. The voluntary codes and controls which UK marketers and advertisers subscribe to are also outlined. The Section beyond that then examines some ways in which the individual organisation might effectively respond to the significant social forces which have just been recorded.

Marketing and the law

Note: The law is stated, in this necessarily brief and general outline, as on 1 May 1985. Since no more than an indication of the law can be provided in a textbook of this kind, the reader is advised to read some of the legal textbooks, as indicated in the bibliography, for a fuller appreciation of the subject.

A great deal of marketing activity is based upon the making of *contracts* and the law stipulates the essentials of a valid contract as being:

1   an intention to create legal relations;
2   offer and acceptance;
3   contractual capacity of the parties;
4   valuable consideration;
5   legality of object;
6   genuineness of consent;
7   possibility of performance;
8   certainty of terms.[13]

The law governing contracts for the sale of goods is governed by the Sale of Goods Acts and by the rules of common law, the general meaning of which is to be found in Curzon's[14] definition: 'the body of law judicially evolved from the general custom of the realm'.

The legal aspects of marketing activity also cover such matters as: the formation of an agency relationship; the carriage of goods; patents, trade marks and copyright; hire purchase agreements; trade descriptions; restrictive trade practices; insurance; negotiable instruments; fraud; banking and financial dealings; company law; partnership; bankruptcy and employment law. This list is by no means comprehensive and statutes may be in force which apply to the specific product or service being marketed, e.g. the Food and Drugs Act 1955, Building Societies Acts 1874 and 1962. Moreover, legislation which may, at first glance, have little or no relationship to marketing activity could in fact prove to be of considerable influence. An example of such a seemingly tenuous connection is provided by the Sex Discrimination Act 1975 and the Race Relations Act 1976; for example, Rowntree Mackintosh were informed by the Greater London Council that stocks of its confectionery would be withdrawn from the Council's youth clubs and other points of sale because of the firm's refusal to complete a GLC questionnaire which, among other things, would provide information upon the employment of females and ethnic groups.

Directly or indirectly therefore the law and its development greatly bear on marketing activity. The purpose of this Section is to review some of the recent legislation which reflects the growing importance of *consumer protection* and the considerable latter-day influence of *consumerism*. The legislation is briefly summarised below (a more extended treatment is provided within *Introduction to Marketing* – see Bibliography).

The Sale of Goods Act 1893 gave the buyer of goods certain implied rights against the seller relating to:

1   the seller's proper title (i.e. his right to sell) to the goods;
2   the buyer's entitlement to 'quiet possession' of the goods;
3   the buyer's entitlement to be supplied with goods which 'correspond with description'; and
4   are of 'merchantable quality'; and
5   are fit for the purpose for which they are brought.

The Supply of Goods and Services Act 1982 implies these same terms into contracts other than for the sale of goods or hire purchase, e.g. leasing contracts. The Act of 1893 also allowed the parties to a sale of goods to agree in the contract that these rights should not operate. This could result in exploitation of the following types:

1   that in some instances the consumer could only buy goods if he was willing to give up his rights; and
2   that in business, as distinct from consumer transactions, small firms might have no option other than to forfeit these rights in order to obtain goods from organisations dominating the supply side of the market.

The Supply of Goods (Implied Terms) Act 1973 (largely restated in the Unfair Contract Terms Act 1977) outlaws the surrender of these rights in a consumer sale and insists on the test of 'reasonableness' for such exclusion clauses in business sales. (The 1893 Act was amended by the Supply of Goods (Implied Terms) Act 1973 and the law has now been consolidated in the Sale of Goods Act 1979).

Trade Descriptions Acts 1968 and 1972

The main purpose of the Acts is to ensure, as far as possible, that when sellers state or imply certain important facts about their goods, prices and services, what they say is true. Under the Acts, it is an offence

1 to apply a false trade description to any goods; or
2 to supply or offer to supply any goods to which a false trade description is applied.

(For example, a book bound with a plastic derivative must not be described as 'leather bound'.)

Fair Trading Act 1973

The Act established The Office of Fair Trading, which investigates in the public interest, monopolies and mergers, collects information on unfair consumer trading practices and is a prime mover in the development of consumer legislation. Consumer trading practices include the terms or conditions relating to the supply of goods or services, the manner in which these are communicated, the promotion or methods of salesmanship, the packaging of goods and the methods of securing payment for the supply of goods and services. The Director General of Fair Trading is empowered to take action against those persisting in conduct detrimental to consumers. The Sale of Goods Act 1893 was a great turning point in the direction of consumer protection. The Fair Trading Act 1973 is thought by many to be of equal, if not greater, significance.

Consumer Credit Act 1974

The objectives of this Act were to provide a uniform system of statutory control with regard to the granting of credit, and the protection of consumers through a system of licensing of persons offering credit facilities.

Goods are deemed as 'protected' under the Act where, though the property in the goods remains with the creditor, the debtor has paid or tendered at least one-third of the total price of the goods and has not terminated the appropriate agreement. Unless the debtor so agrees, protected goods may be recovered only by court order.

Unfair Contract Terms Act 1977

This Act bans 'exclusion clauses', which formerly allowed a trader to limit his own legal liability, arising out of his business, for death or personal injury (such clauses being previously part of the 'small print' of some agreements). The Act also bans terms in consumer contracts which limit the trader's liability where goods fail to meet any description applied to them or which limit liability relating to the quality or fitness of goods supplied. If the exclusion clause is designed to avoid liability for damage caused by negligence, the clause will be subject to a test of 'reasonableness.'

Other important provisions of recent consumer legislation are now very briefly summarised.

1   *Advertisements (Hire Purchase) Act 1967* In advertisements for goods available on hire purchase or credit sale terms, a complete statement of the financial terms must be given if a sum of money is mentioned.

2   *Unsolicited Goods and Services Act 1971* Where goods have been received through the post unordered, the recipient has a right not to have to pay for the goods, nor to return the goods.

3   *Weights and Measures Acts 1963 and 1979* The buyer has a right to be given due weight, due measure (where goods are sold by weight or measure) and an adequate number of items (where goods are sold by number).

4   *The Price Marking (Bargain Offers) Order 1979* Price claims must not mislead or confuse consumers about the value of goods or services.

5   *Resale Prices Act 1976* Consolidating previous relevant legislation, this Act encourages competition, in the interests of consumers, by prohibiting 'resale price maintenance' (although manufacturers are permitted to 'recommend' retail selling prices to traders provided they do not attempt to enforce them)

6   *Restrictive Trade Practices Act 1976* Any agreement by traders to restrict competition among themselves (e.g. by fixing prices) will be prohibited if it is found by the Restrictive Trade Practices Court to be contrary to the public interest.

7   *Competition Act 1980* This Act empowers the Director General of Fair Trading to investigate the business practices of individual

organisations to determine whether they are operating an 'anti-competitive practice'.

Even from this all-too-cursory view of the recent legislation it should be possible for the reader to agree with Curzon[15] that:

Parliament ... has erected a complex structure of law designed to guard the consumer against those who would exploit his lack of knowledge or credulity.

In conclusion, it is also important to note that since the United Kingdom is a member of the European Community it is subject to the provisions of Article 85 of the Treaty of Rome 1957 which prohibits all agreements between business organisations which prevent, restrict or distort competition within the Common Market and to the provisions of Article 86 which declares that the abuse of a dominant position in the market structure is incompatible with the objectives of the Community. These articles provide the basis for the competition rules of the Community and in the collective judgement of Beardshaw and Palfreman[16] 'embody the philosophy of competition more strictly than our own domestic law'.

Consumer protection

UK Institutional structure

Earlier in this Chapter it was mentioned that, in the view of at least one authority, the consumer movement would endure and develop because it had generated an institutional structure of governmental and quasi-governmental agencies to support it. In this Section, something will be said of that structure, as it exists in the UK.

The Office of Fair Trading established by the Act of 1973 is the principal government instrument for monitoring trading practices with the central objective of protecting the consumer against unfair practices. The Director General of Fair Trading:

1   collects and scrutinises information affecting the economic interests and health and safety of consumers, and on trading practices which restrict or inhibit competition and which are in a general sense detrimental to the public interest. He is able to refer appropriate matters to:

(a) the Consumer Protection Advisory Committee;

(b) the Monopolies and Mergers Commission;

(c) the Restrictive Practices Court;

2   encourages the publication of codes of practice by trade associations (see below);

3   takes action against organisations persisting in conduct detrimental to consumers or infringing the laws governing competition;

4   publishes information on the rights of consumers;

5   regulates credit services in general and licenses credit organisations, credit brokers and debt collectors;

6   continually reviews existing law with a view to discovering gaps in the provision of consumer protection and, where necessary, proposes new laws to fill those gaps.

The Monopolies and Mergers Commission

Although this is an independent body it operates under the aegis of the Office of Fair Trading and investigates monopolies or possible monopolies referred to it by the Director General of that Office. Mergers are referred to it by the Secretary of State for Trade, prompted by the Director General of Fair Trading. The acid test is whether such monopolies or mergers are deemed to be, actually or potentially, against the public interest. Its work in the past has ranged over a number of product fields including domestic detergents, photographic film, petrol, and batteries.

Trading Standards or Consumer Protection Departments

These are departments of local authorities which enforce trading laws and extend advice to shoppers and traders. They deal with complaints concerning false or misleading descriptions or prices, inaccurate weights and measures and some issues concerning safety of products. Some local authorities have also established Consumer Advice Centres, which are usually situated within, or near, the main shopping precincts. These also deal with problems and complaints as well as providing shopping advice.

Note: in the matter of safety, the Consumer Safety Act 1978 regulates the composition, design and construction of particular products in order to prevent risk of death or personal injury resulting from their purchase and use. Oil heaters, electrical equipment, nightdress fabric, carrycot stands, electric blankets and paint on toys are examples of products for which minimum safety standards are laid down and for which it is a criminal offence to manufacture, sell or stock goods which do not comply with these standards. The Act enables the Secretary of State for Trade to make *prohibition orders and notices* which it is a criminal offence to disregard.

Environmental Health Departments

These are also operated by local government and deal with complaints on dirty shops and restaurants and unfit food and drink.

Citizens' Advice Bureaux

There is an extensive network of these bureaux in the United Kingdom. They provide advice on consumer complaints as well as on health, employment, housing, domestic, legal and social issues.

The British Standards Institution

Incorporated by Royal Charter, this is a voluntary non-profit-making body which prepares and publishes, for an extremely wide range of products and processes of production, standards for safety, performance, size and testing. The widening field of consumer protection has resulted in a significant increase in this aspect of the Institution's work. Since its incorporation in 1929 it has developed over 7000 British Standards (identified by the Institution's famous *kite-mark*). The acceptance of the Institution's standards, voluntary though it is, has become a notable feature of trade since such standards simplify consumer buying, and the specification of contract details and assist industry to attain economies through the standardisation of products.

The National Consumer Council

Although established by Government in 1975 this is another independent body. It provides an important channel of advice to government and business organisations on consumer advisory services, consumer legislation and the development and improvement of voluntary codes of practice (see p. 491). Its representation on various public and other bodies also assists the development of consumer interests.

Nationalised industries: Consumer and Consultative Councils

The Government has prompted the nationalised industries for coal, gas, electricity, transport and the postal service to establish Councils which enable consumers to influence policy making with those industries – so as to ensure that these giant organisations do not abuse their monopoly position, inadvertently or otherwise. The Councils deal with all matters affecting the consumer interest, including complaints.

These foregoing examples demonstrate that the response of Government to consumerism has been quite serious, significant and extensive. It would now be useful to consider the structures generated by the consumer movement itself.

The Consumers' Association

With over 700 000 members this is the largest consumer organisation in the country. Its magazine, *Which*, carries out comparative tests on products and scrutinises services. Its reports are read with great attention and interest. Its favourable reports on products have virtually become a 'seal of approval' and as such are a significant influence on both consumers and trade, whilst its unfavourable reports have doubtless generated modifications and improvements to products or services which were found to compare unfavourably with competition.

The National Federation of Consumer Groups

There are a large number of Local Consumer Groups in membership of the Federation. Many of the local groups give advice on local retail facilities and prices and concentrate on local issues whilst the Federation organises national campaigns.

User groups; special interest groups

Mention has been made of the consultative councils for the nationalised industries and these are good examples of the user groups which have now emerged. Organisations must also pay heed to the views of special interest groups – landowners' associations, women's institutes, councils for the protection of the countryside, community health councils, sports organisations, parent-teacher associations and the like, for these may have views on consumer and environmental issues that affect current or proposed activities.

Consumer-inspired organisations both national and local are now characterised by their ability to use the communications media and parliamentary spokesmen in support of their objectives. Occasionally too, action groups are formed within a community with a view to accomplishing some particular objective – the curbing of mining or quarrying activity, the re-routing or abandonment of a motorway or an airport project, the provision of a hospital. This may be the result of what has been called earlier the 'frustration-aggression syndrome'. Certainly any. public or private sector organisation, directly or indirectly involved, ignores such trends at its peril!

Industry and commerce: institutional structures serving consumer interests

The final section of this part of the Chapter (which follows) will provide some thoughts on how the individual organisation might, within the broader societal marketing concept already outlined, respond effectively to the twin forces of the consumer movement – consumerism and environmentalism. In this Section we will review just a few of the structural, self-regulatory devices which have been devised by industries or commercial groups and which may be said to serve the interests of the consumer movement.

Voluntary Codes of Practice

By establishing collective, voluntary codes of practice a number of trade associations have gone beyond basic legal requirements in order to provide the best possible level of consumer satisfaction. Trade associations comprise organisations involved in the manufacture and distribution of particular product groups or in the provision of particular services. A number of these associations in the UK have issued guidelines for their members on the quality of service to be provided for customers. They will also assist customers to pursue their complaints. Some of the fields covered by these codes of practice are:

1   cars and car repairs;
2   mail order trading;
3   laundering and dry cleaning;
4   electrical goods and their servicing;
5   package holidays;
6   shoes and shoe repairs.

The advertisement in Fig. 14.1, which recently appeared in the national press, clearly illustrates how one trade association, the Newspaper Publishers Association (NPA) has organised itself to protect the consumer.

Many of these codes of practice have been produced in consultation with the Office of Fair Trading. Because the codes are voluntary, of course, the trade associations cannot apply any sanctions. The Office of Fair Trading therefore exhorts the associations to develop the rigour of such self-regulatory procedures.

The Institute of Marketing's Code of Practice

This was published in 1973 and members are required to adhere to the Code as a condition of their membership. The 'honesty' clause within the Code is to prevent dissemination of misleading, as well as false, information and places responsibility on members for the actions of subordinates. Its rules of professional conduct cover integrity of conduct; injury to the professional reputation or practice of other members and honesty in dealing with both ultimate and intermediate customers. The member is also required to maintain professional standards of behaviour in securing and developing business. The Institute makes it clear that, where appropriate, disciplinary action for breach of the Code may lead to the expulsion of the member.

The British Code of Advertising Practice

The Code, a comprehensive document over eighty pages in length, adapts for use in the UK the rules of the International Chamber of Commerce's International Code of Advertising Practice, 1973. The British Code is supported by advertisers, advertising agencies and media owners, whose representatives constitute the Code of Advertising Practice (CAP) Committee. The Code is said to have two purposes:

THE NATIONAL NEWSPAPER

MOPS

MAIL ORDER PROTECTION SCHEME

MAIL ORDER PROTECTION SCHEME

MOPS is the Newspaper Publishers Association's Mail Order Protection Scheme.

If an advertisement carries the initials MOPS then you are assured that your money is fully protected should that advertiser cease to trade.

MOPS is for your protection. Should you have a query about any mail order advertisement write to the MOPS office in London giving the following information :

1. The date of the advertisement ; 2. The name and address of the advertiser ; 3. What date you ordered and how you paid ; 4. Your name, address, post code and telephone number.

MOPS will make sure your query is investigated.

Full details of MOPS and the excluded categories of advertising can be obtained by sending a stamped and addressed envelope to **The National Newspaper Mail Order Protection Scheme (MOPS), 16 Tooks Court, London EC4A 1LB.**

ORDER WITH CONFIDENCE

Fig. 14.1   *An advertisement published by the Newspaper Publishers' Association*

1   to set out in detail the rules which personnel in the advertising industry agree to follow;
2   to indicate to those outside advertising, the self-imposed regulations designed to ensure that advertisements can be trusted.

If an advertiser or an agency does not agree to amend or withdraw an advertisement, the Code provides that:

1   adverse publicity will be given in the Case Reports of the Advertising Standards Authority (see below);
2   advertising space or time can be witheld from the advertiser;
3   the advertising agency's trading privileges may be withdrawn;
4   other consumer protection agencies may be notified.

The Advertising Standards Authority (ASA), the 'top tier of the control system' is 'an independent body financed by a surcharge on display advertising, set up by the advertising business to ensure that its system of self-regulation works effectively in the public interest'.

The Code states that 'the essence of good advertising' is that all advertisements should be:

1   legal, decent, honest and truthful;
2   prepared with a sense of responsibility both to the consumer and to society; and
3   should conform to the principles of fair competition as generally accepted in business.

In addition to its general rules on legality, decency, honesty, truthful presentation and responsibility to the consumer and society, the Code contains sections on:

1   unacceptable practices connected with advertising (e.g. unsolicited home visits, non-availability of advertised products);
2   health claims;
3   advertising to children;
4   advertising for 'slimming';
5   unacceptable claims – medical and allied areas;
6   credit and investment advertising;
7   mail order advertising; and
8   advertising relating to the hair and scalp, cigarettes, alcohol and vitamins and minerals.

The Code does not extend to advertisements on television and radio, which are subject to a separate code, administered by the Independent Broadcasting Authority (IBA), but closely related to the British Code of Advertising Practice.

A Code of Conduct, devised jointly by The Market Research Society and the Industrial Marketing Research Association became operative in October 1976. The Code 'applies to all forms of market and social research equally including, for instance, consumer surveys, psychological research, industrial surveys, observational studies and panel research'.

Whereas membership of the Society and the Association is comprised of individuals, wherever organisations are mentioned in the Code, individual members have the responsibility to ensure, in so far as they are able, that the organisation fulfils the relevant requirement of the Code. The Code draws a distinction between rules of conduct (which are mandatory) and good practice (which constitutes recommendations to members that, while not necessarily of lesser importance than rules of conduct, cannot be universally applied).

The rules of conduct include provisions on:

1 the anonymity of informants;
2 precautions on the avoidance of adverse effects on informants;
3 the right of informants to withdraw from an enquiry;
4 the maintenance of public confidence in market research;
5 the misrepresentation of other activities as market research (e.g. sales approaches for profit, the compilation of lists for canvassing, industrial espionage);
6 the dissemination of unjustified conclusions;
7 the use of letters after members' names and responsibility to fellow members.

Among the recommendations on good practice are some relating to:

1 the avoidance of unnecessary secrecy;
2 interviews with children under 14 and with 14–17 year olds;
3 security of reports and other confidential material;
4 the distinction between results and opinions; and
5 the need for insurance (e.g. in the conduct of product tests which may involve risks to informants, however slight).

These then are some of the voluntary codes and controls connected with marketing in Britain. Together with the details of the recent legislation given earlier in the Chapter it can be seen that there are powerful forces which now support consumer interests. With regard to the self-regulatory devices just mentioned it can be argued that trade associations and professional bodies have limited power of enforcement – that in fact it amounts to moral suasion, in essence. However, we can see from the details given of the Codes that this understates the case in some instances and that, prompted by the Office of Fair Trading, there is a movement towards greater rigour and the application of clear sanctions. All this makes for a changing social environment for marketing activity. Let us now turn to the implications of that changing environment for the individual organisation.

Note: It is hoped that the conscientious student of marketing will obtain complete copies of the Codes mentioned in this Chapter and other relevant Codes. They should be studied carefully, not least for the implications as to personal conduct they contain.

Society and the individual organisation

The implications of the changing social environment for the marketing actions of the individual organisation should really be seen as the reverse side of the coinage of consumer complaints and concerns that have been described earlier in this Chapter. However, if to be more explicit we were to devise a plan of action based on a broader, more enlightened interpretation of the marketing concept, it would surely contain the points summarised below.

1   Organisational objectives should centre on customer satisfaction but in a manner consistent with public welfare.
2   The product or service must be completely satisfactory in terms of quality, performance, health and safety factors and value for money. Pre-sale and after-sales service must be fully adequate and based on guarantee or warranty conditions that are comprehensive, clear and honest. The product policy should be based on diligent and continuous search for significant product improvements. The design factor must be based on anticipation of consumer limitations and mistakes in using the product and, as far as possible, the design should obviate these. Packaging should be functionally effective, should enhance the image of the product but should not deceive the consumer as to the value or amount of the product. Where appropriate open-dating (the last date on which the product should be sold) and unit pricing should also be a part of the total product offering.
3   Through its advertising, packaging, labelling, and public relations programmes the organisation should try to ensure that the

consumer is an *informed* consumer, with adequate product or service information, realistic expectations and a level of consumer education that enables him/her to purchase as wisely as possible. This implies a communications policy that eschews hyperbole and puffery in favour of a policy that enables consumers to make fair comparisons between products, which assists consumers to keep their credit obligations within reasonable bounds and which assists them to purchase more rationally.

4   The product or service should be made available to the target market in as many points-of-sale as possible bearing in mind the need for striking an adequate balance between marketing costs, an adequate level of accessibility for customers and an adequate level of competition in the market place. Organisations whose target markets include the poorer, less advantaged sections of the community should take account of their limited mobility in fixing their distribution points.

5   The organisation should be continually mindful in all its activities of environmental damage, physical and cultural pollution and of the demands it makes upon finite natural resources. Ecological considerations should extend to its product ingredients, design and packaging as well as to its plant and processes. It should seek to minimise waste in all aspects of its operations.

6   The organisation should adopt a positive, enthusiastic attitude to consumerism and environmentalism and reflect this by adapting the organisational structure where necessary and not least by ensuring that these matters are the ultimate responsibility of senior management.

With regard to point 6, and the organisation's attitude of mind, it is important to recognise that not only must consumerism be taken into account as an environmental force, it can be 'a positive competitive marketing tool – an opportunity for business'[17]. The organisation which developed the first phosphate-free laundry detergent, or the plastic soft-drink container which was biodegradable in solid waste treatment or which pioneered low-lead petrol obtained a competitive edge. The organisation which discovers wasteful procedures may reduce the costs of its fuel and materials. The ecologically superior product may be the one that the market favours now that we are seeing the demise of the 'throw-away culture.' Boone and Kurtz[18] report of a truck manufacturing company which incorporated 140 improvements in one of its models as a result of its 'open' attitude to user

complaints! The consumer movement has resulted in direct
opportunities – some organisations have moved into the expanding markets for pollution control equipment and recycling plants.
The requirement to save energy has resulted in the introduction
of many products, from loft insulation to warmer clothing. Perhaps Peter Drucker[19] had such developments in mind when he
said:

Consumerism actually should be, must be, and I hope will be the opportunity of marketing.

The expanding importance of the social variable in the marketing equation provides an increasing challenge to decision makers.
Yet it is important that such decisions involve greater consideration of the social environment and of the eventual long-run
effects of decision making. The portents are that the influence
of the consumer movement will endure and increase. To ignore
those signs will be socially irresponsible. It will also, for both
profit and non-profit organisations, be managerially irresponsible.

Marketing and tomorrow

If one phrase is used to describe the forces affecting marketing
now and in the future that phrase must be 'environmental
change.' From what has been said throughout this book successful
organisations will adapt to an accelerating rate of change by a
continuous process of 'researching the future', of long-range planning and of socially responsible objective setting and decision
making. It is clear that the consumer of the future will be increasingly decided in his views, more articulate in stating them, less
susceptible to advertising puffery and more ready to take action
in his own cause. Technologies are no longer scarce. As Jonathan
Gershuny[20] has prompted us to remember:

Instead of social shortcomings demanding technical solutions we now
often find multiple technologies chasing scarce applications.

Given a consumer with a wider range of tastes and preferences
and one who is less predictable than hitherto, and given the abundance of technologies there will be little future for the organisation which does not *innovate*. Enthusiastic attention to product
strategy will be a worthwhile investment. Technical research and
development, product and concept testing with continuing marketing research will be critical business activities.

Changes in promotional techniques are upon us in the shape of the computer-based information service which is available to TV owners in the UK through the Post Office. This and the advent of the videophone will change the face of consumer shopping. The cashless society is a near-term prospect. The use of credit cards is already widespread and will be another potent factor in the development of shopping from home. The established network of retail shops is also about to undergo a revolution in accounting and administration. Shops in the town of Northampton have gone 'online' to an ICL 2988 mainframe computer in the UK's first major cashless payments project. ICL and the Anglia Building Society are both funding the project, at a total cost of £1 million. Approximately 200 terminals from the manufacturer, Fortronic, have been installed by Northampton retailers. 70 000 shoppers carry plastic 'Angliacards', with accounting information within the metallic strips on the cards. When the card holder has completed a purchase, the consumer's personal identification number and the details of the transaction are keyed into the retailer's terminal. The card holder's account is accordingly debited and the appropriate amount credited to the retailer's account.

In his paper on Improving Marketing Effectiveness through the use of Modern Technology', Nigel Piercy[21] has also indicated something of the scale of the impact of microprocessors on the the marketing process, reaching as it will into product policy, pricing, distribution and warehousing, marketing communications and marketing information – a 'commodity' that will become cheaper and which will also enable the organisation to respond to the future through analytical information systems leading to model building and market simulation procedures. So that as the 'market' becomes even more dynamic so information technology and data retrieval and transfer mechanisms will enable the individual organisation to respond to that dynamism. In fact, as Markin has outlined, the approach required will be one of constant re-examination of market needs and opportunities in the short and long run accompanied by a capacity for quick adjustment, ready accommodation and organisational suppleness in order to permit the necessary changes in the marketing mix to take place.

On the question of market needs, as Liz Nelson[22] has indicated, the picture is one of increasing fragmentation. Communities are fragmenting not only physically, but also intellectually into the proliferation of minority interests, cultures and religions. With regard to religion, who would have guessed in 1945 that by 1985 the UK population would contain more Muslims than Methodists? Dependent on organisational attitudes this fragmentation can be viewed as either a threat or an opportunity and here technology is again of significance for as Gershuny[23] points out, as technologies develop the advantages of scale accrue to successively smaller productive units. While the National Grid was necessary forty years ago to provide a particular level of service, the same or a higher level of service could be achieved today from much smaller, perhaps city sized, units for generating electricty. And other examples abound in transportation and manufacturing systems. So that while effective marketing was never a function of organisational size, the factor of size will be of even less significance in the future.

The emphasis in the future will be less on products and more on services, with education, transportation, governmental services and communication taking a greater proportionate share of marketing time and effort.

It is also to be hoped that before long the potential contribution of effective marketing to the problems of unemployment and the scandal of poverty and disease in the Third World will be fully realised. We are moved beyond words by the plight of our fellow human beings in the poorest countries – perhaps marketing's contribution to the commonweal will enable the richer countries to do more and that the benefits of enlightened marketing may be realised within even the poorest parts of the world. And it is the developing nations as well as the under-developed ones that will continue to pose problems in the years ahead. Daniel Vining[24] has alerted us to the fact that in some of these countries – South Korea, Ecuador, Algeria, Tunisia, and Indonesia – a demographic problem of serious immediate implications is arising due to the increasing concentration of the population in the major cities – a situation which threatens chaos at the 'core' and dire poverty and disease as the lot of the population at the 'periphery'.

So we can see some of the challenges and opportunities that lie ahead for the marketing approach. To those contemplating a career in marketing, the challenges have never been more pronounced and the prospects have never been brighter. In greater measure than ever before technical competence in marketing will be needed, together with a positive attitude of mind and a determination to rebut the view of Anarchus who believed 'the market' to be 'the place set aside where men may deceive each other'.

Self-assessment questions

1   What consumer rights were identified in the Kennedy Bill of Rights?
2   What is environmentalism? How is it significant for marketing activity?
3   Define the societal marketing concept. How does it relate to the stakeholder theory?
4   What are the aims of the Trade Descriptions Acts 1968 and 1972?
5   What are exclusion clauses? How are they affected by recent consumer legislation?
6   List at least six additional provisions of recent consusmer legislation.
7   Describe the functions of The Director General of Fair Trading.
8   What are voluntary codes of practice? Illustrate your answer with reference to The British Code of Advertising Practice.
9   Identify and explain ways in which the marketing actions of the individual organisation can take account of the changing social environment.
10   Prepare notes for a lecture to be delivered to fellow students on: 'Marketing and Tomorrow'

References

1 Sinclair, Upton. *The Jungle*, Garden City, NY, Doubleday, 1906
2 Carson, Rachel. *Silent Spring*, London, Hamish Hamilton, 1965, p. 39
3 Kotler, Philip. *Principles of marketing*, 2nd edn, Englewood Cliffs, NJ, Prentice-Hall, 1980, p. 608
4 Attenborough, David. *The living planet*, London, William Collins and British Broadcasting Corporation, 1984, p. 307
5 Ibid. p. 308
6 Stanton, William J. *Fundamentals of marketing*, 6th edn, New York, McGraw-Hill 1981, p. 531
7 Kangun, Norman et al. Consumerism and marketing management, *Marketing management* (Marvin A. Jolson) London, Collier Macmillan, 1978, pp. 54–55

8 *Fundamentals of marketing*, p. 531

9 *Principles of marketing*, p. 20

10 Kotler, Philip. *Marketing for non-profit organizations*, Englewood Cliffs, NJ, Prentice-Hall, 1975, p. 47

11 Galbraith, J. K. *The Affluent Society*, Boston, Houghton Mifflin, 1958, p. 255

12 *Fundamentals of marketing*, p. 539

13 Curzon, L. B. *Basic Law*, Plymouth, Macdonald & Evans, 1978, pp. 104–105

14 Ibid. p. 9

15 Ibid. p. 145

16 Beardshaw, John and Palfreman, David. *The organisation in its environment*, 2nd edn, Plymouth, Macdonald & Evans, 1982, p. 386

17 Greyser, Stephen A. and Diamond, Steven L. Business is adapting to consumerism, in *Marketing management*, p. 66

18 Boone, Louis E. and Kurtz, David L. *Contemporary Marketing*, 3rd edn, Hinsdale, Ill., The Dryden Press, 1980, p. 435

19 Drucker, Peter. reported in *Principles of marketing*, p. 626

20 Gershuny, Jonathan. *After Industrial Society?* London and Basingstoke, The Macmillan Press 1978, p. 5

21 Piercy, Nigel. *Improving marketing effectiveness through the use of modern technology*, Cookham, Berks., Institute of Marketing (Professional Paper No. 5), p. 10

22 Nelson, Elizabeth H. *The needs of the citizen in a fragmented society*, (draft paper in the private possession of the author)

23 *After Industrial Society?* pp. 4–5

24 Vining, Daniel R, Jnr. *The growth of core regions in the Third World*, New York, Scientific American, **252**, No. 4 (April 1985), pp. 24–31

BIBLIOGRAPHY

American Marketing Association. *Marketing definitions: a glossary of marketing terms*, Chicago, American Marketing Association, 1960

Argenti, John. *Practical corporate planning*, London, Allen & Unwin, 1980

Attenborough, David. *The Living Planet*, London, William Collins and the British Broadcasting Corporation, 1984

Baker, Michael J. *Marketing: theory and practice*, London and Basingstoke, Macmillan, 1979

Baker, Michael J. *Marketing – an introductory text*, (3rd edn), London, Macmillan, 1979

Beardshaw, John and Palfreman, David. *The organisation in its environment*, (2nd edn), Plymouth, Macdonald & Evans, 1982

Boone, Louis E. and Kurtz, David L. *Contemporary marketing*, (3rd edn), Hinsdale, Illinois, Dryden Press, 1980

British Export Houses Association (BEHA). *Directory of British Export Houses*, London, BEHA, 1978–9

The British Market Research Bureau Ltd. *Acorn – a new concept in marketing*, London, British Market Research Bureau, 1980

British Overseas Trade Board (BOTB). *Marketing consumer goods in France*, London, BOTB, 1977

Britt, S. H. and Boyd, H. W. Jr. *Marketing management and administrative action*, (4th edn), Tokyo, McGraw Hill Kogakusha, 1978

Broadbent, Simon. *Spending advertising money*, (3rd edn), London, Business Books, 1979

Buell, Victor P. and Heyel, Carl, eds. *Handbook of modern marketing*, New York, London, McGraw-Hill, 1970

Cannon, Tom. *Basic marketing – principles and practice*, London, Holt, Rinehart and Winston, 1980

Carson, Rachel. *Silent Spring*, London, Hamish Hamilton, 1965

Central Statistical Office. *Annual Abstract of Statistics*, Norwich, Her Majesty's Stationery Office, 1983

Centre for Physical Distribution Management. *The Director's Guide to storage, handling, freight and distribution*, London, Institute of Directors, 1980

Chisnall, Peter M. *Marketing: a behavioural analysis*, Maidenhead, McGraw-Hill, 1975

Chisnall, Peter M. *Effective industrial marketing*, London, Longman, 1977

Christopher, Martin, Walters, David and Wills, Gordon. *Introduction to marketing*, (3rd edn), Bradford; MCB Publications, 1978

Cooke, Alistair. *America*, London, The British Broadcasting Corporation, 1973

Corbin, Arnold. *Implementing the marketing concept*, London, British Institute of Management, 1966

Crimp, Margaret. *The marketing research process*, London; Prentice-Hall, 1981

Curzon, L. B. *Basic Law*, Plymouth, Macdonald & Evans, 1978

Day, Arthur J. *Exporting for profit*, London, Graham & Trotman, 1976

Drever, James (rev. H. Wallerstein). *A Dictionary of Psychology*, Harmondsworth, Middlesex, Penguin Books, 1971

Drucker, Peter. *Management: tasks, responsibilities, practices*, New York, Harper & Row, 1973

Ehrenberg, A. S. C. and Pyatt, F. G., eds. *Consumer behaviour*, Harmondsworth, Middlesex, Penguin Books, 1971

Engel, James F., Blackwell, Roger D. and Kollatt, David T. *Consumer behaviour*, (3rd edn), Hinsdale, Illinois, Dryden Press, 1978

Enis, Ben M. and Cox, Keith K. *Marketing classics*, Boston, Allyn & Bacon, 1969

Ferber, Robert, ed. *Handbook of Marketing Research*, New York, McGraw-Hill, 1974

Fisher, L. *Industrial marketing*, London; Business Books, 1976

Fitzroy, Peter T. *Analytical methods for marketing management*, London, McGraw-Hill, 1976

Foster, Douglas. *Mastering marketing*, London, Macmillan, 1982

Foxall, Gordon R. *Consumer behaviour*, London, Croom Helm, 1980

Frain, John. *Transportation and distribution for European markets*, London, Butterworth, 1970

Frain, John. *Introduction to marketing*, (2nd edn), Plymouth, Macdonald & Evans, 1983

Galbraith, J. K. *The affluent society*, Boston, Houghton Mifflin, 1958

Galbraith, J. K. *A contemporary guide to economics, peace and laughter*, London, André Deutsch, 1971

Gershuny, Jonathan. *After industrial society?*, London and Basingstoke, Macmillan Press, 1978

Giles, G. B. *Marketing*, (3rd edn), Plymouth, Macdonald & Evans, 1978

Hannagan, T. J. *Mastering statistics*, London, Macmillan, 1982

Harper, W. M. *Statistics*, (4th edn), Plymouth, Macdonald & Evans, 1982

Hart, Norman and O'Connor, James, eds. *The practice of advertising*, London, Heinemann, 1978

Howard, John A. and Sheth, Jagdish N. *The theory of buyer behaviour*, New York, John Wiley, 1969

Institute of Directors. *The Director's Guide to storage, handling, freight and distribution*, London, Institute of Directors, 1980

Institute of Marketing. *Marketing in the construction industry*, London, Heinemann, 1974

Jackson, J. A., ed. *Social Stratification*, Cambridge University Press, Cambridge, 1968

Jolson, Marvin L. *Marketing management*, London, Collier Macmillan, 1978

Jenner, Paul. *Europe: an exporter's handbook*, London, Euromonitor Publications, 1981

Katz, Elihu and Lazarsfeld, Paul. *Personal influence*, New York, The Free Press, 1955

Kempner, Thomas, ed. *A Handbook of Management*, Harmondsworth, Middlesex, Penguin Books, 1977

Kotler, Philip. *Marketing for non-profit organisations*, Englewood Cliffs, NJ, Prentice-Hall, 1975

Kotler, Philip. *Marketing management – analysis, planning and control*, Englewood Cliffs, NJ, Prentice-Hall, 1980

Kotler, Philip. *Principles of marketing*, (2nd edn), Englewood Cliffs, NJ, Prentice-Hall, 1983

Maclean, Ian, ed. *Handbook of industrial marketing and research*, Brentford, Middlesex, Kluwer-Harrap, 1982

Majaro, Simon. *Marketing in perspective*, London, Allen & Unwin, 1982

Markin, Rom. *Marketing-strategy and management*, (2nd edn), New York, John Wiley, 1982

Maslow, A. H. *Motivation and personality*, New York, Harper, 1954

McCarthy, E. Jerome. *Basic marketing – A managerial approach*, (6th edn), Homewood, Illinois, Richard D. Irwin, 1978

McDaniel, Carl, Jr. *Marketing*, (2nd edn), New York; Harper & Row, 1982

McIver, Colin. *Marketing*, (2nd edn), London, Business Publications, 1964

McNeal, James U., ed. *Dimensions of consumer behaviour*, (2nd edn), New York, Appleton-Century-Crofts, 1969

Nicosia, Francesco M. *Consumer decision processes*, Englewood Cliffs, NJ, Prentice-Hall, 1966

Oliver, Gordon. *Marketing today*, London, Prentice-Hall, 1980

Osgood, C. E. et al. *The measurement of meaning*, Urbana, University of Illinois Press, 1957

O'Shaughnessy, John. *Work study applied to a sales force*, London, British Institute of Management, 1965

Proctor, Tony and Stone, Marilyn A. *Marketing research*, Plymouth, Macdonald & Evans, 1978

Pugh, D. S., Hickson, D. J. and Hinings, C. R. *Writers on organisations*, (3rd edn), Harmondsworth, Middlesex, Penguin Books, 1983

Pugh, D. S., ed. *Organisation theory – selected readings*, Harmondsworth, Middlesex; Penguin Books, 1983

Pym, Denis, ed. *Industrial society – social sciences in management*, Harmondsworth, Middlesex, Penguin Books, 1968

Rines, Michael, ed. *Marketing Handbook*, Aldershot, Gower Publishing, 1981

Robertson, Ivan T. and Cooper, Cary L. *Human behaviour in organisations*, Plymouth, Macdonald & Evans, 1983

Rodger, Leslie W., ed. *Marketing concepts and strategies in the next decade*, London, Cassell/Associated Business Programmes, 1973

Rogers, Everett M. and Shoemaker, F. Floyd. *Communication of innovations*, (2nd edn), New York, The Free Press, 1971

Schwartz, David J. *Marketing today – a basic approach*, (3rd edn), New York, Harcourt, Brace, Jovanovich, 1981

Seddon, E. and Appleton, J. D. S. *Applied economics*, Plymouth; Macdonald & Evans, 1978

Seibert, Joseph and Wills, Gordon, eds. *Marketing research*, Harmondsworth, Middlesex, Penguin Books, 1970

Sinclair, Upton. *The Jungle*, Garden City, NY, Doubleday, 1906

Stanton, William J. *Fundamentals of marketing*, (6th edn), New York, McGraw-Hill, 1981

Swindells, Anthony. *Advertising media and campaign planning*, London, Butterworth, 1966

Thomas, S. Evelyn (rev. L. B. Curzon) *Commerce – its theory and practice*, (11th edn), London, Cassell, 1979

Toffler, Alvin. *Future shock*, London, Pan Books, 1971

Walker, David M. *The Oxford Companion to Law*, Oxford, Oxford University Press, 1980

Walsh, L. S. *International marketing*, (2nd edn), Plymouth, Macdonald & Evans, 1983

Webster, F. E. and Wind, Y. *Organizational buyer behaviour*, Englewood Cliffs, NY, Prentice-Hall, 1972

Wentworth, Felix, ed. *Handbook of Physical Distribution Management*, Farnborough, Gower Publishing, 1981

Williamson, R. J. *Marketing for accountants and managers*, London, Heinemann, 1979

Willsmer, Ray L. *The basic arts of marketing*, London, Business Books, 1976

Wilson, Aubrey. *The marketing of professional services*, London, McGraw-Hill, 1972

Wilson, Aubrey. *The assessment of industrial markets*, London, Cassell/Associated Business Programmes, 1973

Wilson, R. M. S. *Management controls in marketing*, London, Heinemann, 1973

Worcester, Robert and Downham, John, eds. *Consumer Market Research Handbook*, (2nd edn), New York, London, Van Nostrand Reinhold, 1978

INDEX